# IMPERILED INNOCENTS

PRINCETON STUDIES IN AMERICAN POLITICS:
HISTORICAL, INTERNATIONAL, AND
COMPARATIVE PERSPECTIVES

SERIES EDITORS

IRA KATZNELSON, MARTIN SHEFTER, THEDA SKOCPOL

A list of titles
in this series appears
at the back of
the book

# IMPERILED INNOCENTS

## ANTHONY COMSTOCK
## AND FAMILY REPRODUCTION
## IN VICTORIAN AMERICA

*Nicola Beisel*

PRINCETON UNIVERSITY PRESS

PRINCETON, NEW JERSEY

*LIBRARY OF CONGRESS CATALOGING-IN-PUBLICATION DATA*

BEISEL, NICOLA KAY.
IMPERILED INNOCENTS : ANTHONY COMSTOCK AND
FAMILY REPRODUCTION IN VICTORIAN AMERICA / NICOLA BEISEL
P. CM. — (PRINCETON STUDIES IN AMERICAN POLITICS)
INCLUDES BIBLIOGRAPHICAL REFERENCES AND INDEX.
ISBN 0-691-02779-X
ISBN 0-691-02778-1 (PBK.)
1. UNITED STATES—MORAL CONDITIONS—HISTORY—19TH CENTURY.
2. CHILD REARING—MORAL AND ETHICAL ASPECTS.
3. COMSTOCK, ANTHONY, 1844–1915. 4. CENSORSHIP—UNITED STATES—
HISTORY—19TH CENTURY. 5. SOCIAL MOBILITY—UNITED STATES.
6. UNITED STATES—SOCIAL LIFE AND CUSTOMS—1865–1918.
I. TITLE. II. SERIES.
HN90.M6B45  1997
306'.0973—dc20     96-3013   CIP

*For My Parents*

# CONTENTS

# ACKNOWLEDGMENTS

THIS BOOK began life as a doctoral dissertation. Many people have contributed to its growth, and to mine. My thanks first of all to William Sewell, Jr., for being a wonderful dissertation chair and mentor. Bill's scholarship provides a vision of what is to be gained from interdisciplinary work; his capacity to foster intellectual courage I can only hope to emulate. Nicholas Dirks, Mayer Zald, William Mason, and Renee Anspack all provided helpful comments on the dissertation. I am especially grateful to Terrance McDonald for helping make an American historian out of an historical ignoramus. Finally, I would not have continued my graduate studies were it not for the support of James House and Rosemary Sarri, nor would I have started them without the encouragement of Craig McEwen. I am grateful to them for helping me find my calling.

A number of colleagues have engaged me in useful conversations about the ideas in this book or have commented on various parts of the manuscript. I would especially like to thank Paul DiMaggio, Wendy Griswold, Pamela Walters, William Gamson, William Roy, Neil Fligstein, Gerald Marwell, Wendy Espeland, Carol Heimer, Marc Steinberg, Vera Zolberg, Jonathan Teaford, Sonya Rose, Elizabeth Hovey, Jane Mansbridge, and Christopher Jencks for sharing their insights. Michele Lamont, Kristin Luker, and James Oakes generously read and commented on the entire manuscript. It was much improved by their labors. Arthur Stinchcombe again showed what an amazing person and colleague he is by reading this manuscript three times. I cannot thank him enough for sharing his remarkable intellect.

I am indebted to the institutions that have supported me during the years of research and writing. The Pennsylvania Historical Society and Library Company of Philadelphia provided a summer fellowship that allowed me to collect data on censorship in Philadelphia. I thank the University of Michigan's Institute for the Humanities, and especially the Hunting family, for the fellowship that supported the final year of dissertation writing. Northwestern University provided release time from teaching, as did the Center for Urban Affairs and Policy Research. I very much appreciate their support of my work.

My work has been aided and enriched by, and dependent on, the help and knowledge of librarians and archivists. My thanks to the library staffs at the University of Michigan and Northwestern University, as well as the archivists at the Massachusetts Historical Society, the Harvard Law Library, the Harvard Business School, the Library Company of Philadelphia, and Haverford College. I owe special debts of gratitude to James Green at the Library Company of Philadelphia, to Diana Peterson at Haverford College, and to Edward Weber, retired curator of Michigan's Labadie Collection. I would not have found the minutes of the New England Society for the Suppression of Vice without the help of Lois Stryker and Dwight Strong; I cannot thank them enough for their assistance and trust.

My colleagues and friends at Northwestern University have provided much appreciated intellectual stimulation and support. Special thanks to Orville Lee, Cathy O'Leary, Nancy MacLean, Susan Herbst, Hollis Clayson, Susan Manning, Marla Felcher, Jim Ettema, Marc Ventresca, and Marika Lindholm for their companionship, both social and intellectual. At Northwestern I have been blessed as well with students whose intellect sharpened mine. In this regard I would especially like to thank Amy Binder, Alan Dahl, Brian Donovan, and Tamara Kay for their insights and their faith.

Many of the years spent researching and writing this manuscript were shared with Karl Monsma. I thank him for those years, for hours of conversation about my work, and especially for taking me seriously as an intellectual long before I did.

I have been blessed with friends who have known me for years and love me anyway. My thanks to Mark Porter, Theresa Deussen, Nancy Cauthen, Diane Hastings, Naomi O'Grady, and Elizabeth Wood for sharing life with me. Mary Murrell, my editor at Princeton University Press, gave me encouragement, support, and advice, as well as friendship. Julia Adams has been an invaluable companion on the path of assistant professorhood; I hope every new Ph.D.'s job search yields such a wonderful friend.

My grandmothers, Aldine Mickle and Verda Beisel, would have loved to see this book in print. It is a source of sadness that they did not live to see its completion. My parents, Richard and Adda Beisel, are almost certainly amazed that they did. I thank them for their patience, support, love, and pride in me. This book is dedicated to them, with gratitude and with love.

# IMPERILED INNOCENTS

# 1

## INTRODUCTION: FAMILY REPRODUCTION, CHILDREN'S MORALS, AND CENSORSHIP

*Lust is the boon companion of all other crimes.* There is no evil
so extensive, none doing more to destroy the institutions of free
America. It sets aside the laws of God and morality; marriage
bonds are broken, most sacred ties severed, State laws ignored,
and dens of infamy plant themselves in almost every
community, and then reaching out like immense cuttlefish,
draw in, from all sides, our youth to destruction.[1]
*(Anthony Comstock, 1883)*

OF THE SCORE of literary censorship societies founded between 1870 and 1890, only two left many traces in the historical record. Our language and laws reflect the legacy of these societies, while the issues addressed by these organizations still motivate contemporary political debate. The New York Society for the Suppression of Vice (NYSSV), founded in New York City in 1872 by Anthony Comstock and his wealthy supporters in the Young Men's Christian Association, sponsored passage of a federal anti-obscenity law that forbade use of the postal service for distributing obscene materials, including information about or devices that caused abortion or contraception. Nearly half the states passed similar laws. The overturning of the last of these laws by the Supreme Court in the 1965 *Griswold v. Connecticut* decision formed the judicial precedent for the legalization of abortion. Comstock's standards for decency in art spawned the word *Comstockery* to denote prudery. A verdict in one of Comstock's cases created the legal standard for determining obscenity for half a century. In Boston, Brahmin backers of the New England Society for the Suppression of Vice (renamed the Watch and Ward Society in 1890) were such vigorous censors of literature that the term "banned in Boston" came to describe the Victorian literary standards of the city.[2] The power of these censorship organizations originated in the wealth and prestige of their members. More than one-quarter of the anti-vice supporters in Boston and New York were in the *Social Register* or were millionaires, while virtually all the rest were businessmen or professionals.

These nineteenth-century censors should not be dismissed as mere quaint Victorians. The issues they addressed—pornography, abortion, the availability of contraceptives, the corruption of children by libidinous and pervasive popular culture, and indecency in art and literature—echo contemporary political concerns. The rhetoric they employed—that obscenity threatened children—was powerful. But it did not always work. While Boston and New York spawned powerful anti-vice societies, Philadelphia remained quiescent in the field of censorship. The Philadelphia anti-vice effort received so little support that historians and sociologists have incorrectly assumed that the city had no censorship movement.[3]

The anti-vice crusade, like many moral reform movements, gained legitimacy from the claim that children were threatened by the vices reformers sought to suppress. This claim remains a powerful rhetorical tool even for movements not identified with protecting children. The contemporary anti-abortion movement, ostensibly about fetuses, scored a major victory with passage of parental consent laws, which increase parental control of teenage daughters. Persons arguing against gay rights assert that homosexuals actively seek to recruit young people, particularly schoolchildren, to their ranks. Similarly, a century ago the Women's Christian Temperance Union mobilized a powerful movement against the consumption and sale of alcohol by arguing that drunken husbands squandered their wages and neglected and abused their families.[4] Moral reform movements, and reformers claiming that their crusade protected children, have spanned at least a century. This book will focus on two central questions: What makes such moral claims potent, and under what circumstances are concerns about children likely to result in moral reform movements? I will address these questions by focusing on the nineteenth-century anti-vice movement, analyzing its success in New York and Boston and its failure in Philadelphia. I argue that the anti-vice movement succeeded when its leaders connected concerns about the moral corruption of children, occasioned by changes in gender roles and the social meaning of sexuality, to threats to the social position of the upper and middle classes. The latter concern resulted from the growing numbers, social presence, and political power of immigrants. Support for this social movement, like any, can be understood only by examining the political and social issues and anxieties faced by potential supporters within a historical context. However, the dynamics of the anti-vice movement offer insights into moral issues that have emerged in this century.

At the heart of moral reform politics, I argue, is family reproduction, specifically, the reproduction of the next generation. Moral crusades address a crucial issue for parents: whether their children will equal or better their parents' place in the social world. The problem of children's survival and success touches parents' most profound hopes and fears. One aspect of family reproduction is the reproduction of whatever economic privilege the parents have.[5] Parents seeking to reproduce their class position in and for their offspring attempt to teach children values and habits that will lead to success. Parents also provide children with opportunities.[6]

Crusades to protect children from vice address parents' fear that vice will render children unfit for desirable jobs and social positions. This concern can take the form of believing that children will not be hired, or will be excluded from desired social circles, because their habits, reputations, or appearance will make them seem untrustworthy. This is the fear that others will erect what Lamont calls "moral boundaries" against one's children.[7] Related to this is the fear that children will actively embrace habits or lifestyles that parents see as inimical to acceptable work or social habits. Alcohol or drug use, or children's embracing youth culture and rejecting their parents' ethics (as in the rejection of "the establishment" in the 1960s, exemplified by the exhortation to "tune in, turn on and drop out"), might lead to understandable, if unsubstantiated, parental anxieties about children's futures. Fear about children's character was possibly even greater in the late-nineteenth century, when discussions of "character" were rampant, and requirements for reproducing middle- and upper-class social positions even less clear.[8]

Moral corruption of children threatens more than the reproduction of parents' cherished values. At stake for parents is the reproduction of cultural styles, habits, and lifestyles. The transmission of culture is important because the reproduction of social privilege involves the reproduction of social ties. In the family and in school, children are endowed with habits, tastes, styles of interaction, and knowledge of cultural forms such as art and music. This knowledge and sense of style, or "cultural capital," becomes a basis of privilege when people are excluded from valued social positions on the basis of cultural markers.[9] The sharing of both cultural symbols and views of the world is essential in forming social relationships and becoming part of social networks. Social networks and shared cultures are central to family reproduction for both middle- and upper-class people, although the role these factors play differs for each class, as well as within historical contexts.

In the late-nineteenth century as well as in the twentieth, the upper class has consisted of (potentially interconnected) networks constituted by friendships, marriages, and acquaintances. These ties are fostered by locally based institutions such as clubs and boarding schools and by social events such as charity and debutante balls. These ties are the basis of upper-class solidarity and are not predicated only, or even primarily, on shared economic interests. Rather, inclusion in the upper class is based on a shared culture, meaning both a style of life and a set of beliefs about the world. A sense of self, and identification with others, originates in this shared culture. Thus culture is the glue that holds networks together. Persons born into or aspiring to inclusion in the upper class are socialized (or socialize themselves) to incorporate the habits, tastes, and attitudes that make them suitable partners in social relationships that lead to their acceptance in upper-class social clubs and at social events. The ultimate consolidation of such social relationships is familial, meaning marriage to another member of the upper class.[10]

The "robber barons" of the late-nineteenth century, exemplars of rapacious capitalists, were obsessed with family advancement. Wealth, even vast amounts of wealth, did not make a man successful, because it did not give him, his wife, or especially his children a place in "Society."[11] Writing about Philadelphia's upper class, Nathaniel Burt described the importance of family position as follows:

> Even deeper than this feeling of family group and its atmosphere as being the measure of social life and the ideal of social tone, is the sense that family status is the basis of one's own standing in the world. For that venerable Position of which the Philadelphian is so confident is based first of all on family.
>
> The derivation of family status anywhere is fairly uniform: tenure of power and wealth, a record of distinction somewhere along the line, and connections with other such families of status. In this Philadelphia is certainly not different from Rome or Kalamazoo. The way to found a family is traditional and summed up by that formula attributed to Quakers, "In the first generation thee must do well, in the second marry well, in the third breed well; then the fourth will take care of itself." If Philadelphia does differ from other centers it is in its emphasis on that marrying second generation. It is not, as a rule, family founders who are remembered and worshipped, but members of a later generation. What this means is that in Philadelphia inherited position is better than self-made position. Inherited money is better than made money. Where the money came from is something, no matter how honorable or even exciting, that one usually prefers to forget. A real family just *has* money; and almost the same thing might be said of distinction.[12]

The aim of the capitalist was not to accumulate as much capital as possible, but to establish a family embraced by the socially elect. To make it into high society one had to be rich, but being rich did not grant one's family admission; furthermore, a family maintained its position not by accumulating more wealth but by participating in social activities that further cemented ties within the social circle.[13] Marriage remains the most important of these activities: Nelson Aldrich, Jr., scion of an old family, urges us to "consider the implications of referring to the *Social Register* as the 'stud book.'"[14]

The most important implication is that family occupies a central place in upper-class reproduction—perhaps, since failure to marry within the group means to marry down, the family is more important to the upper class than to any other. I will discuss the implications of family reproduction for theorizing class politics and class reproduction in greater detail in the last chapter of this book. I will argue that the central place of the family in the reproduction of classes means that the politics of the family, and of morality, are not peripheral to the "real" objects of class struggle. Families are the stuff of which classes are constructed; it is through families that classes are reproduced. What is at stake in battles over morality are fundamental issues about what classes will be.

This notion of a social class being based on networks tied together by a shared culture is also useful for understanding the dilemma of middle-class parents trying to transmit to children their own social position. Wealthy parents can endow offspring with sufficient income to ensure their survival, even if children fail to learn the habits and manners that enable social acceptance from other members of the upper class. In short, wealthy parents can guarantee the reproduction of a child's economic class position even if they fail to reproduce their social class position in the next generation.[15] Middle-class parents, lacking inherited or inheritable wealth, are faced with attempting to ensure their children's economic survival. While the upper class can be seen as a potentially interconnected network of social clubs and philanthropic boards, of families and people tied together by mutual acquaintances, the middle class is both more vast and diffuse. Middle-class parents are spared the problem of ensuring their children's acceptability to others in a finite and hierarchal network of social clubs and social events, but middle-class success remains predicated on the transmission of a shared culture that facilitates social ties. Middle-class success is defined by achievement in two related realms: school and work. A child must do well in school in hopes of becoming an adult who either succeeds in the labor force or who marries a person capable of supporting him or her. Success in school is partly predicated on the manners and attitudes children bring to the classroom.[16] The skills and credentials gained in school are then, hopefully, translated to employment. Part of this translation involves presenting a self that employers see as both able and trustworthy. Getting a job is also predicated on social contacts; knowledge of available jobs flows through social networks.[17] Thus social networks and shared cultures work to reproduce both upper- and middle-class children. Although parents from these two social classes face different problems in ensuring the success of their offspring, moral corruption can threaten access to valued social networks, and thus to a valued social position, for children of both classes.

## Family Relations and Moral Reform

Moral reform movements, and concerns about children that motivate them, are particularly likely to arise in two specific contexts. One potent source of such movements is changing relationships within the family. Family relations are erected upon power relations between adults and children and men and women. Family reproduction involves, in part, controlling children. Preserving the social position of children is in part a policing process, an attempt to keep children from learning practices that will undermine children's future success.[18] But the power that operates in the family is not only that of adults over children. If children are to be reproduced, someone has to do the work of reproducing them—meaning not only giving birth to them, but feeding, washing, clothing, and watching them. In our time, as in Comstock's, that someone is almost always a woman.[19] But power dynamics within the family can be altered by changes outside it. In recent decades increasing employment opportunities for middle-class women have given them a choice about staying home and raising children; the stagnation of wages has given some women no choice but to work outside the home. But if the reproduction of families, and of appropriately class-socialized children, is predicated on the unpaid labor of women in the home, then changes outside the family that potentially alter the roles within it threaten the process of family reproduction—and create a constituency for moral reform movements. In the contemporary United States the most fervent debate about women's roles has taken place within the context of the politics of abortion. At the heart of this debate, Luker argues, is a controversy about the nature of motherhood. The pro-life position is held by women who are dependent on traditional roles as homemakers; they are opposed and threatened by women whose pursuit of careers depends on reproductive control.[20] Changes in women's roles that generate concerns about family reproduction are not confined to increasing employment. In the final section of this chapter I discuss changes in gender in the late-nineteenth century that led to widespread criticism of women for their presumed abandonment of their maternal roles and duties. Moral rhetoric addresses changes in family relations, particularly gender relations. In such arguments parents, usually mothers, are blamed for inadequately socializing their children, and for the presumed suffering of the innocents of the next generation.

The first part of this book addresses changes in the family that drove and were addressed by anti-vice societies. Comstock's campaign against abortion and contraception, and the historical context in which this occurred, is examined in chapter 2. The anti-vice movement, like the physicians' anti-abortion crusade that proceeded it, linked concerns about sexuality and gender with fear of growing immigrant populations. Comstock made several unique contributions to the campaign to make abortion illegal and unavailable. The anti-obscenity law written by Comstock and passed by Congress forbade using the mails to distribute information about or devices that caused abortion or contraception. In his role as postal inspector, Comstock used this law, along with similar state-level laws, to drive abortion—which was still widely available, if illegal—underground. But Comstock used the debate about abortion to the end of suppressing what he saw as obscenity, arguing that abortion resulted from the sexual debauchery of young people, who had become crazed with lust because of lascivious reading.

Chapter 3 is devoted to demonstrating that upper-class and upper-middle-class people supported Comstock's organization and to explaining this support. Comstock mobilized elite supporters by arguing that obscenity corrupted children. Obscenity endangered elite children because moral corruption threatened to topple them from the peak of the social hierarchy, rendering them unfit for respectable society. This problem, in different forms, potentially plagued both wealthy children and those of more humble origins. Comstock's rhetoric largely concerned the harm that obscene materials could inflict on elite children, but he addressed the effects of such material on working-class children as well. Evil reading, he asserted, made those children dangerous and violent delinquents, and thus a threat to their social superiors.

Women occupied an important role in anti-vice rhetoric, although not, I argue, the one usually asserted in feminist readings of Comstock. Focusing on the very negative effect the Comstock Laws had on women's ability to control reproduction, various authors have asserted that these laws were an attempt to control women by forcing them to bear and rear children.[21] I argue that children, not women, were Comstock's concern, although he assumed that the rearing of morally pure children required women devoted to home and family. The Comstock Laws and the anti-vice movement were thus centrally concerned with women's roles in family reproduction, but historians have been mistaken in attributing the anti-vice movement to a desire to oppress women by forcing unwanted pregnancies upon them. Changes in women's roles had an important place in anti-vice rhetoric, but it was a different place than the one women occupied in the physicians' anti-abortion campaign. In the latter, women were chided for failing to reproduce adequate numbers of babies; laws forbidding abortion were advocated as a means to increase the birthrate of the native born. The anti-vice movement was concerned with the proper socialization of children, not their numbers, and employed rhetoric that condemned "fashionable" women for failing to mother properly.

The problem of reproducing morally pure children concerned not only policing their reading materials (which was the joint responsibility of censors, school superintendents, and watchful parents), but guarding the family as a social institution. Late-nineteenth-century social and moral commentators saw the family facing a variety of travails. A growing sexual subculture made increasingly available pornography and prostitutes, consumed and patronized, sometimes openly, by respectable sons and fathers.[22] Proper society also confronted changes in sexual expression and expectations, particularly in romantic relationships. Love became sexualized; the physical expression of love was an expected part of romance. Furthermore, romantic love subsumed and eventually replaced love of God as the central component of individual identities.[23] The eroding power of the church, the changing nature of love, the new expectations of marriage, and the growing autonomy of women were all seen as causes of divorce, which, once almost unthinkable, became more common. These problems, and Comstock's response, are discussed in chapter 4.

Comstock, not surprisingly, attributed the erosion of the family to the spread of immoral sexual practices and materials. Yet other social commentators offered quite different analyses of divorce, prostitution, and sexual immorality. The free love movement offered the most radical critique, arguing that marriage sexually enslaved women. The institution was maintained, they asserted, by women's forced economic dependence on men and by the church that, in violation of the Constitution, had captured the state to serve its ends. Sexual ignorance led to exploitative relations between men and women, free lovers argued, and they proposed frank discussions of sexuality and marriage as the cure. Comstock found these arguments obscene. He used the anti-obscenity laws to harass, arrest, and sometimes imprison the leading free lovers, who responded by mounting the only sustained attempt to repeal the Comstock Laws. Comstock linked the issue of obscenity to the sanctity of marriage and the power of the church, suppressing a movement that advocated the end of women's sexual oppression.

## Ethnic Conflict and Moral Reform

The argument that the anti-vice movement arose from anxieties about the reproduction of elite children, occasioned by changes in the family and the roles of its members, does not explain why the anti-vice societies arose in some times and places rather than others. A second impetus for moral reform movements comes not from changes within the family, but from changes in the social context in which families reside. If the social niche that children are being trained to occupy is threatened, moral reform movements and rhetoric serve to explain children's failure. Moral crusades thus become a response to the problem of parents' attempts to reproduce children fit for an economic niche that is likely to be undergoing changes beyond the parents' control.[24] Moral rhetoric is thus a response not only to changes in family relations, but to political or economic threats to the social position of families.

In the second part of this book I examine how the success of the anti-vice societies depended on their ability to link rhetoric about protecting children to upper- and middle-class attempts to protect their social niche against the incursion of immigrants. In chapter 5 I examine the history of anti-vice efforts in New York City and Boston, and argue that Comstock connected the problems of obscenity and vice to the influx of immigrants into the city. First, Comstock argued that foreigners were responsible for what he saw as the tide of obscenity. As pornography was increasingly driven from the streets, and as Comstock's arrests were increasingly made among the native born, Comstock turned to the issue of gambling, which, he claimed, destroyed both children and families. Comstock utilized already existing discourses about city politics, which blamed immigrants for the problems (and presumed corruption) of city government, to implicate corrupt police and city politicians in the spread of gambling. In turn, Comstock's campaign gave another weapon to civic reformers who, in response to the increasing domination of city government by immigrants, stripped the city councils (and increasingly, city government itself) of power.

While gambling and its presumed protection by corrupt city officials enhanced the success of the anti-vice movement in New York, in Boston these issues were vital. Founded in 1878 as an offshoot of the New York anti-vice society, the New England Society for the Suppression of Vice (NESSV) was characterized by a lack of direction in its early years caused, in part, by Comstock's success at clearing Boston's streets of obscenity. But while the leaders of the New England anti-vice society had assumed police cooperation with attempts to rid the city of gamblers, they soon found their efforts thwarted by both the police and the police commission. Frustration with the police led the NESSV to join with the Law and Order Society in a successful attempt to remove control of the police from the hands of the mayor and place it in the hands of the governor.

The histories of anti-vice efforts in Boston and New York imply that while the problems of family reproduction and the socialization of children to the (class-linked) values of their parents are always present, the success of the anti-vice societies was predicated on their leaders' ability to articulate a link between the problems of elite family reproduction and the (real or imagined) threat of immigrant communities. The anti-vice societies did not invent nativism or the issue of corruption in city government. Nor did Comstock and the NESSV invoke corruption in city government as a ploy to increase support for the anti-vice societies. Immigrants were often blamed for the ills of the cities, so one does not have to assume that anti-vice leaders were being calculating when they also indicted immigrants. But when the anti-vice societies linked presumed immigrant vices to threats to elite children, potential elite supporters saw obscenity as a threat the anti-vice societies could combat.

In chapter 6 I test this explanation of anti-vice success by looking at the failed attempts to found censorship organizations in Philadelphia. Although Philadelphia's city government was far from free of corruption, it was difficult to link the issue of obscenity to the presumed vices of immigrants because the city government was dominated by native-born Republicans. Comstock's attempts to found a Philadelphia offshoot of his organization were unsuccessful even when he tried to link the issues of obscenity to the corruption in city government. The case of Philadelphia supports the argument that an underlying cause of anti-vice mobilization was the political power of immigrants.

Philadelphian's anti-vice efforts also permit an examination of Baltzell's argument that Quakerism accounts for the lack of a successful censorship organization in Philadelphia.[25] Much of the chapter focuses on the attempts of a prominent Quaker, Josiah Leeds, to rid Philadelphia's streets and theaters of material he considered obscene. Leeds's activities are important because he was a rich Friend who operated with the support of other prominent Quakers and the Meeting. Thus the presumed Quaker values held by Philadelphians cannot explain why Philadelphia lacked an effective censorship organization.

But if immigrant political power explains the success of censorship in Boston and New York and its failure in Philadelphia, was the presumed corruption of elite children by obscenity merely a smoke screen for the "real" mission of the anti-vice societies, which was political control of the cities? I argue that some of the class formation activities of the nineteenth-century upper classes, particularly the founding of major art museums and the use of boarding schools to educate elite children far from city vices, were also linked to the size and power of immigrant communities in the three cities. Not only did Philadelphia lack an anti-vice society, the city was slower to adopt these upper-class institutions. Because Philadelphia's elite youngsters were less likely to be educated in boarding schools, away from the watchful eyes of their parents, anti-vice leaders could not cite the threat of corruption at school as a reason to support censorship.

## Family Reproduction and Class Formation

Concerns about family reproduction drive not only moral crusades that address the erosion of privileged social positions, but also the creation of exclusive social niches. The Gilded Age witnessed the formation of a number of upper-class institutions, such as exclusive social clubs, art museums (and a concept of "high culture" to delineate what should be displayed in them), and boarding schools. Boarding schools were founded with the express intent of protecting elite children from vice; trustees of art museums argued that their institutions would prepare children to appreciate the fine collections of Europe. Thus, concerns about family reproduction helped drive the formation of upper-class institutions.[26]

The rise of high culture, exemplified in the founding of art museums, raises a final question about censorship: What do controversies about art censorship suggest about the place of high culture in the formation of upper-class identities and in the reproduction of the upper class? The issue of art censorship creates yet another puzzle. Comstock's art censorship generated public outrage in New York City, but there was no similar controversy in Boston. Furthermore, the anti-vice society in Boston was more successful and was supported by a larger proportion of the upper class than was the New York anti-vice society. The controversy about art censorship is discussed in chapter 7. While Comstock's claim that the appeal of artistic nudes was erotic may have been accurate, this position was untenable given existing discourses about the nature of art. Because the "high art" that the American upper classes were appropriating consisted in part of Salon nudes, Comstock was ultimately forced to argue that reproductions of art sold to the masses were obscene but works viewed in museums were not. This meant that the obscenity of a piece of art was determined by the social class of the person who viewed it. However, in Boston nudity in art did not generate a controversy about censorship. I argue that upper-class fragmentation explains both the controversy about art in New York and the greater support given to the Boston anti-vice society. In Boston, a more unified upper class reached greater consensus about artistic standards and ultimately about censorship.

In the conclusion I will address how considering family reproduction as a central social activity leads to reconsideration of our understanding of the nature of class and status politics. The literature on moral reform movements has been marred by an erroneous separation of "class" from "status." Examining the process of family reproduction forces us to consider how the reproduction of children is simultaneously a material and symbolic process. Reducing moral concerns to economic factors, or treating concern about children as a "symbolic" rather than a "real" issue, blinds us not only to a fundamental motivator of human action—love for one's children—but leads us to misperceive the causes of a number of significant issues in both historical and contemporary political debate.

## Family, Status, and Class Identity in the Gilded Age

In order to understand the anti-vice movement, the problems of family reproduction must be considered in the context of the late-nineteenth century. Family reproduction necessitated production and reproduction of cultural markers. Cultural consumption within families was largely the province of women. Family reproduction involved issues of class identity, which required differentiating one's family from those above and below. What it meant to be upper or middle class was contested in the nineteenth century, and the requirements for class membership, or for security for one's children, were far from clear.

The social and economic context in which families resided changed dramatically in the nineteenth century, which changed the value of children, particularly in the middle class. While farm families needed the labor of many children, who could contribute to the family income at an early age, the children of an urban middle-class family did not labor but had to be clothed, fed, and educated, thus making them significant expenditures. During the late-nineteenth century, economically costly children were endowed with increasing sentimental value, which eventually created an undersupply rather than a surplus of orphaned infants. But a large family was an unnecessary economic burden, as a smaller number of children could provide the same sentimental value. While the nineteenth century witnessed a dramatic change in the size of the average American family, which decreased from 7 children to 3.5 children by the end of the century, a figure that probably overestimates the average size of families in the city, methods of birth control (other than abstinence) were either unreliable or illegal.[27]

Changes in the roles of women accompanied changes in the value attached to children. Middle-class women, relegated to the home, were responsible for making it a place of beauty and tranquility. They were also charged with training children to take their place in a world in which manners and appearances were increasingly important indicators of social position. It was women's duty to make themselves and their families look like proper members of the middle class.[28] As Abelson argues, "social identity was established through new possibilities of consumption." These possibilities, she notes, were facilitated through hugely expanded production capacities, which forced producers to cultivate new markets. The main target of these marketers was the home. Women's role as orchestrators of home consumption thus made them a linchpin of industrial capitalism.[29] While the economy depended on this expanded consumption, the emphasis on style and concern with fashion that were vital markers of middle-class identities were seen as frivolous at best, and a threat to social order at worst. A *Harper's Magazine* editorial, which sought to explain the decreasing size of American families, blamed middle-class reluctance to reproduce on a trivial obsession with merchandise:

> Wealth and fashion have become too generally the great standards aimed at in life. The plain and simple manner of living, with frugal and industrious habits and slow accumulations once practiced, have given way to a more extravagant, luxurious, and stimulating course of life, and an eager struggle for rapid gains. Young men must now commence life where their fathers left off. While men have been, as it were, wholly absorbed in making money, women have become altogether too much immersed in pursuit of mere pleasure and fashion. . . . Under these circumstances children have come to be considered a care, a burden, and an expense which is thought must, at least to some extent, be dispensed with. In making, therefore, plans for marriage and settlement in life, such troubles are to be avoided as much as possible, especially until the parties get off comfortably in the world.[30]

Condemnations of consumption were particularly focused on women; attacks on fashion were a pointed critique of women's social roles. Women's obsession with shopping, critics argued, suggested female moral frailty. A *New York Times* article condemned shopping as follows:

> The awful prevalence of the vice of shopping among women is one of those signs of the times which lead the thoughtful patriot almost to despair of the future of our country. Few people have any idea of the extent to which our women are addicted to this purse-destroying vice.[31]

Fashionable women concerned themselves with appearances, the display of which was a social event removing them from home. The requirements of middle-class status were thus predicated on the labors of women, who were required to venture into public to acquire from the vast, newly available array of articles those which would signify the social place of her family and herself. This particular labor of women was trivialized, and seen as a peculiarly female vice.[32] Thus condemnations of fashionable women rose in concert with changes in the roles of middle-class women, who were increasingly charged with keeping up the middle-class appearance of their family: women were condemned for a role they were increasingly required to play.[33]

## Gender and Contested Upper-Class Identities

Women occupied a second significant role in the social landscape in which Comstock operated. Issues of social status and class identity loomed large in the lives of people who, like many of Comstock's supporters, were upper class. As with the middle class, issues of upper-class identity revolved around social styles based on consumption, an activity orchestrated within the family, and whose coordination was the province of women. Enormous fortunes were made during and after the Civil War. The makers of these fortunes struggled to translate their money into social esteem. At issue was not only the prestige accorded to ownership of a pseudo-chateau on Fifth Avenue, but the social circles in which one would find acceptance. The premier signal of social acceptance was the marriage of one's children into high-status families—in effect, to families with older fortunes. Simultaneously, however, parvenus used their fabulous wealth to remake the upper class, establishing new cultural (and fiscal) scripts for upper-class behavior. The persons at the center of these attempts to establish family position and permanence, who bore the brunt of criticism for both the excesses of the late-nineteenth century and the unhappiness of marriages wrought for status, were women. While Comstock's rhetoric about threats to elite children referred to pernicious influences threatening wealthy families from below, exactly what social place children should be fitted to occupy was also hotly debated. These struggles within the upper class are important for understanding the anti-vice campaigns for two reasons. First, if we define membership in the upper class as being a millionaire or being included in the *Social Register*—a highly restrictive definition that ignores memberships in clubs and attendance at schools that also denote upper-class status—then at least one-quarter of NYSSV and NESSV supporters were upper class.[34] These supporters were disproportionately important, however, because of the status and legitimacy they conferred on the anti-vice societies. But issues of upper-class social competition also occupied an important role in rhetoric about vice. Comstock referred to, and chided, "fashionable people" in his discussions of child rearing as well as in rhetoric about art. Stereotypes about the fashionable referenced schisms in the upper class, as well as middle-class resentment of the wealthy. When Comstock chided "fashionable women" for not taking adequate care of their children, he addressed not only middle-class women's roles, but also issues of what the upper class—and in particular, the upper-class family—should be.

An examination of writings by and about upper-class people in the late-nineteenth century reveals that social competition, particularly the drama of "inclusion" or "exclusion" from "Society," was rife during the late-nineteenth century. Cleveland Amory has shown that claims that "Society is dead" have been made since the landing of the Pilgrims, invariably by those whose status is being challenged.[35] But the years between the Civil War and the rise of the Progressives, which became known as the Gilded Age because of the fortunes being amassed and the excesses they bred, were the site of especially acute social competition, particularly in New York City. Tensions over what it meant to be upper class ultimately impeded censorship efforts, particularly efforts to censor art.

New York high society was composed of a variety of competing cliques, although the most recognized (perhaps because the most vociferous) were the "Knickerbockers," who claimed descent from the colonial Dutch families who had dominated New York social life since the seventeenth century, and "the Four Hundred," a group of parvenus united with old-money families that was organized in the 1870s. Commentaries by those with old money, as well those with new, indicate that social barriers fell quickly under the onslaught of new fortunes. For example, Mrs. John King Van Rensselaer, a Knickerbocker, wrote in 1924 of how Society had changed since her childhood.

> The early '70s furnished the golden age for New York's aristocracy. They were also the years in which men and women began to climb up to the citadel of social distinction over the newly established trails of wealth and achievement. In the succeeding decades money and achievement, or even notoriety, obtained admission for their possessors into what remained of the city's formerly rigid social structure.
>
> Up over the pathway of wealth the men and women who had no qualifications further than the fortunes they had obtained through luck or inheritance, came thronging to the heights once so carefully guarded. Over the trail of achievement, foreign peasants who had become bankers, newspaper owners who had been and still were common scoundrels, obscure folk who had attained position as merchants, physicians, lawyers, clambered upward to the eminence where a few years earlier only those of patrician heritage has been permitted to stand.[36]

This invasion of the barbarian hordes was not, of course, seen in the same light by the barbarians. Ward McAllister, potentate of the Four Hundred, led the onslaught on the old social order. In 1890 McAllister published his memoirs in *Society as I Have Found It*, which discussed the strategies he employed to break the Dutch stranglehold over New York's elite social life.

At this time there were not more than one or two men in New York who spent, in living and entertaining, over sixty thousand dollars a year. There were not half a dozen *chefs* in private families in this city. Compare those days to these, and see how easily one or two men of fortune could then control, lead, and carry on society, receive or shut out people at their pleasure. If distinguished strangers failed to bring letters to them, they were shut out of everything. Again, if, though charming people, others were not in accord with these powers, they could be passed over and left out of society. All this many of us saw, and saw how it worked, and we resolved to band together the respectable element of the city, and by this union make such strength that no individual could withstand us.[37]

The object was not, of course, to let "everybody" in, but to redefine who was acceptable for associating with "Society." McAllister's ability to play on the emotions of pride, envy, and greed made him a genius in the field of social arbitration. It was clear to McAllister that the Knickerbockers could not be circumvented, but must instead be co-opted. This was accomplished through the formation of a committee of twenty-five men, called (fittingly) "the Patriarchs," each of whom would be responsible for inviting nine guests to a series of balls—the Patriarch Balls. The intent of these balls, first held in 1872, was to mix old Society with new money.

> The object we had in view was to make these balls thoroughly representative; to embrace the old Colonial New Yorkers, our adopted citizens, and men whose ability and integrity had won the esteem of the community, and who formed an important element in society. We wanted the money power, but not in any way to be controlled by it.[38]

Each Patriarch was answerable for the behavior of those he invited. In the event that a guest gave offense, the managers of the balls (presumably McAllister and the other Patriarchs) would make public the name of his sponsor, which would result in the offending Patriarch being "upbraided" by the rest of the community.[39]

The key to the success of the balls was not only the mixture of "Colonial New Yorkers" with "money power," but the social exclusiveness of the events.

> We knew then, and we know now, that the whole secret of the success of these Patriarch Balls lay in making them select; in making them the most brilliant balls of each winter, in making it extremely difficult to obtain an invitation to them, and to make such invitations of great value; to make them the stepping-stone to the best New York society, that one might be sure that any one repeatedly invited to them had a secure social position.[40]

However, people did not wait passively for invitations to events seen as tickets to high society. A good deal of lobbying was involved as well. For example, McAllister's glitzy picnics in Newport (for which he rented sheep to make his farm look more pastoral) were also the object (according to McAllister) of much social politicking.

> Now, do not for a moment imagine that all were indiscriminately asked to these little fêtes. On the contrary, if you were not of the inner circle, and were a new-comer, it took the combined efforts of all your friends' backing and pushing to secure an invitation for you.[41]

Once invited, according to McAllister, the guest was put on "intimate footing" with the best of New York society.

The concerns about social inclusion expressed by Ward McAllister and Mrs. Van Rensselaer suggest that while nineteenth-century economic titans could reproduce their children's economic position by leaving a them a large inheritance, the creation of personal and family social position, and a family legacy, was not merely an economic process. Social acceptance of newcomers was predicated on their proper behavior. However, old money families could not ignore those with new fortunes; old money scions needed to cement their own economic position, as maintaining upper-class appearances was not merely a matter of manners but involved expected expenditures on clothing, furnishings, and entertainment. Yet the process of incorporating new money was fraught with social hazards; one could jeopardize one's old money social status and scandalize one's friends if a new money newcomer misbehaved. This problem was exemplified on New Year's Day of 1873, in an incident in the May family parlor. The Mays were an elite New York City family, and participated in the Dutch New Year's Day custom of having an open house. One of the May daughters, Caroline, was rumored to be engaged to James Gordon Bennett, Jr., heir to seven million dollars and the *New York Herald*. Bennett had not only plentiful new money but a reputation for outrageous behavior and excessive drinking. On New Year's Day, however, he destroyed the social invitations that money had bought by staggering into the May family parlor and urinating behind the parlor door. Bennett was never received in "decent" homes again, spending the rest of his life in Europe. The Mays were chided by their peers for allowing a parvenu to court their daughter.[42] The exchange of money for status, and vice versa, was a process predicated on behaviors acceptable within a given social network—in this case, of New York high society.

Among the losers in the status game were New York's old Dutch families. But certainly their status was disputed. Mrs. Van Rensselaer, for example, argued that without its Dutch forebears, New York Society would not have been so prized.

But it is not the present that brings ambitious hordes to the city. It is rather the glamorous tradition established in the past by aristocratic New Yorkers, now almost entirely obscured by more vivid and better-advertised groups. It is the impress of the old Dutch aristocracy that makes New York to-day the nation's great social center.[43]

But the Dutch were not inviolate. While Mrs. Van Rensselaer wrote of the high esteem in which the "old families" were held when she was young, even then aspersions were being cast against the arrogant Dutch. For example, in 1887 the Society journal *Town Topics* wrote the old Dutch families an unflattering obituary.

Who were the Knickerbockers, anyway? How many distinguished men has the whole tribe produced? They came, and were great only in their own little fussy Dutch opinions; they have gone, and there is not a mourner. What they were, let us judge by the few miserable paupers trotting around the ragged edge of society now with nothing under heaven to thank God for but a name, and that part being forgotten.[44]

As a member of the declining Dutch, Mrs. Van Rensselaer probably felt justified in her insistence that "Society once connoted, first of all, family; its primary meaning at present is fortune."[45] But while the currency of Dutch ancestry may not have bought the social status it once proffered, it was not true that "family" and "ancestry" no longer counted for much in Society. Rather, marriage of one's family members into families of higher status was the primary means of proving and securing social position, while holders of new wealth adorned themselves with the trappings of Europe with the intent of demonstrating that their money was "old."

Nelson W. Aldrich, Jr., has written that money ages at varying rates, so variable that when the children of new money gain entry into old money social circles—are educated at elite schools, admitted into exclusive clubs, and marry the children of established families—the status of their parvenu parents is reevaluated. He cites the example of his great-grandfather, the son of a mill hand who became a wealthy and corrupt Gilded Age politician, who has been accorded Brahmin status in various studies of the era because of his children's social accomplishments. This phenomenon was called "climbing up on the backs of one's children."[46] Mrs. Van Rensselaer cites numerous cases of Gilded Age marriages securing the social positions of parvenu families. For example, Commodore Vanderbilt, the wealthiest man in America, "neither sought nor received acceptance from the exclusive society of his time. His sons and grandsons all married women of assured standing, and in the early '70s the third generation, by grace of the blood on the distaff side of the house, achieved social recognition."[47] Another socially ambitious mother moved her family next door to one of the "oldest of the city's families," who had an ill, but convalescing, son. Her prettiest daughter spent the summer at the invalid's bedside, and at summer's end his shocked family learned of their engagement. Their son married "the daughter of a Shoddyite" over their protests. The social climbing mother engineered prominent marriages for three of her other children. "Bound as she and her husband were by all these carefully adjusted family ties to the city's social system, nothing remained but for that system to recognize him and her. It did."[48]

Many attributed marital breakups to this trade of marriage for status. One commentator writing in the late 1860s called "fashionable weddings . . . mockeries of love, satires on marriage, insults to nature."[49] Such charges became more vociferous as divorce among the upper class became more common. Van Rensselaer claimed that in the middle of the 1870s, "all at once it became fashionable to divorce your helpmeet, and Newport (summer home of the most fashionable) followed the fashion with amazing enthusiasm."[50] Van Rensselaer did not name the persons whose morality she indicted, but she probably referred to the divorce and remarriage of the William K. Vanderbilts and the estrangement of the William Astors.[51]

The eclipse of New York's Dutch families did not create a fashion for all things American. Instead, and in part out of a search for ancestry and legitimacy, the new high society embraced the cultural trappings of Europe. McAllister notes that in the 1870s "we imported European habits and customs rapidly." His claim is substantiated by descriptions of parties whose participants came in the garb of French noblemen, as well as the numerous dinner menus written entirely in French, which were reproduced in his book.[52] Acquiring the trappings of European aristocrats increased the status of families and the marriageability of children. Part of what families sought was what the Knickerbockers had—a claim to family history and permanence. This was exemplified above all by Tiffany's genealogical service, which was started in the Gilded Age and produced largely fictitious genealogies.[53] It was not the reality of the family tree, however, but the fiction of family permanence that mattered. While the Four Hundred pretended to be a nobility, this charade was often mocked. An article in the North American Review commented:

> Very many of them seem to think that they have a place in this country
> corresponding to that of the leaders of society in Europe; for example,
> the nobility and gentry of England. They keep their fathers and their
> mothers hidden away,—in closets upstairs, or in the waste places and
> remote corners of the land,—and set up as people of fashion upon fine
> clothes, bric-a-brac, and champagne.[54]

A more compelling tie to European nobles could be made by marrying one. Marriages of American heiresses to European peers increased dramatically during the Gilded Age. Montgomery argues that marriages to nobles can be interpreted as either an attempt to increase a family's status within New York social circles or perhaps to circumvent the snobbery of New York's "aristocrats" by seeking the endorsement of real nobility.[55]

The social setting of Comstock's crusade was not only a city teeming with immigrants and vice. The city was also home to individuals struggling to be included in an upper class that was integral to Comstock's success, a class in turn engaged in a struggle over its collective identity. While the majority of anti-vice society supporters watched these struggles from afar, the struggle over "Society" was part of the lives of a significant minority of its members.

## Prostitution, Gender, and the Boundary Below

Discussions of women's lives attributed meaning to women's actions not only by condemning vain and pretentious women flitting about at the top of the social hierarchy, but by pointing as well to women at the bottom of society. Discussions of women in public concerned not only their roles as shoppers and socialites, but invoked as well "public women," meaning prostitutes. The specter of prostitution haunted discussions of youthful morality, providing a visage of the threat the city posed to families and to youths.

Prostitutes generated horror, fascination, and a great deal of rhetoric bent on reforming "the social evil." Women selling their bodies challenged Victorian ideologies about women's asexuality and, according to reformers, endangered innocent women and children with the threat of syphilis carried into pure homes by debauched husbands. The specter of women's sexuality represented by prostitution was alleviated by the common belief that many women who became prostitutes had been seduced and betrayed by men.[56] Crapsey's guide to vice and crime in New York City included a description of various brothels, and the claim that the majority of women who became prostitutes did so after having been abandoned by their seducers. He presented the following as a typical account.

> Sir, only a year ago I was a happy innocent girl in my father's house in a town near this city. I had a lover everyone thought was an honorable man, and we were engaged to be married. I adored him, father trusted him, all my friends envied me because of him. Well, I was weak, he was mean, and he betrayed me. After that he deserted me; the consequences

of my sin after a time could not be hidden. Then my father cast me off, and all who had ever known me shunned me. . . . Of course I had to starve or come here. I hadn't nerve enough to kill myself, so I went to the house where you found me to-night.[57]

Popular belief held a prostitute's life was marked by a series of downward steps. Her career began in a "first-class house" located in a respectable part of the city. Neighbors of such houses were often ignorant of the business transacted there. The "wretched life" of the prostitute soon took a physical toll, and women were forced out of first-class houses into ever more desperate and degraded circumstances. Ultimately, inexorably, the high-class courtesan fell, ending life as a drunken and diseased street-walker. These unfortunates died in drunken brawls or drowned themselves in the East River.

> Seven years is the average life of an abandoned woman in the great city. She may begin her career with all the *eclat* possible, she may queen it by virtue of her beauty and charms in some fashionable house, at the beginning, and may even outlast the average term at such places; it matters not; her doom is certain. . . . "The wages of sin is death."[58]

This tale of the demise of fallen women may have satisfied outraged morality, but others writing about prostitution equivocated about the prostitute's inevitable end. The most titillating reports of prostitution claimed that women from respectable families, including wives, frequented houses of assignation.

> The effect has been to intrude prostitution into circles and places where its presence is never suspected. . . . Women of high position and culture, no less than unlettered shop girls, resort to the houses of assignation, which are of every grade, from the palaces in the most aristocratic to the frowsy rooms in the slums. Many of the frequenters of these houses are married women, who are driven by an insane desire for display to thus add to a scanty income.[59]

Prostitution thus operated simultaneously as a terrifying moral tale—that the adulterous wife or the unmarried woman who engaged in sexual intercourse with her lover would inexorably fall through the various levels of the social structure, living an ever more degraded life—and as a symbol of the ambiguous moral state of all women, married or unmarried, of whatever social class.

Discussions of prostitution focused on the character of women, but prostitution was ubiquitous in New York City because of the moral transgressions of men. While young women were forbidden from engaging in premarital intercourse, single and married men from respectable families openly patronized prostitutes. The late-nineteenth century, historian Gilfoyle shows, saw the expansion of "sporting male" culture into all social classes. Concert-saloons, which featured bawdy acts and available prostitutes, were frequented, according to Howard Crosby, by "sons of our best-esteemed citizens—merchants' and bankers' clerks, book-keepers, and tellers of banks, employees of insurance offices, city, county, and State office-holders." In 1869 the writer George Ellington asserted that "fashionable bloods and old fogies, known rakes, and presumedly pious people, wealthy bachelors and respectable married men, fast sons and moral husbands" frequented prostitutes.[60] Brothels spread throughout the city; prostitutes could be seen in most of the city's neighborhoods.[61] As a consequence, "it is said that New York is the wickedest city in the country. It is the largest, and vice thrives in crowded communities."[62]

While much discussion of gender in the late-nineteenth century concerned the social position and moral failings of women, such discussions invoked the roles of both women and men. Rhetoric about vice referred to women's sexual transgressions and their victimization at the hands of men. Women's sexual agency and sexual jeopardy were both invoked in discussions of abortion. Comstock's earliest victories against vice involved the suppression of abortion, which is the subject of the next chapter.

# 2

## THE CITY, SEXUALITY, AND THE SUPPRESSION

## OF ABORTION AND CONTRACEPTION

O N AUGUST 26, 1871, a naked corpse was found in a trunk in the baggage room of New York City's Hudson River Railway. The *New York Times* described the body as that of a "young girl . . . [with] a face of singular loveliness . . . but her chief beauty was her great profusion of golden hair . . . that lay in heavy masses upon her breast." Although the identity of the young woman was unknown, the decomposed flesh of her pelvis marked her as "a new victim of man's lust, and the life-destroying arts of . . . abortionists." The corpse was taken to the morgue of Bellevue Hospital, where the "horrible mass" was placed on ice in the hopes that it would be identified. The decaying body drew hundreds of curious spectators. While the young woman remained un-identified for several days, blame for her death was quickly fixed on Jacob Rosensweig, who was a Polish immigrant and a Jew. The death came a week after the *New York Times* published an exposé of the city's abortion trade, entitled "The Evil of the Age." The article examined the careers of several abortionists, including that of Rosensweig. The corpse was finally identified by her doctor and dentist as that of Alice Bowlsby. Police found a handkerchief embroidered with her initials in Rosensweig's house, seal-ing the case against him. At Rosensweig's trial the district attorney ap-pealed not only for the conviction of a man who perpetrated a criminal offense, but for "the suppression of a crime which strikes at the root of all civilized society."[1] Thus Rosensweig was convicted not only for the acci-dental death of a young woman, but for threatening society itself. Abor-tion, which during the first half of pregnancy had been legal in virtually all of the states until the 1850s, and which by 1870 was, according to physicians, moralists, and historians, still commonly practiced, if illegal, had become symbolic of the collapse of civilization.

This chapter will examine anti-abortion rhetoric in the 1860s and 1870s in pursuit of two goals. One aim of this chapter is to introduce the social and ideological context of Comstock's anti-vice crusade. Comstock recapitulated the central themes of anti-abortion discourses in his rhetoric against vice: sexual respectability and prostitution, the perceived social and political threat of the growing immigrant working class, the problem of controlling the sexuality of adolescents and what this problem implied about the state of the family, and finally, debate over the proper social roles for women. Late-nineteenth-century changes in the family and polity to which anti-abortion rhetoric referred were problems that Comstock promised to ameliorate throught the suppression of obscenity; thus, understanding the sexual and political context of the anti-vice crusade helps explain why the movement succeeded. The second goal of this chapter is discussion of Comstock's crusade against abortion and contraception. While Comstock is best remembered for the "Comstock Laws," which banned the distribution of contraceptives, he was a leading anti-abortion crusader and is credited by historian James Mohr with arresting more abortionists in the mid-1870s than did any other person in the United States.[2] I will argue that the case against abortion concerned not only relations within families, both between men and women and between parents and their children, but also invoked the threat posed to the family by the city and its immigrants. Rhetoric about abortion thus provides an important context for understanding Comstock's lifelong campaign to preserve the purity of America's youth.

## Abortion in the Nineteenth Century

Beginning in the 1840s abortions became increasingly common; physicians estimated that between one in three and one in ten pregnancies were aborted. More alarming to physicians were changes in the characteristics of women seeking abortions. During the early-nineteenth century abortion had been practiced primarily by desperate and unmarried women, but by midcentury married women increasingly used abortion to control the size of their families. Abortions were accomplished either through ingesting medicines that would end "blocked menses," poisoning the fetus without, hopefully, fatally poisoning the mother, or by resort to mechanical means of abortion, such as injecting water into the uterus or rupturing the placental membranes with instruments. While home medical advice books commonly gave instructions for preparing abortifacients, women also used pills and potions produced by a number of firms or compounded by herbalists and druggists. Midwives and irregular physicians (those who did not possess medical training recognized by the American Medical Association) also performed abortions, as did some regular physicians who defied the AMA's dictates. In 1857 the AMA launched a campaign to outlaw abortion, which by 1890 resulted in the passage of laws making abortion illegal in every state. Public opinion did not keep pace with the physicians' crusade, but the 1870s marked a critical change in the treatment of abortion in the press and in the courts. The decade opened and closed with well-publicized deaths of women who perished from botched abortions; during the decade, the *New York Times* reported on many abortion deaths. Abortionists were increasingly portrayed as evil—in part because they were immigrants—and their practice portrayed as likely to cause painful death.[3]

## Single Women, Sexuality, and Abortion

Alice Bowlsby's death, and the rhetoric used to explain it, typifies one aspect of the case made against abortion. Bowlsby was a single woman. Her fiancé, a man named Walter Conklin, committed suicide when he learned the identity of the body in the trunk.[4] After his death the papers recounted his numerous sexual escapades.[5] In summarizing the case against Rosensweig, the district attorney recounted Bowlsby's life and her relations with Conklin.

> He described the situation of a young girl ruined and betrayed; a child of misfortune, she is stricken down with the thought that every day brings her nearer to disgrace. She knows her ruin has been effected, and unless she secretly gets rid of her guilt she had better be buried in the grave. . . . Born in poverty, and with an inheritance of beauty which is sometimes more ruinous than any gift that could be conferred on them, they are daily tempted by the scoundrels and rascals that surround them. . . . Under this terrible temptation, united with the love the man professes, the unfortunate girl falls. Fallen, she does not know what to do. Her betrayer tells her she cannot be his wife, and as a last desperate measure she seeks the aid of unprincipled scoundrels that advertise in the newspapers.[6]

At the center of this account of Bowlsby's terrible death, and at the heart of anti-abortion rhetoric, is the problem of relationships between men and women. Single women who sought, and sometimes died from, abortions were simultaneously portrayed as innocent victims of male lust and guilty casualties of their own sexual desires and transgressions. Anti-abortion tracts conceded that abortions by seduced and abandoned women could be understood and forgiven. In 1870 the physician Augustus Gardner wrote, "We can forgive the poor, deluded girl,—seduced, betrayed, abandoned,—who in her wild frenzy, destroys the mute evidence of her guilt."[7] But descriptions of women whose bodies and trust were violated by their male lovers still did not exonerate these women for engaging in sexual intercourse.

The shame and social downfall associated with an illegitimate birth also explain why abortions, emblematic to some of the destruction of the family, were sometimes procured for a pregnant woman by a family member, who thus became an accomplice to a crime. Such a case emerged during the week when Bowlsby's death occupied the press. Emily Post, a thirty-year-old daughter of a bookkeeper who "was the associate of many of the most eminent men in the City," died from an abortion performed late in her pregnancy. On her deathbed she told the coroner that her "ruin" had been "effaced . . . under promise of marriage" by a man who had concealed his marriage from her. Once her pregnancy became apparent, her brother brought her to the accused abortionist, Dr. Perry, and paid him fifty dollars to have her "attended to."[8] While her brother was not charged, two years later a funeral in Cincinnati was halted on the suspicion that the deceased had died from an abortion. A jury was impaneled and an inquest held in the church; the examination of Belle Worts's remains revealed that she had bled to death from an abortion. Although the persons involved had been of "the most respectable character," the woman's sister, nephew, and lover were all charged for being accessories to the crime of abortion.[9]

The dilemma faced by respectable families with pregnant daughters resulted, in part, from changing notions of women's sexuality and the limits of sexual interaction during courtship. Recent evidence suggests that contrary to notions about Victorian prudery, married women, who were obligated to present a public facade of purity and passionlessness, experienced sexual pleasure and expressed carnal desire with their husbands. During the nineteenth century romantic love became sexualized; indeed, sexuality was both justified by and seen as the expression of true love. While this left married persons free to explore their desires, it created a dilemma for courting couples. A strong taboo remained against premarital intercourse, yet, as historian Karen Lystra argues, the middle and upper-middle classes accepted "petting, caressing, kissing, and other non-genital forms of sexual interaction" as acceptable behaviors for courting couples; indeed, the belief that sexual expression of love was seen as the most authentic expression of the self pressured couples to express their emotions physically.[10] Still, while public and private sexual morality differed in Victorian America, the expectation that middle-class women would be virgins at marriage remained intact.[11]

The guilt attached to sexual intercourse among unmarried women resulted, in part, from the violation of the boundaries between respectable and unrespectable society the act represented. Discussions of abortion evoked a thin line between the parlor and the gutter, evident in reflections on a woman's "character" and the social consequences of her sexual behavior. One strand of these arguments asserted that women who seemed respectable were, by engaging in sex before marriage, actually acting like prostitutes. When the district attorney prosecuted Rosensweig, he portrayed Alice Bowlsby as poor but respectable until a man deceived her. Bowlsby's virginity prior to her relationship with Conklin was implied; clearly she was not a prostitute. But the following year a very different account of Bowlsby's life was given by Edward Crapsey, whose book *The Nether Side of New York* offered a lurid vision of the city and its women. Crapsey cited the trunk mystery to make the case that the majority of abortionists' patrons were unmarried women who only seemed "respectable."

> This young girl had always moved in the most reputable circles, and had never been suspected, even by her most intimate friends, of any impropriety. Yet she was forced, in order to get rid of the consequences of her transgressions, to resort to the man in whose hands she died. Up to the moment when the identity of the corpse in the trunk at the Hudson River Railroad depot was established, there was no young woman of fairer reputation; but the revelations following her death rolled away the closing stone from a whited sepulchre, so that all the world looked in upon a mass of corruption.[12]

In place of a girl ruined and betrayed, Crapsey presented Bowlsby as a woman who lived a life of sexual transgressions. He followed this revision of the life of Bowlsby with a series of accusations about women who patronized abortionists. Many of these young women were, he asserted, members of the "first circles of society." But, as Crapsey was quick to note, while seemingly respectable women were the mainstay of abortionists' business, these same services were sought by prostitutes.[13] Rather than being the bulwark of moral purity, women were morally ambiguous. A woman might look respectable, but one could not be sure. Rhetoric about deception extended to men's character as well; abortion also represented the betrayal of young women at the hands of deceitful male suitors.

While women who procured abortions were condemned for acting like prostitutes, a second strand in anti-abortion writings argued that women sought abortions to avoid becoming prostitutes. The death of Jennie Passmore, the daughter of a respectable Poughkeepsie tailor, was reported under the headline "Seeking to Hide Her Shame," a recurring theme in discussions of abortion.[14] Hugh Hodge, a physician, argued that appeals to preserve the lives of fetuses were often lost on unmarried women, for "to preserve their reputation and escape degradation becomes an all-absorbing idea, and renders them perfectly insensible to all other considerations."[15] Moral rhetoric was sometimes grounded in reality: the death of Nellie Smith illustrated the relationship between abandonment, abortion, and prostitution.

Nellie Smith was a girl from the country; she came to Kingston several months ago. She had a lover, a young man of respectable family and good address. Nellie was accustomed to entertain this lover in a room she had hired at Rondout. The intercourse between the young people developed into wrong-doing, and it is alleged that Nellie, in March last, became pregnant.

Nellie, according to the *New York Times* account, secured the services of an abortionist, but lost both her health and social position, for she ended up ill and in an almshouse. Her health gradually returned. Two courtesans visited her, and Nellie "became an inmate of a den of vice." A few months later she died from the effects of the abortion.[16] If virginity was the boundary between life as a respectable wife and life as a prostitute, then women who had become pregnant before marriage had little choice but to abort.

Thus debates about abortion referenced changes in heterosexual culture operating both in public and in private. Outside the home, there were "public women"—prostitutes—and a male sexual culture that spread sexuality beyond the confines of the family and the dictates of respectability. In private, the sexualization of romantic love changed the behavior of both married and courting couples. For women, the juxtaposition of these cultures posed particular dangers. A philandering husband could infect a married woman with syphilis; an unmarried woman might succumb to false protestations of love and promises of marriage and find herself pregant, abandoned, and socially ostracized.

## Married Women and Abortion

While anti-abortion reformers claimed to understand why an unmarried woman would seek an abortion, abortions by married women were universally condemned. As Gardner wrote, "for the married shirk, who disregards her divinely-ordained duty, we have nothing but contempt." Discussions of abortion by single women concerned women's sexuality, and disruption of proper relations between men and women represented by premarital sexual intercourse; similarly, married women's abortions threatened the bedrock of society, the family.[17]

Rhetoric about married women's abortions centered on two issues. Women were excoriated for murdering their unborn children and shirking their marital duties in order to pursue frivolous activities outside of their homes. Simultaneously, women were exonerated from the crime of murder because their presumed ignorance of fetal development (and acceptance of the quickening doctrine, which held that life began when the pregnant woman could feel fetal movement) left them unaware that an abortion ended a human life. Thus Andrew Nebinger, a physician, argued,

> The act is mainly committed to avoid the labor and expense of raising children, and the interference with pleasurable pursuits, fashions, and frivolities. . . . She tears open her womb, or permits it to be assailed with instruments or emmenagogues, and the little being within its portal to be ruthlessly destroyed, mainly, because she does not comprehend the immoral enormity of her conduct.[18]

Women, according to the anti-abortion propagandists, could not be bothered with children, being more interested in the accumulation and display of fine silks and jewels, in avoiding the pain of childbirth, and in averting the expense of educating a large family. This unwillingness of women to have and rear large families was condemned in harshest terms by abortion opponents:

> Who can express what follows [in the eye of God] with regard to those women who, finding themselves lawfully mothers, prefer to devastate with poison or with steel their wombs, rather than bear the discomforts attached to the privilege of maternity, rather than forego the gaieties of a winter's balls, parties, and plays, or the pleasures of a summer's trips or amusements?[19]

Abortion violated what its opponents believed to be women's essential nature and transgressed God-given roles. This was a fearful threat to society; women were not only capable of murdering their unborn children, they might abandon their families altogether. Abortion destroyed the home:

> A moral and social gangrene pervades the community, and threatens its life, by destroying its very roots which nature intended should cluster around the domestic hearth.[20]

Women obtained abortions, according to its opponents, not only because of their distaste for motherhood and the home, but because they were adulterous. Abortions allowed married women to hide the evidence of their unfaithfulness. Mrs. Grindle, whom the *New York Times* had accused of both abortion and "baby farming"—that is, taking illegitimate infants for a fee and letting them die of neglect—argued that her work saved many homes from scandal.

> Poor unfortunate women! How little the world knows how to appreciate their trials. We think it our mission to take them and save them—a noble work it is, too. But for some friendly hand like ours, how many

blasted homes, scandalized churches and disorganized social circles there would be. Why, my dear friends, you have no idea of the class of people that come to us. We have had Senators, Congressmen and all sorts of politicians bring some of the first women in the land here. Many—very many aristocratic married women come here—or we attend them in private houses.[21]

While most opponents of abortion argued that married women who aborted were cheating their husbands, either of his right of fatherhood or of his right to have a faithful wife, often men wanted their wives to abort unwanted children. While the anti-abortion polemicists were correct in their assertion that the pain of childbirth and the care of children fell on wives, the economic burden of children fell on husbands as well. The dramatic decline in the size of the middle-class family probably reflected decisions about family size reached, and acted upon, both by husbands and wives.[22]

Changes in the size of the American family were a predictable consequence of industrialization and the growth of an urban middle class, but this trend alarmed contemporary observers. The shrinking family was viewed as evidence of moral decline because it implied that women were no longer willing to devote their entire lives to rearing children. Social decay was manifest in more than changes in women's roles, however. As *Harper's Magazine* pointed out in 1869, only families of native-born Americans were shrinking. Immigrant parents produced an increasingly large proportion of the nation's children, particularly in cities such as New York. The County of New York, for example, had 965 American-born women with ten or more children, but 2,850 foreign-born women with that many offspring. *Harper's* noted that these disparities might lead to the growing population of first- and second-generation immigrants controlling municipal governments.[23] The *Harper's* article, which also condemned abortion, thus connected the practice to a growing and increasingly powerful, and thus threatening, immigrant population. The nativism at the heart of this argument was an established feature of anti-abortion rhetoric. Physicians campaigning against abortion claimed that married women who aborted not only failed in their duties as women, but betrayed the interests of all native-born Protestants. In 1870 Dr. Andrew Nebinger cited a number of physicians who observed that Protestant women aborted with impunity while Catholic and Jewish women shunned the practice.[24] Thus one role immigrants played in anti-abortion rhetoric was that of a threatening population outbreeding the native born.

Immigrants occupied another role in condemnations of abortion. While the practice of abortion carried the taint of illicit sexuality, prostitution, and marital infidelity, its practitioners also made abortion vile. Women who sought abortion because they did not know about fetal life, or abandoned and desperate girls who aborted to save themselves from disgrace, might be forgiven their crime. Abortionists, however, were evil, cruel, fiendish—and foreign.

Abortionists exposed by the press tended to be immigrants. Of seven abortionists discussed in "The Evil of the Age," three were immigrants.[25] The prejudice against immigrants and Jews was particularly pronounced in the *New York Times* reports of Alice Bowlsby's death. Rosensweig, the accused abortionist, was often quoted in a fake vernacular. He was portrayed as a brutal and stupid man; at the police station he volunteered, "Yes, I wash dar, but I yust makes fun," simultaneously giving himself away and proving his lack of compassion and humanity.[26] In 1873 Rosensweig wrote the *New York Times* a letter from prison. The *Times* introduced the "disgusting note" from the man who performed the "horrible and cruel" operation that killed Alice Bowlsby by claiming that this convicted "miscreant" was trying to "sneak through the meshes of the law." His letter read:

> Poland has no Freinds—I am a Polander—I have no Freinds—I am poor—God knows that I am not the man who cumitted the terrible deed, the Press are doing all they can to prejudice my case, all I ask is Fair play under the law, will You do as much for an unfortunate man without money or rich freinds as to let these few lines appear in your great paper from a countryman of Pulaski and Koscusky.

The *Times* responded by saying that in order to "discourage this 'Polander' without 'freinds'" from writing again, they wanted it known that they wished that he had been sent to the gallows.[27]

## Abortion and Class Boundaries

While abortionists were portrayed as immigrants, and thus to some degree distinct from respectable native-born people, another strand of anti-abortion rhetoric portrayed its practitioners as those who passed as respectable people. Their crime was all the more insidious because it was not obvious. Abortionists passing as doctors, like seemingly respectable women who were actually prostitutes and married women who frequented houses of assignation, were deceivers. Abortionists claimed a facade of respectability by assuming the title of "doctor," a practice that evoked frequent condemnation. Outrage over false medical titles came in part from "regular" physicians, those who had completed what passed for medical training in the late-nineteenth century. James Mohr argues that the newly formed American Medical Association started the campaign against abortion in the 1850s to secure their position in a field filled with midwives, healers, and homeopaths. Medical training was so poor that "regular" physicians actually had little more to offer patients than did "irregular" doctors. The campaign against abortion allowed regular physicians to claim specialized and new knowledge about fetal development that "proved" the fetus was a human life. The AMA used this supposed superior knowledge to agitate for anti-abortion laws that would drive irregular physicians, who practiced abortion, out of business. No scientific advances justified the American Medical Association's claims, but the campaign against abortion differentiated and elevated the status of physicians trained at medical schools, even though the training offered at these schools was minimal and standards for graduation astonishingly low.[28] Still, by the 1870s one of the charges repeatedly made against abortionists was that they claimed to have medical training that they did not possess. The author of "The Evil of the Age" asserted,

> The men and women who are engaged in this outrageous business are, with few exceptions, the worse class of impostors. Very few have genuine medical diplomas. Some are, or have been, nurses, and thus picked up fragments of knowledge, but are lamentably devoid of scientific education; in some cases they are ridiculously ignorant of the commonest rudiments of ordinary branches of learning.[29]

One interpretation of this charge against abortionists is that medical impostors were more likely to harm their patients. But infection was one of the gravest dangers of abortion, and regular doctors did not universally adopt sterile techniques until the 1890s, so the evidence that a medical degree made an abortion safer is not compelling.[30] This suggests another interpretation of anger aroused by an irregular physician posing as an M.D.: such persons, who claimed to be respectable members of the upper-middle class by virtue of their profession, demonstrated through their ruse that appearances could not be trusted. This undermined claims to respectability by both regular physicians and other members of the upper-middle class. When the district attorney made his case against Rosensweig he stated, "For if a man who claimed to be clothed with the character of a physician, much more one who has no such character, or position in the community, deliberately goes to work to take the life of an unborn child, in [my] judgment he is as guilty of murder as if he took the life of an adult."[31] At issue was not only the crime of killing a fetus, but that of posing as a physician while doing so. Laws regulating abortion gave regular physicians the right to determine when an abortion was medically necessary and to perform the operation in such cases.

As well as undermining claims to social respectability based on professional titles, abortionists undercut claims to social status based on wealth. Abortionists' fortunes were frequently mentioned in anti-abortion rhetoric. Lookup Evans, for example, had amassed "in this nefarious business . . . a fortune of $100,000, a portion of which he had invested in a splendid farm near Jamaica, Long Island," while Madame Grindle and her husband, Dr. H. D. Grindle, were "reputed to have amassed a handsome fortune."[32]

The city's most notorious, and reputedly its wealthiest, abortionist, the woman called "the wickedest woman in New York," was an English immigrant named Anne Lohman, better known as Madame Restell. Restell made her fortune selling abortifacients, called "Portuguese Female Pills," through the mail. The practice of abortion was so identified with Restell that it was also called "Restellism." Lohman served a prison term for manslaughter from a botched abortion in the 1840s, but what made her notorious was not her criminal record, but her ostentatious house. Restell lived on Fifth Avenue at Fifty-second Street, a "very fashionable" neighborhood; her house was "one of the handsomest four-story brown-stone structures on Fifth avenue."[33] The house symbolized the impunity with which abortionists pursued their trade. In January of 1871 the assistant district attorney, summarizing in court the evidence against an accused abortionist, Dr. Wolff, dwelled on Restell's house.

He referred to the prevalence of the crime of scientific abortion, and subsequently said, "I have a right to refer to that den of shame in our most crowded street, where every brick in that splendid mansion might represent a little skull, and the blood that infamous woman has shed might have served to mix the mortar with which that palace of iniquity was built. When I see American mothers with servants in livery, and all the evidence of splendor and wealth, frequenting those bloody courts and contributing to keep up this woman in her extravagance and licentiousness, I, in common with my fellow-citizens, should become indignant at this plot on the otherwise fair name of our City. . . . If there is anything that adds to the atrocity of this crime, it is that the men and women who commit it take professional titles. What right has this infamous woman, by whose den of shame and blood we have to ride to get to the fairest scenes in our City—erected there as the old dragon's castle was, close by the gates of the fabled Eden—to take the title of 'Madame' upon her lips! 'Madame Restelle,' forsooth! 'Madame Murderer, Madame Abortionist'; and 'Doctor' Evans and 'Doctor' Wolff— are they entitled to the name of doctor? Are they regular physicians? The defendant nods his head—then so much the deeper, and darker, and more damning his iniquity!"[34]

Wolff's trial preceded both the trunk mystery and the publication of "The Evil of the Age." The *New York Times* claimed that the case excited special interest because prosecutions for abortion were very rare while the crime was known to be common. Wolff was tried for manslaughter, but the *Times* coverage placed as much emphasis on Restell's wealth as on the suffering and death of a young woman.

The notoriety of Restell's mansion is not solely explained by its having been built with the proceeds of a crime, even if that crime represented to opponents of abortion the deaths of unborn children. Rather, Restell's house made visible the sin and shame of the upper- and upper-middle-class women reputed to be her clientele; it was a monument to the moral failures of New York's upper class. Restell's business survived untouched by the law, claimed abortion opponents, because Restell knew too much about the sins of the rich and powerful.

> Brown stone palaces will continue to be built in the Fifth Avenue, and the business of abortion will thrive, and the rich occupants will snap their fingers at the laws; for have they not the reputations of the wives and daughters of lawyers, juries, aye, even of the judges themselves in their hands?[35]

Restell's house thus linked shame with honor, and invisibility to ignominy. Women and their families maintained their social position and appearance of honor through resort to the house of Restell. The sins of the upper class were rendered invisible in one of the most visible and notorious houses in the city. At the same time, the very visibility of this house, and the shame it represented, made the police and courts avert their eyes. Restell's house was only the most visible manifestation of a practice that saved individual families from social disgrace but represented, at least to its opponents, the destruction of the family; that saved women from prostitution, but by its existence showed that the sexual purity of respectable women was hardly incorruptible.

## Comstock, Contraception, and the Criminalization of Abortion

During the 1870s rhetoric against abortion and arrests of its practitioners increased. It is difficult to estimate how common abortions remained, but its practitioners were increasingly furtive. While the American Medical Association played an important role in the criminalization of abortion, one of the most important actors in the campaign to suppress abortion operated independently from the physicians. Anthony Comstock and the New York Society for the Suppression of Vice (NYSSV) are known for their role in suppressing contraception, not abortion, but the federal and state anti-obscenity acts known as the "Comstock Laws" were a powerful legal tool effectively wielded by the anti-vice society against providers of abortions as well as contraceptives. Comstock's role in the abortion controversy was to link abortion and contraception to the availability of obscene literature on city streets. In the process, Comstock utilized much of the rhetoric of anti-abortion agitators, but his arguments focused more on threats to the purity of children than on the moral failings of women.

Comstock's work was sponsored by the Young Men's Christian Association (YMCA), a partnership that united a pious young man already dedicated to the eradication of vices, particularly obscenity, with an organization that had made an unsuccessful attempt to rid the streets of unclean literature. Anthony Comstock was born in 1844 in New Canaan, Connecticut. His father was a successful farmer who owned 160 acres of land and two sawmills, and who employed as many as thirty men; his mother, Polly Lockwood, was the daughter of a prosperous local farmer. Comstock's mother died when he was ten; following a series of business reversals during the Civil War, Comstock's father lost his farm. Comstock joined the Union army after his brother died at Gettysburg. Much of the twelve months of his service were spent in a peaceful area of Florida, where Comstock attended religious services between four and nine times a week. Comstock's regiment did not have a chaplain, so he devoted his time to scouting the area, looking for clergymen to preach to his regiment.[36] Comstock was not popular among his fellow recruits. His refusal to touch liquor generated considerable resentment, particularly because he poured his ration of whiskey on the ground rather than giving it to someone who did not share his scruples. Upon being mustered out of the army in 1865, Comstock made his way to New York City, became a clerk in a dry goods establishment, and married Maggie Hamilton.[37]

Comstock made his first foray against obscenity in 1868. A friend of his was "led astray and corrupted and diseased," it seems, from buying an obscene book and, during a subsequent visit to a brothel, contracting a venereal disease. Comstock visited the book dealer, a man named Conroy, purchased an obscene book from him, and then brought a police captain to arrest Conroy and seize his stock. Comstock made other, similar arrests of obscenity dealers, but he did not come to the attention of the YMCA until 1872.

The YMCA had not been indifferent to the problem of obscenity corrupting the city's youth. In 1866 the YMCA became concerned with the "depravity of clerks," and attempted to secure a New York State law that would restrict the circulation of obscene material.[38] The Albany legislature finally passed the law in 1868, in time for Comstock to make his first arrest. The efforts of the YMCA, however, seem to have had no effect on the circulation of obscenity on the city streets. Thus Comstock found a receptive audience when he asked the YMCA for help in his one-man campaign against indecency.

Comstock wrote to the secretary of the New York City YMCA, Robert R. McBurney, asking for funds from the association to purchase the obscene plates and books owned by the widow of a recently deceased book dealer. Comstock's letter came to the attention of Morris K. Jesup, a wealthy leader of the organization. Jesup gave Comstock $650 to purchase the stock; more importantly, he founded within the YMCA the Committee for the Suppression of Vice, which (secretly) funded Comstock's efforts.[39]

The Committee for the Suppression of Vice devoted its efforts to the eradication of obscene literature, and approximately two-thirds of the 106 people arrested by Comstock during the first two years of the committee's work were charged with selling obscenity. In the next chapter I will discuss in detail how Comstock and his supporters gathered support for their crusade; these appeals, I will argue, were mainly concerned with the corrupting effect of obscene materials on children. But the Committee for the Suppression of Vice, which separated from the YMCA in 1874 to become the New York Society for the Suppression of Vice, also helped put illegal abortionists out of business. Their efficacy in this regard was the result of their successful efforts to lobby both the United States Congress and the New York State Legislature, and to pass laws that forbade the advertising of abortion and contraception. The anti-vice society's work was the enforcement of these laws.

## Contraception, Antifeminism, and the Comstock Laws

Most analysts of Comstock's activities have asserted that because the Comstock Laws had a devastating impact on women's reproductive freedom, controlling women was their intent. This interpretation has a long history. In 1916 Leta Hollingsworth argued in the *American Journal of Sociology* that the anti-obscenity laws, which included clauses forbidding the circulation of information about or devices that caused abortion and contraception, were intended to force women to remain in their traditional roles of wives and mothers by compelling them to bear and rear children.[40] This remains the dominant understanding of the motivations of Comstock and his followers. Smith-Rosenberg argues that the Comstock Laws were intended to reinforce traditional roles for women, asserting that physicians affiliated with the American Medical Association secured the passage of the Comstock Law by using language that portrayed the aborting wife as an "unnaturally selfish and ruthless" being who victimized her husband. Similarly, Brodie argues that in spite of Comstock's stated goal of protecting children, his real aim was the control of women.[41]

The problem with this argument is that neither the laws themselves nor the rhetoric used by Comstock and his supporters in discussing these issues support this contention. Clinton L. Merriam, the New York congressman who introduced the anti-obscenity bill to the House of Representatives, sought support by appealing to the need to protect children from obscene materials.

> I am sure that this American Congress will not only give all the aids of legislation for the annihilation of this trade, but that the outraged manhood of our age will place, in the strongest possible manner, its seal of condemnation upon the low brutality which threatened to destroy the future of this Republic by making merchandise of the morals of our youth.[42]

Merriam played on obscenity as a threat to manhood, a theme that also occurred in his statement that men who "regard their homes as their sanctuaries" would "fight to protect what they hold most precious in life—the holiness, and purity of their firesides." Implicit in such rhetoric is a role for women—moral mothers who help guard the purity of the hearth. Assumptions about women's proper roles thus permeated arguments about obscenity, but this rhetoric offers little support for the claim that the intent of anticontraception legislation was to force women to bear children. While the law that Comstock helped write and Merriam sponsored is remembered as an act to restrict contraception, the issues of contraception and abortion are almost inseparable from that of obscenity in both the Comstock Law and Comstock's writings. The act passed by Congress read:

> SECTION 148. That no obscene, lewd, or lascivious book, pamphlet, picture, paper, print, or other publication of an indecent character, or any article or thing designed or intended for the prevention of contraception or the procuring of abortion, nor any article or thing intended or adapted for any indecent or immoral use or nature, nor any . . . book, pamphlet, advertisement or notice of any kind giving information, directly or indirectly, where, or how, or of whom, or by what means either of the things before mentioned may be obtained or made . . . shall be carried in the mail, and any person who shall knowingly deposit,

or cause to be deposited, for mailing or delivery, any of the herein-before-mentioned articles or things, or any notice, or paper containing any advertisement relating to the aforesaid articles or things . . . shall be deemed guilty of a misdemeanor.[43]

Congress appointed Comstock as special agent of the post office, charging him with enforcing the obscenity statutes regulating the mails. Although this was to be a salaried position, Comstock refused to draw a paycheck in his capacity as special agent.

While the federal Comstock Law banned obscene materials from the mails, about half of the states passed anti-obscenity statutes banning possession and sale of such materials, including contraceptives. Notably, however, these laws banned contraceptives and abortifacients *along with* other immoral articles. Comstock himself did not see the control of reproduction as an issue separable from obscenity. He made this clear in a letter that Merriam read before the House of Representatives, when the only time contraception is mentioned is in Comstock's claim:

> For be it known that wherever these books go, or catalogues of these books, there you will ever find, as almost indispensable, a complete list of rubber articles for masturbation or for the professed prevention of conception.[44]

Comstock used the term "indecent rubber articles" to describe both contraceptives and devices such as dildoes. His writings link contraceptives to unbridled sexuality; contraception and abortion resulted from unnatural passions aroused by obscene literature. Contraceptives allowed young people, afflicted with lust from reading pornography, to sin while affording themselves and their partners protection from disease and pregnancy. In a New York Society for the Suppression of Vice *Annual Report*, Comstock, who served as secretary as well as agent of the organization, described the targets of his crusade.

> We can only hint at the *nature* of this literature. It consists of books, pamphlets, tracts, leaflets, of pictures engraved on steel and wood, of photographs, cards, and charms, all designed and cunningly calculated to inflame the passions and lead the victims from one step of vice to another, ending in utmost lust. And when the victims have been polluted in thought and imagination and thus prepared for the commission of lustful crime, the authors of their debasement present a variety of implements by the aid of which they promise them the practice of licentiousness without its direful consequences to them and their guilty partners.[45]

As well as asserting that the use of contraceptives resulted from reading immoral literature, Comstock claimed that the availability of contraception and abortion encouraged immoral behavior. He pledged to destroy "books and pictures which excite the passions; articles of diabolical design, cunningly contrived to minister to the most degrading appetites, or to conceal the crime which may be contemplated or perchance already committed."[46]

The connection Comstock saw between contraception and sin was shared by other nineteenth-century moralists, who also saw contraception as an unnatural act. For example, N. F. Cook, a physician who in 1878 published (anonymously) *Satan in Society*, wrote that the only acceptable ways of avoiding pregnancy were to abstain from sex entirely or, to use a means of "doubtful propriety," to abstain from sex for fourteen days following the cessation of the menses. "All other means of prevention of offspring are disgusting, beastly, positively wrongful, as well as unnatural, and *physically injurious*." The author's disgust at other means of contraception was apparently not widely shared, for he asserts that "the crime of Onan" had become "a practice so universal that it may well be termed a national vice," meaning that withdrawal before male orgasm had become a widely known and widely practiced means of limiting fertility.[47] While the use of withdrawal as a birth control method may have been common, clearly it was not uncontroversial. While respectable married couples limited their fertility, the use of condoms was more often equated with prostitution rather than with marriage. Gardner, author of *Conjugal Sins*, argued that "intermediate tegumentary coverings" were ineffective for preventing conception; furthermore, "they are suggestive of licentiousness and the brothel, and their employment degrades to bestiality the true feelings of manhood and the holy state of matrimony."[48] Gardner and Cook both argued that male withdrawal before ejaculation also threatened the holy state of matrimony, asserting that a husband who did so not only violated his wife's modesty, but, by teaching her "the stratagems invented and practiced by libertines," showed her that she could "violate her marriage vows without fear of detection" should her "virtue be tempted."[49] While Comstock did not invoke prostitution or marital infidelity to make his case about contraception, his ability to equate contraception with the corruption of children's morals and pollution of the home was predicated on an already existing discourse that linked contraception to moral impurity.

While Comstock transformed discourses about abortion by applying them to contraception and focusing on children's morals, he sometimes employed more conventional anti-abortion rhetoric. He portrayed women who sought abortions as victims of male lust; simultaneously he claimed that women sought abortion because "the victims" of the practice were determined to "conceal their own lapse from chastity."[50] But when Comstock discussed abortion, he emphasized that a young woman who died of an abortion was the aberrant and lost child of a grieving parent. This strategy was particularly apparent in his discussion of the death of Cora Sammis.

## Abortion, Obscenity, and Parental Authority

Cora Sammis, a twenty-two-year-old Sunday-school teacher, died in February of 1879 from an abortion. Sammis was the well-educated daughter of a prosperous and elderly Long Island farmer who owned a coal and wood business. Bertha Burger, a German midwife, was indicted for the crime, along with Cora's lover and fiancé, Frank Cosgrove, the son of a wealthy cooperage owner. The case, according to the *New York Times*, was one of "particular atrocity"; the assistant district attorney described it as "one of the most important cases ever brought to trial."[51] Newspapers frequently reported abortion-related deaths, so the best explanation of the notoriety of this case is the social class of its protagonists; in any event, the death of Cora Sammis and the trials of Burger and Cosgrove drew extensive press coverage and packed courtrooms.

Sammis and Cosgrove had been engaged for several months when she became pregnant. Fearing that her parents would learn of her pregnancy, she traveled to New York City to visit an aunt. There she met Cosgrove and, as she told the coroner before she died, went with Cosgrove to the house of Bertha Burger, who performed an abortion. Sammis became ill, and when Burger refused to call a doctor, her fiancé went to Dr. Whitehead, a man who had been arrested five times for performing abortions, to ask him to attend to Sammis. Whitehead attended the sick woman and called the police. The next day the coroner visited Sammis and, telling her that she was about to die, asked her to make a statement about the cause of her illness. Burger was brought to her bedside, and Sammis identified the woman as the person who had operated on her. Sammis pleaded for help:

> When Dr. Miller attended to Miss Sammis she put her arms round his neck and begged him for God's sake to do what he could to save her. She also asked that they would kneel down and pray for her, and the Coroner and his deputy say that the scene was one which they hope never to witness again.[52]

Sammis's parents were informed by telegram that their daughter was very ill; they boarded a train for the city the following morning. On the train Mr. Sammis purchased a newspaper and learned of the death of his daughter. Meanwhile, the police learned that another sick young woman had been taken from Burger's house, and finally located Maggie Steel in the tenement-house apartment of Burger's mother. She had been abandoned there, receiving neither food nor medical attention, but she recovered from her abortion.[53]

The trials of Burger and Cosgrove provided yet more drama. Burger offered as her defense the claim, made in "broken English," that she was not an abortionist, merely the proprietress of a "house of ill-fame," and described the inmates of her house using a word the New York Times refused to print. She argued that Cosgrove had rented a room in her house, installed Miss Sammis, and procured the services of Dr. Whitehead to perform the fatal abortion. Thus Burger invoked the relationship between prostitution, sexual dissolution, and abortion as the cornerstone of her defense. The prosecutor asked the jury whether they would believe this account or that given by Cora Sammis, whose statement was made when she "was about to enter into the presence of her God." Burger was convicted and sentenced to twelve years in prison. The prosecution of Cosgrove dragged on for months as his friends tried to use their political influence and wealth to "fix" the case. Cosgrove finally pled guilty and received the lowest possible sentence for the crime of assisting in an abortion. The judge noted that Cosgrove had offered to marry Cora Sammis when he learned of her pregnancy, and that the decision to follow "the unlawful and less honorable course to hide your shame" was made by mutual consent. Finally, the judge noted, Cosgrove had not abandoned Cora but remained with her through her abortion and illness.[54]

A year later Comstock gave a strikingly different account of the Sammis case, one that placed emphasis both on the corruption of children by obscenity and on the damage to the home wrought by the moral pollution of children. In a chapter of his book Frauds Exposed entitled "Obscene Publications," Comstock asks his reader to consider "the anguish of the parent who wakes up to the knowledge that the beloved child is debauched." As an example of the pain inflicted on parents by obscene literature, Comstock recounts the death of Cora Sammis.

> What pen or brush can picture the awful suffering of the father of that once beautiful girl, who recently died in one of the infernal dens in the upper part of our city? On a bright day she left her home and the quiet village on the eastern end of Long Island, ostensibly to visit friends in New York. Never a word of suspicion had been raised against her moral character. It is said that she was a favorite in the home, church, and society. As she left her home, she was to her beloved parents a pure, spotless child. Imagine, then, the anguish of the father when, a few days afterward, having been summoned by telegraph, he starts with

his wife to go to his daughter's sick-bed, and on the cars, when the New York papers are brought in, the first thing to catch his eye is the death by malpractice of his beautiful child. He had the presence of mind sufficient to throw the paper out the window, as though he had lost it, so that his wife may not know of it, till he learns if it indeed be true. He then goes up to this abortion den, and there finds all that is left of his lovely child lying in a filthy hall-bedroom, taken there by the son of a respectable family, whose mind had been debauched, and who, after ruining this maiden, failed to marry her, but took her to this place of human butchery. And what a death! Helpless, alone in a cold, cheerless room, without friends, neglected, brutally murdered by a worse than murderess; for, after inflicting the deadly stab, the victim is tortured by neglect, and left to die in a condition of which the details are too loathsome for publication. Is it any wonder that this helpless maiden, in her last agonies, threw her fair arms around the neck of a godless coroner, and besought him to pray for her?[55]

Comstock's account of Sammis's death is interesting for three reasons. The first is Frank Cosgrove's culpability. Although Cora Sammis could not give her account of their relationship, or of how the engaged couple ended up at Bertha Burger's house rather than at the altar, it is possible that both her "ruin" and her abortion reflected her decisions and desires, rather than the calculations of her debauched fiancé. While accounts of the abandonment of Maggie Steel suggest that Bertha Burger was indeed capable of heartless treatment of her patients, Cora Sammis received medical attention because of Frank Cosgrove. Second, Comstock's attributing Sammis's pregnancy to the affects of obscene publications illustrates how he gained support for his anti-obscenity crusade by playing on parents' fears that their children would be harmed by inappropriate sexual behavior. Finally, this story excites sympathy for the father of the dead girl, rather than for her mother. While, as I will discuss in the next chapter, Comstock often appealed to sympathy for grieving mothers who had lost their children to obscene literature, his focus on Cora Sammis's father suggests that it is fathers who should be particularly concerned about the violation of the sexual purity of daughters. Comstock appealed to men to protect their homes from the pollution of obscene literature and from the consequences of uncontrolled male sexual desire.

The link Comstock created between obscene literature and fatal abortions was predicated on preexisting concerns about adolescents and sexuality. Comstock reiterated themes that the city was a dangerous place, and that one of its chief dangers was sexual. Not only did the city's sexual subculture entice and morally pollute young men, but, as the Sammis case showed, its anonymity served as a place where, away from the eyes of

family and friends, a young person could engage in dangerous and immoral acts. The city also served as a source and locus of a youth subculture that undermined the control of parents. At issue was not only the
sexual enticement of the city, but the production of books and periodicals
that spread immoral ideas far from the city's center, into towns and ham-
lets, where the children of unsuspecting parents would be debauched and
perhaps, like Sammis, destroyed by their effects.

## Arresting Abortionists: Comstock Wields the Law

Between 1872 and 1880 Comstock arrested ninety-seven people for advertising or selling abortifacients or indecent rubber articles, including
contraceptives. Comstock's first arrest, that of Charles Mancher, was typical of many. Mancher, a Catholic physician "of Spanish descent," was
arrested for selling articles for indecent or immoral use; the articles seized
were a "small quantity of circulares, and rubber goods." Thus while
Comstock claimed that Mancher was "a notorious abortionist, doing an
extensive business through newspaper advertisements and the mails,"
Mancher was indicted for the possession and sale of a small amount of
goods. He died before his trial. Another case that never came to trial was
that of Francis E. Andrews, who absconded after being arrested for selling immoral rubber articles and articles to prevent conception, and for
advertising articles to cause abortion. Comstock claimed that this man
was "an abortionist . . . worth about $400,000. [He] gave $27,000 to
YMCA of Albany and other charities. . . . Tried to bribe Comstock." In
this raid Comstock seized five thousand condoms. Yet another one that
got away was Moses Jacoby, "a German or Polish Jew," who advertised
as "Dr. Franklin" and was one of the abortionists discussed in "The Evil
of the Age." Comstock arrested Jacoby for advertising abortifacients and
contraceptives. In his records Comstock noted that Jacoby was "a notorious scoundrel and abortionist. Saw his books where he made $2000 per
month." Jacoby absconded before his trial. Comstock's claim that dealers
of obscene articles also sold contraceptives is substantiated by his records:
for example, Morris Bass, a "Bavarian Jew," was arrested in 1875 for
selling immoral rubber goods. The articles confiscated in this case included, "6 doz ticklers, 200 doz condoms, 12 doz womb veils, 70 doz
obscene microscopic charms, 2 syringes for abortion and 1 vagina." Bass
was fined twenty-five dollars.[56]

But while Comstock harassed abortionists and sent a number of them
to prison, it is clear from his own records that this did not deter them
from practicing when they were released. For example, Paul Davis, arrested in 1873, absconded to Canada, where two years later he was con-

victed for accidently killing a young woman during an abortion. Similarly, Orlando Bradford was arrested in February of 1878 for selling "Betine Pills." These pills, compounded of "alors, Ergotine, Extract of Sabine and Betin" (a decoction of beets), were intended to induce abortion. In October of the same year Bradford was arrested for the murder of Victoria Connors. Comstock noted in his records, "If he had been properly tried on the former charge would Miss Connors now be living? This illustrates the operations of the District Attorney's office under the present administration."[57]

Comstock's arrests of abortionists received some notice in the press, although an arrest on a charge of selling a medicine or device to cause abortion or contraception understandably drew less attention than abortion cases involving the death of a patient, which were investigated by the police.[58] But when Comstock went to Madame Restell posing as a man who had impregnated his lover and arrested her for selling abortifacients, his name became closely linked with the suppression of abortion. Restell's arrest was covered by all of the major papers. Comstock was usually mentioned in the opening sentences of these articles, along with Restell's house. The *Sun* reported:

> Madam Restell is in trouble again. This time it is through the ingenuity and persistence of Anthony Comstock of the Society for the Suppression of Crime [*sic*]. Madam Restell lives in the magnificent mansion in Fifth avenue, well known to all frequenters of the street by reason of its peculiarly rich and showy curtains and great door plate.[59]

Reports of Restell's arrest also mentioned that her fortune, estimated at $1.5 million dollars, was accumulated through abortions, and that members of "the very wealthiest families" in the city were said to be her patrons. Restell played on the reputation of her customers, arguing that she should be released on her own recognizance because "she had several ladies belonging to good families under her charge . . . and that her enforced absence would place them in great danger."[60] Comstock's notes on Restell's arrest suggest that she told the truth.

> At time of arrest a prominent man's wife—mother of 4 children—was there to consult this woman professionally. She was very greatly excited, and pleaded I would not expose her, saying, "she would kill herself first." I told her, Go sin no more. Your secret shall be kept sacredly by me. 2 other women came in also. . . . Her house is furnished throughout in most elaborate style.[61]

Although Comstock may have saved one woman from suicide, he caused another; as he noted in the same record, Restell "committed suicide by cutting her throat [the] morning of trial. A bloody ending to a bloody life."

The death of the sixty-six-year-old abortionist generated lurid accounts of her suicide, which was attributed to Restell's distress about her almost certain conviction and imprisonment. Commentators on the suicide played on three themes. Some echoed Comstock's sentiment that the suicide was just punishment for Restell's crimes. But as Restell had been charged only once for causing the death of a woman through performing an abortion (she was convicted in 1847 and served one year for manslaughter), she was either successful at aborting women without killing them or very successful at hiding their deaths. Restell's wealth suggests that she was skilled at her trade and her "crime" was fulfilling women's demand for abortions. The *World* concluded that the women of New York, who had given Restell her fortune, were as guilty as she.

> The suicide of this notorious woman is even more monitory than the infliction of the penalty which awaited her. ... Even the memory of such a woman is entitled to justice, and we must not forget that every one of this woman's murders required an accomplice, in a woman presumably better reared, better educated, and amenable to a higher moral standard than herself. ... The women whom the mere love of ease and hatred of inconvenience led to this hag's "palatial den," and who created the demand which she supplied are, as she was not, beyond the reach of law and of public opinion. If they are not beyond the reach of conscience also, it is worth their while to ask themselves in what respect, except in its terrible expiation, this woman's blood-guiltiness differed from their own.[62]

Finally, while the *World* condemned the women who supported Restell, some also saw Anthony Comstock as being guilty of a crime. Under the headline "Doing Evil That Good May Come," the *Sun* condemned Comstock for his role in the abortionist's death.

> No matter what the wretched woman was who took her life with her own hand yesterday, her death has not freed the world from the last of detestable characters. Whatever she was she had her rights, and the man who cunningly led her into the commission of a misdemeanor acted an unmanly and ignoble part. ... He had been taunted, he said, with not daring to arrest her. So he deceived and wheedled her into a crime.[63]

Comstock responded to accusations of entrapment by reiterating his claim that abortionists were murderers who encouraged sexual depravity.

> The agent has reason to believe, whether from advertisements or other sources of information, that a certain woman has for years made a trade of destroying ante-natal human beings; has acquired such skill in the use of poisonous drugs to destroy life, that she has made not only a fortune,

but a wide reputation in the business, thus throwing a shield over licentiousness and encouraging its continuance, by freeing its victims from the consequences of their vice. He calls at her office, asks if she can do all this and save the mother, and being assured she can, he buys her medicines and convicts her of violating the law. Does he seduce this murderess to commit crime? Exactly the opposite. . . . She was willing, for so many dollars to take a human life. He paid her the dollars, and stopped forever her pre-natal murders.[64]

Finally, Comstock justified his role in Restell's death by arguing that the suppression of the abortion trade saved young women from sexual exploitation, a recurrent theme in his discussions of abortion and contraception. Four years after Restell's death, Comstock took credit for forcing the abortion trade to be carried on secretly, noting that because he had arrested more than sixty of "these wretches," they were now afraid to advertise their services. But again Comstock utilized a common theme in abortion rhetoric, that of women being simultaneously victims and criminals. Comstock did not refer to Restell by name, but rather to "the gilded palace of death built and embellished by the crime of women, on Fifth Avenue." But "the crime of women" was the result of women's victimization by men: "Maiden virtue was of no account, but nostrums were openly advertised as for sale at this place, by one or more newspapers, to help the rake and libertine destroy the fairest in the land."[65]

Comstock's role in making abortion and contraception illegal illustrates a number of themes that would become important in the crusade against obscenity. His obsession with the control of sexuality resulted from a changing sexual culture manifest in both a public culture of prostitution and in the sexualization of romantic love. But the language Comstock used to discuss the Sammis case focused not on the sexuality of adults, but on that of adolescents. This concern with youth sprang from the growth of cities, where supervising young people was more difficult, and from the increasing need of middle-class children to be educated in order to be economically independent, lengthening their years of dependence and parents' years of responsibility. Comstock's crusade against what he saw as a dangerous sexual culture was manifest in his crusade against abortion and contraception as well as against obscenity. He expressed this concern, as I will show in the next chapter, in terms of controlling and protecting children.

# 3

## MORAL REFORM AND THE

## PROTECTION OF YOUTH

COMSTOCK'S EFFICACY in the crusade against abortion resulted from his position as leader of the New York Society for the Suppression of Vice. This chapter will address two questions: Who supported the NYSSV? And how can we explain this support? I will argue that the NYSSV was a powerful moral reform organization because it mobilized privileged people, many of them wealthy and highly respected, into a campaign to ensure the reproduction of the families and the social world of the upper and middle classes. This campaign sought to ensure the reproduction of children suited to take their parents' places as leaders of society; to protect respectable people, and employers in particular, from the criminal behavior of corrupted and thieving children; and ultimately to preserve the existing social order by protecting the institutions, such as homes and schools, that reproduced it. Thus I will argue that the NYSSV was engaged in a project of family reproduction, which spoke to concerns about keeping the upper and middle classes intact, although that task extended far beyond the problem of generating a system of production or a reliable labor force. Family reproduction is a process of both creating the next generation and providing a secure world in which to raise them. Comstock and his supporters understood this project to include keeping children and homes morally pure—a task predicated on, but not confined to, the labors of moral mothers.

### Who Joined the Anti-Vice Society?
### The Class Basis of Moral Reform

Social scientists have argued that moral reform movements are the province of segments of the middle class experiencing erosion of their position in the hierarchies of wealth or social status.[1] The social backgrounds of the supporters of the NYSSV and its sister organization, the New England Society for the Suppression of Vice (NESSV), challenge this assertion, and point instead to the question of why privileged people supported a moral reform crusade.

TABLE 3.1

Distribution of Occupations of Male Contributors to the New York Society
for the Suppression of Vice, 1872–1892, and the New England Society for
the Suppression of Vice, 1885–1892

| Occupation | New York (%) | Boston (%) |
|---|---|---|
| Upper and upper-middle class | | |
| Merchant, commercial importer[a] | 11.4 | 19.2 |
| Owner of manufacturing or extractive industry | 12.2 | 16.4 |
| Corporate official | 12.8 | 8.5 |
| Banker or broker | 13.1 | 7.1 |
| Judge or lawyer | 9.9 | 6.4 |
| Physician | 5.5 | 2.1 |
| Clergy | 3.5 | 7.8 |
| Publisher | 3.8 | 3.6 |
| Social registrant or millionaire, occupation unknown | 3.5 | 10.6 |
| Resident of wealthy area, occupation unknown[b] | 2.3 | 2.8 |
| Other upper-middle-class occupation | 5.5 | 7.8 |
| *Total percentage of Contributors from upper classes* | *83.5* | *92.3* |
| Other Classes | | |
| Merchant or owners of single-partner firm, possibly upper-middle class[c] | 9.0 | 4.3 |
| Member of lower-middle class | 5.0 | 1.4 |
| Skilled worker | 1.7 | 2.1 |
| Semiskilled and Service Worker | 0.6 | — |
| *Number of men with known occupations* | *343* | *141* |
| No occupation listed | (15) | (15) |
| Multiple entries in directory[d] | (63) | (16) |
| Women | (37) | (40) |
| No information[e] | (142) | (20) |

Notes: Data from a random sample of the 1,283 persons listed as contributors to the
NYSSV and the 523 persons who contributed to the NESSV. The NESSV did not list contributors in their *Annual Reports* until 1885. Percentages are based on the total number of
men whose occupations or status as social registrants or millionaires could be determined.
Most of these men are residents of the cities; however, some lived outside of the city and
worked in it. Occupations are coded from the city directories for the first year the person
contributed. Coding categories are similiar to Thernstrom (*The Other Bostonians*, 290–92).
Women were excluded because, if married, only husbands' names and occupations were
listed in the city directories.

[a] This category represents partners in firms with multiple partners, or single owners who
are millionaires, in the *Social Register*, or who live in a wealthy area (see [b] below).

[b] In New York City includes Fifth Ave., Madison Ave., Lexington Ave., Broadway,
Park Place, Park Ave. In Boston includes Mt. Vernon St., Commonwealth Ave., Beacon St.,
Joy St.

[c] Merchants and owners of single-partner firms, not millionaires, not listed in the *Social
Register*, and not living in a known wealthy area.

TABLE 3.1 *(cont.)*

---

<sup>d</sup> This refers to instances where two or more men with the same name were listed in the city directory. When this happened, the subsequent years when the person contributed to the anti-vice society were checked to see if one person with the same occupation and/or address could be isolated.

<sup>e</sup> The large number of contributors not located in the New York city directory, *Social Register*, or millionaire's list are most likely from out of town. Comstock did not consistently list the towns where people were from, so those not living or working in New York could not always be excluded. Of the persons not listed in the city directory, 29 names included the title "Reverend" and 7 the title "Doctor," occupations of persons likely to appear in the city directory if they lived or worked in the city. The large number of ministers suggests that church networks created national support for the anti-vice movement, even though clergymen were not leaders of the NYSSV.

In contrast to the assumption that the lower-middle class forms the bulwark of moral crusades, over 80 percent of the men who contributed to the New York and New England anti-vice societies, and whose occupations could be located in the *City Directory*, were what Stephen Thernstrom called "high white collar," meaning upper or upper-middle class, including merchants, businessmen, financiers, and professionals.[2]

Clearly, anti-vice supporters were not predominately petit bourgeois. Indeed, the anti-vice society was noted for the wealth and prestige of its supporters. In a *North American Review* forum about the anti-vice society, Comstock explained that he had "neither money nor influential friends" when he started his crusade against obscene literature. Upon contacting the Young Men's Christian Association, an organization "founded for the purpose of helping and saving young men," Morris Jesup organized "a meeting of prominent citizens" to consider the problem. Comstock listed the NYSSV's founders, noting that "since its organization about two hundred and fifty gentlemen of equal respectability have been added as members."[3] Indeed, a high percentage of Comstock's supporters were persons of indisputable wealth and prestige: 28.5 percent of the supporters of the New York anti-vice society and 26 percent of those who supported its Boston counterpart were millionaires, were listed in the *Social Register*, or both. These figures increase if anti-vice society supporters who were not listed in the *Social Register* but whose surnames suggest that they were members of elite families are added. In that case 32.5 percent of the supporters of the New York anti-vice society and 31 percent of the supporters of the New England anti-vice society were from families who had a family member who was a millionaire or who appeared in the *Social Register*.[4]

**TABLE 3.2**
Elite Households Who Contributed to the Anti-Vice Society, by Segment of Elite

| Segment of Elite | New York | | Boston | |
|---|---|---|---|---|
| | Percentage | N | Percentage | N |
| Millionaire and in *Social Register* | 17.9 | 598 | 37.0 | 102 |
| Millionaire, not in *Social Register* | 4.6 | 480 | 10.5 | 114 |
| In *Social Register*, not millionaire | 4.0 | 5,918 | 7.0 | 1,243 |

Source: *Social Register*, New York City, 1892; *Social Register*, Boston, 1890; "American Millionaires," *Tribune Monthly*, June 1892.
Note: Numbers are base Ns for percentages.

Not only were a sizable minority of anti-vice supporters from elite families, some fractions of the upper class also offered high rates of support for Comstock. Table 3.2 shows the cross tabulations of anti-vice society membership by whether a person (or his or her spouse) was a millionaire, and whether the person (or the person's spouse) was in the *Social Register*. The millionaires were taken from the *Tribune Monthly*'s 1892 list of "American Millionaires," which reported reputed millionaires throughout the country.[5] This table shows support for the anti-vice society within three categories of the upper class: millionaires listed in the *Social Register*, millionaires who were not, and social registrants who were not millionaires. If either spouse was an anti-vice supporter, a millionaire, or a social registrant, the couple was counted as being in that category. The number of cases in each cell (*N=*) represents the total number of households in that category. Thus in New York 17.9 percent of the 598 households that had a millionaire and a social registrant contributed to the anti-vice society. Rates of support were much lower in other categories of the elite: 4.6 percent of millionaires who were not social registrants and 4 percent of social registrants who were not millionaires supported the anti-vice society. Similarly, in Boston the greatest support for the anti-vice society was found among couples who were both in the *Social Register* and who were millionaires. In Boston, 37 percent of millionaires listed in the *Social Register* were anti-vice supporters, compared with 7 percent of couples in the *Social Register* who were not millionaires and 10.5 percent of millionaires who were not social registrants. The use of the *Social Register* and the millionaire's list as indicators of elite status is problematic; one could possess a fortune of considerably less than a million dollars in 1892 and still be considered a wealthy person. But if a listing in the *Social Register* indicates social acceptance by the most elite and assets of a million dollars represent great wealth, these figures suggest that support for Comstock was fairly high at the pinnacle of New York and, particularly, Boston society.

The officers of the NYSSV furthered the organization's reputation as a preserve of the wealthy and powerful. Its leaders included Samuel Colgate, the millionaire heir and president of the Colgate soap company, who served as president of the NYSSV from 1878 until the end of the century. Other officers and executive committee members during the NYSSV's first decade included Alfred S. Barnes and Birdseye Blakeman, both publishing magnates; William E. Dodge, Jr., who inherited a fortune made in mining and lumbering; and John M. Cornell and Kiliaen Van Rensselaer, both scions of prominent families.

## Protecting Youth: Comstock's Case for Censorship

If support for the anti-vice society cannot be explained by the presumed status anxiety of the lower-middle class, we are left with the question of why a substantial number of people at the pinnacle of New York and Boston society lent their names and dollars to a campaign to eradicate obscenity. We can examine how Comstock elicited support by looking at the claims he made about obscenity's effects. The overwhelming majority of Comstock's justifications for suppressing obscenity, which are tabulated in table 3.3, concern its effects on children.[6] Eighty-seven of the 235 reasons, or 37 percent, were statements that obscenity led to laziness, immorality, lustfulness, criminality, and sometimes death among youth. Eighteen percent of Comstock's reasons for suppressing obscenity were statements that obscene materials were corrupting schools; and 10 percent of the reasons invoked the corrupting effects of obscenity on homes.

Comstock described the anti-vice society as an organization dedicated to protecting children through eradicating obscene literature.

> *The Suppression of Obscene Literature and articles of indecent and immoral use*, is the one great object for which the Society was created. This literature is found in the form of books, pamphlets, leaflets, songs, pictures, and these articles in rubber, wax, and other materials—all designed and cunningly calculated to excite the imagination and inflame the passions of the youth into whose hands they may come.[7]

To understand the support given to the anti-vice campaign, we must decipher this rhetoric about the effects of obscenity upon children.

Comstock portrayed obscene literature as a "trap" that destroyed children both physically and morally. Licentious literature awakened lustful thoughts in young people and aroused passions they could neither control nor suppress.

## TABLE 3.3
### Reasons for Suppressing Obscenity, NYSSV
*Annual Reports, 1872–1884 (N = 235)*

*Control of Youth (37%)*
  Leads to youth becoming immoral (32)
  Leads to youth becoming criminal (7)
  Makes youth dissipated or lazy (4)
  Leads girls to prostitution (1)
  Leads to death of youths (10)
  Corrupts youths (17)
  Ruins youths (8)
  Other youth-related reasons (8)

*Morality (12%)*
  Encourages unchaste behavior (8)
  Conceals lapse from chastity (5)
  Leads to masturbation (3)
  Corrupts people (9)
  Other morality-related reasons (3)

*Preservation of Social Institutions (40%)*
  Material threatens schools (42)
  Material threatens homes (23)
  Material corrupts other institutions (4)
  Material causes social breakdown (17)
  Other reasons about social institutions (6)

*Other Reasons (12%)*
  Creates market for irregular physicians (3)
  Persons spreading material are criminal (24)
  Creates lower-class criminals (1)

*Note:* Reasons coded from the New York Society for the Suppression of Vice, *Annual Reports*, 1872–1884. Percentages represent the percentage of reasons in each category; the numbers in parentheses represent mentions of each specific reason. Due to rounding error, the percentages do not sum to 100 percent.

The boy's mind becomes a sink of corruption and he is a loathing unto himself. In his better moments he wrestles and cries out against this foe, but all in vain; he dare not speak out to his most intimate friend for shame: he dare not go to parent—he almost fears to call upon God. Despair takes possession of his soul as he finds himself losing strength of will—becoming nervous and infirm; he suffers unutterable agony during the hours of the night, and awakes only to carry a burdened heart through all the day.[8]

This passage alludes to what Comstock saw as the most harmful effect of obscene literature: it induced masturbation. Comstock argued that the most "deadly effects" of obscene literature are "felt by victims in the habit of secret vices."[9] Obscene literature could "poison and corrupt the streams of life, leaving a moral wreck, a physical deformity, [and] an enervated system."[10] The dangers of masturbation were not confined to boys; Comstock also discussed girls at "celebrated female colleges" in New England "ruined by the vile things found in their possession."[11] Comstock and his supporters asserted that lust could lead to insanity. The Reverend J. M. Buckley, speaking at the anti-vice society's annual meeting, asserted

> There is no passion as strong with many as the passion which is stimulated by obscene books. One of the leading editors of this city said to me not long ago, that he saw an obscene picture at boarding school when he was fourteen years of age, and that his mind never became free from that picture until he was thirty-five years of age. I acted, at one time, as Chaplain for one of the largest Lunatic Asylums. In my conversations with these persons, I found that such of them as had been made lunatics by licentious vices, nearly all had been corrupted by obscene books, and thus led into the most terrific vice, ending in lunacy. This vice which is so stimulated by obscene books, is that which this Society works directly and indirectly to suppress.[12]

Comstock's assertion that obscene literature led to a potentially fatal habit of masturbation was based on a common fear of autoeroticism.[13] Tracts on "the secret vice," widely circulated during this period, claimed that masturbation caused physical, psychological, and moral debility. Cook, a physician and anonymous author of *Satan in Society*, described the case of a watchmaker who began masturbating at age seventeen.

> At that time he delivered himself to masturbation which he repeated three times a day, and the consummation of the act was always preceded and followed by a slight loss of consciousness. . . . In less than one year he began to experience great weakness after each act. This warning was not sufficient to drive him from the danger. His soul, already wholly delivered to this infamy, was no longer capable of other ideas, and the repetition of the crime became every day more frequent, until he found himself in a condition which led him to be apprehensive of death. Wise too late, the evil had made such progress that he could not be cured, and the genital organs became so irritable and so feeble that there was no longer required the act to produce seminal emission. . . . The spasm which formerly occurred only at the consummation of the act and ceased at the same time, had become habitual, and often seized him without apparent cause, and in so violent a fashion that during the whole time of the paroxysm, which sometimes lasted more than fifteen hours and never less than eight, he experienced in the back of the neck such violent pains

that he commonly raised, not cries merely, but howls. . . . I learned his condition; I visited him; I found less a living being than a corpse groaning upon the straw; emaciated, pale, filthy, exhaling an infectious odor; almost incapable of any movement. He lost often a pale and watery blood by the nose; a constant slime flowed from the mouth; attacked with diarrhea, he rendered his excrements in his bed without knowledge of the fact; the spermatic flux was continual; . . . he no longer had the faculty of motion; the pulse was extremely small and rapid; the respiration very labored; the emaciation excessive.[14]

This unfortunate case ended in death a few weeks later, a fate Comstock alluded to when he cited the case of a thirteen-year-old schoolgirl who had been exposed to "obscene matter" and brought "very near death's door from the direct results of this curse upon her mind."[15] In addition to being occasionally fatal, the secret vice was common; Comstock cited a college professor who claimed that not fewer than 75 percent of adolescent boys were victims.[16] Masturbation was an ever-present danger, made worse by licentious publications. Comstock cited a "prominent citizen of Cincinnati," who, "speaking of the effects of these books and pictures on the mind of the youth," claimed:

Self-abuse is a thousand times worse where it is occasioned by obscene plates. . . . when the excitement is made on the mind by obscene plates it is indelible, and the images remain throughout life. . . . I cannot write out my feeling of disgust on these damnable creatures in human shape who vend or deal in obscene literature. Their infernal trade destroys the manhood and womanhood of millions of our race, annually, over the earth.[17]

Adolescent sexual arousal had other frightful consequences. Comstock alluded to the dangers of prostitution, particularly in his campaigns against the theater and "bawdy playhouses." The popularity of plays increased, he claimed, with the foulness of language, the shamelessness of the actors, the scantiness of apparel, and the lasciviousness of the performance, which made youth "inflamed with lust." After a visit to such a play, Comstock argued, boys often go directly to the brothel.[18]

Death from syphilis contracted from a prostitute seems a more plausible threat than death from masturbation. Comstock's repeatedly voiced concern for protecting youth could explain the roots of the anti-vice campaign; so too could the threat of sexually contracted disease and the growth of commercialized prostitution. But reducing the anti-vice crusade to a campaign against prostitution is unsatisfactory for several reasons. The New York anti-vice society never systematically attempted to eradicate prostitution, and with the exception of a few notorious arrests of brothel inmates, Comstock left work on "the social evil" to other organizations. A sustained campaign against New York City prostitution was not mounted until 1892, when the Reverend Charles Parkhurst, pastor of the Madison Square Presbyterian Church and a vocal supporter of Comstock, founded the City Vigilance League.[19] Furthermore, in the 1880s the NYSSV abandoned the issues of abortion, contraception, and obscene literature in favor of persecuting gamblers and corrupt city officials. An explanation of the anti-vice movement based on sexual commerce could not explain the connection between these issues. And finally, while Comstock invoked danger to children as the reason to suppress vice, the question of whose children were endangered remains. Why did elite people support Comstock, and whose offspring were they worried about?

The answer to the last question provides the key to understanding the anti-vice movement. Three themes in Comstock's writings suggest that members of the upper and middle classes supported anti-vice efforts because of the problems of family and class reproduction faced by privileged people. The most important theme, I will argue, was control of middle- and upper-class children. Elite adults supported Comstock in part because of concerns about children of their own class. But it was not merely the real or imagined threat of sexual diseases that frightened parents and their peers. Vice raised the specter of the permeability of class boundaries and the possibility of children falling in the class system. A second theme raised fears of the lower classes. Comstock threatened potential supporters with the specter of lust-crazed juveniles committing various violent crimes and gambling-obsessed workers stealing from their employers. In addition to invoking these twin problems of class reproduction, Comstock cited the effects of obscenity on the reproduction of society as a whole. This theme concerned not only the dangers of the perversion of the next generation, but the corruption of social institutions, including home, school, and church, that reproduced the existing moral and social order.

## Elite Children and Family Reproduction

From the beginning of his campaign Comstock argued that obscene literature threatened all children, including those with wealthy parents.

> No language can describe the utter disgust and loathing with which pure minds must regard the traffic, and yet so shrewd and wily are the dealers, so hidden their mode of advertising their wares, so stealthy and persistent in their circulation, that in hundreds of our schools, seminaries, and colleges, yes, in thousands of the refined and Christian homes of our land they have succeeded in injecting a virus more destructive to the inno-

cency and purity of youth, if not counteracted, than can be the most deadly disease to the body. If we had the ear of all the teachers, parents, and guardians, in our land we would plead with them, "Guard with ceaseless vigilance your libraries, your closets, your children's and wards' correspondence and companionships, lest the contagion reach and blight the sweetness and purity of your homes."[20]

Comstock's claims that wealthy children as well as the poor were vulnerable to moral corruption were particularly pointed in his discussions of boarding schools. While Comstock argued that obscene literature was spread through many conduits, he asserted that obscenity was distributed primarily through the market pornographers found in schools: "leading up to all the institutions of learning in this country there are broad thoroughfares of communication; along these avenues these scoundrels are continually setting traps to capture the young."[21] Obscenity dealers solicited from postmasters the names of children residing in exclusive boarding schools, paying a small fee for each name.[22] Catalogs printed by the schools, listing the names and addresses of students, also yielded names of potential customers. After compiling lists of names, dealers of obscene literature sent children advertisements for their wares. Elite schools, Comstock asserted, were almost universally afflicted with this problem: "There is scarcely a prominent school or seminary for either sex in our land in which there could not be found if an exhaustive search were made, more of less of this literature familiarity with which enfeebles the mind, destroys the body, and ruins the souls of its victims."[23]

Schools posed several dangers. First, there was the sheer concentration of a market for obscene literature utilized, Comstock argued, by pornographers. Second, there was the problem of good children being exposed to bad ones at school. In 1879 Comstock wrote,

> In one school, in a neighboring city, our agent found over one-third of a department of forty girls under sixteen years of age, of good families who either had in possession, or had recently had, the most obscene matter in their hands. In another school of 100 boys, sixteen of the number had been supplied with obscene pictures and printed matter, which they had given away or sold to other boys.[24]

Comstock often wrote of tracing bad books to one or two troublemakers.[25] A third problem was the corruption of students by teachers. One particularly interesting case was that of G. H. Gaulier, a professor of French in "several of the leading institutions of learning," who, Comstock wrote, made a practice of secretly showing "the vilest books, pictures, and articles ever made," which the professor had brought from France, to his pupils. Comstock did not reveal in the *Annual Report* that

Gaulier was convicted of sodomy as well as of dealing in obscenity, or that the NYSSV had appealed to New York's governor to keep Gaulier imprisoned. In his appeal to Governor Alonzo Cornell, Comstock wrote:

> He was at time of arrest and had been for years prior thereto a Professor of French and Languages in several of our best Institutions of Learning in New York and Brooklyn. While so engaged and enjoying the confidence of our best families he was in the habit of showing most obscene and filthy books, pictures, etc., to the boys to excite them, and then he practiced the Italian vice on them. . . . Aside from this, I seized over one hundred pictures, books, figures, and images, of most obscene character in his possession at the time of arrest. Besides his efforts on the students, he was in the habit of frequenting Cooper Institute, and there soliciting or enticing young men to his room.[26]

School supervisors were also suspect: Comstock cited the example of an Iowa school superintendent who had written a letter to an obscenity dealer "asking for vile pictures."[27] The pollution of schools made all children vulnerable to sexual corruption. The problem, according to Comstock, was vast, and no child was safe.

> A publisher sends out a circular to all the postmasters of the country. He professes to be preparing a directory of schools and school-children of the United States. He will give five cents a name for every list sent him. The unwary postmaster falls into the trap and sends on the list. The wary postmaster possibly suspects, but shuts his eyes, and pockets his fee. The list is sent. Then circulares are sent by the hundred thousand to these children—boys and girls—worked with a devil's skill to pique the curiosity, stimulate the imagination, inflame the passions. You think your boy is safe. No boy is safe. How do you know that his last pocket-money did not go out in answer to such a bait as this?[28]

This points to a particularly grave danger in boarding schools: the lack of parental supervision of children's activities. Nineteenth-century literature on masturbation frequently discussed this danger, which stemmed from a belief that only ceaseless vigilance and unerring supervision on the part of parents could protect children from vice.[29] Comstock's stories of youths being "ruined" in boarding schools played on these fears, as well as on fears that the schools, which had been sought as a means to ensure upward mobility, would be responsible for morally (and consequently, economically) wrecking children:

> What is more beautiful in all the world than the youth of manly form, elastic in physical exuberance, his face radiant with the bloom of a pure blood, a countenance bespeaking a conscious rectitude and an un-

yielding integrity. How many such youths can be found in the various households of the land! How proudly the father of such a boy places him in some select institution of learning, where he can be qualified for future positions of trust and honor! He cheerfully makes every needful sacrifice. How the mother's heart beats with suppressed emotion as he leaves for the first time the parental roof! After he is gone, how the fond parents console each other in the assurance that all is well; there need be no fears for him; character is too well established * * Wait a little. The boy's name comes to the knowledge of such miscreants as we arrest. What then? . . . the susceptible mind of the boy receives impressions that set on fire his whole nature. His imagination is perverted. A black stain is fixed indelibly upon it, and conscience, once a faithful monitor, is now seared and silenced. The will, which once raised a strong barrier against solicitations to evil, no longer asserts itself, and our bright, noble boy too often becomes but a wreck of his former self.[30]

Claims that obscenity spread in boarding schools hit a particularly vulnerable spot in the psyche of upper-class parents, for boarding schools were founded, in part, to shield children from the vices of rapidly growing cities. The sheer size of the cities and the growth of slums made parents ever more concerned about influences on their children; thus boarding schools in little country towns were attractive because of their isolation from the city. Comstock alluded to the problem of children being corrupted in cities when he noted, "with the thousands in our large cities who will do anything for money, catering to the lowest appetites and passions, there is no safety save in eternal vigilance."[31] One of the main goals of St. Paul's headmaster, Henry Coit, was to preserve the "childhood innocence" of his students, largely by isolating them from the outside world and rigidly supervising their activities at school.[32] Not only were the schools intended to be a haven from immorality, they served as well to impart culture and refinement to children of the newly wealthy.[33] Comstock's picture of a father making sacrifices to send his son to school invokes schools as a means of upward mobility. Perversion of children in these schools was a potent threat. The sexual pollution of schoolboys was, anti-vice advocates argued, an indelible stain that tainted both childhood and married life.

The boy will dream over a book or picture until it becomes so fixed upon his mind that nothing but the grace of God will remove it. Frequently I have heard gray-haired men say, "I have never had to pray for anything so much as to be rid of the visions of an obscene book which I saw as a boy at school. These visions come back to haunt the mind; the holiest moments are shadowed by them, the most sacred hours are cursed by these vile phantoms intruding themselves before the mental vision."[34]

Comstock's claims that children could be corrupted in boarding schools were predicated on the notion that a parent's respectability did not confer immunity to the child from either sexual vices or temptations to criminality. The problem of children going astray despite the good character and intentions of parents cut across class lines. "Respectability" could refer both to honest, hardworking, and morally upright (meaning married) members of the working class as well as to (the more likely to be assumed moral) families of the middle and upper classes. In his 1883 book *Traps for the Young*, Comstock wrote that cheap novels and papers such as the *Police Gazette* incited criminal acts. One story he tells is of three boys, "all sons of respectable parents," who had come under the influence of this "murderous literature." One night the three burglarized a saloon. When the owner came downstairs to "protect his property," the eldest boy shot and killed him. Upon hearing that his victim had died, the boy seemed indifferent and pleased that he had proven himself a "tough" by "downing his man." The boy was hanged for the crime, a death Comstock attributed to the influence of debasing literature.[35]

Many of the incidents in *Traps for the Young* refer to children coming under the influence of bad company because of reading crime stories; he relates as well stories of sexual depravity caused by reading obscene literature. Comstock follows the above story with two incidents concerning children with ambiguous class backgrounds, one a twelve year old who shot and killed a friend who accused him of cheating at cards, and another a sixteen year old who placed a tree across a railway track because having read about train wrecking, he wanted to see one.[36] Having made his point about the danger to society posed by juvenile delinquency, Comstock tells a story of a judge's son to illustrate his theme of how novels corrupt elite children. The tale is long and obviously fabricated, for in it the protagonist utters many of Comstock's favorite phrases. The story is about the son of Judge W., of Mississippi, who ran away from home and a year later was severely beaten in a drunken brawl. The boy stabbed a man who insulted his parentage, but his victim in turn beat him over the head, and the boy received fatal wounds. The dying and homeless boy was taken in by a woman who nursed him. When the woman asked if she should contact his parents, he told her how adventure stories had caused his downfall. When asked if he had run away from home because his parents were unkind to him, he replied:

> Oh, if only I could remember a single harsh or unjust word from them. That would be a little excuse, you know. No, they were only too indulgent. I was a little wild then, and I'd heard father say after I'd sowed my wild oats I'd come out all right. It's been a heavy crop, hasn't it? I think he forgot that if you sow the seed you're bound to gather in a harvest. This is mine.

Here Comstock introduces one of his favorite themes, the culpability of parents who do not guard the morals and reading of their offspring. When asked why he left a good home and good parents, the boy cited adventure stories, explaining:

> My parents did not disapprove of these books, and never questioned me about them. They did not suspect how tired I was growing of my dull life, and how I longed to imitate some of my plucky young heroes. I thought as soon as I was free, adventures would pile in upon me.

The woman asked the boy how he could be influenced by "that trash" when he had been "carefully educated," particularly when he appreciated "the beauties of classical literature." Comstock makes several points in this passage. One is that these "loving parents" are to blame for their son's death, because they did not appreciate the dangers of reading adventure novels and because they gave their son too much freedom. Second, the parents did not suspect that their son would attempt to imitate the story, clearly a threat that children might run away without warning—because parents do not suspect that novels make children discontented. And finally, Comstock uses this story to argue that education does not provide protection from debasing literature.

Comstock concludes the sad story of Judge W.'s son with a final point about how easily children could fall. When asked why he had not returned home, the boy answered:

> I got down so low, with drinking and gambling and low associates, that I didn't even like to think of home. Can you understand it, for I can't? I had been carefully raised. My associations were among refined and virtuous people, yet I went down into that hog's wallow as if I had been born to it.

After mourning the memories of his debauched life that came between himself and the memory of his precious mother, the boy asked his nurse to "warn all young people whom you know to let those foolish books alone. They're very silly, but they do harm to many, and they've ruined me. They take you one step down a bad road, and the rest comes quick and easy."[37] The implications of this story for the duties of parents to protect their children from bad reading are clear, but what is not clear from Comstock's tale is why "the rest comes quick and easy." The fall of elite children, Comstock explained, was a consequence of both evil companions and innate depravity.

Comstock asserted that "low associates" preyed on wealthy children. Sometimes profit was the motive assigned to those who taught rich children evil habits or benefited from children's already acquired vices. For example, Comstock extended his campaign against persons advertis-

ing medicines that caused (or were purported to cause) abortion or contraception to those selling treatments for mysterious sexual ailments.
Given widespread belief in the medical consequences of masturbation,
Comstock's claim that young men who were worried about their sexual
habits comprised a large market for fraudulent cures is plausible. Comstock tells of one young man about to be married, who paid two hundred
dollars (and gave a note for fifteen hundred dollars) to a quack "who
frightened him into believing he had not long to live, but that he could
be cured if he could pay the price." Fraud often became blackmail;
Comstock told of a young man who confessed to a nostrum dealer his
ailments and how he acquired them. He was blackmailed out of over fifty
thousand dollars after the swindler threatened to reveal this young man's
story to his wealthy friends.[38] The profit motive was also assigned to saloon keepers, who enticed boys with "glittering allurements" that included "lascivious works of art."[39] Comstock described the effects on
boy patrons:

> Thronging into them may be seen through the wide-open doors hun-
> dreds of bright, healthy, well-dressed and genteel-appearing young
> men. These are greeted by the persuasive creature in attendance whose
> business it is in the most enticing manner to secure patronage for the
> bar. So long as good clothes and money hold out, polite attention
> may be expected. Non-attention grows apace as the victim's purse de-
> creases. As the face becomes bloated, the dress soiled, the money scarce,
> the rougher grows the usage, until at last, clothed in rags, the one
> welcomed so cordially at first is, by the hand that has wrought his
> ruin, led to the back door, and with oaths from the lips that once were
> so honeyed, he is kicked out, to fall at last into an unknown or drunk-
> ard's grave.[40]

Blackmailers and barkeepers had a clear motive—profit—although,
notably, in both cases Comstock claims that men prey on wealthy children by pretending to be helpful or friendly. Evil companions who led
youth to ruin lurked on the streets, plotting means to relieve rich children
of their money and morals. This specter played on the antebellum image
of the "confidence man," a person with a respectable appearance but vile
character who gained the trust of unsuspecting youths, particularly those
new to the city, and robbed them. Fear of the confidence man arose in
concert with the growth of cities, where people operated in a world of
strangers whose character could not be reliably assessed on the basis of
their appearance.[41]

Comstock sometimes attributed to vice peddlers no motive other than
the desire to corrupt elite children. The distribution of pornography assumed the character of indecent exposure.

A beautiful little girl, not quite 14 years of age, was returning from one of the select schools up-town to her home. While waiting for a car a miscreant approached her and handed her a paper parcel, telling her to take it home and look at it alone by herself. This sweet, confiding child took the parcel home to her mother first. The mother opened it and was shocked beyond expression to find that several pages of the most abominable matter had thus been placed in the hands of her beloved child. The father sent this package to our office, and the utmost vigilance has thus far failed to discover this worse than vampire, who sought in this manner to debauch and ruin the child.[42]

Comstock might mean to imply that the miscreant intended to "ruin" the child by seducing her at a later time, presumably because the literature would awaken her sexual interests and make her vulnerable to sexual advances. At times Comstock assigned this rational motive to men who give away pornography, yet he also suggested that men spread pornography solely for the thrill of knowing that it had been seen by rich children. In 1881 he noted, "In a large and very prominent girl's school in a neighboring city, most obscene matter was found which had been thrown into the grounds of the school, where it would fall into the hands of the young girls."[43] Polluting the parlors of the wealthy was reward in itself.

### Lustful Crime and the Problem of Delinquency

Another theme in Comstock's writings concerned the effects of bad reading on children who clearly were not offspring of the elite. Sociologists and historians often assume that members of the capitalist upper class, such as the one that supported the NYSSV, are motivated by two concerns about the working class—the stability of the labor force and the restiveness of oppressed and potentially rebellious people.[44] Comstock played on these fears about the lower classes, in the process citing problems faced by employers with dishonest employees, but he raised concerns about the working class that pointed far beyond the workplace. The concerns were particularly apparent after 1880, when the NYSSV launched a campaign to rid the streets and the mails of "Boys' Papers," most notably the *Police Gazette*. Such papers, Comstock argued, were ubiquitous and cheap—any child had access to and the financial means to acquire papers filled with "stories of criminal life," in which "the leading characters are youthful criminals, who revel in the haunts of iniquity. Many of these stories are written with a vein of licentiousness throughout, debasing the mind of youth as totally as the baser sort of books and pictures. . . . they educate our youth in all the odious features of crime."[45] Because of criminal papers "the knife, the dagger and the bludgeon used in the sinks of iniquity, and by hardened criminals, are also found in the school-room, the house and the playground of tender youth. Our Court rooms are thronged with infant criminals—with baby felons."[46] Comstock cited several examples of bad reading breeding crime, usually perpetrated by boys modeling their acts after those in the papers.

> A lad about 16 years of age in Buffalo, from reading these stories, as he afterwards confessed, conceived the idea of robbing his employer's safe. In accordance with the description of the story, he makes an impression of the safe key, takes the same to a locksmith, orders it made. The locksmith knowing the lad, informed his employer. He then makes the key, leaving it imperfect. The lad takes it, tries it, and coolly brings it back to be altered. He tries again and is arrested. Then, defiantly informs them that it is lucky they caught him as they did, or he would have had his fortune and been off.[47]

Comstock also used examples of successful juvenile criminals, citing cases where there was no evidence that the boys involved had ever read criminal stories.

> Two boys were recently arrested in this city trying to steal a ride West on the railroad. One had robbed his employer of some 15 dollars. They had armed themselves, one with an old rusty revolver, and another with a dirk, or knife, and were starting West to seek their fortunes.[48]

Because these boys' actions followed a plot in some of the story papers, Comstock imputes their criminal actions to harmful elements of youthful culture—that is, story papers.[49] Comstock cited rampant juvenile crime to garner support for his crusade. A discussion of Boys' Papers in the NYSSV *Annual Reports* closed with these examples of youthful criminality.

> In Paterson, N.J., last fall, three young lads under 20 years of age killed an old man in the public streets. They first assaulted him with their fists, knocking him down, and then one of them shot him.
> The same day, in one of our large business houses, two young employees engaged in a dispute, when one drew a knife and stabbed the other.
> In Syracuse, a young man 22 years of age, maddened by lust and jealousy, shot and killed a young lady.
> November 27th, in this City, a young lad 16 years of age stabbed another young man, because of a fancied insult to his sister.
> In November last a bright, handsome boy ran away from a good, respectable home and became a thief.[50]

Comstock played on fears of working-class criminality in searching for supporters. He sought to link the violence and crime of the city to the literature he sought to suppress, in the process invoking employers' concerns about the honesty of their workers as well as fears for their personal safety and that of their families. The suppression of vice controlled crime.

> The corrupt printing press, the gambling hell, the liquor saloon, the dive of iniquity and lust, are turning out annually a large army of criminals, and there are few, even of the most hardened character, but can trace their downfall to rum, lust, or gaming. The safety and highest welfare of the community lies, not so much in severely punishing these as in meting out with severity and rigor the penalties which the law provides against the makers of these criminals.[51]

But to argue that support for the anti-vice society was motivated solely by a fear of, and the desire to control, the working class requires ignoring the dominant strain of Comstock's arguments. Comstock's claims about the effects of crime stories on boys invoked fears of violent delinquents; however, the problem of Boys' Papers did not appear in Comstock's writings until 1880, eight years after Comstock began his work. The threat of working-class criminality became interwoven with Comstock's more dominant claim, that obscenity posed a threat to children from respectable, indeed wealthy, families.

## Moral Pollution and Family Reproduction

Comstock played on upper-class anxieties about the impermanence of their class position. High social position did not protect elite children from exploitation by depraved people. More importantly, wealth did not eradicate inner weakness that made people vulnerable to vices that could destroy their social position, nor did it protect from influences in the home and community that undermined moral purity.

Comstock frequently discussed inner weakness, particularly sexual weakness, that could cause youthful depravity and social disgrace. In one scenario, Comstock tells of a boy in boarding school who receives an advertisement for obscenity and, out of curiosity, sends away for it. While the boy is ashamed of the package that arrives in the mail and considers discarding it, the Devil urges him to open it.

> So urged, the boy breaks the seal and lets the monster loose. The hideous appearance at first shocks the pure mind, and the poor victim would fain put it out of existence. But the tempter says, "It can't hurt you; you are strong. Look it over and see what it is. Don't be afraid." Thus

beguiled a second look, and then a mighty force from within is let loose. Passions that had slumbered or lain dormant are awakened, and the boy is forced over a precipice, and death and destruction are sure, except the grace of God saves him.[52]

The inner forces that led children to abandon a morally upright life for life in the gutter were not only sexual. Comstock argued that gambling was caused by innate and almost universal greed.

> There is planted in almost every breast a desire to possess riches. From the time when first the tiny hand of the infant is stretched out toward the lighted candle until old age, there is constantly active an impulse to get possession of things which charm the fancies or that the appetite craves. To be rich and have a home, luxuries, and position in society is the thought likely to be uppermost in the human heart after the mind is expanded sufficiently to comprehend the condition of others in these respects. ... It requires but a slight bend in this current to turn the youthful mind away from honest labor and healthful occupation. ... [Satan] sets his signboards along the avenues of honest trade and commerce, and seeks to turn aside all classes by the glittering allurements of *easy fortunes*.[53]

In such passages Comstock suggests that the distance between classes is not very great. If the inner natures of rich children differed little from those of the poor, the task of ensuring that the rich would not become poor was difficult. This was made more problematic by the tendency of those with little money to ape the manners and dress of people with established wealth.

> Many a youth of inexperience imagines that because he has money to clothe himself in fine apparel and deck himself with glittering ornament, he thus puts himself upon a level with those who, by years of industry and application, have acquired wealth, culture, and position. The passion for money and prominence has rendered such a one the caricature of a man; has blunted his finer sensibilities, and degraded the higher qualities of his nature.[54]

While social pretenders might be harmed by their pretensions, children from good families were Comstock's special concern. For example, in *Traps for the Young* Comstock discussed the corruption of boys in billiard halls. In 1882, he claimed, a "prominent gentleman" from Brooklyn asked Comstock to help find his nephew, who had stolen a gold watch and silverware from his mother and eighty dollars from his uncle because "he had been crazed with this kind of pool." Comstock searched for "this deluded boy ... to reclaim him if possible." Another boy, also crazed by billiards, ran away to Boston, where he was arrested and sent to prison for larceny. His father, a former member of the New York State Legislature, discovered him there. Ruination of boys from good families came not only from gambling and the theft it inspired, but from the low companions billiards fostered.

> The game invites intemperance and but few young men can indulge long in the practice of playing "pool for drinks" without sinking themselves in the social scale, and forging a chain of habits that they will find it a hard matter to break asunder. It associates our youth with profane and obscene companions. Many men throng into these places well dressed, with plenty of spending money, who, making a respectable outward appearance, seem to think it a mark of a smart man to swear loudly or to gather a group of listeners about them while they regale their hearers with licentious and foul stories. . . . Parents, such an atmosphere is dangerous to your son. The contagion of sinful influences fills the air, and the poison will corrupt the better nature of your boy. Under such influences he will almost inevitably be led away from integrity and honorable pursuits.[55]

Morally pure youth had to be kept from their social inferiors. But policing class boundaries was difficult when those dressed like the elite were not necessarily members of it, when the city made contact between the classes ever more frequent, when depraved members of the lower classes were ever available to corrupt the rich, and especially when a literature glamorizing lust and crime circulated freely. Concern about the fluidity and permeability of class boundaries partially explains elite support for moral reform; in particular, the problem of class pollution may explain Comstock's oft-expressed concern with purity and the pollution of children and of homes.

## Polluted Institutions and the Problem of Social Reproduction

While the elite was urged to support the anti-vice society to protect their children from moral degradation, and their economic interests from thieving and corrupt employees, Comstock also argued that bad books in their various guises threatened the reproduction of society as a whole. Immoral reading "strikes at the foundations of [our] civil, social, and religious life" because it "*attacks specially and fatally the youth.*" The destruction of children endangered society: "What shall be the society of twenty years hence if the boys and girls of to-day are smitten by this leprosy?"[56] The concern about children was partially a concern about reproducing responsible citizens. Dr. Thomas, a guest speaker at an annual public meeting of the NYSSV, remarked, "Whatever strikes at the youth, whatever pollutes the fountain head, strikes at the heart of the Republic."[57] Such remarks related the issue of obscenity to concerns about the nature of the citizenry as a whole: the spread of obscenity was a crime "which by slow and unobserved steps sap[s] the foundation of society and implant[s] the principles of decay and certain death in the body politic."[58]

The problem of reproducing a moral citizenry led Comstock and his supporters to address the corruption of a variety of social institutions. Rather than ensuring the purity of children, schools and other institutions became venues for villains to spread obscene literature and pervert youth. In his speech at an annual meeting of the NYSSV the Reverend W. J. Tucker "called attention to the fact that [obscenity dealers] are using the very organizations that good people have built up for the defence and security of society—schools, seminaries, colleges—for carrying on their nefarious work."[59] Lust blighted churches and seemingly respectable businesses.

> A sexton of a church manufactures his licentious photographs in a room separated from the parish school only by folding doors, employs men or boys to sell them on the street as they walk about in the crowded thoroughfares. A dealer in jewelry passing among the trade supplies the young men with libidinous microscopic charms. Still others, frequenting the steps of banking houses in Wall and Broad Streets, furnish the sons of the wealthy classes with the highest libidinous art. . . . Newsboys on railroads, porters in steamboats and hotels, boys and young men in schools and colleges all spread the contagion, and in such stealthy form as oftentimes to escape detection.[60]

No longer bulwarks against the spread of vice, schools and churches became pathways through which vice spread. Comstock's rhetoric combined metaphors about disease with concerns about the social and class mixing facilitated by the city. His frequent invocation of disease, cancer, and contagion recalled fears of cholera and syphilis and echoed the arguments of his moral predecessor Sylvester Graham, who exhorted the public to avoid cholera by reducing indulgence in sexual intercourse to at most once a month, thus avoiding the weakening effects of coitus on their constitutions.[61] Vice, Comstock argued, afflicted ever more members of society, eventually destroying it. Lust spread when a diseased person contacted an unafflicted one. Social class did not insure immunity from vice, and no place was safe, not even the home.

So shrewd and wily are the dealers, so hidden their mode of advertising their wares, so stealthy and persistent in their circulation, that in hundreds of our schools, seminaries, and colleges, yes, in thousands of the refined and Christian homes of our land they have succeeded in injecting a virus more destructive to the innocency and purity of youth, if not counteracted, than can be the most deadly disease to the body.[62]

The language of disease and cancer applied to the problem of vice suggested its cure—the surgical removal of the diseased part to protect the whole. Thus anti-vice crusaders demonized their opponents. The Reverend Dr. Crosby used such rhetoric to explain the necessity of extralegal organizations to eradicate vice.

I have come to believe that it is an absolute necessity in a free country like ours to have something more than the official machinery to overpower and crush vice. I am convinced that we need in every community men who are respected and known by their fellow citizens to be above low ambitions and false motives; men whose character is open before all, and honored by all, who shall be the Vigilance Committee of the community to see that the officers of the law perform their duty, and see the laws enforced.[63]

The need for organizations to enforce their supporters' interpretation of the law lay in the analogy of vice to cancer. Crosby continued,

I have come to the same conclusion that [the anti-vice society has] come to, that there is no way whatever to cut out this cancer which is eating away the heart of society, but to put in the knife and tear out the venomous part; and let every citizen in the city of New York help us by his moral endorsement and pecuniary support. . . . Gentlemen! let us purify this city if it be by the fire and sword—the fire and sword of stern, invincible, inexorable Law.[64]

But while Comstock and his supporters invoked the breakdown of social institutions, the destruction of homes and of the church, and the corruption of the citizenry, children remained the anti-vice society's chief concern.

The result of this literary poison, cast into the very fountains of social life, is found everywhere. It is infecting the pure life and heart of our youth. They are becoming weak-minded, vapid, sentimental, lustful, criminal. Parents are mourning over the distaste of their children for all that is sensible and useful. The teacher finds study irksome to them; romantic tales, narratives of love, lust, hate, revenge, and murder are to their taste. They assimilate what they read, and so down, down our youth go, weaker and weaker in all the *mental* and *moral* elements of true manhood and womanhood. . . . Let fathers, mothers, and teachers watch closely over the pockets, desks, and rooms of their children. Be sure that the imagery and seeds of moral death are not in your homes and schools.[65]

## Protecting Children: Moral Mothers and Vice Crusaders

While the anti-vice society took responsibility for protecting children by policing the streets and the mails, the question remained of how the home would be guarded. Comstock invoked moral mothers as guardians of the home and defenders of children's purity. His descriptions of motherhood suggest that traditional motherhood was the basis for moral behavior and the reproduction of society. Children's moral purity demanded traditional and restrictive roles for women.

Comstock wrote of mothers and motherhood as a moral buttress against vice. Memories of mother and the lessons she taught, particularly the habit of prayer, were a corrupted youth's last hope against a life of dissipation.

> Let not the mother's heart faint nor grow weary. Instil in early youth thoughts of God. Train your children to habitual calling upon God in prayer, and you will thus start a little fire that will perchance burn its way through the accumulated follies of youth, and in after years reclaim your otherwise lost child.[66]

However, the "sainted mother" bore responsibility for more than prayer supervision. Comstock's passages on parental obligation imply that both fathers and mothers had a responsibility to protect children from vice and from improper reading. However, while the following passage discusses the duties of parents, it follows directly after the preceding passages about mothers, implying that mothers bore the blame for immoral children:

> A terrible responsibility rests upon parents who fail to early store their children's minds with wholesome thoughts, and protect them from the foul and criminal literature so fearfully prevalent.[67]

While Comstock never asserted that women's rights advocates were wrong in their claims that women should have a role in public life, his writings were replete with implications that women should remain at home. When Comstock discussed motherhood it was clear that woman's place was by the cradle:

As soon as the babe is born the duty of the mother is changed. A human soul is placed in her hands to care for, instruct, and bring up for the Master. A high and sacred duty. Fashionable society no longer should have a control over her. This gift from heaven is not a small thing, to be intrusted to some ignorant and often vicious servant girl, but constant care is required to preserve its precious form.[68]

But how were mothers to protect their children? Certainly they were to stay home and teach their children virtuous habits, with the hope that, even though boys "may go wild despite all such influences," such a son would remember his devoted mother and his memories would "cause him to awaken, rise up and call her blessed."[69] But what about women's direct participation in movements against obscenity? Given the context in which the anti-vice movement occurred, one would expect women to be active and important participants. The Women's Christian Temperance Union (WCTU) was demonstrating the power of extending women's role as moral guardian in the home to one of policing public morality; at the same time, women were active in antiprostitution movements in the United States and Britain.[70] But the officers of the NYSSV were slow to realize that women could be valuable allies.

Comstock had a quick change of heart about women's participation in the anti-vice movement. In April of 1885, when Comstock held a meeting to attempt to organize a branch of the NYSSV in Philadelphia, the call for a meeting stated that "gentlemen only" could attend.[71] When Comstock presented the *Annual Report* in January of 1886, however, he described in glowing terms the attempts of women to suppress obscene literature. These activities included the formation of a Bureau of Literature by the WCTU; the success of a group of women in Manistee, Michigan, at petitioning newsdealers to not sell the *Police Gazette*, *Police News*, and dime and half-dime novels; and the efforts of a New Hampshire woman who called the offices of the NYSSV for a draft of a law to be introduced in the New Hampshire state legislature. Comstock credited her efforts with passage of the law two months later.[72] Women's initiatives against obscenity inspired changes in NYSSV policy about their participation. At the January 1887 annual meeting, two speakers, General Clinton B. Fisk and Noah Davis (former chief justice of the New York State Supreme Court), took issue with the exclusion of women from the public meeting of the society. Still, women were not admitted to the meetings until 1891.[73]

It was not simply male chauvinism that barred women from the anti-vice societies. One of the few surviving letters from the New England Society for the Suppression of Vice is from a woman who wrote thanking the gentlemen of the society for their work, of which "most men are lamentably indifferent." In spite of her words of encouragement, she asked that her name not be published. Perhaps upper-class women considered it shameful for their names to be associated with obscenity.[74]

Women thus occupied an ambiguous role in the anti-vice campaign. While Comstock invoked the issue of "protecting" women as a justification for his activities, clearly women did not start the campaign, nor was their participation in the anti-vice societies particularly welcomed. While writings about "separate spheres" in the late-nineteenth century tend to assume that morality was the province of women, this campaign against obscenity was the province of men. Yet women played a vital role in anti-vice rhetoric. The issue of protecting children was framed in terms of women's primary (and virtually only) role as that of mother. The anti-vice society was thoroughly patriarchal in its assumptions, including the belief that women should not sully themselves with the issue of obscenity. As a result, while the leaders of the anti-vice movement justified their actions by invoking the protection of women, women were given few opportunities for expressing the need for or nature of these protections.

## Morality, Reality, and Class Reproduction

Comstock's threat that children would be sexually corrupted by obscene literature, his warning that moral pollution would cause children's social and economic downfall, and his claim that mothers must protect children from the dangers of evil reading lead to consideration of the rationality of the fears Comstock addressed. It is tempting to dismiss the issues Comstock raised as an irrational expression of underlying social conflict; the literature on moral reform has typically pointed to status competition as the cause of moral crusades and claimed the issues addressed by the organizations were ephemeral to the "real" cause of the social movement. To so dismiss Comstock is especially tempting when he argued that obscenity would lead to potentially fatal masturbation, an absurd claim to the mind of the contemporary observer. But a better approach to understanding moral reform movements is to consider how real fears addressed by such movements, such as harm to children, are shaped by the historical and cultural context in which they occur. Comstock's rhetoric points to real and rational problems faced by his supporters. It points as well to the ways that cultural and ideological lenses distorted and obscured the issues faced by Comstock's supporters, who included, but were not confined to, parents.

The desire to ensure the future of beloved children is rational and understandable to contemporary observers—middle-class children became priceless in the late-nineteeth century, a status that spread to children of all classes and that they still maintain.[75] To the extent that reproduction of the family's social position is predicated on access to social networks, and that moral or cultural criteria are determinants of such access, then concern that children's moral lapses might undermine their futures seems rational. But rhetoric about children's morals can also point to the larger social context in which parents are trying to raise their children. Parents face the problem of reproducing their children's social position in a political and economic context over which they have no control. Gilded Age parents of all classes had reason to fear for their children—the Depression of 1873 heralded a worldwide economic crisis and widespread economic stagnation. During the late-nineteenth century the boundaries around the middle class and the requirements for securing middle-class social positions were far from clear.[76] Similarly, what it meant to be upper-class and the cultural requirements for upper-class positions were also vague and contested.

This suggests that fears that children would be excluded from valued social networks because of moral failings can be rational fears based on a clear assessment of the requirements of family reproduction. But if fears that children will fall in the social structure are a response to economic or political conditions that parents do not control or understand, then we should also consider how ideological structures lead to moral interpretations of economic or political conditions. Katherine Newman has shown that children's failure to succeed can be blamed on their moral shortcomings, as when Depression-era parents blame their baby boomer children's inability to reproduce their parents social position on children's inability to delay gratification rather than on the GI Bill and cheap housing loans that made the Depression generation prosper.[77] Alternatively, the moral failings of others can be blamed for the precarious social position of children: in the nineteenth century, as I will show in chapter 5, Comstock blamed immigrants and corrupt politicians for driving up taxes and ignoring the gamblers that preyed on elite children. In our time, Newman argues, the presumed shiftlessness and greed of welfare recipients are blamed for the economic problems of the boomer generation.[78]

Comstock's invocation of the moral mother as the buttress against vice suggests another source of anxiety about family reproduction. Not only were nineteenth-century parents trying to reproduce their families in an era of economic uncertainty and unpredictable requirements for middle-class inclusion and prosperity, they faced as well a situation in which expectations of men, women, and family life were changing. While Comstock did not address arguments about women's rights, his claims that mothers had a duty to protect their children from vice, a duty involving constant supervision, points to a contested politics of gender. Comstock's arguments about the dangers of sexuality are anachronistic—we no longer believe that masturbation is potentially fatal—yet the underlying issue he referenced, control of children's desires so that they become responsible citizens and respected members of society, was (and remains) a real parental concern. The seemingly irrational elements of his arguments, such as the claim that obscenity could kill children, help us understand the ideological structures through which Comstock and his supporters perceived the world.

# 4

## ANTHONY COMSTOCK VERSUS FREE LOVE:

## RELIGION, MARRIAGE, AND THE

## VICTORIAN FAMILY

THE POWER WIELDED by the New York Society for the Suppression of Vice and its position as one of the nineteenth century's most influential moral reform movements resulted from the support given to it by wealthy and influential men. But while Comstock often appealed to the upper class by framing issues of youthful corruption in terms of problems that could befall wealthy children, the issues of protecting children and preserving the family also concerned persons of more modest means. Comstock sought support among these classes as well. He did this, in part, by linking the corruption of children by obscene materials to other issues already established as "social problems," such as prostitution, abortion, and juvenile delinquency. Comstock also linked his movement to changes that potentially affected all respectable families, particularly to two issues that social commentators feared were undermining the foundations of the Victorian family: the changing role of religion, in particular the declining authority of the church and increasing emphasis on individual emotional expression, and a concurrent change in the meaning of romantic love, which gradually supplanted love of God as an individual's most important source of identity. The threat to the family represented by changes in religion and romance and by the weakening of the institutions of church and marriage were exemplified in one of the great religious scandals of the nineteenth century, the adultery trial of the Reverend Henry Ward Beecher. Comstock's arrests of the women who broke the scandal, Victoria Woodhull and Tennessee Claflin, were his first highly publicized activities. The arrests also marked the beginning of his long crusade to suppress the free love movement.

While Comstock argued that obscenity lay at the root of problems of sexual disorder, free lovers offered a radically different analysis of these problems. Free lovers argued that women were sexually enslaved by the existing institution of marriage. They asserted that neither the church nor the state had the right to regulate sexual relations. Comstock used the obscenity laws to arrest and imprison free love advocates, in the process

becoming the movement's chief target and enemy. The free love movement mounted the only sustained attempts to repeal the Comstock Laws
and discredit the anti-vice movement. Comstock's harassment of the free
love movement illustrates not only his attempts to gain support by linking
his concerns about obscenity to larger social issues such as the sanctity of
marriage and the power of the church, but also his use of the law to
silence a movement that advocated women's freedom through the end of
sexual oppression.

On November 2, 1872, Comstock arrested Victoria Woodhull and
Tennessee Claflin for publishing in *Woodhull and Claflin's Weekly* the
charge that Reverend Henry Ward Beecher had committed adultery with
his parishioner Elizabeth Tilton, wife of Beecher's close friend Theodore
Tilton. Famous as an advocate of women's rights and notorious for her
advocacy of free love, Woodhull had leveled her charges at a minister
who routinely drew three thousand people to his Sunday sermons and
who was considered the "most eminent preacher of the country." Theodore Tilton, former editor of the *Brooklyn Eagle*, was also a well-known
writer and lecturer. Beecher and Theodore Tilton were renowned aboli-
tionists, and both had embraced the cause of women's rights: Beecher
served as the figurehead president of the American Woman Suffrage Association, while Tilton was elected president of Elizabeth Cady Stanton's
National Woman Suffrage Association.[1] The scandal precipitated by
Woodhull's charges culminated in 1875, when Theodore Tilton filed
charges against Beecher for adultery and for alienating his wife's affec-
tions. The six-month trial monopolized public attention, with the principals' testimony reported and letters reprinted in newspapers around the
country. Although the jury failed to reach a verdict about Beecher's guilt,
the scandal was one of the major moral dramas of the nineteenth century,
spawning a public reexamination of the meaning of "love" and its
bounds within marriage. Historians have credited the scandal with solidi-
fying public support of moral and social restrictions, presumably including the activities of Comstock, with finalizing the split between women's
rights advocates and sex reformers, and with hardening public disdain for
the arguments and goals of free lovers.[2]

The free love movement did not die of its own accord. The Woodhull
and Claflin arrests marked the beginning of Comstock's campaign
against free love advocates, which resulted in the arrests of many leading
sex reformers and spawned the judicial decision that would be the basis
of obscenity law for more than fifty years. While Comstock's animus
against free love originated in his beliefs about the roles of marriage and
religion in maintaining social order, the Beecher-Tilton affair illustrated
the danger that the passions glorified by free lovers—and more importantly, by the emerging culture of romance—posed to the family and

church.[3] Comstock's suppression of Woodhull and his successful prosecution of Ezra Heywood, one of the country's most famous critics of existing marital and gender relations, bolstered the traditional family by suppressing debate on women's family roles. Comstock did not act against persons advocating expanded public roles for women, but the free love doctrines Comstock censored examined the sexual side of women's liberation, particularly a woman's right to control her reproduction, to refuse intercourse with her husband, and to express her sexuality outside of marriage.

## Woodhull, Claflin, and Social Reform

In 1869 Victoria Woodhull and her sister Tennessee Claflin became the first women stockbrokers on Wall Street, as well as the founders and editors of *Woodhull and Claflin's Weekly*. Their paper advocated a variety of social reforms, including organized labor, relaxation of divorce laws, and free love. Rumor held that the money for these ventures came from Commodore Vanderbilt, a friend of the sisters.[4] In 1871 Woodhull became the first woman to testify before the House Judiciary Committee, where she argued for women's right to vote. This earned her the friendship and support of Susan B. Anthony and Elizabeth Cady Stanton, the country's leading women's rights advocates, who introduced her to Beecher and Theodore Tilton.

Woodhull and Claflin soon announced their support of socialism, becoming leaders of the two New York–based sections of the International. When the sections issued a document advocating free love and the expulsion of immigrants from the communist movement, Karl Marx purged the sisters from the International. Woodhull attempted to replace Marx as the leader of the Communist Party by forming a new Communist Party with herself at its head. In the course of Woodhull and Clafin's short-lived involvement with communism, they published the first English translation of the *Communist Manifesto* in the United States. By 1872, however, Woodhull's outspoken free love views earned her increasing censure. Denounced by Stanton and Anthony, Woodhull responded by forming the Equal Rights Party, which nominated her to run for president of the United States on their ticket.[5]

In 1871 Woodhull became president of the American Association of Spiritualists. Spiritualism was hugely popular in the pre–Civil War years, and while the movement was never well organized, making attempts to accurately estimate its size futile, contemporary observers estimated the number of Spiritualists at between a few hundred thousand to eleven million. Spiritualists believed that divine truth was directly accessible to individuals through spirit communication, eliminating the need for the church. Spiritualists believed that the church perpetuated repressive social conventions that inhibited an individual's quest for truth. They shunned the subjection of individuals to the authority of others, denouncing the "authority of churches over believers, of governments over citizens . . . of masters over slaves, and, most of all, of men over women."[6] Women gained a particularly prominent role in Spiritualism, and as spirit mediums performed much of the early public speaking done by women. Spiritualists argued that women were forced to marry because they were denied means to support themselves, protesting that within marriage a woman lost the right to refuse sex with her husband and to avoid the pregnancies that resulted. Many of these beliefs were shared by the free love movement, but Woodhull's election excited considerable discord in the American Spiritualist Association. The organization itself was quite weak, as many women saw it as an attempt by men to take over the Spiritualist movement; few people attended the convention that elected Woodhull, who gained the presidency by garnering forty-three votes.[7] Some members were horrified by Woodhull's open advocacy of free love, and others believed that Woodhull, who had not previously identified with Spiritualism or attended a convention, attended this one only to further her political ambitions. Upon her reelection in 1872 (this time with thirty-one votes), Woodhull defended her principles.

> I only proved that the real liberty of women consisted in an exact equality of rights, privileges and duties with those exercised by man. I also asserted that, in the economy of Nature, before she had been enervated by false civilization, woman was as capable of self-sustenance as man, and that, until woman is made to be self-sustaining, she cannot be really independent. And I do not forget, if she do no other labor than to continue to be the architect of the race, that, alone, should entitle her to one-half of the wealth of the world. . . . In a word, every child is worth a certain sum to society, and it must pay for the services rendered in its production.[8]

Spiritualists should support her, Woodhull argued, to spare their daughters from forced maternity at the hands of men "debauched by drunkenness, degraded by the fruits of licentiousness, or undermined by the use of tobacco." The children of such unions would be "abortions upon nature." Thus Woodhull, like other nineteenth-century feminists, made claims for women's rights using the language of women's responsibility as mothers. She also echoed the sentiments of women's rights advocates who argued that woman should have the right to refuse sexual intercourse with their husbands, claiming that no woman should be obliged to "bear children by a man whom she loathes and hates."[9]

Woodhull aired the Beecher-Tilton affair at a Spiritualists meeting in September 1872. Dissatisfied by the muted response to her revelation, she published the charge in the November 2 issue of *Woodhull and Claflin's Weekly*, in which she stated:

> The fault with which I . . . charge [Mr. Beecher] is not infidelity to the old ideas, but unfaithfulness to the new. He is in heart, in conviction and in life, an ultra socialist reformer; while in seeming and pretension he is the upholder of the old social slavery, and, therefore does what he can to crush out and oppose me and those who act and believe with me in forwarding the great social revolution. . . . Speaking from my feelings, I am prone to denounce [Mr. Beecher] as a poltroon, a coward and a sneak; not, as I tell you, for anything that he has done, and for which the world would condemn him, but for failing to do what it seems to me so clear he ought to do; for failing, in a word, to stand shoulder to shoulder with me and others who are endeavoring to hasten a social revolution he believes in.[10]

Comstock had the sisters arrested on charges of circulating obscene literature. Upon their release from Ludlow Street Jail a month later, Woodhull and Claflin were immediately rearrested on a slander charge made by L. C. Challis, a stockbroker. Woodhull had again accused an elite man of sexual misdeeds; in this case, that Challis had attended the French Ball, an event notorious for salacious behavior, with a fifteen-year-old virgin, and seduced her afterward at a brothel.[11] In June of 1873 the sisters were finally tried and acquitted. Judge Blatchford charged the jury not to convict, explaining that "under the [obscenity] act of 1872 newspapers were not included, the act of 1873 being specially framed to cover the omission and meet the present case, and that therefore there was no evidence to sustain the prosecution."[12]

While Woodhull and Claflin opened the Beecher-Tilton affair to public scrutiny, the scandal did not assume its prominent public place until 1874, when the Plymouth Church dropped Theodore Tilton from its membership rolls, claiming that he had slandered Beecher. Tilton responded by publicly accusing Beecher of adultery; the preacher asked for and obtained a committee of church members to investigate the charge.[13] Beecher defended himself and explained some incriminating documents by asserting that his only wrongdoing had been to urge Elizabeth Tilton to leave her unhappy marriage. Plymouth Church, not surprisingly, found Beecher innocent of adultery; the civil adultery charges initiated by Tilton ended, as noted above, in a hung jury. While historians continue to debate Beecher's guilt, the trial revealed how Tilton's attraction to the doctrine of free love had destroyed his marriage. But while free love doctrines were already subject to public censure, the trial also caused the condemnation of Beecher's popular "Gospel of Love." Beecher's gospel was erroneous and dangerous because it strayed too close to the central tenet of free love, namely that individuals should follow and express their feelings of love outside of the confinements of social institutions, including marriage.[14] The trial thus prompted public examination of the strains in marriage wrought by the sexualization of love.

Theodore Tilton's transgressions were twofold: he had severed his ties to the church and he supported free love. Elizabeth Tilton refuted her husband's claim that their marriage had been happy before her friendship with Beecher:

> The implication that the harmony of our home was unbroken till Mr. Beecher entered it as a frequent guest and friend, is a lamentable satire upon the household where he [Tilton] himself, years before, laid the corner-stone of Free Love, and desecrated its altars up to the time of my departure; so that the atmosphere was not only godless, but impure for my children. And in this effort and throe of agony, I would fain lift my daughters, and all womanhood, from the insidious and diabolical teachings of these latter days.[15]

Elizabeth's discussion of the desecration of her home and marriage was a veiled charge of adultery, the "corner-stone of Free Love." Theodore Tilton had simultaneously made their home godless, presumably because of his religious and political opinions.[16] Elizabeth, the wronged and suffering wife, linked Tilton's marital transgressions to his religious infidelity.

The thin line between sexual infidelity and the advocacy of unconventional ideas about religion and marriage emerged in the church committee's interrogation of Theodore Tilton. Tilton refused to answer questions about his "alleged acts of immorality" or whether he had brought "certain women" to his home when his wife was not there, but was greatly agitated when asked if his "intimacy with public women had not greatly disturbed Mrs. Tilton, and made her life unhappy." When Tilton replied, "What do you mean, Sir, to talk to me of public women," he almost certainly had interpreted "public women" to mean prostitutes. Another member of the committee placated Tilton by explaining that the questioner "does not mean public women in an odious sense. He means so-called reformers." Thus the term "public woman" carried two meanings: prostitutes, women who sold their sexuality to men (that is, the public); or women who advocated women's rights in the public sphere. Theodore Tilton's relationship with women reformers had indeed strained his marriage, for he found his wife dull and intellectually inferior to women such as Anthony and Stanton. There were rumors of his having sexual liaisons with women reformers as well.[17]

While the examination of the Tilton marriage exposed Theodore Tilton's presumed infidelities, the central issue of the trial concerned his wife's faithfulness. Tilton simultaneously defended his estranged wife's honor and purity while accusing her of adulterous acts with Beecher by asserting that Elizabeth was unaware of the sinfulness of her actions. Beecher, he testified, had used his pastoral authority to seduce Elizabeth, so that when Elizabeth had confessed her adultery, she explained that Beecher had declared their liaison pure:

> Mr. Beecher's arguments and reasonings with her to overcome her long maintained scruple against yielding to his desires, and declaring that she had committed no wrong to her husband or her marriage vow, quoting, in support of this opinion that her pastor had repeatedly assured her that she was spotless and chaste, which she believed herself to be. She further stated that her sexual commerce with [Beecher] had never proceeded from low or vulgar thoughts, either on her part or his, but always from pure affection and a high religious love.[18]

Tilton's charge that Beecher seduced his wife using the argument that sexual love was not necessarily sinful reflects both the gospel that Beecher preached and the changing nature of romantic love it spoke to. Beecher's enormous popularity derived from his Gospel of Love, in which "God's wrathful judgment and the believer's scrutinizing conscience were replaced by God's universal acceptance and humankind's joyful response."[19] Beecher discussed moral development in terms of lower and higher spheres. In the lowest stages of moral development, fear of God and of social sanction guided behavior. But highly developed individuals were freed from institutional imperatives: "Instead of reason, he recommended emotion; instead of organized religion, love; instead of duty, spiritual affinity."[20] This disdain for institutional constraints on emotional expression suggests a Spiritualist influence on Beecher's theology, and created similarities between Beecher's gospel and Woodhull's.[21] For both Beecher and Woodhull "it was inappropriate to feel guilt about following one's feelings."[22] This made more plausible Theodore Tilton's claim that "for a period of a year and a half or thereabouts, [Beecher] maintained criminal intercourse with [Elizabeth Tilton], overcoming her previous modest scruples against such conduct by investing it with a false justification as sanctified by love and religion," as well as Woodhull's argument that only Beecher's hypocritical public statements differentiated his conduct from her own.[23] The free love and anti-church beliefs of Woodhull and Theodore Tilton were condemned during the trial, but Beecher's doctrine and his romantic (even if chaste) love for Elizabeth Tilton were condemned as well.[24] The *New York Times* complained of the language and behavior of the scandal's principals, noting that "all these people seem to live in a world of their own, and it is useless for an ordinary man to attempt to understand their sayings and doings." Regarding Beecher's claim that his encouraging Elizabeth to leave her unhappy marriage had made him "filled with morbid intensity at the very shadow of it," the *Times* noted, "Should any spiritualistic humbug of the next generation ever profess to summon the spirit of Mr. Beecher, he can hardly make him talk more extraordinary gibberish than this."[25]

The Beecher scandal highlighted changes and contradictions in nineteenth-century notions of romantic love. Karen Lystra argues that in the nineteenth century, romantic love replaced love of God as a person's most powerful and compelling emotion. Individuals discovered and created their identities not through religious worship but through romantic love—a change she calls the "new theology of self."[26] Couples expressed love using religious metaphors that made sacred sexuality as an aspect of love. The replacement of love of God by romantic love is evident in Elizabeth Tilton's letters to her husband, in which she wrote: "Do you wonder that I couple your love, your presence, and relation to me with the Savior's? I lift you up sacredly, and keep you in that exalted and holy place where I reverence, respect, and love with the fervency of my whole being. Whatever capacity I have I offer it to you."[27]

Others besides Victoria Woodhull perceived the similarity of Beecher's doctrines to those of free lovers. In January of 1872 Thomas Munnell published an article in the *Christian Quarterly* that linked "Beecherism" with "free-loveism," arguing that the "tendency in religious thought" that Beecher represented endangered both church and society. Beecher's sermons suggested that the ceremonies ordained in the New Testament were necessary only for weak persons: "If you can not, in your present stage of development, rise to the absolute and direct communion with God, he [Beecher] will administer to you either of these ordinances; but if you can get along without them, there is no condemnation in disregarding them."[28] While Munnell argued that Beecher would not advocate the abolition of the marriage ceremony (a doctrine that "would not only shock the moral sense of all right-minded people, but would ruin the family, society, and the world," which was advocated only by "those sewers in the system of moral reform—the free-lovers"), he condemned Beecher for believing that "love is the only power to move men to do right. . . . he has very little use for law, penalty, or fear as even primary incentives."[29] Thus Beecher erred in according too little importance to the rules and ceremonies of the church, offering instead a doctrine that love alone was the animating force of Christianity. In doing so he epitomized the crisis of authority of the church in regulating the lives of the populace.

Beecher's rumored affair and the Tiltons' resulting divorce raised not only Beecher's relationship to free love but issues of love and marital stability more generally. Rhetoric about divorce concerned the relationship between women, the family, and the state. While Comstock rarely addressed the issue of divorce, his statements about protecting the family and his arguments that parents' primary duty was to guard their children's morals resonated with widespread social concern about women's changing roles and the future of the family. At issue was whether the heart of marriage was romantic love or the reproduction of the next generation of citizens; and if the latter, if marriage was a duty to be preformed for the state, what was implied about women's rights?

Noah Davis, a justice on the New York State Supreme Court who at various times was a vocal supporter of the anti-vice society, addressed this issue in 1883. Davis asserted that "marriage alone is the mother of the family; and the family is the organic unit of civil society, and the sheet-anchor of its social order." Divorce threatened children with loss of "their rights of heritage and heirship, of lineage and name," and society with the specter of "the race turned loose in a pandemonium of selfish and indiscriminate lusts and crimes."[30] But marriage not only channeled and constrained sexual desire; it assured the reproduction of the next generation.

> That [marriage] is not a mere copartnership of individualities created to intensify individual advantages and enjoyments, but a God-ordained union of bodies, hearts, minds and souls consecrated to the perpetuation of the race by the creation of the family, through with organized society obtains its surest and holiest guarantees of happiness and progress. . . . Therefore, in considering the subject of divorce, the interests of society are first and paramount; those of individuals are subordinate and secondary.[31]

Persons who were "modern advocates of free-and-easy divorce" did a disservice to society and to women. Their advocacy of more easily obtained divorce "ignore[d] the family, exaggerate[d] the individual, and wholly discard[ed] the claims of the State." This emphasis on the desires of the individual "has always been a central ideal of barbarism." If divorces were more easily obtained, women would become "the slave . . . bought and sold at the price of lust." Davis echoed the concerns of Comstock when he argued that divorce harmed the "public mind" and "public morals" through the medium of the press, which "teems with scandalous reports of such suits, often giving prurient and disgusting details, which the youth of neither sex can safely read."[32]

But while Davis argued that increasing numbers of divorces damaged society and loosened marital bonds, he simultaneously argued that they were caused by the decreasing size of families: "a large family of children is a safeguard against divorce." Large families were sacrificed to "petty conceptions of individual ease"; emphasis on material desires created barrenness. In an analysis similar to physicians' anti-abortion arguments, Davis utilized anti-Catholic sentiment to assert: "And so we Americans by descent are fast handling over our country with all its mighty interests to the races of immigration and their descendants who are happily taught obedience to the laws of nature as a religious duty."[33] Protestant families disrupted the "natural" purpose of marriage, the bearing and rearing of large numbers of children; family breakdown and loss of political power and social influence to Catholics followed.

Davis's analysis of divorce exemplified concerns about the family spawned by industrialization. Middle-class family size shrank as children became increasingly costly; the industrial economy drew increasing numbers of immigrants, who threatened the political power of the native born; and the growth and spread of popular culture, exemplified by the yellow press, made it ever more difficult for parents to control their children. Comstock raised similar issues in discussing obscenity (his use of anti-immigrant rhetoric will be discussed in the next chapter); Davis's analysis also shares themes with physicians' construction of abortion as a social problem. Changes in the family, interpreted by some as evidence of family breakdown, was a theme expressed in a variety of venues in the late-nineteenth century, and were a source of Comstock's support and power.

In the Beecher affair the country witnessed the authority of religion being undermined by the doctrines of the country's leading cleric and the institution of marriage being undermined by both his actual and rumored actions. Although he played a small role in the Beecher affair, Comstock addressed the issues raised by the scandal during the next two decades of his work. His desire to protect marriage and religion were most strongly pursued in his harassment of those who openly advocated free love doctrines.

## Free Love and Free Speech

To free love advocates the Beecher affair exemplified the errors of a social system based on marriage. Elizabeth Tilton's treatment by Beecher and his allies, particularly Beecher's claim that he had been drawn into moral misdeeds by Mrs. Tilton, outraged free lovers. Ezra Heywood, editor of the *Word*, a leading free thought and free love journal, commented, "So Beecher now represents himself as the victim of the many affectionate sisters who, he says, passionately love him. His overflowingly attractive nature has gone out into so many gladdened channels that he cannot now gather himself up into orthodox or respectable limits. And the women are to blame for it!"[34] Elizabeth Cady Stanton reiterated this theme, arguing that Beecher had persuaded Elizabeth Tilton to love him and be his lover, and that Elizabeth acted nobly when she defied "law, gossip, [and] conventionalism" to leave her husband.

> Thus leaving husband, children, home, she went forth to vindicate the man she loved, making his friends her friends, his God her God! With what withering cruelty, then, his words must have fallen on her heart— "She thrust her affections on me unsought"; though a mutual confession of love is revealed in the course of the investigation, and recognized in the verdict.[35]

Comstock arrested Woodhull for airing the scandal but could do nothing about most of the coverage that followed. He arrested John A. Lant, editor of the New York–based *Toledo Sun*, for printing a humorous poem likening the affair to a naval battle. The *Word* urged readers to sign a petition for Lant's pardon; under the heading "National Gag-Law," Heywood warned:

> People are generally not aware of the unlimited stretch of despotism embodied in the Congressional "law" of which religio-sectarian tyranny secured the passage, and which *enables one man to obstruct the freedom of the U.S. mails and suppress well-intentioned efforts to discuss the Social Question.*[36]

Two organizations challenged Comstock's obscenity prosecutions. The National Liberal League (NLL) held its first meeting in Philadelphia in July of 1876. The preamble of the constitution of the Liberal League stated that although the United States Constitution is "framed in accordance with the principle of the total separation of Church and State," this separation was in many instances violated. Demanding total secularization of the United States government, the Liberal League advocated taxation of church property, the end of religious instruction in public schools, and repeal of all laws enforcing observance of the Sabbath. The NLL also advocated changes in the enforcement of the Comstock Law.

> Resolved, That this League, while it recognizes, the great importance, and absolute necessity of guarding by proper legislation against obscene and indecent publications, whatever sect party order or class such publications claim to favor, disapproves and protests against all laws, which by reason of indefiniteness or ambiguity shall permit the prosecution and punishment of honest and conscientious men, for presenting to the public what they deem, essential to the public welfare, when the views thus presented do not violate, in thought or language the acknowledged rules of decency; and that we demand, that all laws, against obscenity

and indecency, shall be so clear and explicit, that none, but actual of-
fenders, against the recognized principles of purity shall be likely to
suffer therefrom.

Resolved, That we cannot but regard the appointment and authoriza-
tion, by the government of a single individual to inspect our mails, with
power to exclude, therefrom whatever he deems objectionable, as a delegation of authority, dangerous to public and personal liberty, and utterly
inconsistent, with the genius of free institutions.[37]

The National Liberal League maintained that anti-obscenity laws were
necessary, although flawed in their present enforcement, until 1878,
when controversy about the issue tore the league into two separate organizations. Comstock's prosecutions of Ezra Heywood, editor of the
*Word*, and D. M. Bennett, editor of the *Truth Seeker*, led to this breach.

## Cupid's Yokes: The State and Conjugal Life

In 1877, Comstock arrested Ezra Heywood for publishing *Cupid's
Yokes, or, The Binding Forces of Conjugal Life*, a tract advocating the
abolition of marriage on the grounds that women were enslaved and love
demeaned by the institution. Heywood analyzed women's role in society
and its maintenance through women's economic dependence on marriage. His assertion that women should have the right to control their
reproduction enunciated, a century early, a central tenant of twentieth-
century feminism. It was also, according to Comstock, obscene.

Heywood argued that marriage harmed women, love, and society as a
whole. The popular idea of virtue, which included premarital chastity
and fidelity afterward, rested on a series of laws that were both "intru-
sive" and made by men. Heywood asked how "coition" could be pure
only if "sanctioned by priest or magistrate" when the clergy had been
sullied by Beecher's adulterous affair and politicians were corrupt.[38] Instead of letting the church and state legislate love, Heywood proposed
that individuals be taught about sexuality and entrusted with the regulation of their sexual conduct.

Heywood argued that marriage enslaved women. The belief that a wife
was her husband's property meant that she could be "overpowered" by
him and forced to endure "selfish" and "invasive" love. In marriage
women could be and were raped, while outside marriage the "right to
control of and dispose of her own person" at least nominally protected
women.[39] But marriage also victimized women who were not raped. Sexual ignorance made married lovers "prey on each other." The consequence of ignorance was unwanted pregnancies that made women "ema-

ciated wreck[s]," while men's health suffered from too much intercourse.[40] Marriage thus gave men and women "legal license to invade,
pollute, and destroy each other."[41]

The "tyranny of lust" victimized married women for, denied political
and economic rights, they were martyred to the sexual license granted
men: "Marriage attempts, by legal means, to furnish food for his savage
nature; and we have but to lift the roofs of 'respectable' houses to find the
skeletons of its feminine victims." Women suffered the consequences of
lust but were blamed by people like Henry Ward Beecher for its existence.
When embarrassed by the scandal resulting from his sexual peccadilloes,
Heywood noted, Beecher blamed his paramour for the couple's sins. Men
were exonerated by the ideology that they were not responsible for their
actions when under a woman's spell: Adam was only the first to blame a
woman for his sexual misdeeds. Yet sexual savagery was not innate to
men's nature; rather, a barbarous and erroneous "marriage theory" created a "social hell" inflicted upon both women and men.[42] Sexuality was
socially constructed; therefore, abuses in the existing system of love and
marriage were socially caused and changeable.

Heywood equated marriage with prostitution because women's low
wages—lower than those given to men doing the same work—forced
them to sell their bodies either to a husband or in the brothel. But women
sold sex not only for money but to satisfy desire: the "fraud" of marriage
forbade "natural intercourse," giving women the options of selling themselves for a night or for life. Capitalism thus turned "natural desire" into
a "marketable commodity"; the "profit system" and marriage were
"twin-relic[s] of barbarism."[43]

Heywood specified the social consequences of the existing marriage
system as well as its economic and social causes. The perversion of sexual
desire by marriage and the stifling of sexual knowledge by prudery and
the Comstock Law created a supply and demand for prostitutes, encouraged the spread of obscene prints and pictures, and fostered the evils
of celibacy, which included "involuntary emissions, celibate abstinence
and solitary vice."[44] Licentiousness resulted from sexual ignorance and
from the state's attempts to regulate what individuals alone should control. Unwanted children were another social burden resulting from sexual
ignorance. Following Malthus, Heywood asserted that famine would
check a population not controlled by other means.[45] But unlike Malthus,
Heywood advocated widespread use of birth control, which would lead
to perfect and wanted children, although the only method Heywood
found acceptable was sexual abstinence during women's fertile days. Unfortunately, Heywood's proposed rhythm method calculated women's
fertile period incorrectly.[46] Heywood condemned more effective means

of contraception: "artificial" means, such as the use of barriers and with-drawal, were "unnatural, injurious, or offensive," while abortion was "murderous."[47]

Heywood called privacy "sexual rights," asserting that the state had no right to regulate the private lives of its citizens.

> Why should the right of private judgment, which is conceded in politics and religion, be denied to domestic life? If government cannot justly determine what ticket we shall vote, what church we shall attend, or what books we shall read, by what authority does it watch at key-holes and burst open bed-chamber doors to drag lovers from sacred seclusion? . . . The belief that our sexual relations can be better governed by statute, than by individual reason, is a rude species of conventional impertinence, as barbarious and shocking as it is senseless.[48]

These arguments reflected Heywood's anarchist roots and identified a specific enemy—Anthony Comstock. Heywood railed against the Comstock Acts, arguing that congressional attempts to suppress obscene books and pictures were motivated by good intentions, but that legislators failed to understand that demand for such literature sprang from sexual ignorance. A bad law was worsened by its enforcer: Congress had empowered the "religious monomaniac" Comstock, whose actions Heywood likened to "fires of the inquisition."[49]

## The Arrests of Heywood and Bennett

Comstock arrested Heywood in November of 1877 for distributing *Cupid's Yokes* and Thrall's *Sexual Physiology*, a popular medical manual containing instructions about contraception. Comstock obtained the pamphlets by sending a "decoy letter," requesting the material using an alias. Shortly thereafter Comstock arrested D. M. Bennett on charges of obscenity and blasphemy for mailing *How Do Marsupials Propagate?* by H. B. Bradford, and Bennett's tract *An Open Letter to Jesus Christ*. The former was a "scientific pamphlet," while Bennett's tract attacked the beliefs of Christianity and the actions of the church and its members.[50] In the annual report to members of the NYSSV Comstock announced:

> Another class of publications issued by free-lovers and free-thinkers is in a fair way of being stamped out. The public generally can scarcely be aware of the extent that blasphemy and filth commingled have found vent through these varied channels. Under a plausible pretense, men who raise a howl about "free press," "free speech," etc., ruthlessly

trample under feet the most sacred things, breaking down the altars of religion, bursting asunder the ties of home, and seeking to overthrow every social restraint.[51]

While Heywood denied the authority of the church in matters of marriage and sexual morality, the blasphemy Comstock complained of was most pronounced in Bennett's *An Open Letter to Jesus Christ*. The tract ridiculed religion, mocked the church as filled with licentious clergy and hypocritical followers, and advocated the replacement of religion with science. Bennett's letter to Christ asked, "Have you ever doubted whether your first miracle, changing water into wine, at the wedding in Cana, was well advised, especially as the guests were already drunk?" Bennett asked if Christ approved of the "Holy Inquisition," during which malicious priests slowly tortured the innocent and defenseless: "Could you hear the cries and groans of these poor, helpless, tortured wretches, hour after hour . . . century after century, and never feel a particle of sympathy for the sufferers, and never stretch forth your hand or lift a finger to stay these most accursed wrongs? . . . If you did not aid in all this most infernal business transacted in your name, and by your church, were you totally unconscious of it?"[52]

Bennett indicted the morality and sincerity of church leaders and members. He recounted the sins, particularly sexual sins, of various popes, asking, "How did you like John XXIII in the fifteenth century, who was proved to have been guilty of seventy different kinds of crime, among which were sodomy, simony, rape, incest, and murder, and with having illicit intercourse with over three hundred nuns?" Bennett followed his recitation of past sins with an inquiry about present ones: "Have you not often had occasion to blush with shame and to redden with indignation at the base conduct of hundreds—yes, thousands of licentious hypocrites who try to pass themselves as shepherds and leaders of your flock? Are not the ewe-lambs specially exposed to their seductive wiles and artifices, their sensual plots and lascivious designs?" Clerics not motivated by sexual lust were driven by greed: "Is not money, which in your book is called 'filthy lucre—the root of all evil,' the main incentive which induces your clergy to engage in your cause? . . . If there was no paying would there be so much preaching and praying?"[53]

Finally, Bennett attacked wealthy churchgoers, asking, "Are not the fashionable churches of the day mere aristocratic associations for an exclusive class, where they can foster pride, arrogance, and self-righteousness?" He claimed that the "magnificent church places where Mr. Moneybags, Mrs. Grundy, and Mrs. Uppercrust meet to worship alike the unknown God and the god of fashion" should be converted into industrial schools and hospitals for the aged and crippled. Bennett concluded:

"In a few words, is not Christianity, as known and practiced in the world, a cheat, a fraud, a costly and expensive luxury which mankind could well spare, losing nothing by its rejection," and that "false gods, base devils, useless saviors, and degrading creeds" should be abandoned and replaced by practitioners devoting themselves to improving the world and encouraging the pursuit of human happiness.[54]

The charges against Bennett were dropped, but shortly thereafter the legal fates of Bennett and Heywood became intertwined. Heywood was convicted in January of 1878 for selling *Cupid's Yokes*, at a trial held before Judge Daniel Clark of the United States Circuit Court in Boston. The trial was remarkable for how little defense Heywood was allowed. The prosecutor was not required to show evidence of the alleged obscenity in court, and, arguing that the passages in question from *Cupid's Yokes* were too obscene to appear in court records, chose to give the passages to the jury only after they had entered the jury room. Heywood was not allowed to argue about the nature of obscenity, as the judge deemed that the judgment of the jury was to be uncontaminated by the defendant's arguments. The sole question to be argued in court was whether Heywood had indeed mailed *Cupid's Yokes* and *Sexual Physiology*. Judge Clark, in charging the jury, told them that Heywood's free love doctrines would turn Massachusetts into a house of prostitution. The jury found that *Sexual Physiology* was not obscene but that *Cupid's Yokes* was.[55]

Heywood's case was appealed to the Supreme Court, but was delayed pending a decision on another case, that of *Ex parte Jackson* (1877). This case concerned the power of the Congress to regulate the content of the mails. Although the case referred to the exclusion of lottery material from the mail, the Supreme Court opinion specifically referred to the Comstock statute as an example of congressional power to regulate the mail, thus implicitly upholding the Comstock Law.[56] Heywood was sent to Dedham Jail upon losing his appeal. Bennett responded by advertising *Cupid's Yokes* in his paper, the *Truth Seeker*. Comstock arrested Bennett, and the trial generated a landmark obscenity decision.

Bennett was convicted in this case by Judge Samuel Blatchford, sentenced to thirteen months in prison, and fined three hundred dollars. The Blatchford decision formed the basis of obscenity law in the United States for more than fifty years. Blatchford drew on a decision in the British courts, *Queen v. Hicklin* (1868), which asserted that the test of obscenity was "whether the tendency of the matter charged as obscenity is to deprave and corrupt those whose minds are open to immoral influences, and into whose hands a publication of this sort may fall." The *Hicklin* case was significant for allowing a work to be judged obscene on the basis of isolated passages; furthermore, the judgment of obscenity was based on the presumed ability of an object to cause libidinous thoughts in the minds of the "young and inexperienced." In addition to upholding the *Hicklin* standard, Blatchford affirmed the precedent of prohibiting discussion of the allegedly obscene matter in court, as had been done in Heywood's trial. The purpose or social value of an indicted work was irrelevant in determining whether it was obscene.[57] The Blatchford decision was remarkable for its substantiation of Comstock's definition of obscenity as material that could potentially corrupt youth, and for the power it gave Comstock to impose his standard on persons who intended neither to corrupt youth nor to profit from children's sexual curiosity.

## Challenging Censorship: Repeal Attempts and the Indignation Meeting

Comstock's persecution of Heywood resulted in both a concerted effort to repeal the anti-obscenity law and the formation of the National Defense Association, which endeavored to defend people prosecuted by Comstock. In March of 1878, after Heywood's conviction but before his ultimate imprisonment, a group calling itself the Committee of Seven, for Fifty Thousand Petitioners, appealed to the United States House of Representatives' Committee on the Revision of Laws for repeal of the Comstock Acts. The signatures of the fifty thousand petitioners appeared on a two-thousand-foot-long petition. The petitioners argued that the anti-obscenity laws had been "enforced to destroy the liberty of conscience in matters of religion, against the freedom of the press and to the great hurt of the learned professions."[58] The House Committee denied the appeal of the petitioners, stating: "In the opinion of the committee, the post-office was not established to carry instruments of vice or obscene writings, indecent pictures, or lewd books." The committee further argued that the obscenity acts did not violate the constitution of the United States, and should not be repealed.[59]

On August 1, 1878, the newly formed National Defense Association, a group founded to stop "pernicious and outrageous application of certain special laws by the agent of a "Society for the Suppression of Vice," held an Indignation Meeting at Boston's Faneuil Hall to protest Heywood's imprisonment. Six thousand people attended the meeting, which was devoted to a series of speeches examining the constitutionality of the Comstock laws and the morality of Comstock's actions.[60]

Heywood's defenders largely ignored the content of his arguments, pursuing what they considered the greater issues of free speech and freedom of the press. The Reverend J. M. L. Babcock addressed the issues of morality and free speech by arguing:

Some people seem to have fancied that we must here take up free speech and morality as rival questions, and balance the conflicting claims of each; and that we can after all allow ourselves only so much of the luxury of free speech as may be found consistent with due legislation against immorality. But we are reduced to no such pitiful dilemma. We are not at liberty to weigh out one of these things against the other. Essential as morality is, not even legislation to promote it can be permitted to restrain or impair free speech. . . . We have no business to inquire as to obscenity to-night. Mr. Heywood was tried and condemned for his opinions. . . . If a man has a right to publish his opinions, and his right is assailed, it is simply impertinent to ask what his opinions happen to be.[61]

The Comstock Law violated not only the right of free speech, but the separation of church and state. Theoron Leland based this claim on the presumed relationship between Comstock and the church.

Heywood has invaded no human rights, nor harmed any individual; and this punishment of him for his published opinions is the work of the Christian Church, in spiteful revenge for outspoken dissent from their works and ways. The State has played only the subordinate part of tool and accessory in the business. The Church is responsible for Comstock. He is her agent. He does her bidding, and earns the salary which she pays; and her clergymen rush to his defense when he falls into difficulty, or gets criticized in the newspapers. The Church owns Comstock, and he runs the United States Courts.[62]

Heywood's defenders did not trust the courts to properly defend constitutional rights. A particularly potent theme in the Indignation Meeting was the relationship of law to the only recently abolished institution of slavery. The meeting was held on the anniversary of the emancipation of the slaves in the West Indies. Comstock's treatment of Heywood was likened to the legal treatment of fugitive slaves: "As we found in the case of the Fugitive Slave act, it usually happens that a merciless statute is administered in a merciless manner." Thaddeus Wakeman declared that while the Supreme Court might be the "final legal tribunal," it was not the final moral tribunal: the Supreme Court "settled that Dred Scott was a slave; but the people thereupon decided that every other Dred Scott should be free. That the post-offices are decoy traps and under the 'moral' espionage of the officials is the sum of this decision: the people may demand that the post-offices must be free, equal, and safe to all!"[63]

Speakers at the Indignation Meeting reviled the anti-vice society and its officers, particularly Comstock. Comstock's critics accused him of entrapment and of a flawed character that led him to pursue his work. "Anthony Comstock does not, it seems, undertake to detect crime already committed: he goes cunningly at work, in the use of the vilest arts, to induce people to violate the law in order that he may punish them. All his convictions, by his own testimony, are for infractions of the statute which he has caused. It is a work no honorable man would do. He is a professional falsifier; and he seems to lie from pure love of lying." Speakers lambasted the other officers of the NYSSV as well. Samuel Colgate, president of the New York Society for the Suppression of Vice and owner of the company that distributed Vaseline, came in for particular criticism. Colgate had been embarrassed by an advertisement touting the contraceptive properties of Vaseline mixed with salicylic acid. His company withdrew the advertisement, but free lovers used this as an example of the NYSSV's hypocrisy. Rawson, president of the National Defense Association, argued:

> I have no doubt that, if inquiries are made, you will find Mr. Colgate just as ignorant of Comstock's method as he was of what was printed about the virtues of his vaseline. . . . And I am charitable enough to believe that the other gentlemen of the society are ignorant of the fact that their agent is associating with criminals, and, by their aid, bribing people to break the laws, to the end that business can be done under the auspices of their very unique society, which seems to have Ignorance in the presidential chair, Bigoted and Criminal Zeal in its secretary's [Comstock's] pen, and Indifference in its board of management. After all, I do not condemn the legitimate object of the society, which was intended to do a needed work. But, when it turned aside from its proper work to attack a class of citizens who differed from it in opinion, it did violence to the common sense of the people, and forfeited the esteem of all good men.[64]

The assemblage passed resolutions that Comstock should be dismissed from his post in government and that Heywood should be released from prison. Then the crowd demanded to hear Moses Hull, a leading free love advocate and editor of *Hull's Crucible*. Hull called for the deliverance of "honest people out of the hands of the mob called government," and rebuked Comstock:

> When I trace out the life of this man, I honestly conclude that, if there is an endless hell, where the devil reigns because he is the greatest sinner that ever lived,—when Anthony goes to that place, his Satanic Majesty will arise, doff his hat, make his lowest bow, and say: "Mr. Comstock, you have beaten me; please take the chair."[65]

The National Defense Association dispatched Laura Kendrick to Washington to attempt to persuade President Hayes to pardon Heywood. Hayes did so in December of 1878, citing Heywood's failing health and the requests of many citizens for his release. In his diary, however, Hayes noted that "in my judgment the law was not in fact violated—the pamphlet was not obscene matter," and stated,

> Indeed, I think the real objection to Heywood's act is not that he discussed a question in an objectionable manner, but that he was on the wrong side of the question. That he maintains the wrong side of the question as to marriage I entertain as little doubt as those who assail me. But it is no crime by the laws of the United States to advocate the abolition of marriage. . . . Pamphlets or books on the wrong side of that question may be obscene publications, so also may writings on the right side of the question. In this case the writings were objectionable but were not obscene, lascivious, lewd, or corrupting in the criminal sense.[66]

Heywood's clemency was granted before the landmark *Blatchford* decision imprisoned Bennett. Bennett was an elderly man in poor health; his friends and supporters feared that his thirteen-month prison sentence might kill him, and they asked Robert Ingersoll to approach President Hayes and ask for Bennett's pardon. Ingersoll was the country's leading proponent of "free thought," meaning atheism, although Ingersoll claimed that he did not support the opinions of free lovers, merely their right to express them. Given that Hayes had pardoned Heywood for publishing *Cupid's Yokes*, Ingersoll was confident that Bennett would be pardoned for mailing it. Ingersoll met with Hayes several times to argue for the pardon, but Hayes, who had received a great deal of criticism for his pardon of Heywood, buckled under pressure from Comstock and other social purity supporters and refused to pardon Bennett.[67]

## Sexuality, Religion, and the Social Order

Comstock responded to the Liberal League's and National Defense Association's challenges to his work with three arguments. In response to the attacks on his character he flung slanders of his own. Challenges to the constitutionality of the anti-obscenity laws were met with extensive discussions of legal precedents. And in response to free lovers' claims that social problems such as prostitution, abortion, and masturbation resulted from sexual ignorance spawned by religious doctrine, and from the perversion of nature resulting from marriage and restrictive social and sexual roles for women, Comstock claimed that atheist and free love doctrines destroyed the foundations of society.

Comstock attacked his opponents by deriding their characters. While Heywood's defenders argued that Heywood was an educated and principled man who sought to improve society through an honest representa-

tion and critique of its institutions, Comstock painted him quite differently. Heywood's arrest, which took place after Heywood's speech at a
free love convention, was portrayed by Comstock as a daring quest into
a den of lust.

> I went up to the convention, bought a ticket, and as I entered the hall
> heard the speaker railing at "that Comstock." I took a seat without
> being recognized. The address was made up of abuse of myself and dis-
> gusting arguments for their cause. I looked over the audience of about
> 250 men and boys. I could see lust on every face. After a little while the
> wife of the president (the person I was after) took the stand, and deliv-
> ered the foulest address I ever heard. She seemed lost to all shame.[68]

The National Defense Association, founded to defend those "arrested
for dealing in obscene publications [and] articles for immoral use," was,
Comstock claimed, "composed of ex-convicts, free-lovers, and other
creatures that seemingly believe neither in God, religion, or morals." The
persons attempting to repeal his law were "long-haired men and short-
haired women [who defended] obscene publications, abortion imple-
ments, and other incentives to crime." While the National Liberal League
opposed "doctrines that make men better and keep the community pure,"
the leaders of such organizations were persons whose "lives are hollow
and rotten to the core." This rottenness was exemplified, according to
Comstock, in the character of A. L. Rawson, president of the National
Defense Association, who was an "ex-convict, thief, and bigamist."
Rawson's former convict status resulted from Comstock's efforts. Comstock substantiated the charge of bigamy in *Frauds Exposed*, where he
reprinted Francis Abbot's claims that Rawson, a leader of the repeal element that took the leadership of the National Liberal League from Abbot,
had committed bigamy.[69]

Comstock augmented charges about the disreputable characters of his
opponents with discussions of the obscenity law's constitutionality. A
chapter of his *Traps for the Young* was entitled "The Question of the
Unconstitutionality of the Law Answered." His case rested on the Supreme Court's interpretation of article 8 of the Constitution, which
granted Congress the power to establish a post office. Comstock quoted
the Supreme Court's decision in *Ex parte Jackson*.[70]

In response to the entrapment charges, Comstock declared that he
never requested obscene materials from a suspect unless there was cause
to believe that the law was being violated, and he, like every citizen, had
the right to "purchase whatever he sees advertised," as well as the "right
to do what he sees fit" with the purchased article. He differed from someone who purchased obscene articles "from a baser motive, and keeps

[them] to the defilement of his own mind, and in many cases that of others," for Comstock donated them to the government's prosecuting officer "to prove the business of the man who has voluntarily set himself up in a traffic that violates the above statute."[71]

Comstock's claims about the effects of free love doctrines reflect his understandings about the nature of social order and the sources of social stability. Social order rested on the twin pillars of religion and marriage; in the absence of these institutions, unleased human desire would cause social chaos. Likening religion to sheep fencing, Comstock argued,

> To let down a pair of bars in a field is to encourage the flock of sheep to leave their pasture and roam abroad. So, to break down religion, license wrong-doing, blaspheme God's name, and make light of sacred things, is to induce thoughtless ones to give freest scope to those vices which destroy the soul and degrade society.[72]

Atheism, according to Comstock, was cruel: it taunted the mother of a dying child by telling her that there was no Savior; it sneered at the wife of a drunken husband who prayed for help, "There's no God for you to take comfort in, or from whom succor can come." To the widow who looked forward to reunion with her husband in heaven, "Ingersollism" proclaimed no life after death.[73] Religion offered both public order and comfort from private travails.

Comstock asserted that the greatest danger of atheism and free love was that they furthered the corruption of children that had begun with obscene publications. He equated persons who challenged the existing social order with pornographers, arguing, "These Liberal publications and blasphemous rantings are the mortar that fills up the space between the stones of vice and crime, laid up about our youth by master hands— the publishers of criminal reading."[74] Likening free love doctrine to the accumulation of filth in a sewer, Comstock argued that adherence to such ideas turned homes into brothels and humans into animals:

> With them, marriage is bondage; love is lust; celibacy is suicide; while fidelity to marriage vows is a relic of barbarism. All restraints which keep boys and girls, young men and maidens pure and chaste, which prevent our homes from being turned into voluntary brothels, are not to be tolerated by them. Nothing short of turning the whole human family loose to run wild like the beasts of the forest, will satisfy the demands of the leaders and publishers of this literature.[75]

Comstock defined humanity by the control of sexuality, but sexual restraints clearly were fragile. Not only was the boundary between human and animal sexuality tenuous, but sexual indulgence threatened to blur the lines separating male from female, evidenced, according to Comstock, by the physical state of Ottoman Turks. Comstock quoted an article in the *Saturday Review*, which stated:

> One of the direct results of this sensuality is that the Turks have degenerated physically during the past two hundred years. That the conquerors of Constantinople were a hardy race of great physical strength there can be no doubt; that the great majority of modern Turks are of an effeminate type is equally certain; very many of them are persons of fine appearance, but they are physically weak, without elasticity, giving the impression of men who have lost their vitality. The same may be said even more emphatically of Turkish women; they are small in stature, of a sickly complexion, easily fatigued by slight exertion, and become prematurely old. After the age of forty all feminine beauty is gone; the eyes have become sunken, the cheeks hollow, and the face wrinkled; and there remains no trace of the activity and physical strength often seen in English women of sixty-five or even seventy years of age.[76]

While the sexual consequences of widespread adoption of what Comstock styled as free love doctrines were dire, the greatest danger of free love was its effects on individuals, especially children. "Victims" of free love ideology faced "sure ruin and death." Comstock praised mothers for guarding their children against the perils of "Infidelity."[77] In the name of these parents Comstock made his final claims about the constitutionality of the Comstock Laws, asking, "Where is the life, or property interest to debauch the morals of the young to be found in the Constitution?" Comstock concluded that parents' "inalienable right to the pursuit of happiness" included the "right to defend the morals of one's children."

> What greater joy, what more precious happiness, than to be assured that one's children are pure and clean, honest, intelligent, and honorable? To corrupt a child, or lead a youth astray from virtue's path is to destroy all the happiness in the parent's heart.[78]

## A Woman's View of It: Angela Heywood and Reproductive Freedom

Comstock continued to harass Ezra Heywood until Heywood's death in 1893, arresting the editor three more times on obscenity charges. The first arrest, which occurred in October of 1882, involved a direct confrontation on the issue of contraception and spawned a remarkable series of articles written by Ezra's wife, Angela Heywood.

In 1882 Heywood challenged Comstock on two issues—the obscenity of Walt Whitman's poetry and the legality of contraceptive devices. Acting on Comstock's advice, the leaders of the New England Society for the Suppression of Vice (NESSV) stopped publication of a new edition of Whitman's *Leaves of Grass* on the grounds that several of its verses were obscene. These included two entire poems: "A Woman Waits for Me" and "Ode to a Common Prostitute." Heywood reprinted the censored poems in the August 1882 issue of the *Word*; Comstock responded by arresting him on four counts of violating the federal obscenity statute. The charges included mailing the poems, and two counts of mailing a contraceptive device—a douching syringe that Heywood had named "The Comstock Syringe."[79]

Heywood's arrest was the culmination of his increasingly vocal advocacy of women's right to contracept. In June 1878 the *Word* responded to the arrest of Sarah B. Chase, a graduate of Cleveland Medical College, on charges of selling articles designed to cause abortion, by printing an editorial titled "Irresponsible Parentage." In this editorial Heywood (probably in conjunction with his wife, Angela) argued that while they opposed abortion, women must have the right to control their reproduction. In doing so, they became two of the few voices in the nineteenth century acknowledging that women might have good reasons to abort. The Heywoods placed blame for abortion squarely on the shoulders of lascivious men and the system of marriage that bred their licentiousness:

> Asserting the "right" of men to use the persons of women irresponsibly, (which "right" is the animating principle of marriage) legislators in their laws against abortion and "obscenity" are savagely severe on efforts of women to destroy the fruits of this monstrous imposition. Yet whether a man by request gives woman the seed of life, semen, or forces pregnancy, it is unquestionably right, imperative duty and an unavoidable necessity for her to control what thereafter inhabits her person. . . . While we do not believe in abortion and are doing our utmost by liberation and enlightenment to make parentage desirable, instead of an irresponsible disaster, we utterly deny the assumed "right" of men to dictate to women what they shall do with the life-seed they give to or force upon them. Foeticide and abortion are unnatural inhuman actions; but what shall be said of men who freight a woman with offspring, deprave her to think child-murder right or desirable, and then make laws to punish others for the results of their own lascivious indiscretion?[80]

During the months between Ezra Heywood's arrest and his ultimate acquittal on the obscenity charges, Angela Heywood wrote a series of articles entitled "A Woman's View of It." The articles are remarkable not only for their advocacy of women's right to control their reproduction and their sexuality, but for the language in which this case was made. As Jesse Battan has argued, Angela Heywood believed not only in women's right to control their persons, but in their right to language to discuss and appropriate sexuality. Hence Comstock's revulsion at Angela Heywood's address to the free love convention: what Comstock saw as a woman "lost to all shame" was Angela Heywood creating a language for claiming sexuality.[81]

The first article of the series argued that "the will of man to impose vs. the Right of Woman to prevent conception is the issue." Arguing that "Heism" limited women's right to contracept, Angela Heywood claimed that "Sheism" should have a say in the issue as well.

> Shall we submit to the loathsome impertinence which makes Anthony Comstock inspector and supervisor of American women's wombs? This womb-syringe question is to the North what the negro question was to the South: as Mr. Heywood stood beside the slave demanding his liberation, so now he voices the emancipation of woman from sensual thralldom. Clergymen tell us we must "bear the cross," that is the penis; Congressmen vote our persons sluice-ways for irresponsible indulgence, empower Comstock to search bureaus and closets,—lest by means of a syringe, or otherwise, we resent the outrage! As well might woman vote that man shall flow semen only when she says; that he must keep his penis tied up with "continent" twine; that he shall constantly hav [sic], nearby, specified strings to assure "virtue,"—the which, if he is found without, he shall be liable, on conviction by twelve women, to ten years in prison and $5000 fine; that a feminine Comstock shall go about to examine men's penises and drag them to jail if they dare disobey the semen-twine "law."[82]

Angela Heywood continued to excoriate Comstock in her writings about contraception. Two months later she argued that "Sexuality is an ever-present, irresistibly-potent fact," and given its power, must be controlled by an educated sense of moral obligation. Instead, the Republican Party "employs a sensual savage and allows him to ride free over all U.S. mail routes to 'stamp out' Intelligence in sexual well being." Comstock, "the pious fraud," was the same person who "carries rubber penises to ministers, congress[men] . . . legislators, judges, and prates of the degeneracy of American girls and women who seek artificial purity, rather than be infected with the syphilis-dripping Heism 'Society' now offers them!"[83]

In advocating women's sexual empowerment, Angela Heywood argued that "pure ignorance [and] idiotic virtue unable Girls to speak of the beauty, fullness, exhilarating & creative value of the Penis; but they are tongue-tied only at the expense . . . of an over-charged, vibrating Womb (her word for vagina) unduly craving the natural offices of our Savior, the

Penis." But the power to name extended beyond the right to know about sex and to engage in it; Angela Heywood also offered a different view of the possible products of conception.

> So unlearned are we that new-born, innocent babes are called "illegiti-mate;" as if the babes had illegitimated themselves; as if they were not fathered & mothered quite naturally; as if a penis did not giv [sic] and the womb receive & take care of what was given, refusing to hold it foreign or unfit. The seed planting is "illegitimate" & the planter criminal if he skulks, fails to face & provide for the fruit of his action; the mother cannot skulk; intrusted, quickened with new Life, her size, form, habits, needs & maternal instincts speaking truth of the situation, she must carry, deliver & nourish being.

By hiding the secrets of sexuality in "dark places of their church and state, the great & little men, born of our bodies, still hold us underlings."[84]

This case against Ezra Heywood ended differently than the last had: the judge threw out the charges against *Cupid's Yokes* and *Leaves of Grass*, leaving Heywood to defend himself on two counts of mailing a contraceptive syringe. In this instance the judge, T. L. Nelson, allowed Heywood to present a defense of his character, work, and ideas, including a five-hour summation to the jury that discussed issues of free speech and women's right to control their bodies. The judge directed the jury to find Heywood innocent if they had any doubts about Comstock's truthful-ness, as the government's case was almost wholly Comstock's testimony. The jury acquitted Heywood.[85] Shortly thereafter Comstock rearrested Ezra Heywood for mailing a pamphlet reprinting parts of "A Woman's View of It," but the judge dismissed the charge.[86] A fourth arrest in 1887 resulted in charges being dropped by the United States district attorney, but in 1890 Comstock's fifth arrest of Heywood finally resulted in his prey serving a stiff sentence.[87]

In this final case Heywood was convicted for reprinting one of the series of articles, "A Woman's View of It," a letter entitled "A Physician's Testimony," which discussed oral-genital sex, and a letter printed in the *Word* in which an anonymous mother wrote about educating her chil-dren about sexuality. The judge, George M. Carpenter, did not allow Heywood to discuss his work or to present character witnesses; he charged the jury that the offense at issue was "the foulest, meanest, lowest offense of which a human being can be guilty."[88] Heywood, who was sixty-one years old, was sentenced to two years at hard labor. A request for a pardon was denied by President Harrison, and Heywood served all but two months of the sentence. Often sick in prison, he died a year after his release.[89]

## Competing Family Politics in the Gilded Age

Like the free love movement, social purity movements such as the New York Society for the Suppression of Vice responded to changes in the family and gender relations. Both offered analyses of issues that troubled the upper and middle classes, and attempted to gain support for their organizations by arguing that if their organizational goals were supported, problems such as prostitution and abortion would be solved. Free lovers also offered an analysis of the rising divorce rate, arguing that the state should have no say in regulating sexual relations, nor did it have the right to force incompatible people to stay together. But free lovers based their arguments on the premise that women were oppressed and exploited, a condition rooted in women's exclusion from most positions in the economy and in the control men wielded over their bodies, their sexuality, and their reproductive capacity.

By asserting that problems in sexual relations would be solved only if sexuality was freed from the strictures of religion and the state, the free lovers' position competed with, and was diametrically opposed to Comstock's. The NYSSV sought to preserve youthful purity by increasing the power and scope of state laws and wielding them in accord with their vision of a pure society. Comstock used the power of the state invested in him as agent of the post office, as well as the power of law and legal precedent, to harass, arrest, and imprison his most vehement critics. He also used their opposition to benefit his organization. This irony was noted in 1890 by E. B. Foote, Jr., an officer of the National Defense Association, whose father had been among those arrested for distributing contraceptive information.[90] After the final arrest of Ezra Heywood, Foote responded to a supporter who desired to repeal the Comstock Acts by saying:

> You ask if there is any way by which we can secure the repeal of the infamous Comstock law. Some years ago you are doubtless aware that we made a very decided effort for its repeal and it seemed to result more in strengthening Comstock than in giving success to our attempts. He made a great handle of it, and has made a great handle of it ever since. It is about as hard to get an egg back after the hen has laid it, as to repeal a law that has for its ostensible object any moral purpose.[91]

Comstock utilized the power of the state to defend the power of the church. While he viewed the family as the ultimate basis of social order, the church and state were, in his view, essential institutional means for reproducing the family. His arrest of Woodhull for charging Beecher with adultery was an early and exemplary instance of Comstock using the power of the state in accord with his religious beliefs, in this case, to protect a man who was a pillar of nineteenth-century Protestantism. Yet the Beecher case exemplified two problems that motivated anti-vice activity: the problem of individual rights and desires versus the power of the church and state, and the expression of this conflict within the family.

Changes in the family were most dramatically expressed in new roles for and expectations of women. The urbanization of the population, and the rise of a middle class that reproduced itself by imbuing its children with various forms of cultural capital changed children from economic assets to economic liabilities. This decreased the economic value of women's reproductive capacity but made for an increasing emphasis on her role in socializing children and supervising the middle-class consumption patterns of her family.

The family played a vital role in class reproduction: it produced the next generation of class members and endowed children with the cultural capital that would allow them to reproduce their parents' class position. But while upper- and upper-middle-class support of Comstock can be explained by their concern with their children, and the likelihood of their children inheriting (or improving on) their parents' class position, this does not explain why support for a moral crusader such as Comstock would be strong in some historical periods and not others, or in some locales rather than others. I have argued that the timing of anti-vice support can be explained by changes in the family and in women's roles; and that upper-class social competition helps explain why many of its members supported Comstock. But another feature of the historical and social context, I will argue, explains why the anti-vice movement was strong in some cities and weak in others. The next two chapters will consider the role of immigrants, and in particular immigrant political power, in explaining the success of the anti-vice movement.

# 5

## IMMIGRANTS, CITY POLITICS, AND CENSORSHIP

## IN NEW YORK AND BOSTON

I HAVE ARGUED that support for the anti-vice movement stemmed from the willingness of influential members of New York City's upper class to see obscenity as an issue of family reproduction. Comstock posed the problem of obscenity as a problem of protecting children and families from moral corruption, and argued that institutions intended to protect children were not as impenetrable as parents hoped. But knowing that the anti-vice societies were concerned about children does not explain why this concern was strong enough to generate anti-vice movements in the 1870s and 1880s, nor why Boston and New York, but not Philadelphia, had such movements. Furthermore, identifying youth as the target of obscenity does not identify its presumed source. This chapter will focus on the purported causes of youthful corruption in New York City and Boston. I will show that the source of corruption was seen in the growing populations of immigrants, located predominately in the working class, which posed a dual threat to the reproduction of the upper classes. Comstock argued that foreigners threatened to pervert the "high" culture of the upper class, an issue that will be examined in chapter 7. But immigrants also posed a threat to the political power of the upper and middle classes. Anti-vice societies succeeded when reformers linked the problems of reproducing the elite in the next generation to the incursion of immigrants, which involved appeals to nativism as well as to the need to save the city from political corruption. The political power wielded by immigrants, and the charge that abuse of this power inhibited efforts to arrest the vicemongers corrupting respectable youths, became a crucial issue in campaigns against vice. Furthermore, in addressing the increasing political power of immigrants, the moral crusade against obscenity acted to preserve the social niche for which elite children were being prepared.

Although from the beginning of his crusade Comstock connected obscenity with the corruption of youth, it was not clear in his first report to his supporters in the Young Men's Christian Association who the target of his actions against obscenity would be. With the publication of the first *Annual Report* of the New York Society for the Suppression of Vice in 1875, Comstock made it clear that, while universal human weakness made elite children susceptible to the effects of pornography, the source of pollution was slums, not mansions. Foreigners and immigrants were blamed for the tide of obscenity. Comstock noted: "Of the entire number of persons arrested, 46 were Irish, 34 Americans, 24 English, 13 Canadian, 3 French, 1 Spaniard, 1 Italian, 1 Negro, and 1 Polish Jew, showing that a large proportion of those engaged in the nefarious traffic are not native American citizens."[1] The following year Comstock cited similar statistics, commenting: "It will be seen at a glance that we owe much of this demoralization to the importation of criminals from other lands."[2]

Not only were Comstock's targets mostly immigrants, he repeatedly claimed that the people he pursued were dangerous. At stake was the public perception of Comstock's work—Comstock's most famous early targets, Victoria Woodhull and Tennessee Claflin, excited public scandal but little fear. But blaming obscenity on immigrants raised the specter of fearsome mobs; the Irish, in particular, were associated with public violence. Arrests made in the 1863 New York City Draft Riots had been overwhelmingly of Irishmen, and in both 1870 and 1871 the Irish had staged pitched street battles with Ulster Protestants during parades celebrating the victory of William of Orange in the Battle of Boyne.[3] In an 1883 article in the *North American Review* entitled "The Abuse of Citizenship," Edward Self invoked the violence of the Irish in making the case that persons of Irish descent might be unfit for American citizenship, asserting, "The murders and other atrocities committed by the Fenians in Ireland, and the Irish Molly Maguires in Pennsylvania, stamp them with a strong family likeness."[4] The NYSSV *Annual Reports* praised Comstock's "fearless courage" in pursuit of his dangerous immigrant foes. The NYSSV reported that in October of 1874 "a desperate attempt was made upon [Comstock's] life" when he tried to arrest Charles Conroy for mailing obscenity from sixteen post offices using nineteen different aliases. Conway stabbed Comstock twice, the second stab "laying open his face, severing four arteries, and inflicting a terrible wound."[5] Comstock recovered but became a martyr: "His blood thus shed in the cause of purity cries out in a thousand hearts for justice upon the wretches who are sending blasting mildew and death into the schools and homes of our land."[6]

After 1876, Comstock stopped reporting the nationalities of his captives, in part because he was increasingly arresting people born in the United States. Between 1872 and 1876, 30 percent of those he arrested were born in the United States; this figure rose to 49.5 percent between

1877 and 1881.[7] Still, Comstock played on fears of the city, and of the people who lived there, asking in 1878: "How many fair girls are transferred from beautiful country homes to dens of infamy and shame in our great cities, through the influence of this accursed traffic?"[8] This passage invokes the possibility of sexual corruption, and ultimate prostitution, of "fair" native-born girls by the city's foul influence.

Comstock played on a potent source of discord in American social relations when he invoked immigrants as the source of a tide of obscenity threatening upper- and middle-class children. While immigration caused little comment early in the nineteenth century, and immigrants were seen as a source of wealth, by midcentury the concentration of immigrants in cities and the association of immigrants with poverty and crime created the perception that the city's immigrants were "collectivities of strangers inhabiting social netherworlds."[9] The extreme poverty of tenement dwellers in the heart of Boston, Chicago, Philadelphia, and especially New York was not blamed on low wages and periodic economic recession but on the presumed "shiftlessness" and "intemperance" of slum dwellers.[10] In an 1872 exposé of New York City crime entitled *The Nether Side of New York*, the journalist Edward Crapsey attributed lawlessness in New York City to immigrant communities. Noting that over four million immigrants had arrived in New York's port between 1847 and 1868, he commented:

> Of these millions nothing, with few exceptions, but the dregs settled in the metropolis where they landed. All the rest, representing nearly all that was valuable in this avalanche of humanity, was poured into the untilled lands of the West, where a mighty empire sprang from their loins. . . . The thrifty emigrants who came to us forehanded and determined to wring competence from the new republic, merely made New York their stepping stone to fortune; the emigrants who exhausted their stores in securing their passage, and landed penniless perforce, staid [sic] with us to add to the dissonance of this mixture of peoples. In time many of these became self-sustaining, and they or their children pushed forward into the ranks of our most substantial citizens, but a large proportion, as was inevitable, became public burdens, and permanent additions to the vice, crime, or pauperism of the metropolis.[11]

Writers such as Crapsey linked problems associated with the growth of a major city to the immigrants who provided New York with the majority of its labor force. By blaming the spread of obscenity on immigrants, Comstock utilized already existing ideologies about the city and its inhabitants to construct obscenity as a threat.

## City Politics and Immigrant Corruption

Largely as a result of Comstock's efforts, the stream of obscenity appeared to be running dry by the end of the 1870s. Comstock's campaign against gambling began in 1879. His biographers claim he attacked gambling because of the increasing paucity of pornography.[12] By 1878 Comstock had seized 202,214 obscene pictures and photographs, 21,150 pounds of books, and 63,819 "articles for immoral purposes, rubber, etc" (meaning contraceptives, abortifacient instruments, and articles to enhance sexual pleasure). During 1878 he seized only 2,100 pounds of books, 465 obscene pictures, and 175 rubber articles.[13] Taking on gambling changed the nature of the immigrant threat battled by the NYSSV. Blaming social corruption on immigrants was no longer a matter of conjuring fears of dirty (and foreign-born) miscreants corrupting children. Instead, the decay of the city's political institutions because of corrupt hordes of immigrants became a theme in anti-vice rhetoric.

Whether or not Comstock turned to the issue of gambling for want of obscenity, he phrased the campaign against gambling in terms similar to those used to justify the crusade against pornography. Gambling, like obscenity, caused the corruption of youth. Comstock claimed he encountered the problems of gambling after one of the "gentlemen of this Society" discovered that an employee was stealing from him, and the thief confessed that the money was used to buy lottery tickets. At about the same time, he asserted, a woman starving to death because her husband spent all his money on lottery tickets appealed to Comstock for help, but the gambler "was so infatuated that even his wife's suffering could not check him in his mad career."[14]

Campaigning against avarice rather than lust left Comstock with the problem of justifying gamblers as an appropriate target for the NYSSV. Comstock depicted gambling as an economic threat to businesses, as well as a threat to upper- and middle-class children. Gambling, Comstock argued, threatened the purses of the propertied by creating a class of criminals whose costly imprisonment increased taxes. Thus Comstock linked gambling not only to corrupt police but to the tax rate, making an explicit plea to the pocketbooks of potential supporters:

> Members of this Society and gentlemen of New York, as a matter of business, will you not spend a little time and money to enforce the laws that shall check crimes, and reduce taxes; will you go on indifferent, while each year you are taxed more and more, to provide enlarged prison populations for the advancing army of young criminals?[15]

The "army of young criminals" gambling generated was composed of the sons of respectable families, both middle and upper class. Instead of arguing that gambling led to increased thefts from business in the form of burglary and robbery, Comstock suggested that young embezzlers posed the real threat to business. Gambling made paupers of the poor but criminals of the rich. Gambling, like obscenity, originated in the lower classes, but threatened children from good families. Comstock told many stories of gambling-addicted, defrauding clerks who threatened their employers with financial ruin and their families with social ruin. One early discussion of gambling reported:

> In November last, a man who held the trusted and responsible position of cashier in one of our city banks, was discovered a defaulter to about $35,000. He made a written confession, admitting that he had spent from $400 to $500 per day in a certain policy shop on Broadway, spending thousands and receiving back but a few hundred.[16]

Comstock argued in many cases the "victims of these nefarious schemes" were "the young man from the counting-room, the store, the bank, and the office, and in some instances the school and college."[17] Gambling, like obscenity and criminal papers, victimized women and children as well as men because men addicted to gambling would destroy their families to pursue their vice. Again, mothers were powerless to save their sons.

> A poor mother called a short time ago to have us save her boy. He was a young man, married, with one child—a babe—-scarcely two years of age, who, although he held a high position of trust in a prominent business house, on a good salary, failed to provide for his family. When questioned, he frankly confessed to patronizing lotteries.[18]

Comstock made the same claim about gambling and masturbation: both unleashed uncontrollable desire. Other writers equated gambling with lust; in 1882 O. B. Frothingham argued that the problem with gambling was the uncontrolled passion it aroused, which reduced men to the level of beasts. To add excitement to their lives, Frothingham declared, some men gambled, others patronized wine shops or prostitutes, and still others listened to "lascivious music."[19] Furthermore, while a gambler overtaken by animal passions lost his sense of the importance of money, particularly his sense of "the divine import of money as a sign of man's supremacy over the lower spheres of nature," gamblers simultaneously believed they could put themselves on the same level as the best men by "wearing the finest clothes, the shiniest hats, the most immaculate boots and gloves."[20] The gambler's crime was his caricature of persons to whom he should defer. In this way gambling posed a problem of class reproduction similar to that represented by immigrant leaders in public office: wealthy gamblers, like political bosses, supplanted the upper class.

Although Comstock equated gambling with masturbation, masturbation threatened self-destruction, while gambling destroyed whole families. Like obscenity, gambling rendered upper-class children unfit to take their parents' place as the leaders of business and society. The ultimate disgrace occurred when young men from good families became criminals, toppling their families from positions at the top of the class system into the morass of criminals at the bottom.

> Many sad cases have come to us of families ruined; wives and children beggared; young men made thieves; and persons in responsible and trusted positions suddenly discovered to be defaulters, thus hurling their families from a high position in social life to a disgraceful obscurity. We speak of lottery, policy and gambling schemes operating through the mails and in other modes.[21]

Children squandered inherited wealth in gambling schemes; Comstock told of a young man who lost six hundred dollars from a trust fund in a gambling hall and, returning to his hotel, committed suicide.[22]

Gamblers were associated in the public mind with three potent sources of sin—alcohol, the Irish, and corrupt city politicians. From the beginning of the campaign against gambling Comstock argued that gamblers were protected by corrupt city officials.[23] In 1881 he asserted: "From facts coming to the knowledge of the Committee within the last few months, it is hard to escape the conviction that these gambling hells are in some way under the protection of those whose duty it is to arrest and punish the guilty operators."[24] The campaign against gambling and the accusation that corrupt politicians protected gamblers' haunts raised the specter of Irish politicians. It was commonly believed that a Democratic political machine, directed by Tammany Hall, controlled New York City politics. In 1871 New Yorkers witnessed the scandalous fall of the "Tweed Ring," which collapsed when the mayor, "Boss" William Tweed, was accused of stealing millions of dollars from the city treasury. Tweed attempted to flee to Europe, but was apprehended to face trial and die in a New York prison.[25] Popular belief held that the Tammany Machine still thrived. Crapsey noted in 1872 that New York's "political rascals" were native born (Tweed was born in the United States), but he claimed the politically corrupt "achieved their bad pre-eminence by the fact that more than half the population of the city which they mastered were the easy prey of unscrupulous demagogues because they were not rooted in the soil by birth or by competency acquired on it."[26] Six years later Francis Parkman argued that universal suffrage had failed because the indifference of Irish and Irish American men to the public good made their votes "a public pest"; in particular, Parkman charged, the Irish allowed themselves to be used or bought by demagogues and priests. "His inalienable right [to vote] may perhaps be of value to him for the bribe he gets out of it; but it makes him a nuisance and a danger to the state."[27] This vehemence resulted from the growing political power gained by the Irish during the 1870s. The city's Democratic Party was increasingly seen as the party of "rum and Romanism."[28] In 1882 journalist James D. McCabe, Jr., author of *New York by Sunlight and Gaslight*, explained the workings of New York City politics:

> The professional politician is generally an Irishman, or of Irish descent. The immense Irish population of New York, which constitutes at least one-fifth of the total number of the inhabitants of the city, comprises the ruling element in metropolitan politics. It is also the most ignorant, as well as the most reckless class in the great city. It is blindly devoted to its leaders, and obeys their orders implicitly, and without care of consequences. . . . Its leaders are men who have risen from the grogshop, by the exercise of bribery and sheer knavery. Its headquarters are the numerous bar-rooms with which the city abounds; and votes are bought and sold; incompetent men are put in nomination and elected, and the whole system of free government in municipal affairs is thus placed at the mercy of a few leaders, who are in their turn subject to a central authority, who is commonly known as "the Boss."[29]

This image of city politics was widely shared by members of New York's (and Boston's) upper class, but it obscures the struggle for political influence taking place within these cities. The nineteenth-century image of the "machine" rests on two premises: that city aldermen were powerful and that the mayor's office controlled and coordinated politics at the ward level so that vast sums could be spent on political patronage, creating an unofficial welfare system that bought votes to sustain the machine. The much-maligned political boss headed the machine and ran city government for the enrichment of himself and his minions.

> The political boss is conqueror, entitled, by right of conquest, to absolute dominion over the political estate, which he may sublet to his partisan helots and henchmen, upon such terms and conditions of service as he may choose to impose. No matter how base the services required, this feudal system in our politics breeds multitudes of camp-followers and political tramps, who are willing to take the oath of fealty to any political boss for an office, or a contract, or for a promise of one forthcoming.[30]

Integral to ideological constructions of the machine and the political boss was the belief that the machine employed innumerable immigrants in superfluous jobs that, in combination with widespread graft on the part of city officials, drove up taxes, a burden that fell disproportionately on the city's property holders. Concern about municipal finances focused not only on taxes but on municipal debt. Arthur Blake Ellis noted that while the national debt, as well as the debts of states and counties, decreased in the 1870s, the debt of cities more than doubled. The debt of New York City, he argued, was one-nineteenth of the national debt, and greater than the debt of all New England's cities combined. Blame for the debt was laid on those who voted based on "political partisanship," with the consequence that voters "devote themselves to money-getting, and lose all sense of civic pride, while the hungry professionals in politics are making their municipal budgets and confiscating their property."[31] This vision of city politics, and the image of the machine, promulgated by upper classes trying to "reform" city politics, is imbedded in histories of the era.[32]

Stories of political corruption were an upper-class response to the increasing presence of immigrants in city government, particularly in the city councils. While Tweed may have been a thief, the image of a machine resting on the power of aldermen vastly overstates their authority. Aldermen controlled their wards, but their power was manifested in minor deeds, such as allowing constituents to hang signs or erect stands and water troughs, and in minor public works such as paving a few blocks of street.[33] Aldermen were transients; city councils were characterized by rapid turnover of their membership.[34] Aldermen generally could not determine city policy—or city payrolls. As city councils became increasingly dominated by immigrants, they were increasingly stripped of their power. For example, in 1884 the state legislature gave the mayor of New York City absolute power of appointment, with no aldermanic veto, following Theodore Roosevelt's investigation of city government corruption and introduction of a reform bill. Roosevelt complained that the aldermen were a group of liquor dealers "who from their vices should be the lowest in the social scale" but "are allowed to rule over us."[35] E. L. Godkin, editor of the *Nation*, supported passage of the Roosevelt bill using a similar argument:

> We have learnt all that the lowest tribe of demagogues ever seen in a civilized community can accomplish through a large body of immigrant voters. We have actually seen the creation among us, as Judge Davis forcibly pointed out, of an aristocracy or oligarchy of liquor-dealers— that is, of members of one of the most odious and disreputable of modern callings. . . . The present condition of New York exhibits the working of this system under peculiarly favorable conditions. The success of the Roosevelt bill would go far to overturn it. It would not bring in the Millennium, or drive the liquor-dealers out of politics, but it would strip them of their power over municipal administration, and reduce them to insignificance.[36]

Boston enacted legislation similar to the Roosevelt Bill in 1885, when a new charter gave the mayor the power to nominate executive officials and, by imposing a ceiling on the city tax rate, denied councils the power to raise revenue.[37] The effect of stripping power from the city councils was to concentrate it in the hands of the mayor, a man almost always "respectable," meaning rich and native born.[38] In advocating the Roosevelt Bill, Godkin argued that, because liquor dealers, the forces of "ignorance, vice, and corruption," would always lose elections to men representing "intelligence, virtue, and order," the bill would grant governing power to "a man identified with some one of the reputable interests of the municipality, and more or less eminent in talents and character."[39] Throughout the rest of the century "respectable" men did tend to win the mayoralty: although both New York and Boston elected their first Irish mayors in the 1880s, Boston elected only one Irish mayor in the late-nineteenth century and New York City elected two.[40] While New York City's mayors were almost always Democrats, control of the mayoral office in Boston shifted between the Republican and Democratic parties.[41] Finally, the image of a machine obscures the struggles that took place between ward leaders and within parties themselves. The Tammany Machine that supposedly dominated city politics in New York competed with the Irving Hall organization and the County Democracy. Throughout the 1870s and 1880s Tammany Hall lacked secure control of the Democratic Party.[42]

Concern about political machines reflected not only upper-class concern about their economic interests, but spoke as well to fears that they were no longer honored as the rightful leaders of their society. For example, in 1878 Godkin editorialized in favor of an amendment to the New York State Constitution that would allow only taxpayers to elect members of city boards of finance. This, he noted, would be in violation of the principle of universal suffrage, but it would "put the city treasury in the keeping of a board of citizens of character and repute." In contrast, he argued, if the New York City Board of Finance was elected "without the restricted suffrage . . . it would become, in short, from the very first a ring of jobbers drawn from both parties . . . probably most of them men without property, and animated by that contempt for property-holders which seems to be the latest fashion among American demagogues."[43] The relationship between control of city government and respect for propertied men was articulated more forcibly by Francis Parkman, who in 1878 argued that "hordes of native and foreign barbarians, all armed with the ballot" have taken over the state.[44] In the increasingly populous cities "the weakest and most worthless was a match, by his vote, for the wisest and best," but worst of all, "every day more and more the masses hug the flattering illusion that one man is as essentially about as good as another."[45] The success of "indiscriminate suffrage," Parkman argued, depended on "whether the better part of the community is able to outweigh the worse." This condition was no longer met in the cities.

> A New England village of the olden time—that is to say, of some forty years ago—would have been safely and well governed by the votes of every man in it; but, now that the village [has] grown into a populous city, with its factories and workshops, its acres of tenement-houses, and thousands and ten thousands of restless workmen, foreigners for the most part, to whom liberty means license and politics means plunder, to whom the public good is nothing and their own most trivial interests everything, who love the country for what they can get out of it and whose ears are open to the promptings of every rascally agitator, the case is completely changed, and universal suffrage becomes a questionable blessing.[46]

The masses' lack of respect for their social superiors was most grievously expressed in their unwillingness to vote for them.

> The masses have grown impatient of personal eminence, and look for leaders as nearly may be like themselves. Young men of the best promise have almost ceased to regard politics as a career. . . . In fact, the people do not want them there. The qualities of the most highly gifted and highly cultivated are discarded for cheaper qualities, which are easier of popular comprehension and which do not excite jealousy.[47]

Reformers such as Parkman played on upper-class fears that city government no longer represented their interests. Mobs led by demagogues would destroy the interests of the propertied either through the legal machinations of government or, perhaps, by rioting in the streets. Concern about alien interests leading city government reflected concerns about the city being a dangerous place for respectable people.

## Political Machines and Vice Reform

While New York City's government may have been less corrupt than reform groups suggested, Comstock used the widely held beliefs that city politicians were grafters and city cops crooks to link children's morality to corrupt government. Between 1880 and 1885 discussions of gambling dominated the *Annual Reports* of the NYSSV. Having made the accusation in 1881 that gambling was protected by the police, Comstock claimed some victories against gamblers in 1882. He asserted that his investigations of gambling began in 1877, but that little progress was made until 1880, when Alonzo Cornell, New York's governor, called for the enforcement of antigambling statutes. Comstock claimed numerous victories against gamblers: in 1880 there had been 9 lotteries and 600 policy shops operating in New York, but following the governor's proclamation, the NYSSV was able to arrest 122 gamblers and close 50 policy shops and all 9 lotteries. The enactment of a new Code of Criminal Procedure, Comstock claimed, made it impossible for the police to interfere with arrest warrants obtained by the NYSSV.[48]

Either Comstock's victories against gamblers were short-lived or the issue was too popular to drop. In spite of his claims of victories against gambling, Comstock dwelt upon the issues of gambling and political corruption in *Traps for the Young*, published in 1883. Arguing that "the modern politician virtually bargains away the people's rights," Comstock offered the following fictitious dialogue between a politician and a saloon owner. Comstock utilizes almost every stereotype about political corruption in this interchange. It begins with the politician saying:

> You manufacture voters for me and my party, and I will secure the passage of an act that shall violate public policy and outrage every sentiment of humanity, make it legal for you to transform your fellow-men into brutes and criminals at a handsome profit to yourself; provided always you respond when called upon for political purposes, and that you support my nomination.
>
> *Rumseller.* That is capital! We are bound to make criminals, but there's money in it, if only you legalize it.
>
> *Politician.* Of course, criminals must be provided for. Courts, police officers, jails, State Prisons, and reformatories must be supported by the public; but these are minor considerations if only you make money and I have a fat office.[49]

Comstock raised three issues in this discussion between the saloon owner and the politician. First, this dialogue plays on the belief that the saloon was the basis of city politics. This was not an unfounded fear—in 1882 the *New York Times* reported that half of the city's twenty-four aldermen were either currently or formerly "keepers of gin mills."[50] The prevalence of bar owners on the city council, Comstock implied, protected the liquor trade and its abuses. On the heels of connecting the city council to the city's saloons, Comstock raised the issue of taxation. Taxes supported jails for criminals (and offices for corrupt politicians).

The dialogue between politician and rumseller continues with the rumseller complaining that patrons with "sensitive and high-strung nervous temperaments" sometimes became raucous after only a couple of drinks, which engendered police raids on his establishment. The remedy suggested by the politician was to pay the police to not prosecute or to thump the troublemakers on the head. The rumseller replied that he did this often, but sometimes when patrons were maimed or killed, the police were forced to act against him. Comstock implies that boys, and presumably elite boys, were more "sensitive" patrons, and could be victimized freely and, unless they were grievously injured, with impunity. Not only did the saloon manufacture votes and increase criminality among the working class, it threatened the destruction of "respectable" boys who might venture there. Not content to stop his accusations with the police, Comstock indicted the judicial system as well. Comstock incriminated the district attorney and the courts, both widely believed to be under the influence of political machines, in the following:[51]

> *Politician.* In such case send for me, and I will go your bail, and then will see the District Attorney, and tell him not to prosecute you, as you control the primaries in your ward, and you and your neighbors in the same business carry your district at all elections. But remember, you have to pay out liberally for all this.

In the event of prosecution by an honest district attorney, a prospect raised by the rumseller, the politician suggested that both the judge and the jury could be bought. And when respectable citizens rose against political corruption, the politician argued that their efforts could be defeated by hiring a "gang of repeaters," who, in combination with votes bought with liquor, ensured the victories of corrupt candidates.[52]

In this diatribe against liquor and politics, Comstock exploited existing public sentiments about city councilmen to engender support for his work. Comstock did not arrest liquor dealers, but used the same rhetoric of corrupt politicians protecting saloon owners, who preyed on respectable boys, to explain his campaign against gambling. In spite of his pessimistic assessment of the ability of good citizens to control the governmental apparatus of their cities, Comstock often claimed victories against gamblers. His most important work in 1883, he asserted, was the routing of pool gamblers from Long Island City. This tale of good overcoming the forces of evil in government featured Comstock as its hero. In Long Island City, officials colluded with gamblers, the coroner owned a saloon, and the mayor embezzled seventy-five thousand from the city treasury. Concerned local citizens banded together in a Law and Order Association, but were helpless to intervene—until they applied for help from the New York Society for the Suppression of Vice. Comstock obtained arrest warrants for twenty-one gamblers and search warrants for four gambling dens, and claimed to have closed down gambling in Long Island City.[53]

Gambling still thrived in spite of Comstock's heroic victories. In 1884 Comstock complained about lenient sentences imposed by judges, and asked petulantly, "Bowing with deference to the Judge on the bench, we cannot refrain from asking why this leniency to the convict whose business breeds criminals?"[54] However, in 1884 the agents of the NYSSV were called before the Roosevelt Investigating Committee, where they testified about the workings of the New York City Police Department. They enumerated their experiences with police protecting gambling dens, of officers telling gamblers of impending raids, and police officers found in gambling establishments.[55] With the passage of Roosevelt's bill Comstock's complaints temporarily abated; the following year he claimed the New York City police cooperated wholeheartedly with the anti-vice society's efforts, and that the law had triumphed over the gambling fraternity and corrupt politicians.[56]

Comstock insinuated that gambling, like obscenity, was a problem ultimately to be blamed on immigrants—in this case, on immigrant-supported political machines. By attacking gambling, he translated concern about criminal foreigners, who sought to pervert children by spreading pornography, into fear that the police force and the courts, institutions designed to protect respectable people from crime, were defiled. Referring to gambling dens, Comstock says:

> The laws against the crimes we fight must be enforced, if you would save our youth from crime, our homes from sorrow and shame, the community from the dangers and burdens that a vast of army of criminals necessarily bring. If you would preserve our sacred institutions in the future, you must save the youth of to-day. From their ranks come the men of to-morrow.
>
> For any political leader or official to make a league with these crimes for personal gain, is *infamous*. But to make such a league for party preference, thereby jeopardizing the interests of society, defying the laws and trampling underfoot the Constitution of the State, is practically *high treason*, and should be punished accordingly.[57]

Comstock's attack on city government may have resulted from his careful framing of issues to best gain the support from the city's upper classes. But fear and distrust of immigrants, and outrage over their control of city government, did not originate with Comstock. Without an exploding immigrant population, and without nativists and civic reformers interpreting the growth of these populations as a threat to the native born, Comstock could not have framed the anti-vice crusade as a response to social corruption caused by immigrants.[58] Comstock responded to immigrants with a crusade whose stated motivatation was the protection of children, but in so doing he acted to protect the political power of the elite. The reproduction of families also reproduced the power of the dominant class. The argument that anti-vice mobilization depended on portraying the campaign against vice as a response to the immigrant threat is strengthened when one examines the successful anti-vice campaign in Boston and the failure of Comstock and other reformers, especially Josiah Leeds, to establish an anti-vice campaign in Philadelphia.

## City Politics and the Campaign against Vice in Boston

The fate of the anti-vice society in Boston also hinged on the issues of gambling and city corruption. While attacking gambling helped Comstock sustain the New York society, the issue of gambling gave Boston's anti-vice crusaders its primary mission and public support. The case of Boston illustrates most clearly the ties between the growth of immigrant populations, the decline of upper-class political power, and the success of moral reform.

In 1875, Comstock met in Boston with the Monday Morning Ministers Meeting. The group funded Comstock's travels to Boston to arrest pornographers, and in 1878 founded the New England Society for the Suppression of Vice (NESSV), an organization better known as the Watch and Ward Society, the name they adopted in 1891. The New England anti-vice society, like New York's, was an elite organization. Its officers included the presidents of exclusive colleges and universities such as Yale, Brown, Amherst, and Dartmouth. Other vice presidents included Edward Everett Hale, pastor of Boston's most elite Unitarian Church, and Bishop Phillips Brooks, pastor of Boston's most elite Episcopal congregation, the Trinity Church.[59] Following in the shadow of Anthony Comstock, who began arresting Boston's obscenity dealers during the early years of his campaign, the leaders of the New England anti-vice society found themselves with little to do. The NESSV's second *Annual Report* stated:

> Owing to the repressive influence of our Societies and Mr. Comstock's active surveillance of all advertisements, the grosser form of obscene publications are pretty nearly suppressed. The fact that comparatively few such offenders are now seized and convicted, proves, not that Mr. Comstock's influence is superfluous, but precisely the contrary. While he lives it is known to be unsafe to offer such works for sale.[60]

In the second year of their organizational existence the leaders of the NESSV found themselves doubting the necessity of their efforts. In spite of the paucity of obscene publications, they found some objectionable books and papers to remove from newsstands.[61] The NESSV also began the work for which it became famous, claiming that "we have in several cases secured of booksellers the withdrawal from sale of objectionable books, upon calling attention to their immoral character."[62] In 1879 all the books discussed at the Executive Committee meetings were dime novels. While the Executive Committee discussed the possibility of attempting to get a city ordinance "for the suppression of impure literature," the only action taken in 1879 was petitioning the public library to produce a list of books suitable for young readers.[63]

The Executive Committee found an outlet for their work in railway stations, succeeding in removing some papers from newsstands and in having "indecent inscriptions" removed from station privies. The Committee on Prevention of Improper Inscriptions in Railway Stations was so successful that not only were the walls cleaned, they were subsequently sanded to make the painting of graffiti more difficult.[64] The fledgling society seemed greatly demoralized in 1880, when so little was accomplished that the executive committee did not issue an annual report. Early in 1881 the society employed the Reverend Canfield to "make a survey of our City to discover what need there may be for the further actions of our Society."[65] Canfield found enough vice to warrant the continuation of his employment, but he was replaced in 1882 by Henry Chase, who became the permanent agent of the NESSV. Upon employing Chase the NESSV refused a request from the New York Society that it send more money to fund Comstock's work.[66]

In spite of this declaration of independence from Comstock, the NESSV remained an organization looking for an issue. Book censorship, the issue that ultimately made the organization notorious, was pursued with some vigor; in 1881 the society campaigned against the impure literature available in the public library, and reported in March of 1882 that "the District Attorney has at our insistence notified a number of booksellers that a certain immoral book, which had hitherto been freely exposed for sale, comes within prohibition of the law, and that any further sale will render the dealer liable to prosecution."[67] The book at issue was a new edition of Whitman's *Leaves of Grass*, which the Executive Committee had chosen to prosecute after considering several books, including Balzac's *Droll Stories* and Boccaccio's *Decameron*, as possible targets.[68] The suppression of Whitman, and its implications for understanding the role of high culture in reproducing the upper class, will be discussed in chapter 7.

Forcing Osgood to halt the publication of *Leaves of Grass* and restricting its distribution was a triumph for the NESSV, but not one the society publicly acknowledged. While the organization made its disapproval of *Leaves of Grass* clear, the NESSV did not take credit for the censorship of Whitman for many years.[69] Afraid to take credit for censoring high culture, and with street pornography too scarce to justify their existence, the organization faced a crisis of mission. The problems facing the NESSV are illustrated by an article published in 1882 by the society's president, Homer Sprague. Sprague's article, "Societies for the Suppression of Vice," appeared in *Education* magazine. The article is remarkable for the extent to which it relies both on Comstock's rhetoric and his accomplishments, offering little in the way of what the New England anti-vice society had accomplished and almost nothing to indicate where the NESSV might be heading. Sounding like a pale imitation of Comstock, Sprague fulminated:

> There is a hydra-headed evil, malignant, unresting, yet, for the most part, invisible; allying itself with kindred destructive agencies; subsidizing the strongest appetites and passions; making the youth of the land its especial victims, sparing neither high nor low, dragging them by thousands to mental, moral, and even physical disease and death; existing from time immemorial, but increasing year by year till it has reached gigantic proportions; a frightful pestilence walking in darkness, a horrible destruction wasting at noonday![70]

Perhaps what is most interesting about Sprague's article is that the *Annual Reports* of the NESSV did not contain such Comstockian diatribes. The invocation of Comstock did not end with imitating his rhetoric, for much of Sprague's article recited in admiring terms the story of Comstock's youth and his rise to the position of leader of the NYSSV. While Sprague's article was certainly intended to bolster support for the New England anti-vice society, what it shows most clearly is that the society was faltering under his leadership.

The turning point for the NESSV came in January of 1883, when the society attempted to close the Royal Gambling Club on Tremont Street.[71] The directors of the NESSV assumed the police would cooperate in their campaign against gambling. In February of 1883, they met with the police commissioners to discuss the best way of proceeding against gambling houses.[72] In March, when the NESSV reported on their activities in the past year, the society praised the police for cooperating with their efforts against gamblers and congratulated themselves on closing a gambling house.

> In response to our solicitation, the Police Commissioners ordered all the gambling saloons of the city to be closed. After a while, as the proprietors began to resume operations, evidence was quietly obtained, and successful raids made on a number of these places. We are grateful to assure our citizens of the co-operation of the Police Commissioners, and their pledge of active and unremitting hostility to these establishments.[73]

By the end of the year, however, the NESSV had encountered considerable difficulty in getting the police to cooperate in their campaign against gambling, and were disgusted with the police and the police commission. In December they submitted an affidavit to the court asserting that the Executive Committee:

> Understand[s] that the Constables are appointed by the Court and hold office during good behavior. They desire to ask if the offenses herein specified do not tend to bring the administration of justice and the execution of our laws into contempt. It is well known that there are peculiar difficulties in bringing some classes of law breakers to merited punishment. The Executive Officers of the Court should be required to assist instead of resisting or thwarting those who endeavor to secure the enforcement of law.[74]

The directors of the anti-vice society continued their public crusade against the police administration in 1884. In February they visited the district attorney "for the purpose of bracing him up," and in their March *Annual Report* called for "radical and thorough" reforms in the police administration.[75] The NESSV discussed at length police obstruction of their attempts to raid gambling houses. The *Annual Report* also recounted the following from their meeting with the police commissioners.

> On that occasion the Chief Commissioner said that raiding the gambling houses would only result in driving out the "honest gamblers," and bringing in those who would play a "skin game." His opinion was that the result of a more vigorous enforcement of the law against gamblers would be a reaction; that gambling would continue, and the most that could be done was to regulate it; indeed, it was no worse than many other employments,—buying stocks on margins, for example; and that many of the gamblers were good and honest men. There was, in short, no word of condemnation for the proprietors of common gambling houses, while much was said in regard to the wrongdoing of other people; and, although he assured us our warrants should be faithfully served, the agent could not refrain from asking him how we could expect the officers to execute the law according to our ideas, while such was the sentiment of the Commissioners.

Warrants were obtained, but the NESSV learned that all the gambling houses in the city had been closed, with the explanation that "a little bird flew over the city two hours before."[76]

The directors' frustrations mounted. Agent Henry Chase's report of his summer activities highlighted "the difficulties experienced, the lukewarmness of officials and authorities, the bribery and perjury of witnesses, and the expense and peril of the work accomplished." The NESSV decided to join with the Law and Order League in an attempt to give the governor control over Boston's police force.[77] Under this plan, police commissioners would be appointed by officials of the state government who were mostly native-born Republicans, rather than by city government officials who were mainly Irish Democrats. Robert Treat Paine, a member of the NESSV Executive Committee (who bore the name of a ancestor who signed the Declaration of Independence), testified at a hearing of the state legislature in support of this legislation.[78] The legislation passed, and remained a source of tension between Boston's native born and Irish for decades.[79]

In Boston, as in New York, municipal reform efforts pitted the native-born elite against an increasingly Irish City Council. And as in New York, the success of the Democratic Party was blamed on corrupt and ignorant Irish immigrants. The *Boston Evening Transcript*, the Brahmin daily, editorialized:

> If politics are necessary to the existence of Irishmen, they can get plenty of the needful in this country, in some parts of which they vote so soon as they touch the soil. Our Celtic friends are good at voting, they vote early and sometimes often, and as a general thing can be relied upon for the whole Democratic ticket.[80]

The timing of anti-vice society agitation for municipal reform was particularly telling in Boston, where Hugh O'Brien, Boston's first Irish mayor, was elected in 1884. O'Brien had proceeded to horrify Boston's native Protestants by announcing that Boston had become "the most Catholic city in the country," and by closing the public library, the board of which was one of few elite bastions in city government, on St. Patrick's Day.[81] The NESSV's efforts at municipal reform may explain why the organization shared a significant number of members with the civic reform association, the Citizen's Association of Boston. Twenty-six percent of the members of the anti-vice society also contributed to the Citizen's Association in 1889, the first year that the latter organization published its list of supporters. Tackling the issue of gambling gave the anti-vice campaign direction and funding. Contributions, which had languished at $617 for the year ending in March 1882, rose to $1,777 for the year ending March 1884.[82] In both Boston and New York, the anti-vice campaigns led to governmental reforms pitting the power of state governments, dominated by the native born, against immigrant-dominated city governments. And in both cities, the presence of large and increasingly powerful immigrant populations was crucial to the success of anti-vice campaigns.

## Prostitution, Skating Rinks, and City Government

In March of 1886 the leaders of the NESSV announced their satisfaction with the new metropolitan police: "Judging from the manner in which the laws are now enforced against those crimes in whose suppression we are interested, we believe the appointment of the present Police Commission to be one of the greatest blessings ever conferred upon the city."[83] But however great their satisfaction with control of the police being wrested from Mayor O'Brien, the leaders of the NESSV were again faced with the problem of what to do with their organization. Now, however, the Executive Committee was armed with influence in the police commission, and they used this power to pursue two foes of good morals: houses of prostitution and skating rinks. These targets appear at first to have little in common. But according to the NESSV, skating and prostitution both encouraged the sexual corruption of respectable children by lower-class seducers. Furthermore, both targets were vulnerable to police action, and allowed the NESSV to utilize their newly won powers to further protect youth.

The problem of the skating rink was brought to the attention of the Executive Committee in January of 1885 by E. O. Warren, who served as visitor to the poor for Trinity House, a charity run by the Trinity Church. Warren wrote to the society about how his efforts to improve a poor family were "baffled" by the Argyle Skating Rink.

> The family stood better than the average visited for the same time in as much as no drink and always working. The mother told the daughter she should inform me if the visits at Skating Rink were not discontinued. . . .
> I went to the Rink. The man who seemed to know all about it said the girl always got her fare paid in, but he would not let me look in after her without a fare. I found they were drinking beer in the Rink although he said they were all gentlemen and ladies, he used abusive language of the girl's mother, for trying to prevent the girl from coming.
> One night the girl failed to go home until morning and her story is this, a man she met there gave her drink. She had not seen him there before. The drink was what made her unconscious but if taken there or after coming out I cannot tell. She found herself locked into a room on Eliot Street near Washington. Her mother gave her a beating and the Skating Rink man made a complaint at the Station House of the mother's abuse. The girl has become a mother and a sad one, with a babe four months old for her mother to care for while she is but seventeen.[84]

The NESSV successfully petitioned the police commissioners not to renew the Argyle Skating Rink's license.[85] But the NESSV did not confine their concern to poor girls like the one victimized at the Argyle Rink. Instead, they seem to have been impressed by a news clipping enclosed with Warren's letter, entitled "The Immoral Skating Rink." Warren urged the NESSV to publish a similar appeal with the aim of making skating rinks unpopular. The clipping made several charges against the rinks:

> We . . . know enough about the skating rink to know that it is frequented by some of the most moral and estimable people. But is it not also frequented by some of the most immoral class, prostitutes and libertines, both married and unmarried? And which class is the more likely to be influenced by the other? . . . Does it improve a young girl's modesty or morals to fall in a heap on the skating rink floor, with perhaps her feet in the air and her clothes tossed over her head? Is it good for her proper training to even see other females in such a plight?
>
> The skating rink is a bad institution even if it did nothing but keep young people out late at night. Do parents *know*, or simply think, that their maturing children are at the skating rink *every* night *they say* they are? We would simply here remind parents that it is within the province of newspaper men, as it is of detectives, to know of many social matters of which they disapprove.[86]

The problem of knowing where children were and who was influencing them resonated with the already existing concern about the effect of reading on children's morality. In warning the public of the dangers of skating rinks, the NESSV stated the problem not in terms of threats to the deserving poor, such as to the girl who became pregnant as a result of being drugged and raped by the stranger she met at the rink, but rather in terms of polluting influences seeping across the class boundaries:

> We believe that most of [the rinks] in the city are tolerably conducted, and that the proprietors try to suppress the inevitable evils that seem to follow the promiscuous mingling of all classes. . . . In general it is for the conscientious proprietor and the watchful parent to reduce the real dangers to a minimum, if the rink is to continue to be one of the most popular places of amusement for the young.[87]

This tepid endorsement of the skating rink was revoked a year later, when the *Annual Report* of the NESSV stated:

> The skating rink, which at first received the approval of many of our best citizens, and which it was hoped might prove both innocent and beneficial as a place of amusement for the young, seems to have very rapidly

degenerated. Deserted generally by those who alone could give it character, it has become more and more the resort of the most disreputable. . . .
we feel it our duty to warn parents of the dangers which now surround
their children at the rink.[88]

The campaign against skating rinks involved exercising the power of the
state to help enforce boundaries between classes, specifically, to minimize
contact between privileged children and the poor. Such appeals for the
maintenance of class boundaries were similar to those made earlier by
Comstock.

In their campaign against prostitution the NESSV again cited the danger posed by lower-class seducers to upper-class children. In 1887 they
justified their efforts against prostitution by noting the large number of
college-aged people living in Boston:

> We must remember, however, that there are in the schools and colleges
> of this city and its immediate vicinity twenty-five hundred young men,
> and in our shops and stores thousands of young persons of both sexes,
> with a constant influx from all New England. Many of these are with-
> drawn from the reach of parental influence, and it is our duty to shield
> them, as far as possible, from special temptation.[89]

The pursuit of prostitution involved negotiating with the police commissioners the appropriate policy to be taken toward "the social evil." In
June of 1886 the NESSV wrote to the Commissioners advocating a strong
policy against prostitution.

> The policy to be pursued towards all such houses should be recognized
> as one of earnest and vigorous antagonism.
>
> They should not be allowed to consider themselves tacitly recognized
> as a necessary evil. The directors urge that constant raids should be made
> upon such houses at night and that this should be done frequently
> enough to impress upon both the inmates and visitors to such houses a
> sense of peril and insecurity.
>
> In order that whatever information the officers have or may gain as to
> the character of such houses may be made most effective the directors
> especially urge that the entire force be given to understand that active
> warfare is contemplated, that as far as possible the business be driven
> from houses that have become notorious: that no special localities may
> be granted immunity as legitimately devoted to this traffic.[90]

While the NESSV had been pleased with the efforts made by the reformed police commission against gambling houses, their campaign
against prostitution was repeatedly thwarted. In 1887 the Executive
Committee decided to submit to the daily papers a report of the activities

of the NESSV that would acknowledge what had been accomplished by the police commission against gambling houses and urge similar activity against houses of prostitution, in particular the raiding of "notorious houses."[91] The campaign against "bad houses" dominated the discussions of the Executive Committee in 1887. In June the committee concluded that the district attorney was a particular obstacle to their efforts, and that he wielded a "vast and irresponsible power"; by November the society had collected evidence that the proprietors of houses of prostitution were paying police officers for immunity from prosecution.[92]

In 1888 the NESSV attempted to wield its influence in city government to suppress prostitution. In January the committee received a letter from Mr. Whiting, chairman of the Police Board, requesting that the NESSV urge the governor to reappoint Mr. Edward Osborne to the board overseeing the police. The NESSV equivocated, expressed its dissatisfaction with police actions against prostitution, and threatened the commission with a public crusade if more rigorous policy against prostitution was not pursued.

> In the matter of repression of houses of prostitution they are convinced that far more might be done than at present. They therefore prefer to wait a month or two before urging the reappointment of any member of the present board. They recognize the obstacles and difficulties in handling this matter. Still they cannot forget that your predecessors used the same language concerning the gambling houses. You have converted their impossibility into a possibility for which we are very grateful. We trust however that it may not be necessary to look to others to achieve by devotion and earnestness what you shrink from.[93]

The frustration generated by the campaign against prostitution led the leaders of the NESSV to take two actions in the spring of 1888. First, the society moved to cooperate with the Law and Order Society in circulating a petition urging that the manner of appointing a district attorney be changed from election to appointment.[94] Second, the society circulated a petition urging the governor to appoint police commissioners who would pledge themselves to "vigorous and aggressive warfare . . . against all houses of prostitution."[95] The letter attached to the petitions reiterated the policy that the NESSV had suggested to the commissioners in 1886, contrasting their suggestions to what they claimed was the policy of the police commission. Police policy, the NESSV claimed, was the following.

1. No place, however notorious for years as a house of ill fame, shall be disturbed, unless its inmates are disorderly and noisy enough to make the house a public nuisance. (In other words, all houses which

ply their infamous traffic quietly are granted as complete immunity as though they were licensed).

2. An exception is made where the neighbors are able and willing to bring explicit and open charges against such a house. (Owing to the reluctance of neighbors—sometimes being ladies—to appear publicly in such cases, and the fear of depreciating their property, such concerted action of neighbors is seldom obtained.)

3. It is urged that the difficulty of obtaining adequate legal evidence against such houses makes vigorous action against them impossible. (When there was a manifest *special* reason for suppressing such a house, we have never found the difficulty in obtaining evidence [to] stand in the way of the prompt and effective action of the Board in cleaning out the place.)

4. It is objected that if these houses were summarily closed, the evil would be scattered and the inmates less under the surveillance of the police. (Our statute contemplates no such local immunity from interference; the executive arm should enforce the law, not substitute for it a wiser policy.)

5. Lastly, it is said that public sentiment would not sustain any vigorous and aggressive warfare upon quiet houses of bad character; that they are a necessary evil, and that ideal purity cannot be looked for in a great city.[96]

The anti-vice leaders obtained over six hundred signatures on their petition, but it took several years to obtain the desired cooperation from the police. Not until 1895, when General Martin was made chairman of the police commission, were the leaders of the NESSV satisfied that the police cooperated with their efforts.[97]

## The Political Culture of Moral Reform

The histories of the New York and Boston anti-vice societies suggest that their successes were predicated on the political contexts in which they operated. Leaders of the anti-vice societies mobilized support by linking moral reform efforts to the perceived political impotence of the native born in cities increasingly dominated by immigrants. Understanding the political context requires that we disaggregate the actual political power of the upper classes from extant political discourses about that power. The anti-vice societies thrived in an environment where the elites felt beleaguered; however, agitating for the suppression of obscenity is hardly an obvious response to immigrant political power. Furthermore, while the upper classes in Boston and New York perceived themselves as increasingly subject to the reckless rule of Irish immigrants, the ability of elite civic reform organizations like the Citizen's Association to strip control of the police from Boston's mayor and control of finances from its councilmen shows that the upper classes responded to their declining power at the municipal level by wielding the power that they still held at other levels of government.

The political impotence of the upper classes in Boston and New York became a source of power for Comstock, and for his allies in Boston, because they linked their concerns about the corruption of youth to the increasing social presence of immigrants and to the political power immigrants wielded. The translation of elite political frustrations into anti-vice success was the consequence of anti-vice leaders mobilizing elite support by framing obscenity and gambling as dangers to youth caused by immigrants. Thus while the political position of the upper classes is crucial in explaining anti-vice success, these structural factors can explain human action—such as support for the anti-vice societies—only when we take account of the cultural frameworks that people used to understand their social position. A central source of Comstock's power was his ability to manipulate these cultural resources.

But Comstock's efficacy as a crusader against vice was also predicated on elite political power wielded in other political arenas. As postal inspector, Comstock was an agent of the federal government; he gained both this position and the law he wielded because his wealthy supporters had considerable influence with federal lawmakers. The passage of state anti-obscenity laws depended on anti-vice supporters using influence with sympathetic state senators and representatives. The enforcement of these laws depended also on anti-vice society access to agents of the state: Comstock's ability to get convictions in more than half his cases depended on cooperative judges. Thus the political context of the anti-vice movement encompassed not only declining elite influence in cities such as New York and Boston but the continuing influence wielded by the elites in New York and Massachusetts state government, as well as with the federal government. Anti-vice leaders mobilized support for their crusade by playing on elite fears of immigrants' increasing social presence and political power in cities; simultaneously, the efficacy of their crusade was predicated on elite power in the state and federal levels of government.

# 6

## CENSORIOUS QUAKERS AND THE FAILURE OF THE
## ANTI-VICE MOVEMENT IN PHILADELPHIA

THE SUCCESS of the anti-vice societies in New York City and Boston sprang, in part, from their ability to connect fears about the corruption of children and families to corruption in city government. The link between sexual depravity and dirty politics was, in both cities, the protection of gambling by corrupt police and city officials. Anti-vice crusaders portrayed gambling, like obscene literature, as leading the children of middle- and upper-class families to associate with bad companions and acquire habits that would topple them from the pinnacle of society to its depths. Gambling, obscenity, and city corruption were effects of immigrants flooding the city, threatening its moral and social fabric as well as its political institutions.

Like Boston and New York, Philadelphia was one of the five largest cities in the country and shared a history as a colonial seacoast city. But Philadelphia differed from Boston and New York in one respect crucial for this study: it did not have a strong or successful anti-obscenity movement in the late-nineteenth century. Historians and sociologists assert that Philadelphia had no anti-vice movement at all.[1] This assertion, I will show, is false, but Philadelphia's anti-obscenity movement was less successful and less supported by the elite than were the anti-vice societies in Boston and New York. This chapter discusses the history of censorship in Philadelphia and the reasons for its failure. I suggest that political conditions in Philadelphia, in particular the continuing domination of the city government by Republicans, rendered arguments that generated anti-vice support in Boston and New York ineffective there. Furthermore, Philadelphia's upper class enjoyed relative immunity from the social presence of immigrants, which retarded the formation of institutions, such as boarding schools, that were intended to insulate the upper classes of New York and Boston from their social inferiors. Thus Philadelphians were less invested in the institutions for class reproduction that in Boston and New York, Comstock argued, were threatened by obscenity.

In contrast to the success of the New England Society for the Suppression of Vice, Comstock's attempts to start an anti-vice society in Philadelphia met with repeated frustration and failure. Comstock lamented his problems in Philadelphia beginning in January of 1877, when he reported that while Philadelphia harbored a large business in obscene pictures, arresting its proprietors was useless. He cited the case of two dealers of obscene literature who carried on their business "beneath the shadow of the walls of Girard College," but who, upon pleading guilty, were imprisoned for only two weeks. As Girard College was a school for white orphan boys, this activity must have seemed particularly heinous to Comstock, but he reported that the men in charge of anti-vice work in Philadelphia did not respond when he communicated the facts to them. In consequence, Comstock abandoned work in Philadelphia.[2]

These reports of Philadelphians' complacency may have had some effect on anti-vice efforts in Philadelphia, for Comstock reported that on March 20, 1877, a "large meeting of leading citizens," organized by the Reverend John Hall, had founded the Pennsylvania Society for the Suppression of Vice.[3] But this group vanished as quickly as it appeared, leaving no traces.

What explains Comstock's failures in Philadelphia? One way to address this question is to compare the situation of Philadelphia's elite to that of elites in Boston and New York. In the previous chapter I argued that mobilizing the threat of immigrants, and in particular the political power of immigrants, was vital for the success of the anti-vice societies in both New York and Boston. The nature and size of the immigrant communities of Boston, New York, and Philadelphia suggest that Philadelphia's upper class was less threatened by immigrants. The 1890 census reported that 80.5 percent of New York City's white population were either foreign born or had immigrant parents. In Boston, 68 percent of the white population were first- or second-generation immigrants, while the corresponding figure for Philadelphia was 57 percent.[4] More important for political and social outcomes in the cities was the geographical distribution of immigrants. Boston's immigrants were more concentrated in ethnically homogeneous districts. By 1890, eight of Boston's twenty-five wards had populations that were more than 40 percent foreign born; in Philadelphia only four of thirty-three districts had such high concentrations of immigrants.[5] Philadelphia's immigrants, particularly the Irish, were less concentrated in unskilled laboring occupations than were their counterparts in Boston.[6] The occupational distribution of Philadelphia's Irish community may explain why they divided their allegiance between the Democratic and the dominant Republican parties, a division that kept the Irish from being a major force in city politics until the twentieth century.[7]

The demographics of immigrant communities in Philadelphia versus Boston and New York translated into greater political power for Philadelphia's upper class. Philadelphia was not free of political corruption, nor did it lack organizations trying to eradicate it. To the contrary, Philadelphia's "Gas Ring" was notorious among civic reformers. Philadelphia differed from Boston and New York in that city government remained dominated by native-born Republicans throughout the nineteenth century.[8] While the upper classes of Philadelphia, as in Boston and New York, complained that the "best people" no longer had power in city government, the elite was more active in Philadelphia's government than in the other cities'. In 1895, 39 percent of Philadelphia's councilmen were listed in the city's blue book, a directory of the elite that listed about 10 percent of the city's families. In Boston, where 15 percent of the city's families were in the blue book, only 8 percent of the city councilmen were listed, and the proportion for New York was even lower.[9] In 1903 Lincoln Steffens argued that the relative power of the upper class and Philadelphia's lack of an immigrant-dominated city government made the upper class of Philadelphia more complacent about vice in their city.[10] Governmental corruption in Philadelphia meant that the native born quarreled among themselves about city services, and that those who made fortunes from service contracts and public monopolies were native born rather than Irish. Philadelphia's upper and middle classes maintained control of city government, benefited from city services, and acquiesced to political abuses.[11]

A remarkable document, entitled "The Union League and the Political Situation in Philadelphia," was written in response to the "Republican Ring" by "A Republican Member of the League." As in other cities, Philadelphia's Union League was a club patronized by elite men concerned about city politics. In New York the club was a haven for "good government," meaning those who sought to reform the immigrant-dominated city government.[12] But in Philadelphia, charged the anonymous Republican, the Union League was an accomplice in election frauds perpetrated by the Republican Party. As a result, "the people of Philadelphia are no longer a free people, enjoying the right of self-government." Furthermore,

> Having permitted itself to be made the tool of a circle of professional politicians, who have managed to control the Republican party in this city, the League has made itself responsible for all the frauds that have been perpetrated under their sanction, and made itself a sharer in the disgrace which attaches to them. It has even so far assumed the responsibility of the Republican party in this city as by its committee to denounce as renegades all Republicans who failed to support the whole ticket, making no exceptions of the many thousands of Republicans, who, from the highest and purest motives, supported a local ticket formed upon a non-partisan basis with a view to much needed reform.[13]

The political situation in Philadelphia was not congruent with the discourse of evil immigrants corrupting city government that Comstock and his allies employed in Boston.

Comstock's final attempt to mount an anti-obscenity campaign illustrates the futility of attempts to link censorship to city government corruption in Philadelphia. In 1885, Comstock's third attempt to establish a Philadelphia branch of the NYSSV was heralded by a letter to Josiah Leeds, the local purity crusader, announcing that "strong political influences in favor of this vileness" were inhibiting anti-vice efforts. Comstock recruited people sympathetic to such views to the organizational meeting of the new anti-vice society.[14] Eight of the thirty-three people, or 22 percent, who signed Comstock's call to found an anti-vice society were also members of the Committee of 100, an overlap between civic and moral reform agencies similar in magnitude to that in Boston. However, while Boston's elite was well represented in the NESSV, only three of Comstock's supporters in Philadelphia were in the *Social Register* and none was a millionaire. This feeble response to Comstock's attempt to use strategies for mobilizing support that had worked in Boston and New York suggests that the relative security of Philadelphia's upper class accounts, at least partially, for elite indifference to anti-vice efforts in Philadelphia.

While this explanation is consistent with the historical facts, it is unsatisfying and incomplete. It is difficult to point to a historical circumstance, like the relative absence of immigrants, to explain the failure of a social movement. Social movements are made by actors operating in a social context. While that context offers opportunities and constraints, the link between social circumstances and the success of an anti-vice crusade is made by sometimes idiosyncratic individuals making appeals for support. Comstock left virtually no record of his efforts in Philadelphia, making it is hard to construct a compelling story about his failure. But the efforts of other moral reformers to stamp out vice in Philadelphia give us more clues about why censorship failed there.

Philadelphia's own proselytizer for purity was Josiah W. Leeds, a rich man who in 1870, at the age of twenty-nine, joined the Society of Friends, married Deborah Ann Crenshaw, and began crusading against his neighbors' vices. Leeds's trail of good works is chronicled in his scrapbooks, consisting of correspondence and newspaper clippings that he assembled and annotated from the early 1870s until his death in 1907.[15] One of Leeds's first published complaints about vice appeared in 1875, in a letter protesting the "shameless can-can," and the proliferation of "nests of unclean birds," apparently a reference to theatrical plays and dance exhibitions.[16] Three years later Leeds made his first forays against two other sources of sin, immoral reading and tobacco.

The campaign against immoral reading began with a complaint to the Pennsylvania Railroad that improper reading materials were being sold to schoolboys on the train. This generated a sympathetic letter from the company but no action against the sales.[17] But a protest to the Philadelphia, Wilmington, and Baltimore Railroad Company resulted in the firing of a company newsboy who had offered to sell Leeds an "obnoxious paper."[18]

Leeds's crusade against tobacco was linked to his hatred of the theater. He complained to R. C. Brown and Company, a "segar" company, about their "objectionable illustrated advertising card." Leeds asked the firm to stop mailing such cards "in view of our accountability in Eternity for acts done here."[19] Unsympathetic company agents responded to Leeds because his "choice verbiage" betrayed him as a person of "more than ordinary intelligence."

> We defy you or anyone else to point out to us any obscene point in our card and we deny that the mere exposure of limbs on our advertisement is sufficient to precipitate any sound minded person into dissipation; moreover, we are quite content to stand the consequences at the bar of "Eternal Justice."

Furthermore, the company argued, it was "quite evident" that Leeds had not seen "certain masterpieces of paintings and sculptures which are to be seen even in this country," implying that artistic prints used for advertising purposes were protected from censorship because they were "art." Finally, Leeds was invited to call the company offices and get a "Capadura segar" to smoke, in order to restore his good humor.[20] Leeds's response to this letter betrays the origins of his complaint. Using arguments similar to Comstock's, Leeds asserted that the proliferation of "pernicious" papers and prints was "destroying the virtue and happiness of families." Concerning the claim that artistic ignorance explained his response to the advertising cards, the Quaker asserted that in spite of his limited acquaintance with the arts he knew that: "It would be impossible to conform the chaste productions of a Raphael (in painting) or a Thorwaldson (in sculpture) with the lewd figure of the card—one which yourselves can but know is of the same class of representations with those which advertise the low variety theatres."[21]

In 1884 Leeds introduced legislation into both the Philadelphia City Councils and the Pennsylvania State Legislature that forbade the sale of indecent materials, or of crime-story papers, from newsstands. Leeds's campaign in Philadelphia's city hall offers an interesting contrast to the success of the NESSV in Boston. The recalcitrance of the Boston City Council, and especially the police commission, provided the NESSV with an issue that increased the success, and ultimately the political power, of the association. While Leeds received greater cooperation from Philadelphia's mayor and city council, I suggest that he ultimately wielded less power than did Comstock and the leaders of the NESSV because the Philadelphia city government was still in the hands of Republicans. Neither Leeds nor Comstock could connect obscenity on Philadelphia's streets to the presence of immigrants or to the presumed corruption of a city government dominated by immigrants.

Leeds's campaign for the passage of censorship laws began with a project to fight corruption in the halls of city government—but in this case, corruption came in the form of papers of an "immoral or pernicious tendency" being sold at a newsstand in the east-west passageway of the new city hall. Leeds's complaint, presented to the city councils in June of 1884, claimed that a similar stand closed by order of a grand jury in 1882 had recently reopened, and requested that the councils send a resolution to the commissioners of public buildings prohibiting the sale of such literature in city hall.[22] A investigative subcommittee purchased the offending papers, and reported that Leeds's claims were truthful and that the Public Building Commission should require newsdealers to exclude such materials from their stands, which they did.[23]

Emboldened by this success, Leeds moved to clean up newsstands located in the post office. This time Leeds demonstrated ambitions that transcended reforms in Philadelphia (and trespassed on Comstock's turf) by asking the secretary of the treasury to prohibit the sale of "immoral" papers at any stand in a post office owned or leased by the federal government.[24] A response from the assistant secretary of the treasury C. E. Coon claimed that only three or four newsstands existed in the post offices, making a general order unnecessary, but promised that prompt steps would be taken whenever such a complaint was made. Coon also instructed the custodian of the Philadelphia post office to issue instructions prohibiting the sale of materials of the "character mentioned" in Leeds's letter.[25]

## Censorship Laws in Philadelphia

Satisfied that pernicious papers would not be sold in the post office but thwarted in his attempt to act on a national scale, Leeds returned to problems of moral depravity in his home city, and particularly to the effects of the theater. Leeds successfully petitioned Mayor William B. Smith for the removal of a "highly objectionable, large-size" theater poster, whose display "should no more be permitted than should any case of personal indecent exposure."[26] Leeds found theater posters a continuing vexation; in a letter to George Scattergood, a member of Philadelphia's most prominent Quaker family, Leeds reports that he called on

Mayor Smith to complain of yet another poster. Again the mayor ordered the poster removed. Leeds complained to Smith that, because there was no penalty for putting up the posters, they could be replaced as quickly as they were taken down. According to Leeds, the mayor responded that "he had seriously thought of petitioning councils to enact some measures which would relieve the sidewalks of both the scandalous posters and the pernicious papers." Leeds suggested that if he wrote a law, it could be sent to the councils with the mayor's recommendation, a plan Smith seemed to approve.[27] Scattergood met with the mayor the following week, and sent Leeds news that the mayor seemed "entirely in sympathy" with Leeds's proposed ordinance.[28]

Encouraged by the mayor's support, Leeds petitioned the board of education to submit his proposed law to the city councils. He claimed that a "Christian Mother of this city" had recently written to him, distressed about the display and sale of "pernicious posters and periodicals" that rendered the public sidewalks "morally unsafe." The mother feared for the moral purity of children exposed to such matter, and "though herself (was) but a weak woman, she could at least supplicate for a blessing upon all right endeavors to rid our fair city of this abounding pest of demoralizing pictures and prints."[29] Arguing that several cities had taken measures against such literature, Leeds requested:

> Believing that the Board of Education recognize, and are not indifferent to, the obviously mischievous influence upon the school children of the debasing, brutalizing and crime-inciting pictures and publications to be seen upon or about our sidewalks, your addresser respectfully and earnestly suggests that, as a body watchful of the best interests of our public school population, you submit this matter to the City Councils.

Leeds assured the board of education that the mayor was "very desirous that a prohibitory measure of general character . . . be enacted" against objectionable papers and posters. Since the city councils had unanimously voted to prohibit the sale of the *Police Gazette* and similar papers on "certain city property," Leeds asserted that they would act favorably on this matter as well.[30]

In spite of this statement of faith in the city councils, Leeds attempted to circumvent opposition to his proposed legislation. He asked allies on the Select and Common Councils to direct his resolution to either the Committee on Schools or the Committee on Law. He specifically asked that it not be referred to the Committee on Police, because McMullen and some others who "would not give right relief" were members.[31]

The board of education cooperated, citing danger to youth in their request that the city council pass laws limiting the circulation of objectionable papers and posters.

There can be no doubt as to the direct agency of these pernicious papers and pictures in inciting to insubordination, violence and lust, to the disregard of parental restraint, contempt for the authority of teachers and infractions of the public law—and that all these lamentable results are obviously on the increase.[32]

Leeds did not confine his lobbying to the city councils. The *Philadelphia Inquirer* printed a resolution from the workers at the Baldwin Locomotive Works, one of the country's largest manufacturers of locomotives, which supported the proposed law, expressing concern that men of "depraved minds" who spread demoralizing pictures were immune from prosecution. The resolution, signed by several hundred employees, had been accompanied by a note apologizing for the "necessarily soiled appearance of the document" which the signers "trusted . . . will be overlooked."[33] Leeds had carefully orchestrated this show of support from humble laboring men concerned about their families.[34]

Mayor Smith's support was not unequivocal. In an interview with the Philadelphia *Press* the mayor stated that he could request, but not force, the removal of theater posters.

If anything is to be accomplished in this direction it must be by legislation. I am willing to aid in the passage of a law that will give to the Mayor and to the Police Department jurisdiction over the flagrant violations of decency in the posters. This is a question, however, as I told Mr. Leeds, upon which the public will not agree when such fine distinctions are involved.[35]

The mayor also stated misgivings about censoring theater posters. The plays, he noted, were attended by "plenty of our best citizens," who did not consider the performances harmful; illustrated papers such as the *Police Gazette* caused far greater injury to public morals. Finally, Smith asserted that the posters themselves did not call for specific action, but that the formation of a society "like that controlled by Anthony Comstock in New York" would reach other, and greater, evils.[36] The mayor realized what Leeds would not—that the success of anti-vice efforts depended on gaining the support, and not the antagonism, of members of the upper class.[37]

Leeds instead sought support from the Baptist, Presbyterian, and Methodist Ministers' Meetings, and received it from the first two groups. J. G. Walker of the Mantua Baptist Church contacted Leeds, telling him that the Philadelphia Conference of Baptist Ministers had appointed a committee to lobby the city councils about his proposed anti-obscenity legislation. As chairman of this committee, Walker sought Leeds's instructions.[38]

Representatives from the Baptist church, as well as from the Friends, came to support Leeds when the Committee on Law of the Select Council discussed his proposed legislation. The *Press* opened its report on the hearing by observing:

> A delegation of benevolent faced Friends sat in the back row of the seats in the Select Council Chamber yesterday afternoon during the session of the Committee on Law. Some of them wore their broad-brimmed hats all through the afternoon. Several Baptist ministers sat on the seat in front of the Quakers.[39]

The delegation of Friends was noteworthy for containing "some of the most influential members of the society."[40] While Leeds was able to mobilize some religious groups, most notably the Quakers, he appears to have ignored the Episcopalians, the religious home of many wealthy families who had left the Friends.[41]

J. H. Graham introduced the anti-obscenity ordinance into the Select Council. The proposed bill made it illegal to maintain a stall for selling newspapers on any public street without a permit signed by the mayor. To obtain a permit the seller must agree that he:

> Will not sell, lend, give away, or offer to give away, or keep, or exhibit to view any obscene or lascivious, or manifestly indecent book, magazine, pamphlet, newspaper, story paper, writing paper, picture, drawing, or photograph; that he will not sell, lend, give away, show, or have in his possession . . . or advertise any book, pamphlet, magazine, newspaper, or other printed paper devoted to the publication, or principally made up of criminal news, detailed police reports, or accounts of criminal deeds, or pictures and sensational stories of deeds of bloodshed, lust or crime, and that he will not hire, use, or employ anyone to sell, give away, or distribute such publications.[42]

The law mandated fines for violations of the law, payable to the Pennsylvania Society for the Protection of Children from Cruelty, and imprisonment for anyone failing to pay the fines.

Newsdealers argued that the legislation was both too broad and too vague, but a legal technicality tabled (and ultimately defeated) the law. The proposed imprisonment was not legal, because the council derived its powers from the state and could not pass laws mandating prison sentences.[43] The proposed ordinance was referred to a subcommittee, where it died. An amended bill introduced a year later also failed, although Leeds did not lobby for the bill a second time.[44]

## The Citizen's Representative Committee and Censorship in Pennsylvania

The New England Society for the Suppression of Vice acted as an organization, with no one of their members singled out as its leader. The New York anti-vice society was known as Comstock's organization, but the staunch support of wealthy and influential men, some of whom served as the organization's executives, was widely acknowledged. While Leeds was wealthy (although not a millionaire), he usually acted alone. In 1885 Leeds came as close as he ever did to leading an organization for moral purity. The Society of Friends received a letter announcing a meeting of representatives from several churches and charitable organizations whose goal was to found an organization to suppress vice and immorality.[45] The Friends decided not to be formally represented in the new organization, because, according to Leeds, "on account of the different way which Friends have thought advisable to pursue in religious and philanthropic service . . . their position has at times been greatly misapprehended." Leeds opined that the city would benefit greatly from a Society for the Suppression of Vice, and hoped that such an association would be comprised of "not necessarily men of repute for their attainments, respectability, or wealth, but . . . those that fear God and love their fellow men."[46]

The meeting resulted in the formation of the Citizen's Representative Committee (CRC). Leeds lent his support to the new organization and his name to the Executive Committee.[47] One early victory of the Committee was the prohibition of a boxing match, which was stopped after Leeds consulted with the city solicitor and mayor about its legality.[48]

The Citizen's Representative Committee should have been an effective organization. Its leaders included the bishops of the Protestant Episcopal and Reformed Episcopal churches, and ministers from the Presbyterian, Baptist, Methodist Episcopal, Lutheran, Dutch Reformed, German Reformed, Unitarian, and United Presbyterian churches, as well as Leeds from the Friends. Representatives from the Law and Order Society, the Pennsylvania Society to Protect Children from Cruelty, the Philadelphia Tract and Mission Society, the Home Missions, the Bedford Street Mission, the Sabbath Association, and the Beneficent Building Association also sat on its Executive Board.[49] In short, the CRC had the potential to unite many of Philadelphia's Protestants into an effective reform organization. The constitution of the organization stated that its aim would be to cooperate with all efforts to suppress vice and immorality, and that it would be composed of "representatives appointed by each of the various religious, philanthropic, and charitable organizations" in Philadelphia, with room for only ten additional representatives from the community at large.[50] While the directors of philanthropic organizations were often wealthy, this structure realized Leeds's wish that the organization be made up of men chosen for their religious devotion, rather than for their wealth.

Leeds worked with the Citizen's Representative Committee but briefly. After stopping the boxing match, the CRC, represented by Leeds, lobbied for a state anti-obscenity law. Upon learning that the Pennsylvania House of Representatives was debating an anti-obscenity bill, Leeds mailed a letter to George S. Graham, chairman of the Committee on Vice and Immorality, requesting, from his position as chairman of the Citizen's Representative Committee, that another section be added to the proposed law.[51] The new section would accomplish what Leeds had failed to gain in the city council:

> The Mayor of any city or the Burgess of any borough shall remove or cause to be removed, any poster, pictorial hand bill or other article or articles coming within the description or descriptions of articles mentioned in any of the foregoing sections of this Act, whenever the same shall be exposed to view on any public street or passage way, or in any window fronting on, or in any door way, vestibule or other entrance opening upon any public street or passage way.[52]

Leeds claimed that Mayor Smith was anxious to have the power in the proposed law; but the law as written would have compelled mayoral action, which Leeds may have intended but the mayor probably did not.[53] Leeds's lobbying did not help. Before Leeds had sent his proposed amendment, he had been informed that the bill was in its second reading and probably would pass. The bill did not pass until 1887, when it became law without Leeds's proposed amendment.[54] Leeds abandoned the Citizen's Representative Committee shortly thereafter. One month later Leeds had William J. Gilmore, manager of the New Central Theatre, prosecuted for posting obscene show bills. Leeds told the press that he acted "solely in his individual capacity" in filing the complaint against Gilmore.[55] Leeds also acted on his own in yet another foray against objectionable papers sold at stands in city hall. Members of the city council treated this request less kindly than earlier ones. When Leeds appeared before the Building Commission and asked that the papers be removed from the stands, he was rudely interrupted and told to put his request in writing, which, Leeds explained, he already had. The commissioners told Leeds to write a new statement, and when Leeds left the room, "one of the commissioners replaced on the table a copy of a sensational paper which he had been reading before the crusader's advent."[56]

Leeds's next attempt to employ the powers of city government against vice met with more success, but cooperation from city officials was again wanting. This time Leeds, in alliance with the Citizen's Representative Committee, requested removal of a series of frescoes from the Girard House. The frescoes were ultimately removed, but Leeds was quite irritated at his treatment by District Attorney George Graham.[57] The Citizen's Representative Committee collapsed shortly thereafter.[58]

The election of Mayor Edwin Fitler in 1887 accelerated Leeds's loss of influence in city hall. Fitler was the candidate of the Committee of 100, a group of middle-class civic reformers who had successfully lobbied for the Bullitt Reform Bill, which was intended to eliminate the city's notorious "Gas Ring" and other perceived sites of corruption. In May of 1888, when Leeds complained that the superintendent of police refused to remove an objectionable poster on display at the Chestnut Street Theatre, he noted that the police really could not be blamed for laxity in this matter, as often defendants in such cases had been discharged or acquitted. This "weakening of the public conscience" was caused, Leeds asserted, by discussion of theater performances and stage gossip in the secular papers, which increased attendance at plays. Attendance was further boosted by consumption of tobacco, which brought cards adorned with pictures of actresses into public circulation.[59] Frustrations with city government and the conviction that the theater bred immorality led Leeds to publicly attack Mayor Fitler in December of 1890, when he charged that Fitler refused to suppress the ballet because he was a director of one of the city theaters.

> And so it has happened that we have continued all the sensualities of the spectacular drama and opera, not excepting the displays of the notorious American Opera Company, which was allowed to come and go without hindrance on the part of the authorities, although public protests were made thereagainst by individuals in the community.[60]

Leeds's frustration suggests the inefficacy of his strategy of acting alone as a "concerned citizen" exhorting city government officials to enforce the law according to his preferences.

While Leeds's problems with city government were shared by the leaders of the New York and New England anti-vice societies, there are striking differences between events in Philadelphia and those in New York City and Boston. Foremost among these is that Leeds did not mobilize public opinion by arguing that his pleas for a war on vice were ignored because the city government was corrupt. Furthermore, he did not appeal to civic reform organizations to unite with him against corrupt city officials, the strategy the NESSV pursued. While in Boston the success of municipal reform organizations increased the power of the anti-vice society, in Philadelphia the opposite occurred. In 1892 Leeds asked Thomas Meehan, who had been an ally on the council when Leeds tried to get the anti-obscenity law passed, for assistance. Meehan responded that he thought that the issues Leeds raised were important, but unfortunately, because of the new city charter, which was passed "expressly to take out of the hands of Councilmen all executive duties," he could be of no help to Leeds.[61]

Without an organization to back him, Leeds was brushed aside. The failure of the Citizen's Representative Committee suggests that it was not a religious organization that was needed, but instead an organization of upper-class citizens, like that led by Comstock. Leeds resisted such a strategy. His forays against art represent one of the few times that he was able to cooperate with members of the upper class against a foe of good morals.

## Art and Upper-Class Support for Leeds

That members of the upper class ever cooperated with Leeds on an artistic issue was remarkable, for Leeds was unremittingly hostile to artistic displays. The skirmish over the removal of the Girard House frescoes in 1885 suggested his attitude toward public art; he made these objections explicit in a complaint to Samuel Biddle. Biddle was a member of Philadelphia's first family and a partner in Bailey, Banks, and Biddle, a jewelry store. In March of 1886 Leeds wrote to Biddle, complaining about three statuettes in his store window that had a "morally hurtful tendency." Such displays by a wealthy man were a particular problem, because "in endeavoring as a private citizen to do something to discourage the pernicious in print, in pictures, etc, I have found that the pleas as to what, of immoral tendency, may be seen displayed in the galleries of the wealthy, is a defense often the first to be made." Leeds concluded by noting that several months earlier he had asked a Jewish merchant to remove a number of statuettes—much smaller than those displayed by Biddle—from his window, and the merchant had complied. Leeds hoped that Biddle would see the reasonableness of this complaint and withdraw the figures in question. Biddle answered Leeds the next day, asserting that the windows were decorated by a young man hired from another firm, who had been instructed not to use such figures again.[62]

Leeds's next forays against "art" were less successful. He swore out a warrant for the arrest of George Senn, a cigar dealer, for displaying in his store window 250 photographs of actresses in scanty costumes, which were samples of cards packed with cigarettes. At Senn's trial, Leeds picked out several pictures he considered most offensive. The attorney for the defense noted that one photograph was of a "work of art" known as "The Beautiful Diver," which, he claimed, could be seen in many art stores on Chestnut Street. The magistrate acquitted Senn, noting that there was nothing worse in the photographs than could be seen on the stage.[63] Leeds had prosecuted these cases by himself, without seeking support from the district attorney. Shortly after Senn's acquittal, District Attorney Graham wrote to Leeds, claiming that he should have been consulted, for he agreed with Leeds about the pictures. Graham suggested that another case be brought before a different magistrate. Graham offered to try the case himself if the magistrate agreed to bring the case to trial.[64] In October Leeds prosecuted another cigar dealer, John Walker, for displaying pictures of actresses. The grand jury refused to indict Walker and charged Leeds with court costs. Leeds was ultimately relieved of the costs because Graham argued the case in a second hearing, but Walker was never tried.[65]

In November of 1887 Leeds's fate became intertwined with Comstock's crusade when the latter arrested one of New York City's leading art dealers, Edward L. Knoedler, for selling photographic reproductions of obscene art. One consequence of this arrest, which will be discussed in the next chapter, was the sale of a special edition of the *New York Evening Telegram*. The paper's front page was covered with sketches of artworks supposedly seized by Comstock, most depicting nude women. While Comstock was unable to try the vendors of the *Telegram* in New York, three men were arrested in Philadelphia for importing copies of the paper and selling them for five cents apiece. The *New York Herald* noted that Leeds, "an amateur detective of vice and a notorious busybody," was in the crowd, but reported that the detective who made the arrest claimed that he had seen the boys selling the paper, and his superiors ordered the arrest.[66] The newsboys were held over for trial, which took place in April. In the meantime Leeds brought yet another case to court. This time a saloon owner, Robert Steel, was arrested for displaying a copy of Garnier's *Temptation of Saint Anthony*. Steel was dismissed because the new state law against obscenity, finally passed by the legislature in 1887, specifically excluded "works of art."[67] The case also yielded a smug letter from Comstock stating "it seems to me that the law has been purposely and intentionally weakened in your state, and ought to be changed at the coming Legislature. If I had been consulted in the matter I think we could have prevented such a catastrophe to the great Commonwealth of Pennsylvania."[68]

Three days later the newsboys were acquitted for selling the *Evening Telegram* without the jury's ever leaving their seats. The judge instructed the jury:

It is not my function, gentlemen, nor yours to pass upon any particular school of art, but I think the modern French school from which these pictures have been taken, is open to the most severe criticism.

But if they are works of art, and are so accepted and considered by the community in which we live, the sale of them under the Act is not punishable. If they are considered works of art, the sellers are entitled to protection under the Act of Assembly. . . . I do not think the evidence would warrant a conviction.[69]

Some newspapers attributed this prosecution to Leeds, although Leeds noted in his scrapbooks that the superintendent of police was responsible for the arrest of the newsboys.[70]

After losing four cases concerning art and photographic prints, Leeds turned to other issues. His influence at city hall had almost disappeared, and Leeds found organizations such as the Citizen's Representative Committee to be of little use, although he did became vice president of the Social Purity Alliance. But while Comstock cultivated wealthy supporters, Leeds was never savvy about the uses of power or the usefulness of powerful people. Leeds's unwillingness to turn to the wealthy is particularly remarkable given an incident in 1891, when Leeds's views of art received rare favorable commentary in the press, largely because of the support of Philadelphia's wealthy women.

In March of 1891 the Philadelphia Academy of Art staged its largest annual exhibition ever, a show of six hundred works of modern art, which generated the one of the most successful sales of artworks in the academy's history.[71] The Academy of Art was the city's only venue for regular art exhibits, although it possessed few permanent works. The nudity exhibited in some of the show's paintings appalled women from some of Philadelphia's wealthiest families, as it did Josiah Leeds. In a letter to the *Philadelphia Inquirer* Leeds asserted:

> It is occasion for great regret that the "Jury of Selection and Hanging" of the Philadelphia Academy should have taken the new departure they appear to have done in placing pictures on public exhibit, which, were they to appear in any of the ornate drinking saloons of the city, would seriously imperil the application of their proprietors before the Board of Licensing Judges. The Academy authorities cannot have seriously considered, I think, the encouragement which they hereby give to the exposures of vulgar and indecent prints on the public thoroughfares.[72]

This time Leeds was not alone in his complaint, for a group of wealthy women, claiming to represent over five hundred Christian women, sent the following protest to the Hanging Committee:

Gentlemen: While thanking you for the many beautiful pictures with which you have decked the wall of the Academy, we desire, in the name of the womanhood of Philadelphia, and as voicing the expressed sentiments of very many—several of whom are stockholders in the Academy—respectfully to protest against the flagrant indelicacy of many of the pictures now on exhibition.

It is the general sentiment that never before in Philadelphia has modesty been so ruthlessly assailed. As Christian women, as modest women, we feel this to be an offence to our womanhood, an attack on the delicacy of our daughters and the morality of our sons.[73]

An unsympathetic Hanging Committee retorted:

Heaven forbid that the delicacy and morality of children should be so poorly established as to be in danger of overthrow by the contemplation of the pictures you have selected for censure. . . . In finally disclaiming any intention to affect injuriously the morals of the community, by placing these pictures on the Academy walls, we cannot refrain from expressing our sincere pity for that man or woman who finds in all the beauty and purity of the human form nothing but immodesty, indelicacy, and, alas, indecency.[74]

In spite of this rude reply, the women prevailed. Edward H. Coates, director of the academy, wrote to Leeds, saying that while he might disagree with him about the appropriate "artistic treatment of the human frame," he agreed that several of the canvases should not have been exhibited and assured Leeds that "you are not likely to have so much cause for disapproval in future exhibitions."[75]

While the New York City press reacted with outrage to Comstock's raid of Knoedler's gallery, and asked if Comstock would raid museums as well, in Philadelphia, upper-class women and Leeds selected a museum's pictures for censure and received the support of the press. The *Philadelphia Inquirer* attacked defenders of the nude by asserting:

All persons conversant with art realize the necessity, importance and value of the nude under certain circumstances. The wholesale defenders of the exhibition have taken the ground that European ideas of the art are the best; that the Europeans admit the nude and consequently the local committee was justified in its selections. This reasoning is so fallacious on its face as to require no expert logician to show its errors. . . .

The only excuse for the nude in art is where desired attainments of beauty in thought and expression can be secured equally well in no other way. That end is seldom attained, but when it is the result is always pleasing to art lovers except the uncompromising prude, and to this last class we are sure the good women who have protested against the Academy pictures do not belong. As a matter of fact the pictures referred to have shocked the modesty of noble-minded, cultured and refined men and women, for it is a mistake to suppose that women are alone in this matter.[76]

While this defense of art censorship was much stronger than anything published when Comstock was censoring, Leeds noted that the *Philadelphia Inquirer* poked fun at censors. His scrapbooks include a cartoon that shows women "At the Academy of Fine Arts," dressed in dowdy clothes, swooning, and covering their faces in front of a display of nudes. The right side of the cartoon shows two scenes: "At a Bon-Ton Affair," where women expose their backs and cleavage in fashionable gowns, and "At the Seashore," where young women play in wet, clinging bathing costumes[77] (see figure 1). Leeds commented that the *Inquirer*'s supportive editorial was of no account, because the paper published pictorial illustrations of nude pictures at the Academy "all for <u>sensation</u>."[78]

Leeds was not satisfied with the effects of his protest. In 1892 he wrote that, although some of the directors of the Academy of Fine Art seemed inclined to respond favorably to the "appeal for purity" generated by the display of 1890–91, the next exhibit was just as bad.[79] The immediate effect of the protests was to generate enormous publicity for the paintings, and "the Academy was besieged by a great crowd of people, all of whom sought for the objectionable pictures."[80]

When Philadelphia's wealthy joined Leeds in protesting obscene art, he avoided public ridicule, but he did not see this group as potential supporters. He returned to his solitary protests against the immoral. In November of 1891 he sent a letter to the Treasury Department, asking that the Rochegrosse painting *The Fall of Babylon* be prevented from entering the country. The department responded by stating that while they had to guard against narrowness of judgment, it seemed that the painting was a "flagrant violation of decency and morality." The customs authorities were ordered not to admit the painting if Leeds's description was accurate.[81] Leeds's collection of clippings contains several negative notices about this action but no positive ones. One cites the special deputy collector in New York, recipient of the instructions to stop the entry of the painting, as saying, "We have received a communication in reference to the picture from Washington . . . but we will not let our judgment as to the morality of the painting be in any way influenced by the opinion of people of Comstockian tendencies."[82]

Another clipping states that while Leeds had been severely criticized, he was no doubt sincere in his actions and thought he did a public service by having the painting excluded—but on the other hand, he may have

Figure 1. An exhibit of nudes at the Philadelphia Academy of Arts in 1891 drew protests from wealthy women as well as from Leeds. The *Philadelphia Inquirer* satirized the ladies' protest in this cartoon, which shows the women swooning in front of the paintings, then exposing their bodies in revealing gowns and bathing costumes.

been "disposed to look at it only from the point of view of an Anthony Comstock."[83] And the most severe criticism defended the picture because refined Europeans liked it:

> This picture, "The Fall of Babylon," has been seen by thousands of the most refined and educated people of Europe, who saw nothing in it, because they were not like Leeds, morally depraved themselves, for only one whose nature is depraved could see anything immoral in such a picture. This man Leeds, and that hypocritical knave Anthony Comstock, are a nuisance to society and should be suppressed. Leeds may be entitled to some sympathy because he is simply a crank, who means well, but Comstock is a hypocrite and a knave.[84]

This attack on Leeds raises a question about his legacy. Leeds was frequently derided by being equated with Anthony Comstock, but a century later nobody remembers Leeds, while *Comstockery*, a noun describing overzealous censorship of literature and the arts, remains part of our language. But the issue of Leeds's failure transcends lapses in our historical memory. Comstock arrested 3,731 people, and over 55 percent of these arrests resulted in conviction, reflecting the national scope of his powers as postal inspector. Leeds arrested approximately fifty people, and convictions were rare.[85] It is not surprising that Comstock achieved national fame. But the New England Society for the Suppression of Vice, while not a national movement, nor empowered by the federal government, was still effective, and the notoriety of their censorship is still recalled in the phrase "banned in Boston." Leeds's obscurity reflects the lack of force he wielded relative to the accomplishments of censors in New York and Boston.

The remainder of this chapter will explore the question of why Philadelphia never had an effective censor or censorship organization. I will examine various causes of Leeds's ineffectiveness as a defender of public morality, including his hostility toward upper-class diversions, his Quakerism, and the issue of competition with Comstock. The final part of the chapter will return to the situation of Philadelphia's upper class, and explore the possibility that the more secure political and social situation of Philadelphia's upper class made them slower to adopt both boarding schools and high art as institutions of class reproduction. The retarded growth of these upper-class institutions, I suggest, deprived Philadelphia's potential censors of another source of appeals for elite support, namely, that such institutions had become a venue for corruption of children.

## Leeds as Leader

One explanation for why Leeds never mobilized the upper class to support him in a censorship movement was his hostility to the tastes of the upper class. This attitude, grounded in Leeds's devotion to the "plain" style of Quakerism, made him loath to appeal to more lavish members of the elite, and the latter unlikely to respond if he had.

On many occasions Leeds expressed his distaste for the pleasures of the wealthy. Upper-class patronage of the theater generated some of his most vituperative statements. Leeds kept his misgivings private at first, although he did not shrink from attacking one of Boston's most sacred upper-class institutions, Harvard's Hasty Pudding Club. Leeds lamented a production of a "pronounced theatrical sort" staged at Haverford College, and expressed concern that if amateur theatrical productions were not strongly discouraged, "our students may even go so far as to the length of those at Cambridge and have an audience coming from Philadelphia—as they [have] from Boston."[86]

Leeds did not confine his misgivings about upper-class theatrical entertainments to his letters. In 1887 he began a campaign against the ballet, appealing to the Presbyterian and Baptist Ministers' Meetings to request that the mayor and chief of police forbid a performance by the National Opera Company, which was to be staged at the Academy of Music, on the grounds that it was a violation of laws forbidding an "offense to common decency," and furthermore asking that "the law of the State be so amended as that a ballet and all other public stage dancing by women be disallowed, and, further, that all professing Christians be encouraged to give no countenance in any way to such entertainments, no matter under what guise they may come."

Leeds justified this request by arguing that the police had recently refused to close a "notoriously disreputable music hall" near the Academy of Music. He argued against a double standard regarding sensuous dancing for the poor and ballet dancing for the rich:

> It may be well to seriously ask ourselves whether it is possible to close or keep closed the so-called *low-class* music and dance resorts, while the performances, permitted and unspoken against, at the halls patronized by those who claim to be of a better or higher standing in society, are almost or equally as sensuous and debasing.

The Baptist and Methodist ministers did not sign the condemnation of the ballet or of the Academy of Music that Leeds requested. But they did ask the mayor to enforce and the legislature to pass laws to "provide against all public displays of the human form that involve the degradation of women, and appeal to the baser passions of men," leaving the status of the ballet open to interpretation.[87]

Leeds won a partial victory. The ballet was danced undisturbed, but some patrons were disturbed by the dance. Before the performance, Leeds noted, the *Ledger* had asserted that the protesting ministers would find "nothing but pure delight" in it. After the performance Leeds quoted the *Ledger*'s review:

> the postures, etc., of the dancers, in their immodest, scant attire, was "simply revolting," and as to the participants in the shameless bathing scene, the unpitying wish was expressed that they might "all be drowned," so that they might certainly never "come on again."

Leeds concluded that his charges that the ballet was "sensuous and debasing" were fully sustained.[88]

Leeds condemned the ballet's audience as well as its performers. Four months after the National Opera Company's performance he triumphantly announced that the company intended to stop performing the ballet because of the "notoriety of its badness," adding:

Many people, rated high up in society, will not scruple to attend a place of diversion where the character of the entertainment is sensuous and obviously demoralizing, provided there is an abundance of respectability there to keep them company, and to stand by them in condoning the evil. But when the fact of the badness becomes notorious, and it may appear in "bad form" to attend, then considerations of expediency may attend to keep a goodly percentage of these pleasure-seekers away. Loyalty to the Holy One, and a regard for the best interests of families, should incite us to leave them alone altogether.[89]

Disdain of the wealthy also appeared in Leeds's diatribes against the charity ball, objectionable because the price of the lavish gowns far exceeded the proceeds to charity, and in his attempt to outlaw the favorite sport of America's horsiest upper class, fox hunting.[90] The campaign against the latter foundered when the agent of the Society for the Prevention of Cruelty to Animals explained that arrests for fox hunting were impossible because the agents for the SPCA would have to ride with the hounds for fifteen to thirty miles to see the kill. "At the death, they would witness a fox torn to pieces by the hounds, and the latter we cannot prosecute."[91]

Potential upper-class supporters must have found Leeds's unremitting self-righteousness almost as annoying as his campaigns against their amusements. Those who did not question their own purity were subjected to Leeds's scrutiny and advice. For example, in 1886 Leeds wrote to John Wanamaker, the department store magnate whose devout Presbyterianism had earned him the nickname "Pious John," in regard to his associations on the board of directors of the Girard Trust Company. Leeds noted "with sorrow" that an advertisement he found in the papers (presumably for the Trust Company) showed Wanamaker "in intimate business relations with the leading beer brewer of the city, with its leading distiller, and its most moneyed ... theatre owner." Leeds admitted that he did not know any of these men personally, but thought their occupations were such that their company could not be recommended to any of the two thousand Sabbath school children that Wanamaker helped supervise. Leeds explained that he was only sending this as a friend, "in remembering the warrant—to look upon the things of our neighbor for his good." For his part, Wanamaker was cordial in his response to Leeds but hardly apologetic for sitting on the board of the Girard Trust Company:

I had never thought of it in that light before but enjoyed the association with two of my old friends in the Board who are Elders in the Presbyterian Church and two others who are leading men in the Episcopal Church. I would be pleased to talk the subject over with you and have you explain how my friend Garrett, the President of the Girard Trust and a Preacher in Twelfth St. Meeting, reconciles your views with sitting with me in his Board, and on the other side of him the largest brewer in the city.[92]

Leeds's watchfulness for the failings of his neighbors made him willing to criticize his closest allies. Wanamaker's exasperation with Leeds must have reached new heights when, upon being appointed to the office of postmaster general, he received a letter from Leeds asking him to censor the *Christian Statesman*. The paper was a strong supporter of Leeds, printed many of his articles, and published editorials favorable to his work. Leeds's attempt to act against it must have been seen as utmost ingratitude. Wanamaker replied that he would not censor the *Christian Statesman*: "I need not, therefore, say to you that the Department is powerless to prevent the circulation of the "Christian Statesman" simply because it contained an advertisement which is believed to be of a lottery scheme."[93]

## Quakerism and the Failure of Censorship in Philadelphia

Leeds was a difficult person, but his social and organizational failings do not explain why censorship organizations that operated independently of Leeds, particularly Comstock's, failed in Philadelphia. But Leeds's righteous scrutiny of the flaws of his potential allies raises the question of the role of religion in explaining the failure of censorship in Philadelphia. The only sociologist to ask why censorship was successful in Boston but not in Philadelphia, E. Digby Baltzell, argues that censorship failed in Philadelphia because of the city's Quaker history. Quakerism, he argues, produced in Philadelphia an "anti-authoritarian" ethic, adopted by the city's residents whether or not they were Friends. This ethic induced "excessive tolerance" in Philadelphians, making them loath to censor.[94]

The problem with this theory is that nineteenth-century Quakers censored willingly. Leeds was a devout Friend, and he acted with full support of the Meeting. Not only did some of the city's most influential Friends show up at the city council meeting to support the passage of the unsuccessful censorship bill, but shortly thereafter the Committee of the Representative Meeting of the Religious Friends for Pennsylvania, New Jersey, and Delaware sent a petition to the city council, urging them to pass legislation suppressing "demoralizing literature."[95] Contrary to Baltzell's assertions, it was not Quakerism that hindered censorship in the late-nineteenth century, for Quakers were strong supporters of censorship.

However, at times Leeds's Quakerism hurt the censorship movement. Leeds sometimes claimed that as a Quaker he could not cooperate with other organizations promoting censorship. As we have seen, Leeds told the founders of the Citizen's Representative Committee that the Friends would not be organizationally represented in the association because of historic misunderstandings of Quakerism. Leeds lost interest in the CRC, but was asked again to become a member of the Executive Committee when the CRC united with the Law and Order Society. Leeds "declined on account of dull leaning, tho I do not unite with all their methods," meaning that the primary reason for his refusal was again Quakerism.[96]

If Quakerism did not impede censorship but was used as an excuse to thwart organizational cooperation, perhaps organizational issues explain the failure of censorship in Philadelphia. In particular, perhaps conflict between embryonic censorship organizations explains the lack of successful censorship in Philadelphia. Leeds competed with Comstock for the censorship turf at various times. Comstock's third attempt to found a censorship organization in Philadelphia, in 1885, coincided with Leeds's attempts to get the Pennsylvania Legislature to pass a law against obscene literature. Comstock wrote to Leeds, asking for a copy of the law being considered by the legislature. In his letter he announced that in two weeks he would be holding a meeting of Philadelphia gentlemen interested in this subject. Although invited to attend the organizational meeting of the Pennsylvania Society for the Suppression of Vice and Crime, Leeds did not. Comstock's call to the meeting, intended to alert "Pastors, Fathers, and other Married Men" to the "appalling facts" about the publication of books that threatened the purity of youth, and to begin "immediate and vigorous action" to "stay the plague," did not mention Leeds's efforts in this regard.[97] With or without Leeds's help, Comstock again failed in Philadelphia.

For his part, Leeds trespassed in regions that Comstock probably considered his alone, particularly the mails. In 1887 Leeds wrote to the postmaster general, requesting that the *Police Gazette* be excluded from the mail, and was told that mailing this paper did not violate any existing statutes.[98] When John Wanamaker was made postmaster general, Leeds hoped to suppress the *Police Gazette*, assuming that his social acquaintance with Wanamaker would allow him to "communicate with him with a view of suppressing some of the great mass of indecent prints that, despite the law, are carried in the mail."[99] Leeds asked Wanamaker to meet with him to discuss the possibility of banning the *Police Gazette* and the *Police News* from the mails.[100] Wanamaker referred the matter to the law officer of the Post Office Department, who wrote to Wanamaker saying that because no former law adviser to the department had declared the *Police Gazette* unmailable, he could not advise Wanamaker to do so either. Furthermore, he noted that Comstock had raised this issue repeatedly.

> Mr. Anthony Comstock, who has long been commissioned by this Department as an Inspector to exercise espionage over such publications, has often applied to the U.S. District Attorneys in New York to find indictments against the publisher of said sheet, all of whom have believed that it was not indictable. I will address Mr. Comstock with an inquiry covering this presumed fact, and communicate his answer to you. In the meantime your correspondent might obtain more specific information by corresponding with Mr. Anthony Comstock.[101]

One problem with attributing the lack of a viable censorship organization in Philadelphia to competition between Comstock and Leeds is that they appeared to be interested in different constituencies. The only time Leeds expressed an interest in forming an organization at all was when he stated his support of an organization of men who fear God. Comstock was certainly God-fearing, and his organizational base in the Young Men's Christian Association meant that his supporters were powerful and influential Christians, but the power wielded by Comstock presumably came from the wealth and social status of his followers and not from their relationship to God. Perhaps Philadelphia was not large enough for both Leeds and Comstock to have organizations, but they did not appear to divide the same constituents. Instead, neither reformer found much support.

## Leeds, Comstock, and the Women's Christian Temperance Union

The connection between Leeds, Comstock, and the Women's Christian Temperance Union (WCTU) raises another issue of organizational politics and anti-vice society success. In 1886 Comstock claimed that the WCTU founded a Bureau on Literature after he brought the problem of obscenity to their attention. Comstock addressed the National Convention of the WCTU twice in 1885, and reported frequent communications between the WCTU and the NYSSV.[102] Letters from the WCTU to Josiah Leeds tell a different story about the efforts and inclinations of the temperance leaders.

Leeds forged a connection to the WCTU in 1885, when he learned that Lucy Holmes, national superintendent of the WCTU's Department for the Suppression of Impure Literature, had praised Leeds's pamphlet "The

Theatre." Leeds responded by sending her his pamphlet "Concerning Printed Poison," offering to send as many copies as she would like to distribute.[103] Between 1885 and 1887 the WCTU reorganized its efforts against obscenity. In 1887 Leeds's wife, Deborah Crenshaw Leeds, received a letter from Francis Willard, national president of the WCTU, telling her:

> Between you and me and the sign post I want you for the national superintendent of the effort to put down impure literature, etc. You and Brother Josiah can work that department admirably together. . . . Of course I am not empowered to say that you will be elected, but I am permitted to hope so.[104]

Deborah Leeds denied Willard's request, saying that "she didn't have the strength at this time to undertake it and her husband was engaged in behalf of the maintenance of decency in Philadelphia."

Willard was not easily dissuaded. In October the Leedses received a letter from H. W. Smith, written at Willard's behest, trying to persuade them to lead the WCTU's efforts against demoralizing literature. Smith argued that they would be more effective in this office than if they were working alone, and pointed out that, as part of the WCTU, they would "have the cooperation of all our women everywhere."[105] It is not clear how the Leedses responded to this letter, but in November Deborah Leeds received a letter from Mary Woodbridge, recording secretary of the WCTU, telling her that at the National Convention a "Department of Impure Literature" had been created and that she had been placed in charge of it.[106] For his part, Josiah Leeds gave Willard his "qualified acceptance" of her offer, but told the WCTU that he could not give regular assistance to his wife, and that he preferred the "plain style."[107]

Deborah Leeds's report of the activities of the Department for Suppression of Impure Literature of the Women's Christian Temperance Union for the year 1888 chronicles the efforts of a very weak department. She reported that the department had no superintendent in almost half of the states and territories, and that only eight of twenty-two state superintendents sent reports of their activities to her. She attributed this problem to two causes: first, people might need to feel that they were doing the Lord's bidding when undertaking such sensitive work, and "the unwillingness to put one's hand unbidden upon work with which we may not have been divinely charged" might account for why only twenty-two states had superintendents dealing with impure literature. Why so few superintendents had work to report was also attributed to lack of divine inspiration, for Leeds notes that her instructions for dealing with pernicious literature were vague: "Tabulated 'Suggestions,' relative to the character of the work of this Department were sent out to all my corespondents, but their *directions*, whether to do or attempt much or little, were left to be sought of the Holy Spirit."[108]

It is not clear how Willard responded to this style of leadership, but the Leedses left the WCTU. In 1891 the tumult over the display of nudes at the Academy of Art came to the attention of Willard. Willard wrote to Josiah Leeds, suggesting that he contact Mrs. Martin and Mrs. Webb in the WCTU's Social Purity Department, who would be happy to cooperate with him on the issue of purity in art.[109] When the Philadelphia WCTU joined with the Social Purity Alliance, of which Leeds was nominally a vice president, in petitioning the mayor to prevent displays of immoral pictures and theatrical exhibitions, Leeds did not sign the appeal.[110]

Comstock and the Watch and Ward Society are remembered and Leeds forgotten in part because Leeds was unable to cooperate with other organizations and their leaders. If Leeds had wanted to act on a national scale, he had simply to accept the appeals from Willard to use the organizational resources she offered. But why did the WCTU seek the organizationally inept Leeds rather than Comstock, who was a more effective crusader against obscenity? The reasons for the WCTU's courtship of Leeds and their spurning of Comstock lead to a comparison of Comstock's and Leeds's visions of women and their social roles, and examination of the implications of these visions of gender for the censorship efforts each man championed.

Although Comstock wanted to open the annual meetings of the NYSSV to women and praised women who had acted against obscene materials, after the 1887 debacle of the Knoedler arrest he returned to the issue of gambling, and women's activities received no mention in the *Annual Reports*. But the question of why Comstock did not unite with the WCTU in the 1870s and 1880s is not answered by reference to Comstock's changing targets. Comstock's public praise of the WCTU suggests his willingness to work with them. Willard's appeals to Leeds indicate that Leeds offered something that Comstock did not. What Leeds had to offer was a vision of women's roles that allowed women greater autonomy—a vision manifested in his public support for women's suffrage.

While Comstock believed that women should stay at home to raise morally sound children and thus ensure the perpetuation of society, Leeds did not articulate so restrictive a role for women. Deborah Leeds's leadership in the Department for the Suppression of Impure Literature was not particularly efficacious, but she became well known for her work on prison reform, visiting many prisons and delivering public lectures.[111] Deborah Leeds testified when her husband brought charges against Steel for displaying *The Temptation of St. Anthony*, although this exposed them both to public ridicule. Deborah Leeds's testimony was described in the papers as follows:

> Mrs. Deborah Leeds followed her husband. She said she had seen the painting about a year ago, and lately obtained another view of it through a window. "It was," said the witness with considerable pathos in her voice, "a picture of our sister or mother exposed to view. Tears came in my eyes to think that a man with a mother would expose the feminine figure in that manner. If it were in a gentleman's private parlor I wouldn't object so much."
>
> "You're sentimental," observed counsel. "It is my desire as a mother to shield my children," replied the witness.
>
> "You went and gazed at it, though," persisted counsel. "It was my duty," meekly replied Mrs. Leeds. The woman wept while testifying and was joined by her husband.[112]

While Deborah Leeds cited her motherhood as a reason to act against the display of nude paintings, it is clear that she and her husband believed that, although she was the mother of five children, the duties of motherhood did not confine her to home, and the moral duties of motherhood included working to make the larger society safer for children. Josiah Leeds supported the vote for women because the presence of women in public life would render it more civilized.

> Speaking personally, I will say that it was only about three years ago that I became a convert to conferring the ballot upon women, and it grew out of the circumstance of my appearing before the grand jury in a case wherein the party indicated was charged with exposing a large number of indecent photographs, which had been used to advertise a certain brand of cigarettes. The clouds of smoke puffed out by the assembled jurymen, and filling all the room with a blue atmosphere, appeared to have so befogged or warped their juridical apprehension of things that they had no condemnation to pass upon an exhibit which the Commonwealth's attorney had strongly reprobated as having been made in violation of the law. It then occurred to me that with even a small minority of women occupying seats in the jury room, the atmosphere of the latter would never be permitted to become that of the smoking-car or club-room, while the findings of the mixed company, being of clearer brains, would be in accord with the pointings of fairness and decency.[113]

Anthony Comstock and Josiah and Deborah Leeds thus offered two visions of what censorship should accomplish. These visions differed most importantly in the assumptions they made about women's place in society. Both Comstock and the Leedses argued that obscenity was a threat to children and to the family, and they both argued that it debased women. But they differed in assumptions about whether protecting women meant confining her to the home and ensuring the purity and sanctity of the home she would be confined to. The position of the Leedses was more attractive to the WCTU because maintenance of the patriarchal family was central in Comstock's ideology.

## Censorship and Upper-Class Formation in Philadelphia, Boston, and New York

A variety of organizations promoting censorship arose in Philadelphia during the 1870s and 1880s. In addition to Comstock's attempts to found organizations, the Citizen's Representative Committee formed an alliance of Christian churches to ban obscene material, and the WCTU, in coalition with either the Leedses or the Social Purity Alliance, presented a proto-feminist alternative for censorship. Yet none of these organizations succeeded. While Philadelphia's upper class might not have supported organizations affiliated with the WCTU because Willard supported labor unions, this leaves the question of why Philadelphia's elite did not support either Comstock or the Citizen's Representative Committee.[114]

One possible explanation of the indifference of Philadelphia's upper class to censorship efforts is that Philadelphians had different norms or values about art and sexuality than were held by the upper classes of Boston and New York. However, while Philadelphia's upper class did not support a censorship organization, the incident at the Academy of Arts shows that at least some of Philadelphia's elite were no more tolerant of nudity in art than were their Boston counterparts. The five hundred women who signed the petition to the Academy's Hanging Committee represented the potential constituents for a larger censorship movement. That they (and their spouses) were not mobilized into a movement suggests that different norms about obscenity cannot explain the failure of censors and censorship in Philadelphia.

I have proposed that Boston and New York had successful anti-vice societies while Philadelphia did not because the nature of the political and social threat to the upper class posed by the immigrant working class was different in these cities. The upper class of Philadelphia faced a smaller, less miserable, and less well organized immigrant working class than did the upper classes of Boston and New York. The city government of Philadelphia remained in the hands of Republicans, and rich Philadelphians maintained more influence over local government affairs than did their counterparts in New York City and Boston. The relative security of Philadelphia's upper class eliminated one important incentive for supporting censorship, removing the possibility of framing the anti-vice campaign as a counter to corrupt immigrant politicians.

The presence and pressure of immigrants not only offered the opportunity to frame the moral crusade as a response to foreigners, but immigrants helped create another condition that influenced anti-vice success. The threat of immigrants might have helped spawn upper-class institutions, such as boarding schools and art museums, that created an exclusive upper-class sphere isolated from the masses. Philadelphians were slower to send their children away to boarding schools, and they were slower to build art museums to mark their class superiority. As a consequence, upper-class Philadelphians did not have to confront the possible adverse effects of cultural institutions such as high art and elite schools on their children.

In the next chapter I will discuss the role of high culture in class formation, and show how Comstock tried, and failed, to regulate the content of high art using arguments about obscenity and moral threats to children. The dominant classes of New York and Boston, and in Chicago as well, believed in the promised virtues of high art enough to build magnificent public art museums in the late-nineteenth century. But Philadelphians did not erect the Philadelphia Museum of Art, a museum comparable to the Boston Museum of Fine Arts and the Metropolitan Museum of Art in New York, until 1928, more than two decades after the Boston museum moved to its present location on the Fenway. The Philadelphia Museum of Art had its origins in the 1876 Centennial celebration, but during its first decades it was dedicated almost exclusively to "decorative" arts and did not develop its role as a repository of high culture until the twentieth century.[115] The growth of the Metropolitan Museum of Art, founded in 1870, also far outpaced that of the Philadelphia museum.[116]

The practice of sending sons to exclusive boarding schools—in part to protect them from the vices of the city—also arrived later in Philadelphia. Baltzell reports that Philadelphia's scions were sent to these schools beginning in the 1910s, while the growth of these schools, fueled by an influx of Boston's and New York's upper-class sons, was greatest in the 1890s.[117] Comstock's favorite issue, the spread of obscenity in boarding schools, would likely arouse less parental anxiety in Philadelphia, where children were not leaving town for their education. And while the exhibit at Philadelphia's Academy of Art in 1891 certainly excited a great deal of discussion about art, it seems likely that the values promoted by art were of even greater concern to the wealthy people of Boston and New York, who were pouring both dollars and artifacts into public museums with permanent exhibits. The retarded development of upper-class institutions in Philadelphia explains, in part, the failure of censorship there. An important source of this retarded class development was the relative security from the immigrant working class enjoyed by the dominant class of Philadelphia.

But threats to the power and status of a social class, such as that posed by immigrants in Boston and New York, are not translatable into actions such as the building of museums and schools or the support of censorship without cultural maps that enable people, in this case upper-class people, to interpret their situation and act on it. While prevailing ideas about culture and social improvement may explain the investment of upper classes in high culture in the late-nineteenth century, by no means were these cultural actions uncontested. Instead, the process of using high culture to consolidate class power was fraught with the problem of reaching agreement on just what these class symbols should be and what values, if any, the symbols should convey. These areas of contention exploded in New York when Comstock turned to censoring art.

# MORALS VERSUS ART

I HAVE ARGUED that the success of the anti-vice societies was linked to the social presence and political power of immigrants in New York and Boston. Growing cities filled with aliens generated parental fears about children's safety and elite anxiety about immigrant political power, which censors exploited to solicit support for crusades against obscenity and gambling. But in addition to responding to growing immigrant populations with a frontal (and ultimately ineffectual) assault on the power immigrants wielded in city politics, the upper class created institutions that would exclude the masses. Some institutions, such as boarding schools and social clubs, physically kept the rabble from entering. But, driven by status competition and a desire to adopt cultural symbols that denoted exclusiveness and refinement, members of the upper class also became collectors and consumers of art in the late-nineteenth century.

Literature on the formation of the American upper class suggests that the creation of institutions of high culture helped resolve two problems. First, it allowed the upper class to define and control an arena immune to the assaults of immigrants.[1] In spite of much rhetoric that the existence of the Metropolitan Museum of Art would benefit humble working men, workers were not especially welcomed in its corridors. For example, in 1897 the MMA's director, Louis di Cesnola, refused to allow a workman in overalls to enter the museum, telling the press that "we do not want, nor will we permit a person who has been digging in a filthy sewer or working among grease and oil to come in here, and, by offensive odors emitted from the dirt on their apparel, make the surroundings uncomfortable for others."[2]

Even workers with clean overalls had to bear considerable condescension from those who brought culture to them. In spite of the trustees' claim that artisans were among their "most steady and studious visitors," the trustees intended to "improve" these visitors.[3] Art brought to the public in magnificent public buildings came with a definition of "culture" as something old, expensive, and European, available in American cities only because of upper-class munificence and bestowed upon the public for its ennobling and civilizing effects.[4] For example, addresses given at the opening of the Boston Museum of Fine Arts in 1876 included the statement from Mayor Samuel Cobb that:

It will be a favorite resort of the cultured few who find a supreme delight in the creations of art; and, what is most important, all classes of our people will derive benefit and pleasure from barely looking upon objects that appeal to the sense of the beautiful. Even the least favored and least cultivated persons cannot fail to derive some refining and elevating influences from the sight of beautiful things.[5]

In contrast to the definition of culture prevalent during the Jacksonian era, this definition was profoundly antidemocratic. While the early-nineteenth-century upper class patronized art that glorified the American farmer, a symbol of the American character that built democracy, Gilded Age elites patronized art that glorified leisure.[6]

High culture was really intended not to improve workers, but to improve the upper classes. Art helped define class boundaries in an era when vast fortunes were being made and new upper classes were developing in cities around the country. Patronage of the arts showed one worthy of elite company, regardless of family or regional background. The trustees of the Metropolitan Museum played freely with the social anxieties of parvenu millionaires, inviting them show their refinement by contributing to the museum. The tenth anniversary of the museum's founding saw the opening of the Central Park building, at which Joseph H. Choate delivered an address calculated to extract donations from the newly monied:

Probably no age and no city has ever seen such gigantic fortunes accumulated out of nothing as have here been piled up within the last five years. They have been made in this city and out of this toiling people. Now, all these lucky citizens owe something to the city, and to the people out of whom they have made their millions. Their fortunes are not all their own; and where better than here can they pay this debt of gratitude? These Trustees are too proud to beg a dollar, but they freely proffer their services in relieving these distended and apoplectic pockets. Think of it, ye millionaires of many markets, what glory may yet be yours, if you only listen to our advice, to convert pork into porcelain, grain and produce into priceless pottery, the rude ores of commerce into sculptured marble, and railroad shares and mining stocks—things which perish without the using, and which in the next financial panic surely shrivel like parched scrolls—into the glorious canvas of the world's masters, that shall adorn these walls for centuries. The rage of Wall Street is to hunt the Philosopher's Stone, to convert all baser things into gold, which is but dross; but ours is the higher ambition to convert your useless gold into things of living beauty that shall be a joy to a whole people for a thousand years.[7]

The patronage of the arts was not only a means to achieve social acceptance within the upper class. It also increased the acceptability of one's children, both in old-money American circles and by elite Europeans. The *Annual Report of the Trustees* of the Metropolitan Museum of Art argued in 1875 that one of the functions of the museum was to make rich children more sophisticated travelers:

> Young men and women, educated at the best schools, and passing through courses of study which include mathematics, ancient languages, mental and physical philosophy, and many branches of special scientific character, have graduated with what is commonly, though absurdly, styled finished education, without receiving the instruction in the history of art, and without any knowledge which would fit them for travel, and the enjoyment and benefit conferred by it in the great collections of Europe, in which travelers pass so large a portion of their time.[8]

Not only did the educational function of the museum make the children of America's upper classes more suitable for the company of sophisticated Europeans, but scions endowed with refined tastes increased the probability that they would choose an appropriate marriage partner, who either shared refinement from birth or acquired it because of elite schooling. The sense of refinement and privilege bestowed by art patronage may have been especially important to an upper class faced by masses of impoverished but increasingly politically mobilized immigrants, and fostered the belief that the upper class benefited all of society.[9]

In the last chapter I argued that Philadelphians were slower than New Yorkers and Bostonians to build a grand public museum because they were less besieged by immigrants. This argument is purely structural— pressure from immigrant populations generated the impulse to create an exclusive sphere of high art. The problem with this argument is that art is nothing if not symbolic, and to understand the creation of such a sphere, one must consider the ideas and language through which it was created and interpreted. The role of anti-vice crusaders in the formation of the arts was to offer a discourse about morality that contradicted the claims about art made by those attempting to establish themselves as arbiters of high culture.

## The Pollution of Literature: Literature as Pollution

Until 1879 Comstock conducted his assault on obscenity as a war against corrupting influences seeping from the lower classes to pollute children. Then he discovered polluting influences bearing the imprimatur of "high art" and emanating from within upper-class culture itself. Comstock faced the new problem of "the classics." Obscenity dealers, fearing arrest for circulating older forms of obscenity, issued translated, abridged, and illustrated editions of salacious "classic" literature, in particular, works by Ovid and Boccaccio. Comstock's attempts to suppress these books evolved into a campaign against the writings of living (but unnamed) French novelists and, ultimately, a temporarily successful campaign against Walt Whitman's poetry.

Comstock recognized that the authority he gleaned from successful suppression of common obscenity did not translate into jurisdiction over books considered great literature. Upon encountering translated, abridged, and illustrated classics, he consulted publishers and book dealers "of high standing." These presumably more knowledgeable men responded to the sullied classics by telling Comstock, "Any man that does that ought to be prosecuted."[10] Comstock also sought justification for his actions in the law, which, he asserted, allowed the censorship of materials that "corrupt the minds of the youth and awaken lewd and libidinous thoughts, if sold so as to be liable to fall into their hands."[11]

Still, Comstock realized that prudence (and the social class of his supporters) dictated that he not argue for the complete suppression of objectionable "classics." Opting for confinement rather than eradication, Comstock argued that "classics" were acceptable when kept from the general public.

> This society has never interfered with any work of art, classic, or medical work, except to maintain and keep them in their own special sphere. We do not feel that it is interfering with a classic, when we punish a man in the courts for prostituting said book, and making an obscene article of it to serve his own base purposes.[12]

In bounding the "special sphere" of the classics and delimiting obscene versus acceptable uses of such works, Comstock again invoked the vulnerability of youth and the threat of foreign influences. But when censoring common obscenity, Comstock argued that he erected a barrier between polluting materials and the pure children of the elite. Classic literature, however, denoted sophistication. As part of the cultural capital of the upper class, the classics were not mere status symbols. The classics were part of "high" culture, a sphere endowed with the power to elevate and purify those who consumed it.[13] Thus in making arguments that abridged and translated classics were obscene and should be suppressed, Comstock was forced to concede that the classics were not inherently bad. Instead, the classics were both polluting and polluted when used inappropriately by certain audiences.

Just as he had argued that common obscenity was most dangerous to children, Comstock attempted to restrict the circulation of the classics by making arguments about the effect of such literature on youth. While consumption of the classics may have been suitable for elite adults, Comstock argued that children were imperiled by salacious "classics" in much the same way as by common pornography.

> To set our youth wild with passion by the lascivious products of ancient writers, or to fasten the picture of lust painted by some "old master" upon their imagination to defile it, is none the less a crime because these records of crime have outlived their day.
>
> It is the morals of youth of the present and of the future that should most interest every patriot, not of those of the past. These slimy records disclose nothing but that which appeals to our lower natures. They may be warnings. But if such, let them be warnings to parents and teachers. They are too obscene and seductive to be regarded as educators of the young.[14]

Furthermore, Comstock argued, "so-called" classics were marketed in the same way as other forms of obscenity, namely by sending advertisements to children in schools. "Others advertise them precisely as the suppressed books were formerly advertised, as 'rich, rare, and racy,' 'spicy reading for young men,' etc."[15] The marketing of these abridged and translated works to youths was one of Comstock's chief justifications for their suppression.[16]

Comstock's discussions of the effects of classics on children were fraught with contradictions. While Comstock clearly wanted to acknowledge the aura that surrounded such literature, and probably feared that censoring classics would offend his supporters and undermine his work, his arguments revealed considerable hostility toward the literature. Yet Comstock seemed unable to decide if the classics were inherently polluting or if only translated classics caused moral decay. Sometimes he argued the former. He compared classic literature to strychnine made palatable by a candy coating, concluding,

> This cursed literature corrupts the thoughts, perverts the imagination, destroys the will power, renders impure the life, defiles the body, hardens the heart and damns the soul. . . . The practice of spreading impure literature among the young is fast sinking them to the level of ancient heathendom.[17]

Comstock tempered his diatribes against the classics with the acknowledgment that such literature might have legitimate uses. Street pornography, peddled by lower-class miscreants, threatened elite youth with moral ruin that would result in their falling from the top of the class hierarchy to the bottom. The classics, if misused, threatened the same. Comstock conceded that classics could be tolerated when used to satisfy the legitimate demands of elite audiences, but not when corrupted classics fed illegitimate desires.

> These works, heretofore carefully concealed from public view, and kept by booksellers only to meet what some consider the legitimate demand of the student, or gentlemen's library, are now advertised and sold by certain parties as "rich, rare and racy" books, "amorous adventures," "spicy descriptions," "love intrigues on the sly," etc.[18]

But what was the proper place of classics? Comstock maintained that such works should be confined to the "literary world," making classics the sole property of the educated. Comstock made this argument most explicitly in *Traps for the Young*, in which he quoted a professor of English literature who responded to Comstock's claim that translations of classic works should be confined to the literary world.

> You concede too much. The book you are really writing about is an English book, having no "use in the literary world," for you are writing about a translation. You seem to me to admit that an English version of Boccaccio has the rights of a classic. That is not true. The plea for freedom in the circulation of classics is good only for Boccaccio in the *Italian original*. The translation is an English book, which no scholar wants, which nobody wants, for a literary or educational purpose. If there are scholars who want to know the beautiful Italian of Boccaccio, they must, of course, learn to read Italian.[19]

While common obscenity was inherently bad and Comstock sought to eradicate it altogether, the classics were polluting when they left the libraries of educated gentlemen. Furthermore, the classics were polluted by those who popularized them by issuing translations that could be read by all classes. While cultivated people might have a legitimate use for the classics, "they are clearly illegal when so prostituted from what has heretofore been thought their proper and legitimate place."[20]

While those who could speak foreign languages might be allowed to read classic literature, Comstock played on fears of foreigners and foreign culture to justify his attacks on both literature and street pornography. While Comstock had argued that it was foreigners who sold common obscenity to pure, elite, native-born children, in discussions of the classics Comstock asserted that foreign culture could be inherently polluting. Italian classics were "celebrated the world over for their indecencies"; such works had caused, and would cause, the collapse of nations.[21]

In recognizing the claims of art and the classics, we do not recognize the right of any man to explore the records of corruption of past ages, and then serve up that which has helped destroy the nations of old, as a sweet morsel for the youth of our land.[22]

Comstock's campaign against foreign authors was not confined to ancient civilizations. Modern French and Italian novels translated into "popular and cheap forms" were also evil, for "many of these stories are little better than histories of brothels and prostitutes, in these lust-cursed nations."[23] While Comstock condemned foreign novelists, it is not clear that he did much about them, although he did encourage supporters in other cities to peruse the shelves of their public libraries and agitate for removal of offensive literature.[24] Moving from dead authors to living ones allowed Comstock to look for modern literature (unprotected by the aura of "the classics") that might be encompassed in definitions of the obscene. In 1882, Comstock's quest to protect youth from sexuality in print or pictures brought him to the writings of one of America's greatest poets—Walt Whitman.

## *Leaves of Grass* and Fig Leaves

While Comstock had originally portrayed obscenity as works emanating from foreigners and lower-class people that polluted respectable children by arousing forbidden sexual desires, Whitman was the quintessential (although controversial) American poet, and he had many elite admirers. Furthermore, while Comstock justified much of his forty-year career in the anti-vice movement on the grounds that he was protecting children, he never claimed that Whitman's poetry was sold to youths. Comstock was left to argue that sexuality in high culture was demoralizing. Under the heading of "Semi-Classic," Comstock noted

> Another "classic" for which exemption is named, is an attempt by an author of our own time to clothe the most sensual thoughts, with the flowers and fancies of poetry, making the lascivious conception only the more insidious and demoralizing.[25]

The case for suppressing Whitman's poetry would be difficult to make. Rather than risking a battle over publicly censoring Whitman, Comstock turned to his allies in the New England Society for the Suppression of Vice.

In February of 1882 the NESSV's agent, Henry Chase, consulted with the assistant state attorney regarding the prosecution of persons who sold "one or more of several books." The books at issue included Balzac's

*Droll Stories*, Whitman's *Leaves of Grass*, and Boccaccio's *Decameron*.[26] At the next month's meeting the Executive Committee of the NESSV read a letter from Comstock, apparently regarding Whitman's poetry, and unanimously voted that " 'Leaves of Grass,' the volume of Walt Whitman's poems, is a work tending to corrupt the morals of the young. They therefore make their appeal to the publishers, James Osgood & Co., to withdraw said work from circulation or to expurgate from it all obscene and immoral matter."[27]

The NESSV found a willing ally in the district attorney, Oliver Stevens. Stevens contacted James R. Osgood and Company, the firm publishing a new edition of *Leaves of Grass*. The well-respected firm reacted with alarm upon being informed by the district attorney, "We are of the opinion that this book is such a book as brings it within the provisions of the Public Statutes respecting obscene literature, and suggest the propriety of withdrawing the same from circulation and suppressing the editions thereof."[28] Osgood immediately contacted Whitman, telling him they did not yet know what portions of the book were objected to, but that they "are, however, naturally reluctant to be identified with any legal proceedings in a matter of this nature."[29] Before agreeing to publish with Osgood, Whitman had informed the firm that his "sexuality odes" might be controversial, and the terms of his publication agreement included the understanding that these poems would be published in their entirety.[30] But upon being threatened with prosecution, Osgood began negotiating with Whitman about altering his poems. Whitman expressed willingness to delete some passages, until he was told that two entire poems, "A Woman Waits for Me" and "Ode to a Common Prostitute," would have to be removed. When Whitman refused to delete these poems, Osgood refused to print his book. Whitman took his book to Philadelphia, where the furor aroused by its suppression in Boston made it an enormous financial success.[31]

Shortly thereafter, the NESSV issued their *Annual Report* for 1881–82, in which they stated,

> The District Attorney has at our instance notified a number of booksellers that a certain immoral book, which had hitherto been freely exposed for sale, comes within prohibition of the law, and that any further sale will render the dealer liable to prosecution. A prominent publishing firm has, in consequence of a similar official notification, agreed to expurgate one of its books containing much indecent matter.[32]

Forcing Osgood to halt the publication of *Leaves of Grass* was a triumph for the NESSV, but not one publicly acknowledged. While the *Annual Report* of the NESSV hinted at their role in suppressing Whitman, the society did not admit that it had been the force behind the censorship of Whitman until 1895.[33] This may have been the result of unfavorable public opinion about the arrest.[34]

The *Boston Evening Transcript*, the Boston elite's favorite newspaper, strongly supported the suppression of Whitman. In response to the question of why Whitman refused to purge the offensive passages, the *Transcript* asserted,

> to tell the honest, shameful truth the very portions objected to are all that have made the book sell. We feel safe in asserting that not one person in a hundred who ever purchased a copy of "Leaves of Grass" did so with the single and only purpose of literary enjoyment. . . . It would be an exaggeration to say that Whitman has written nothing of poetic merit, but it would not be exaggeration to say that every line from his pen worthy of preservation could be crowded within the limits of half a dozen pages.

The editorial also asserted that Whitman's reputation came largely from the support of his friends in the press. These friends in New York would again assail "Boston prudery."[35]

The president of the NESSV, Homer Sprague, also publicly condemned *Leaves of Grass*. In September of 1882, Sprague published an article in *Education* magazine. In it he constructed the problem of obscenity in the same terms used by Comstock, arguing that obscenity was a "malignant" and "hydra-headed" evil fed by the "strongest appetites and passions." Like Comstock, Sprague used "classic" literature to make the rhetorical bridge between "debasing pictures" and "filthy songs" and Whitman's poems. Sprague argued that translated classics, in which was stored "the vilest . . . Greek, Italian, or French obscenity," threatened to ruin the "afterages."[36] And finally, like Comstock, Sprague's only charge against Whitman was that sexuality rendered his work indecent.

> Next come the dirt-eaters, each rolling before him his darling morsel of literary filth; disgusted with artificialities and linen decencies, and finding nutriment in *Leaves of Grass*, but not in fig-leaves; so much in love with Nature that, like the poor human earth-worms in Xenophon, they wish to do in public what others do in private, [and] abolish all laws against indecent exposure.[37]

Sprague's analogy of Whitman's poetry to indecent exposure probably referred to the celebration of sexuality in some of Whitman's verse. In "A Woman Waits for Me," one of the poems the NESSV proposed to censor, Whitman wrote:

All hopes, benefactions, bestowals, all the passions, loves,
    beauties, delights of the earth
All the governments, judges, gods, follow'd persons of the earth,
These are contain'd in sex as parts of itself and justifications
    of itself.

Without shame the man I like knows and avows the deliciousness
    of his sex,
Without shame the woman I like knows and avows hers.[38]

Those, like the anti-vice crusaders, who anchored the safety of society in the control of sexual passion, saw such verses as an incitement to dangerous behavior. Whitman's celebration of sexual passion was similar to the free lovers', although when Heywood was arrested for reprinting Whitman's poems in the *Word* the poet did not comment, telling a friend, "I shall certainly not do any thing to identify myself specially with free love."[39] Still, when Whitman discussed the censorship of his work in the *North American Review*, he made arguments similar to Heywood's about the social benefits of sexual knowledge and education. In particular, Whitman argued that women's emancipation (also championed in "A Woman Waits for Me") would benefit from intelligent discussion of sexuality. He asserted, "To the movement for the eligibility and entrance of women amid new spheres of business, politics, and the suffrage, the current, prurient, conventional treatment of sex is the main formidable obstacle."[40]

The decision to suppress Whitman thus extended earlier boundaries that Comstock had erected around obscene literature. Whitman's poetry was, to Comstock, similar to abridged editions of salacious "classics"; in addition, Whitman's treatment of sexuality was similar to that of free love advocates. Yet Comstock apparently declined to arrest New York City booksellers who sold *Leaves of Grass*. In 1896 the *Conservator* printed a previously unpublished letter sent to the *New York Tribune* in 1882. The letter asserted, "In August Mr. Anthony Comstock told your reporter that if he found 'Leaves of Grass' on sale in New York, he would certainly take steps to suppress it. August has melted into September, five large editions of 'Leaves of Grass' have been sold under his very nose—his ubiquitous and omni-prevalent nose—and he has taken no steps whatever."[41] Comstock's apparent decision to ignore the sale of *Leaves of Grass* in New York City suggests that he was reluctant to risk censoring a renowned figure from the art world on his home turf. Yet unresolved issues about the acceptability of sexuality in art lingered. They exploded when Comstock arrested the owner of one of the city's leading galleries.

## Indictable Art: Censoring the Victorian Nude

On November 11, 1887, Comstock entered the Knoedler Gallery on New York's Fifth Avenue and arrested the proprietor, Alfred Knoedler, for selling obscenity, specifically, photographic reproductions of paintings of nudes by French artists such as Bouguereau, Cabanel, Henner, and Lefebvre.[42] The event was remarkable for two reasons. First, Knoedler's was, and still remains, one of New York City's leading art galleries. Formerly a branch of Goupil's art gallery of Paris, Knoedler's had been one of the institutions primarily responsible for spreading a taste for European Salon art among America's upper class during the nineteenth century.[43] As notable as Comstock's audacity was the torrent of press coverage proclaiming it. Knoedler's arrest was discussed in all the major New York papers; those which did not leap into the fray on the first day did with the passage of a few more, and almost all added their voices to the howls of outrage, derision, and laughter aroused by Knoedler's arrest.[44]

The Knoedler case clearly (and publicly) marked the limits of power wielded by the NYSSV. Although Knoedler was found guilty of selling obscenity, the case was a public relations failure for Comstock and his society, and the NYSSV abandoned the issue of art censorship for the remainder of the century. In the course of the controversy Comstock made contradictory arguments about Salon art—that nudes painted on canvases were often beautiful and pure, but photographic reproductions of these paintings were a danger to childhood morality and incited lascivious passions in the minds of the uncultured masses. The contradiction in these arguments reflect underlying tensions in the culture of an upper class whose desire to imitate and impress European nobles was at odds with the sexual values that undergirded the Victorian family. Contradictory arguments also speak to divisions within New York's upper class. Competition between factions of New York's upper class was reflected in different attitudes about art. Fragmentation of New York's upper class limited Comstock's ability to censor.

## Censorship Precedents

While Comstock's censorship of reproductions of art on the grounds that they were obscene generated enormous public outcry, his action was not unprecedented. Comstock moved first against cheap photographic reproductions of these paintings, and in 1882 arrested August Muller, an art store clerk, for selling obscenity. Comstock proclaimed his victory against "licentious French art."

We have cleared many shop windows, and checked the tide of obscenity which had been coming from France and other European countries under the specious protection of art. We maintain that Genius has not more right to be nasty than the common mind; that the French artist has acquired no right to debauch the minds and morals of our land, simply because he has conceived in his mind a lascivious picture, and then wrought it on canvas.

It is not a matter of art at all, it is simply this, shall foreigners or others bring lewd, obscene and indecent pictures here and display them in public windows, to the detriment of the morals of our youth?[45]

The New York Court of Appeals upheld Muller's conviction. Comstock considered his victory in this case to be not the destruction of 768 pictures or the fine imposed on Muller, but the definition of obscenity decreed by the Court of Appeals: "It would be a proper test of obscenity in a painting or statue whether it is naturally calculated to excite in a spectator impure imaginations."[46] It was unfortunate for Comstock that he ignored another part of the judicial ruling which stated,

It is evident that mere nudity in painting or sculpture is not obscenity. Some of the great works in painting and sculpture as all know represent nude human forms. It is false delicacy and mere prudery which would condemn and banish from sight all such objects as obscene, simply on account of their nudity.[47]

Comstock interpreted his victory in the Muller case as encouragement to proceed. He gave notice to the public that no art was exempt when he reported in the NYSSV *Annual Report*, "There are many decisions when even paintings and original works of art have been suppressed under the common law. We simply enforce the law."[48] The leaders of the NYSSV claimed that Knoedler's had been given a copy of the law and warned that unless they desisted from selling the pictures, "the same law that punished a clerk in a Barclay Street store would be applied to a big firm in Fifth Avenue."[49] What the NYSSV failed to realize was that in matters of art, address was everything.

## The Press Response to the Knoedler Arrest

The *New York Herald*'s response to the Knoedler arrest was only slightly more vociferous than most. Under the headline "St. Anthony's Temptation: Mr. Comstock's Raid on High Art Denounced as an Outrageous Abuse of the Law," they reported that Comstock was again "on the rampage."

According to Comstock Knoedler & Co. are unable to distinguish between the decent and the indecent in art. They actually are ill advised and audacious enough to sell photographs—not the ordinary, every day sort of photograph which is found in the family album, but costly, elegantly executed reproductions of famous works of art, satisfying to the eye and the aesthetic sense.

But then Comstock, while he has an eye, and a very prying one, too, doesn't run to aestheticism.[50]

In two paragraphs the *Herald* raised the most important issues in the debate over art censorship, which were Comstock's qualifications to censor art and the validity of his artistic judgments compared to Knoedler's. Comstock's standards for art became the object of much discussion and ridicule.

The consensus quickly emerged that, in Comstock's eyes, nudity was obscenity. This was a tenuous position to hold in a country where Hiram Power's *Greek Slave*, which depicted a Christian woman stripped and manacled by the Turks, was the country's (and the Metropolitan Museum of Art's) most popular statue, and Bouguereau's nudes among its most popular paintings.[51] A Fifth Avenue art dealer, T. J. Blakeslee, explained that "a nude picture . . . might be decent and chaste in its conception and treatment and it might be possibly indecent. It behooved Comstock to learn the difference."[52] A writer for the *World* opined that Comstock was "guided entirely in his empiricism by the absence of clothes."[53] A *New York Herald* reporter suggested the solution to Comstock's ignorance when he asked the artist William Chase if he would support a subscription by art patrons to send Comstock to Europe. Chase heartily concurred, asserting that "a careful tour of the great galleries would certainly work a great change, both in his taste and judgment."[54]

These who ridiculed Comstock's artistic standards did not stop with his ignorance, but engaged as well in moral slander. Comstock's attribution of obscenity to nudity in art was in turn attributed to his licentious imagination. General di Cesnola, curator of the Metropolitan Museum of Art, claimed that Comstock saw what his mind predisposed him to see.

While on one hand a statue or a picture may impose reverence or sentiment of the purest and the most tender sort, to another it may merely bring images of base desire and unlicensed indulgence. Must those who look upon art from the standpoint of pure appreciation be deprived of that best of all pleasures because others of prurient and unclean imaginations can find nothing that is elevating in the most perfect types of human beauty?[55]

Cesnola and the other experts voiced the dominant opinion of the nude, which they transmitted from the French artistic community to an American upper class desperate to show its cultural sophistication. Comstock lacked both the class and the artistic credentials needed to refute experts like Cesnola. The opinion of the press was best voiced by the sculptor St. Gaudens, that "the decision as to the morality of a work of art should not be left to a man like Comstock."[56]

This may have been true enough, but Comstock did not act alone. The Executive Committee of the NYSSV sent a letter to all the city's newspapers, stating that the pictures confiscated at Knoedler's had been submitted to "the highest law official of this county, Mr. Martine" as well as to Judge Kilbreth, who issued the arrest warrant for Knoedler. In response to the imputations that Comstock was merely a dirty-minded man who acted alone, the leaders of the NYSSV stated, "Mr. Comstock simply obeyed the orders of the Executive Committee of the Society for the Suppression of Vice in making this seizure, and as Chairman of that Committee I distinctly state that we are ready to assume the entire responsibility of that action." The letter was signed by Samuel Colgate, president of the NYSSV, Henry E. Simmons, chairman of the Executive Committee, and J. M. Stevenson, secretary.[57]

The social standing of the leaders of the NYSSV—virtually all of the officers were listed in the *Social Register*—did not quash the fury of the press. The *Evening Post* argued that the issue of immorality in art should not be left to Comstock and his detectives or to "the respectable offices of the Society which employs them," for the latter had "plainly showed their utter incompetency in matters of art" in their letter to the press.[58] The following day the *Evening Post* asserted that while the leaders of the NYSSV had approved of and made themselves responsible for the raid on Knoedler's, this "did not help matters much, because the public will not recognize their names as those of persons who are authorities either on art or indecency."[59]

While the press would not concede that the social status of the leaders of the NYSSV gave them authority to censor, the consensus was that the standing of Knoedler's, and that of its customers, should grant them immunity from charges of obscenity. Knoedler was quick to point this out.

> Certainly we do not seek to pander to any depraved taste, or anything of that sort. Our patrons are among the most respected in the community. . . . We do not wish to sell any pictures, prints, or photographs which it is unlawful to sell. But I imagine that no one will contend that all nude pictures are immoral. If so, many people who now stand high in the community would be convicted of vicious taste.[60]

The *New York Times* also used the social class of Knoedler's patrons as the criterion to judge the nature of their merchandise. Describing Knoedler's as "a respectable house that has furnished respectable citizens with good pictures for more than a generation," they asserted that Knoedler's was not a legitimate target for Comstock because "everybody knows what sort of pictures Knoedler & Co. sell; they have no relation to vice or the stimulating thereto; the best proof of which is that they are not sought for by persons of vicious life or inclinations.[61]

The issue of class revolved, in part, around the issue of artistic authority. In the week after the arrest of Knoedler it seemed that everybody in New York's art world had an opinion about the arrest of Knoedler and few of them were favorable to Comstock. The conflict about Knoedler's was not only over what classes purchased art, but over who determined its moral content.

## The Art World Responds to Comstock

Art dealers, predictably but not unanimously, were furious about the arrest of one of their own on charges of dealing in obscenity. Herman Schaus, owner of a Fifth Avenue art gallery, stated that "it was an outrage for a man to come into a respectable house of the standing of Knoedler & Co. and seize pictures representing works of art." T. J. Blakeslee, another Fifth Avenue art dealer, opined that "it would be positively amusing if it were not so outrageous."[62] However, at least one gallery owner conceded that photographic reproductions could violate obscenity laws. Arthur Elliott, of the American Art Gallery, stated:

> My own view is that the law, as it stands, should be enforced. Colored photographs of pictures are sometimes very different from the originals. The original may be a fine work of art. The photographs may be touched up in such a way as to be offensive to any refined and decent taste, and indeed this is too often the fact. . . . The taste for these photographs is growing, and in my opinion its growth is not altogether due to an increasing love and appreciation of art.[63]

Knoedler's standing in the community still protected the firm in the eyes of Mr. Elliott, who continued by saying that he did not think that Knoedler's would deliberately violate the law.[64]

While it was possible to find an art dealer who supported art censorship, the artists themselves offered almost universal denunciation. The Society of American Artists met on November 15 and condemned the Knoedler arrest.[65] They made three arguments in their statement. Noting that reproductions of some of the foremost living painters were the object of Comstock's raid, they asserted that "the study of the nude is necessary to the existence of any serious art whatever, and that the proper representation of the nude . . . is refining and ennobling in its influence." Furthermore, "the popularization of such works of art by photography [is] of the greatest educational benefit to the community." Finally, the artists concluded:

> We protest against the actions of the Society for the Suppression of Vice as the work of incompetent persons, calculated to bring into bad repute one of the highest forms of art, and denounce such action as subversive of the best interests of both art and morality.[66]

Newspaper editors and reporters sided with the artists in their claims that artists, not Comstock, should determine when art violated morality. The *New York Post* asserted that the petition from the Society of American Artists, coming as it did from a group including a number of leading sculptors and painters, should be honored by "the great number of intelligent people in this city whose cultivation, however advanced it may be in other respects, is deficient in matters involving questions of aesthetics." If questions of morality in art were left to the Society of American Artists, it would exercise a "capable and discriminating censorship."[67]

Artists also defended the French Salon against Comstock. John LaFarge, "an artist whose opinions have very great weight," acknowledged that some of the art of the modern French school might "verge too closely upon immoral suggestiveness," but asserted that the committee that granted painters the right to exhibit in the Salon would not allow any improper pictures to be shown.[68]

Debate about the proper display of nudes had raged in Parisian art circles for more than twenty years. In Paris, the criterion for satisfying the demand that nudes display the beauty of women's bodies yet remain nonsexual was the portrayal of prostitution. Paintings that depicted a woman selling sex, such as Manet's *Olympia*, which scandalized the Salon in 1865, or Gervex's *Rolla*, banished from the Salon in 1878, were censured by the Parisian art world. On the other hand, the typical Salon nude, which portrayed naked women in mythical or "classical" settings, cavorting with satyrs, cupids, and goats, was pure. Thus, Parisian discourses about obscenity in art concerned the commercialization of sex in an increasingly class-divided city and were motivated in part by fears of the effects of prostitution on the family and society.[69]

American artists and critics, following their French counterparts, conceded that some art might be immoral, but asserted that people educated in art (as Comstock was not) could tell a pure nude from an impure nude. But they rarely gave examples of an impure portrayal. Daniel Huntington, president of the Academy of Design, described a painting that violated Parisian moral codes—it showed Jupiter showering a nude girl with gold. "There was nothing obscene or immoral in the nudity of the girl, but the idea that was suggested, seduction by the gold, made it objectionable to many."[70] The power of Parisian moral discourses derived from American upper-class concern about European opinion.

Knoedler's supporters repeatedly threatened supporters of censorship with the scorn of the French. Under the subheading "How Paris Will Laugh!" Charles Sedelmeyer, who was in town exhibiting a painting, asserted

> When the details of the arrest are learned in Paris there will be a great laugh there at the expense of your institutions here. To think that reproductions of works of art which have been hung in the Paris Salon to be admired by men, women and children of all nationalities and of all conditions of life should be confiscated here as objects likely to impair public morals, why it seems ridiculous.[71]

Fear of European reaction was also incited by the curator of the Metropolitan Museum of Art, General di Cesnola, who laughed heartily and sneered:

> It is only another example . . . of a spirit of ignorance and prejudice which I myself have had to contend against for years past in the management of the Metropolitan Museum. It was formerly many times worse than now, but the American public still needs an immense deal of educating in the general principles of art before it will be able, as the most ordinary small shopkeeper in an continental city may, to distinguish between a pure nude and a suggestive nude.[72]

Clearly the way one was to view the nude was in accord with how the French saw it.[73] Not only was Comstock passing judgment on the art of modern French painters, but, the *Herald* asserted, Comstock also had to explain how the works of "Old Masters . . . whose pictures adorn the churches of the Old World" would be treated when he wielded the law.[74]

While artists vehemently defended reproductions of the nude, art collectors were more ambivalent. At issue was the fear that their cultural symbols might be degraded by reproductions. One painting drew particular attention in the discussion of the Knoedler raid. Many reports of the arrest stated that a reproduction of Cabanal's *Birth of Venus* had been seized by Comstock, and although both Comstock and the leaders of the NYSSV denied that this was the case, the confiscation of this painting was frequently cited to illustrate the absurdity of Comstock's actions.[75] Henry Gibson, a Philadelphia financier who owned a (presumably painted) reproduction of the painting, was interviewed by the *Star*, which published the article under the heading "Cabanal's Great Painting: What Its Owner Has to Say about the Comstock Raid." Surprisingly, while Gibson was piqued at the idea that he would display impure art, and although he expressed low regard for Comstock, he sympathized with the notion that reproductions could be indecent.

> Many of the costly works of art are subverted to low objects by people who copy them for certain classes of advertisements, in which they are given a suggestiveness that makes them more or less indecent. This may be the case with the engraved copies of Cabanal's painting. It makes a difference the light in which they are viewed. In the painting itself there is not the slightest suggestion of immorality. . . .
>
> These Comstock people are after every form of nudity. They might as well take the warpath against some of the finest works of sculpture in existence on that basis. I don't care anything about what they do, for that matter. . . . When these pictures are distorted for the purpose of appealing to vulgar and depraved instincts, they deserve to be condemned. But to make an attack on a pure and simple reproduction of a nude representation in art is ridiculous.[76]

Gibson's ideas contradict those of the artists. Torn between wanting to join Cesnola in deriding Comstock and fearing the degradation of cheap artistic reproductions, he equivocated about censorship.

Remarkably, the only paper that supported Comstock's censorship was devoted to art. The editor of the *Art Amateur* conceded that Comstock may have made some mistakes, but expressed strong support for the aims of the NYSSV. He repudiated the arguments that photographic prints were art and that Americans should accept Parisian standards of morality.

> It has been urged that some of the prints seized were those of paintings from the Paris Salon. That says little for their decency. Let us hope that Parisian toleration of lewdness under the guise of art will never set the standard of decency in this country. Every year there are canvases by the score in the Salon which should be taken out and burned by the police; and, as a rule, the worst of them are photographed and imported into this country to be reproduced in cheaper form, so that your little boy or your little girl can buy them out of their pocket-money if they choose to do so.[77]

The *Art Amateur* supported Comstock's claim that cheap photographs of nude painting were liable, like any other sexual photograph, to corrupt the morals of children. The journal refuted artists' claims that photographic reproductions of nude paintings furthered their craft, insisting that every artist knew this assertion to be absurd. Painting the original may have helped the technical education of the painter, but it was a "pity that the wretched fellow did not put his education to better use." But a photographic reproduction was not art. Furthermore,

Its cheapness makes it dangerous; and in this, I think, we have some-thing like a key to the proceedings against Messrs. Knoedler & Co. I have it on good authority that while Mr. Comstock would not formu-late the distinction that would guide him in determining what prints of the nude those dealers might and what they might not sell, he indi-cated it pretty clearly, on the occasion of his official visit, by passing by high-priced etchings and engravings and seizing prints of the same subjects in cheaper form. Anything costing $10 or more was safe from seizure.[78]

The *Art Amateur* supported censorship if carried out by a board of artists and connoisseurs rather than by the NYSSV, but this editorial, as well as Gibson's condemnation of the use of cheap reproductions to make adver-tisements, contains a strand of support for Comstock. Both of these writ-ers are expressing concern about the cheapening of art. The *Art Amateur* approved of the suppression of photographic reproductions; Gibson ap-proved of the suppression of "vulgar" reproductions. Comstock cited the cheapening of art by vulgar audiences in his search for support.

## Comstock Explains Censorship

The debate carried on in the press between Comstock and his critics was lopsided—the critics were given pages to voice their views, while Com-stock and the leaders of the NYSSV were waiting either for the storm of condemnation to pass or for Knoedler's trial, or perhaps they were simply denied space. Given that most papers published the NYSSV Executive Committee's letter supporting Comstock, it seems likely that the censors were intentionally quiet.[79] However, in December Comstock explained his actions in a speech to a group of Baptist ministers. The *New York Times* printed the text of this speech; in revised form it appeared later that month as a tract entitled *Morals versus Art*.[80] Comstock attempted to placate his upper-class supporters by making several appeals to their class interests, arguing that art should be protected from its appropriation and exploitation by uncultured people, presumably the working class; that failure to restrict the circulation of artistic nudes would engender disre-spect for upper-class women; and that improper values expressed in art-works would harm children, especially elite children. Comstock's argu-ments were contradictory, but I maintain that this was caused by the need to appeal to an upper class holding contradictory ideas about the proper use of art.

When asked if he would seize all works of art that he would define as obscene pictures, Comstock replied:

These photographs I have seized, sir, are not works of art. They are sold wholesale at fifty cents a piece to small dealers. These dealers sell them to our youth—boys and girls—-and by these very sales encourage that very lasciviousness against which this law is provided. A grand oil painting, with its massive coloring, its artistic surroundings, its grand shadings and streaks of light, all of which create a work of art, ceases to be such when represented in a photograph, which gives mere outlines of form, and that is all. Again let me add, if you please, that the very cost of art precludes it from being gaped at—stared at by the masses, who have no conception of the grandeur of the merits of such a work—and would, if they had a chance, merely admire the very form, the bare nudity if you so call it, without letting their minds or their eyes, even if they could, rest upon the grand surroundings; in fact, upon the work of art as an entirety.[81]

This passage outlined Comstock's arguments about what art was, how it should be viewed, and most importantly, by whom it should be viewed; furthermore, he brings up the issue of the effects of art on children, although he does not explain why black and white reproductions would cause greater harm to children than the originals on the walls of rich peoples' homes.

Comstock's critics devoted more time to ridicule than response, but they did address the issue of the obscenity of reproductions. "Nym Crinkle," columnist for the *World*, thought Comstock's argument about originals curious.

His argument that a work of art that hangs in a gallery may be allowed on account of its place and its color, but that a photograph of it given to the public must be condemned, is a curious attempt to show that there are grades of morality in material. Thus canvas may not be as wicked as card-board, and a salon is not as immoral as a cellar.[82]

Charles Sedelmeyer also wondered about the wisdom of suppressing black-and-white photographs, which one might reasonably argue were less obscene than the full-color originals. He asserted that if Comstock was so opposed to nudity, he "might better seize the original paintings, which contain the tones and colors making them more like life than the photographs, which lack the colors altogether."[83] Both of these writers missed the point, which Comstock clarified in *Morals versus Art*.

In the artist's picture the figure is chaste in expression and posture, and surrounded by a beauty and harmony of blended colors and attractions that practically clothes it. These accompaniments certainly demand attention and divert the mind of the observer from the nude figure, so that in contemplating the work as it left the artist's hands, one is scarcely aware that a nude figure is thus exposed. This figure thus exhibited to cultured minds in an art gallery, where it legitimately belongs, is a very different thing from what it appears to be to the common mind on the public streets in the shape of a photograph.[84]

The seemingly silly argument that Comstock makes about how a painted background "clothes" the nude attempts another argument: when those with "cultured minds" looked at paintings of nudes, they saw "art," not naked women. Obscenity was determined by the social class of the beholder, and what distinguished high art from obscenity was the "culture" of the people who looked at it. Comstock argued that reproductions should be suppressed because they drew too much attention to the nude women depicted in them. Such art, Comstock argued, should be available only in art museums, which he considered a tolerable venue with a suitable audience. Museum hours, and their treatment of poor patrons, effectively kept them as bastions of the rich, which justified Comstock's assertion that only "cultured" minds would be found there.[85] The inaccessibility of art to the working classes did not disturb Comstock, for not only did he argue that photographic reproductions should be suppressed, he asserted that only "cultured" people should look at nudes.

> Let the nude be kept in its proper place, and out of the reach of the rabble, or those whose minds are already tainted or diseased with licentiousness, and its power for evil will be far less.[86]

Comstock's main complaint against Knoedler, then, appears not to be that he sold reproductions of nudes, but that some of the reproductions were ultimately acquired by the uncultured masses. Although Comstock excited considerable outrage by his actions, the arrest of Knoedler should not be interpreted as the actions of an excessive, obsessed, or isolated individual. Comstock's tactical error lay not in restricting the sale of reproductions, but in arresting someone who sold them to the rich. The arrest of Muller aroused neither public fury nor the condemnation of New York's art world. Even the arrest of Knoedler found some support among those who agreed that cheap reproductions were a different thing from "high art." Until Comstock arrested Knoedler there was little public comment on activities such as Comstock's forcing a candy dealer to remove a reproduction of Hans Makart's *Triumph of Charles the Fifth* from his window. The picture showed Charles riding into Antwerp, his horses led by nude boys.[87] Comstock commented on this action in 1879.

> What artist would be flattered to have his grand picture copied and used to advertise taffy in a confectionery store window? No; these things have their proper and legitimate spheres, and there they are safe under the law.[88]

While Comstock argued that his suppression of this print should be supported because an artist would not want his painting used to sell candy, implicit in this action is the rationale that the upper-class supporters of the NYSSV should not want their art cheapened for vulgar commercial purposes because this demeaned its symbolic value as a marker of upper-class taste and sophistication. In doing so Comstock reiterated a common complaint about use of art for crass commercial purposes. The *Art Amateur* editorialized,

> It is a pity that one cannot punish the course-grained clown who is ever ready to sacrifice decency for the sake of advertising his wares. A pork-packer has recently published as his trade mark the cherubs of Raffaelle with heads of suckling pigs in the place of those of the lovely children we all know so well. The comedians Robson and Crane, it may be remembered, set the example by inserting their own portraits in the spaces now occupied by their swinish successors.[89]

During the controversy over Knoedler, Comstock argued that he was defending art. The *New York Times* published a letter that Comstock had sent to Henry Gibson, the person who owned the reproduction of *The Birth of Venus*. Comstock wrote to tell Gibson that reports of his censoring the painting were false, but attempted to justify the suppression of photographic reproductions by pointing to those published by the *Evening Telegram*. The *Evening Telegram* had responded to the Knoedler arrest by covering its front page with photographs of art supposedly seized (See figure 2). While the NYSSV denied that these were the pictures in question, the *Telegram* did a booming business in the issue, selling extra editions of their two-penny paper at five cents a copy for several days.[90] In his letter to Gibson, Comstock asserted:

> I am sure you will draw a striking distinction between the beautiful work of art which you possess and the monstrous caricature upon it published by the *Evening Telegram* of this city, and that you will equally object to having the most objectionable feature of your picture, as a work of art, taken out and substituted by those who formerly advertised "rich, rare, and racy pictures," and have these photographs made under this head.
>
> I submit these facts for your consideration, because we are not wanting in our desire to protect art, nor in the still stronger desire to protect the youth of this country from the demoralization that must come from such photographs as have been sold of late in this city.[91]

If we could believe that Comstock was sincere in his desire to protect art from profanation, one could argue that the NYSSV's art censorship was merely an attempt on the part of the upper class to protect their cultural capital. Yet if Comstock sincerely desired to keep art from being

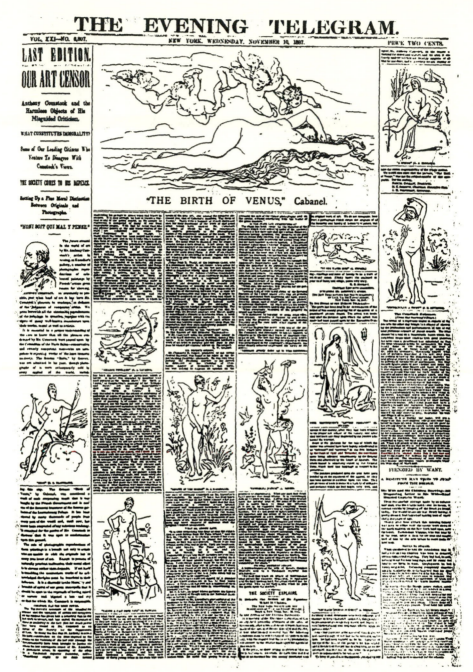

Figure 2. The *Evening Telegram* responded to Comstock's raid of Knoedler's gallery by covering its front page with sketches of the artwork supposedly seized in the raid.

profaned, there was a more obvious target in town. But this one Comstock did not touch. As Cesnola pointed out to the *New York Herald*, Bouguereau's painting *Nymphs and Satyr* was hanging in a local saloon at the same time that Comstock arrested Knoedler.[92] The painting, which shows four naked young women dragging a reluctant satyr into a brook, is probably Bouguereau's best-known work. Twentieth-century critics have commented on its sexual content. T. J. Clark describes the painting as an image of "outright and imperative lust . . . in which the nymphs take their revenge on an all-too-human satyr."[93] The *Art Amateur* moralized about the painting slightly less harshly when they noted, "The exhibition of the big Bouguereau in an up-town bar-room has paid because the peculiar character of the subject makes it popular with frequenters of the place and, altogether, it may be said that the picture is happy in its surroundings."[94] An artist commenting on Comstock's censorship also mentioned Bouguereau's painting:

> I believe the immorality of most of the pictures which contain nude figures consists principally in the manner in which they are used. The very same picture which I would rejoice to see in a friend's parlor, and would contemplate with enthusiasm, I would unhesitatingly condemn as immoral if used in a place where the nudity was simply made a thinly-disguised source of exciting immoral or lewd thoughts.
>
> Take, for example, one which is known to all in this city. I feel, and I have no doubt the artist Bouguereau feels, for he must know of it, the burning disgrace of having his lovely picture hung in a prominent bar-room. I stated, when I first heard of it, as I state to-day, and I am sure I am upheld by all the artists in this city whom I care to meet, that were it my best work I would rather have it burned and lost for ever than to have it so placed. Bar-room associations are not the accompaniments for a proper appreciation of such a picture. Yet, I have no doubt, many will view it as I did, even since it has been placed there, with actual pleasure and benefit, as far as the picture and my own personality alone were concerned.[95]

If Comstock wanted to choose a case in which art was profaned by not being confined to museums, this was an obvious choice. But instead he arrested Knoedler. Perhaps prosecuting the saloon owner who displayed *Nymphs and Satyr* would have been equally unsuccessful. That Comstock went after Knoedler implies that he thought he could successfully prosecute dealers of photographic reproductions no matter what their class or clientele, but that original canvases were off-limits. He was mistaken. In any case, Comstock's weak arguments that he was trying to protect art from profanation are belied by his other statements about the paintings he was supposedly protecting.

## Photographic Demoralization and Evil Nudes

Comstock was ambivalent about art. His statement that the "power of evil" of the nude would be far less if it was kept "in its proper place" suggests that, while political pragmatism kept Comstock's censoring hands off original oil paintings, he dearly wished that Bouguereau's paintings had stayed in France.[96] Before Knoedler's arrest Comstock had expressed contempt for admirers of the nude, and the most protection he could offer was exemption from his own censorship.

> Art has no right to trample on virtue, and excite lascivious passions in the minds of youth, certain to lead to vicious practices. The silly cant of modern apostles of "high art" and "aestheticism" deserves, and as we are glad to see it is receiving, the contempt of an intelligent public. Even if specimens of "high art" according to the fleshly school are to be tolerated in picture galleries and museums, there is no justification for their exhibition in shop windows on our public thoroughfares.[97]

The power for spreading evil inherent in nudes was realized when they were available to the general public, but Comstock and the leaders of the NYSSV were uncomfortable with nudes in originals as well. Comstock and his supporters disdained the ideal of aestheticism, and argued instead that art was beautiful only when it was moral. Morality had priority over aesthetics; furthermore, the promotion of morality created aesthetic pleasure.

> The closer art keeps to pure morality the higher its grade. Artistic beauty and immorality are divergent lines. To appeal to the animal in man does not inspire the soul of man with ecstasies of the beautiful. Every canvas which bears a mixture of oil and colors on it is not a work of art. The word "art" is used as an apology for many a daub.[98]

Comstock cited the president of Rutgers College, Merrill E. Gates, who asserted that the "cry of art for art's sake" is made by those who "fail to understand the first principle of all art," that it must suggest "the beauty of holiness."[99] Using this logic, Comstock asserted that nudity might be acceptable but nudes inciting sexuality were not, and that nudity could not be tolerated when "the brow" is "insincere" or "the physical beauty suggests moral ugliness."[100] Judging artistic value on the basis of sincerity and moral purity gave censors a say in artistic content and display.

Comstock was angered at his censure by the Society of American Artists, and one goal of *Morals versus Art* was to refute the artists' claim that Knoedler's arrest and the suppression of photographic reproductions damaged art. Referring to the argument that photographic reproductions educated the public's taste, Comstock retorted,

It is said the exposing to public view of the nude figures of women is "an educator of the public mind." It may educate the public mind as to the form of beautiful women, but it creates an appetite for the immoral; its tendency is downward; and it is in many cases a blight to the morals of the young and inexperienced.[101]

Not only did the NYSSV attack the claim that a public educated to hold more refined artistic taste would embrace rather than condemn the nude, they attacked aestheticism. The Reverend Charles Parkhurst defended the society against the condemnation of artists by saying

We will assume that these artists are honest, and that what they have said is not put forth because they wish to defend that which is vile. We do not need to believe that. But they have an overmastering art sense. They can look at a picture that in its very constitution is devilish and nasty, without any sense of the vileness that is in it, being so controlled and mastered by the aesthetical sense, which asserts its absurd authority over all the others.[102]

Clearly this was a battle over who would judge the content of art. In contrast to press assertions that artists should censor because they were artistically trained and thus qualified to judge art, Parkhurst argued that constant exposure to nudes had numbed the artists' moral sense. If art must be moral, then the censors had a say in artistic content: the leaders of the NYSSV were not qualified art critics but they were qualified moral police. Samuel Colgate, president of the NYSSV, asserted:

But we are "incompetent persons." They mean we are not expert judges of fine art. Perhaps so. That is not our business. It is not Art that is on trial; but Immorality. If the picture is calculated to carry impure ideas, or tends to excite prurient passions, and thus destroy the character of our youth, that picture is condemned, however artistic the work may be. We are not incompetent to judge of the moral quality of the picture, having received a fifteen years education in this work.[103]

In making such arguments the leaders of the anti-vice society recapitulated a controversy about the nude that had raged in elite American periodicals a decade earlier. In 1879, *Appleton's Journal* published an editorial complaining about "certain literary and art folk" who condemned their opponents as "Philistines."

To take a literary view of art—which means, we believe, to judge of a picture by its motive and story rather than by its *technique*—is to be a Philistine; to assume that art and poetry are not the highest things in life is to utter rank Philistinism; to intimate that morality should be a force and a factor in the arts is to show oneself wholly incapable of discerning the high purpose of aesthetics, and as a consequence to merit being cast into the darkness and dreariness of Philistinism for ever. No art topic is so dangerous in this way to laymen as that of the propriety of nudity in art.[104]

In a later issue *Appleton*'s editor asserted that artists were particularly incompetent when it came to judging morality in art—the public could look to artists for education in the principles of art, but should look to moral experts for standards of artistic morality.[105] Two issues were at stake in the struggle over the nude in art. One was control over the use of nudes as a cultural symbol: Would the nude be a vehicle of profit for hucksters and pornographers, or would it be a symbol of the upper-class aesthetic sense? The second issue was control over the content of high art. This involved the place of artists in determining the upper-class symbolic repertoire. Was the object of art to illustrate and support the moral values of the upper class, or did the privileged positions of artists in the realm of aesthetics mean that art could subvert the values of the dominant class? The role of art in the reproduction of the upper class was a particular concern of NYSSV.

## The Nude and Class Reproduction

Comstock raised three distinct issues of class reproduction in the struggle over art: the first was family reproduction and the proper socialization of elite children; the second, the reproduction of the social relationship between the upper class and the masses of workers; and the third, the reproduction of social relations within the dominant class, in particular, whether the values of the newly monied would subvert the values of the old.

Comstock explained art censorship with the same argument used to justify arresting pornographers—he was protecting the chastity of children. When art promoted sexual dissolution, it threatened children's morals.

> There is nothing on earth more chaste or beautiful than a modest and chaste woman, unless it be that of innocent childhood, and *that chastity every chivalrous man ought to defend and protect.* The nude in art is a menace upon this chastity. The youth of this country to-day are being cursed by the dissemination of pictures where woman is exposed to vulgar gaze, through the medium of photography and art. There is nothing more repulsive than an unchaste woman; there is nothing more seductive than a beautiful woman. Art has been employed to reproduce and represent all of these characteristics. And when art lends its charms to the seduction of the harlot, the law stretches out its strong arm over the heads of innocent children and says, "You shall not approach these innocent ones to contaminate them."[106]

When art excited youthful sexuality, Comstock argued, it could "fan the flame of secret desires," a particular problem for young men "cursed with secret vices."[107] Thus art, like common pornography, threatened children, including upper-class children.

Fear of the working class suffused Comstock's discussions of art. He implied that the spread of artistic nudes could diminish the social distance between the dominant class and their inferiors. Comstock argued that many children "inherit tendencies to lust and intemperance," and that exposing such "weak ones" to nudes could damage their susceptible minds.[108] But it was not charity for the poor that dictated keeping photographic reproductions of French nudes from their vulnerable hands. Working-class boys who looked at nudes were a threat to "respectable" girls and women.[109] Asking the reader to "consider the throngs about windows where nude or partially nude figures are exposed," Comstock raised the issue of how boys looking at such art would look at women.

> Nude in art unclothes beautiful women. To thus expose her in public is to rob her of that modesty which is her most beautiful mantle. It is food for impure imaginations, and provokes comment among the evil-minded. . . . By what right does a few selfish men. . . . denude woman for the inspections of others or seek to put these representations of nudity upon the open market for all classes to gaze on?[110]

Comstock connected his attack on art to nativism by arguing that youth were endangered by "a foreign foe" in the form of "lewd French art."[111] This linked nativist sentiments directed against immigrants in American cities to foreign art—which he implied was yet another dangerous import.

The attack on French art met with one major obstacle: the upper class of New York collected it. Clement Bowers, a painter, noted that Comstock, "if left alone . . . will probably take another of his moral fits and walk into the mansions on Fifth Avenue and seize the paintings hung there."[112] Knoedler's brother pointed out that Comstock's supporters owned pictures of nudes—indeed, he claimed, they owned the originals of the pictures Comstock seized.[113] Comstock partially evaded this problem by defining "pure" nudes as beautiful, not diabolical, but this left the problem of impure art, which could appear in originals as well as reproductions. Comstock attempted to resolve the contradictions between the class that patronized him and the art they patronized by playing upon divisions within the upper class. New York was home to the Four Hundred, a clique of parvenus and scions of older fortunes with a taste for extravagant living; the city was a magnet for those with new fortunes. Comstock attempted to justify his attack on art imported from France by defining it as a product of parvenu taste. He quotes the following from an address entitled "Some Growing Evils of the Day," published by the Religious Society of Friends of Philadelphia.

With the cultivation of what are known as the "fine arts," and through the opportunities which wealth affords, there have been introduced on this side of the Atlantic many works of the acknowledged masters in painting and sculpture, which are commended as models of art, and have thus been accepted as a standard to be followed. Some of these, which are in keeping with modes of life and a code of morals utterly at variance with the pure teachings of the gospel, are tolerated and admired in cultivated society, forgetting that no cover of artistic excellence or stamp of classical reputation counts for anything in the divine sight as an excuse for that which prompts unholy thoughts.[114]

When Comstock argued that "pure minds" or a "noble character" were not made by "elegant dress, lavish expenditure, proud position, and arrogant ways," he alluded to resentments within the upper class. Elite fragmentation explains Reverend Charles Parkhurst's attack on the upper-class critics of the NYSSV.

The readiness with which they take sides when anything is brought up in the way of criticism upon this Society, and ally themselves on the side of filth, is, indeed, amazing. I find in the houses of persons connected with my congregation, pictures on the wall that I would not look at after the rest of the family came in. . . . I am not speaking of simple nudity. I am talking about pictures that cultivate the most diabolical animal instincts in the mind of the beholder. The Bible gives us to understand that men and women are to be clothed. There is to-day, in the homes of the "best families," what are called "works of art," but which I call obscenity. In them women are stark naked. What are you going to do, with these scenes prevailing in the very centres of society? How can these parents expect to do the work of the Lord Jesus Christ, with such agencies working their hellish influences in the minds of the children?[115]

Parkhurst questions the validity of art as a means of class reproduction, opposing the arts to biblical morality (and Victorian ethics). Furthermore, he suggests that competition within the upper class over who would control the nature and content of cultural capital was at issue in the controversy over Knoedler's gallery.

While Comstock equivocated about the nude in an attempt to avoid offending his elite supporters, some defenders of censorship had no such qualms. The Reverend Dr. Howard Crosby, a vocal supporter of both censorship and Comstock, disparaged persons who displayed nudes.

Fashionable people buy these pictures because they are nasty. They make a pretense of buying them because of their artistic beauty, but this is all a farce. Fashionable people want to be as nasty as they can and still stay out of prison, and I think that the suppression of all such paintings, or copies of them, is perfectly right, and I hope that all these voluptuous pictures of the last Paris Salon will be among the first to be suppressed.[116]

For years the NYSSV had been sustained by the contributions of persons who were willing to be identified with Comstock's attacks on pornographers. These wealthy supporters were certainly unwilling to see themselves as consumers of obscene materials. During the campaign against common pornography, ideologies about immigrants and the poor allowed for its construction as a threat to the purity of respectable children. The arrest of Muller for selling cheap photographic reproductions of paintings in a poor section of the city was a plausible extension of the crusade against the impure. But the arrest of Knoedler, one of the city's leading art dealers, questioned the purity of the upper class itself. By arguing that the reproduction of pure children and pure families was endangered by the sexuality prevalent in art, Comstock ran afoul of another aspect of class reproduction, namely, the formation of a separate sphere of high culture. While attacks on gamblers and immigrants had united the projects of family reproduction and class reproduction, with the censorship of Knoedler, Comstock found himself caught in a contradiction between these two projects. Class issues permeated the controversy about Knoedler, arising in discussions of Knoedler's and its patrons, the identity of consumers of photographic reproductions, the effects of nude art on upper-class children, and in who would be blamed for the appearance of Salon art within factions of the upper class itself.

## Art and Justice: Knoedler and the Court

The law had been on Comstock's side in the Muller case. A jury in New York City's Oyer and Terminer Court, presided over by Judge John R. Brady, convicted Muller. The case was appealed to the general term of the Supreme Court of the State of New York, which unanimously upheld the conviction, and then sent it to the Court of Appeals, where it was again upheld.[117] When Comstock indicted Knoedler for selling obscene pictures, including four that had been the basis for the conviction of Muller, he must have assumed that convicting Knoedler would be a simple matter. It was not. Within days of the arrest, Comstock's legal support began unraveling.

First to defect was Judge Brady. In an interview with the New York *Herald* he stated that the jury had determined the pictures to be obscene, but that one must "read between the lines" of the decision of the Court of Appeals in order to understand the implications of the Muller case. Brady pointed out that the pictures themselves were not entered as evidence in the appeals, so none of the higher courts had ever ruled on whether the paintings were obscene. Brady went on to criticize the law itself.

> My position, of course, prevents me from speaking with freedom on this subject, but I may surely say that if I had been a legislator I would never have voted for this law. Originally designed to cover vulgar and obvious violations of morality in art and literature, it is framed in such a way that it is impossible to draw a general line of distinction between what in nude art is legally permissible and that which is not. I think that too large and too dangerous a discretion is lodged in the hands of the officer who is charged to see that the law is obeyed.[118]

While Comstock lost the support of Brady—indeed, according to Brady he would never had it—the retired Supreme Court justice Noah Davis, who had previously spoken on behalf of the NYSSV, offered his support.[119] While the *New York Herald* merely reported Davis's comments, the *Star*, a Democratic daily with a circulation of fifty-five thousand, lambasted Davis because of his earlier rulings on the sale of liquor on Sundays. Davis had asserted that there must be no discrimination in the application of the law, a comment the *Star* editorial deemed "sapient." Davis asserted that there was a great difference between an original picture and a photograph, to which the *Star* replied,

> The ex-Judge evidently believes that there is a great difference between a photograph and an original, because in his own drawing room hangs a study of female figures to which Mr. Comstock might properly take objection. As to discrimination in the law, it is very properly shown in every criminal trial. Assuming that Knoedler & Co. have unwittingly violated its provisions, would Mr. Davis subject them to the same punishment that he would a peddler in the Bowery, whose customers brought the same photographs because they were studies in the nude, and not because they were representations of works of art.[120]

The withering attacks by the press were apparently too much for District Attorney Randolph Martine, who on November 20 released to the press two letters from Comstock and his own reply. The first letter from Comstock asks Martine to examine the November 16 edition of the *Evening Telegram*, which displayed the nude sketches on its front page. Comstock requested Martine's assistance in this matter:

As it is a personal attack upon me I do not deem it wise for me to appear as a prosecutor, or to take action until the matter is submitted to you for your judgment and advice. Is not this a proper matter to submit to the Grand Jury, which is now in session?

Receiving no response, Comstock sent another request the next day, pleading for help. The *Herald* printed this letter under the subheading "Anthony Crawls," not an unfair comment on its tone.

I am ready to do anything that you shall direct or command in the premises, but having failed to hear from you or see you when I called, I have not taken any action, except to submit the matter to you.

I want you to feel, dear Mr. Martine, in this matter that I am simply anxious to serve you, and will go to any extent that you shall designate. Of course, if you do not think it wise to take any steps in the matter it would be foolish for me to inaugurate a prosecution that you disapproved of.

Mr. Martine did not think it wise to prosecute the *Evening Telegram*, and probably did not appreciate being credited with approving the arrest of Knoedler. In any case, Comstock was told that he could proceed with the case before a police magistrate but not a grand jury.[121] Martine's unwillingness to proceed against the *Telegram* curbed Comstock's willingness to make yet more arrests in the Knoedler matter, and he retreated to prepare his next salvoes, the publication of *Morals versus Art* and the trial of Knoedler.

*Morals versus Art* displays Comstock's conviction that the law was on his side, in spite of Judge Brady's warnings to the contrary. Much of the text is a primer of legal precedents for the Knoedler arrest, beginning with English common law. Comstock attempted to establish that Knoedler's arrest did not exceed the limits of the law. Given the NYSSV's successes in getting legislatures to pass laws and in using the legal system to combat gambling, Comstock was confident that the law would also be on his side in this case. He told Josiah Leeds:

The issue is now sharply drawn. It is whether the lewd and indecent of the Salon of Paris may break from their bonds, cross the water and debauch the minds of the children of this country, or whether law shall be enforced and the morals of our youth protected.

I have been through a week of the grossest misrepresentations and attacks from the Press, evidently with the design on their part to divert public attention from the question in issue; but I beg to say, that I am not dismayed, and I assure you that we have the law and Right on our side.[122]

## The Press Responds to the Knoedler Decision

Technically, Comstock won the Knoedler case. Judge Kilbreth decided that the defendants should be tried on two counts of selling obscene material. The press announced Comstock's victory, noting that Kilbreth had declared two of the thirty-seven pictures seized by Comstock, *Rolla*, and *Entre Five et Six Heures en Breda Street*, obscene.[123] But this left the matter of thirty-five other pictures, including four that had been the basis of the decision against Muller.[124] Judge Kilbreth chided Comstock in court, saying that, with the exception of the two paintings named in his decision, he could not find anything in the others that was obscene or lewd.[125] When Comstock protested that young people might be corrupted by such paintings, Kilbreth retorted: "Oh, the minds of the young haven't anything to do with it. . . . If we conduct ourselves only with consideration for the minds of the young we wouldn't do a good many things we do."[126] Thus Kilbreth undermined both Comstock's claims about the legal precedents for this case as well as his fundamental claim for art censorship, which was protecting youth. Comstock declared that the judge had erred and that he would still prosecute persons who sold the four pictures found obscene in the earlier trial.[127]

Comstock won the case but lost the moral battle. Kilbreth's decision upheld Parisian criteria about morality in art. In Paris, only realistic portrayals of prostitution rendered a painting obscene, and it is likely that both *Entre 5 et 6 Heures en Breda Street* and *Rolla* violated this criterion. Although the former painting seems to be lost, Breda Street was the center of Parisian prostitution, so sexual commerce was a likely theme of that painting. Gervex's *Rolla* was thrown out of the 1878 Salon as indecent. The painting depicts Rolla, a debauched son of the bourgeoisie, about to commit suicide after spending his last money on a night of pleasure with Marie, a beautiful young prostitute.

The press continued to take a dim view of Knoedler's arrest. The *New York Times* opined that since thirty-five of thirty-seven canvases that Comstock had based charges on were declared not obscene, his judgments were wrong 94 percent of the time, and his powers should be reduced.[128] The *Star*, a Democratic daily paper (the same paper that accused Judge Noah Davis of hypocrisy on the subject of nudes), took the occasion to take another swipe at the rich:

> This morbid Procrustes would not only destroy many of the masterpieces of the world in painting and sculpture and gut the galleries of Europe, but play sad havoc with canvasses and statues which grace the houses of our own wealthy connoisseurs. The same principle carried

a little farther would make Mr. Comstock the sumptuary dictator of fashions in female costume. People mingling much in fashionable society see gleaming necks and marble busts exposed with generous liberality. Certainly this living rose-tinted statuary is, in the Comstockian sense, quite as demoralizing as the painted or marble counterfeits of the human form divine. The nude in art indeed cannot compare in its appeal to the amorous emotions with the breathing loveliness clasped in gowns which "half concealing, reveal the more." Imagine the picturesqueness of a scene at a police court when Comstock carries his logic to the last result in practice! A throng of beautiful virgins and matrons netted by the police and scrutinized by the judge as to whether they are decently attired or not.[129]

Given Comstock's pronouncements that nudes should be kept away from the masses, this sarcasm seems warranted. Yet in spite of the snide comments about the rich, even the *Star* ultimately supported the anti-obscenity efforts of the NYSSV, stating that Comstock's excesses in the area of art were unfortunate because "in spite of all his faults, the public cannot afford to have him make a laughing stock of himself." This was a curious endorsement, as Comstock had gained considerable support by attacking the Democratic Party.[130]

Although Comstock claimed that he would still try to prosecute the persons selling reproductions of the pictures that had been the basis of the Muller conviction, the Knoedler fracas convinced the NYSSV to turn to other issues The coffers of the organization suffered somewhat from the Knoedler prosecution, although given the irregular pattern of contributions, the Knoedler case was not especially devastating (see table 7.1). Comstock dropped the issue. The Knoedler case was not discussed in the NYSSV *Annual Report* for 1889, the first report to be made after Kilbreth rendered his decision. The only mention of art censorship was the arrest of a man who sold photographs composed of the bodies of French nudes and the faces of "reputable" girls, presumably a prosecution that the upper class would support.[131] Comstock returned to the prosecution of gamblers, the issue that had boosted his campaign in the early 1880s.

The Knoedler case was a spectacular rebuke to the New York anti-vice society's attempt to further extend their domain. Comstock's defeat came not only from a poor tactical decision to arrest an art dealer who was one of the leading arbiters of high culture in New York City. It came as well because the role of high culture in forming upper-class identities was contested. Comstock and his supporters offered an image of an upper class that showed its morality by shunning displays of artistic nudes. Comstock attempted to circumvent criticism by turning to the issue of originals versus reproductions, but at various times he stated the issue as one

TABLE 7.1
Contributions to the NYSSV, 1873–1893

| | Amount ($) | | Amount ($) |
|---|---|---|---|
| 3/1/72 to 1/28/74 | 7,508.25 | 1884 | 7,909.07 |
| 1874 | 2,844.00 | 1885 | 7,729.39 |
| 1875 | 5,185.93 | 1886 | 8,776.49 |
| 1876 | 6,240.40 | 1887 | 7,941.16 |
| 1877 | 6,979.75 | 1888 | 8,003.74 |
| 1878 | 6,631.30 | 1889 | 6,758.78 |
| 1879 | 7,168.44 | 1890 | 8,942.03 |
| 1880 | 7,563.58 | 1891 | 7,637.15 |
| 1881 | 7,462.11 | 1892 | 9,343.17 |
| 1882 | 7,978.52 | 1893 | 6,971.32 |
| 1883 | 9,462.14 | | |

Source: NYSSV, Annual Reports, 1873–93.

of containing the power for evil that was inherent in paintings of naked women. In doing so he followed the lead of Howard Crosby, the minister who had started the American debate about the nude in art in 1879 and who had vehemently supported Comstock during the Knoedler case. Defenders of the nude responded to critics by quoting the scriptural text, "Unto the pure all things are pure." Crosby used this text to attack those who collected nude art.

> Instead of justifying a man's praise of a Titian's Venus, this Scripture declares that a pure man would not possess such a libidinous picture. It is under such false quotations as this, and under a sickening cant about "high art," that Christians are filling their parlours with statuary and paintings calculated to excite the lowest passions of the young. There is a natural pruriency that is charmed with this dilettantism among indecent things, as the polite distance to which refinement can go in licentiousness. It would be apposite to ask how many youth is unable to restrain within these bounds, after having thus far inflamed their desires. God has clearly shown us that the human body is to be covered. Art comes forward and declares, in direct opposition to God, that the human body shall be stark naked. Christians leave God and follow Art. Then when we tell these Christians that they are aiding vice, they ridicule our verdancy, and call on the world of culture to join them in the laugh.[132]

Art censorship reflected a struggle over what it meant to be upper class. The NYSSV's attempt to define the nude as an inappropriate symbol of upper-class culture clearly failed. It failed because a substantial fraction of New York's upper class sought to justify and sustain their privilege by adopting European high culture as their own. The conflict over Knoedler, and Comstock's failure, is thus partially explained by the cultural process of the formation of upper-class identities. But the Knoedler fracas also resulted from competition between New York's upper-class cliques. Rhetoric about "fashionable people" used to disparage Salon art and its collectors referenced resentments generated by competing segments of the upper class, as well as middle-class resentment of the fabulously wealthy. The importance of upper-class fragmentation in New York City in explaining the trajectory and success of censorship is underscored when one examines the censorship activities of Comstock's compatriots in Boston.

## Art Censorship in New York and Boston

The comparison of Comstock's censorship with that of the New England anti-vice society reveals that organizational, structural and ideological factors influenced the success of censorship, and ultimately of the two organizations. The Boston anti-vice society was more adept at handling the publicity that might result from controversial censorship actions; furthermore, the cohesion of Boston's upper class made censorship less controversial.

The leaders of the NESSV preferred to censor without publicity. The most striking example of this is that they did not admit that they were the force behind the suppression of Whitman's *Leaves of Grass* until more than a decade later.[133] The threat of prosecution seemed to ensure the cooperation of Boston's booksellers; in New York, when Comstock threatened Knoedler with arrest for selling obscene reproductions, his warning was ignored. The NESSV's shunning of publicity can be interpreted in two ways. It could have reflected organizational tactics that differed from Comstock's. But the silence of the NESSV could also have reflected its strength. The NESSV drew more support from Boston's upper class than the NYSSV drew from New York's elite; this difference, I argue, not only influenced the success of the two societies but reflects underlying structural differences in the two cities.

Organizational differences are reflected in the nature of the *Annual Reports*. The reports of the NESSV are shorter and tend to factual statements of the activities of the society. In contrast, the reports from the New York society contain elaborate justifications for anti-vice work, diatribes about art, and anxiety-arousing exposés about threats to the reproduction of the upper class. Comstock's efforts to create a consensus about his work reflect the underlying lack of consensus in New York's upper class about what constituted appropriate upper-class culture.

New York's upper class was less cohesive than Boston's. In part, this was a matter of sheer size: in 1892 New York was home to 1,078 millionaires, Boston to 216.[134] But more important than size was New York's role as the mecca of newly minted millionaires. The status competition in New York's upper class fragmented consensus about high culture. Upper-class fragmentation in New York City made the formation of cultural symbols more contentious, which was particularly problematic in an era when institutions of high culture were being established. The Metropolitan Museum of Art remained an institution separate from the venerable New York Historical Society because the trustees of the latter organization considered the pedigrees of the founders of the Met too unfashionable; similarly, the Metropolitan Opera was founded when Vanderbilt was unable to buy a box at the Academy of Music.[135] The barbs Comstock aimed at "fashionable society" and Reverend Parkhurst's attack on nudes on the walls of the homes of New York's "best families" may reflect their perception that flashy new millionaires embraced Salon nudes as their status symbol. This may have been the case—art historian E. P. Richardson has credited the Four Hundred with popularizing Salon art in the United States.[136] If New York's new money looked to Europe to gain status, then the claim raised by various defenders of Knoedler that Paris would laugh at them and their cultural institutions must have stung.

Bostonians displayed more public prudery in matters of art than did New Yorkers, which implies more consensus about matters of nudity in art. Before the Museum of Fine Arts could be opened it took two special meetings to decide what to do about the genitals on the museum's statues—after rejecting the suggestion that men and women should be admitted to these exhibits on separate days, the directors outfitted the statuary with fig leaves.[137] The difference in upper-class consensus about art in Boston and New York was perfectly exemplified in 1896, when MacMonnies's statue *Baccante and Infant Faun*, commissioned for display in Boston's Public Library, was driven from town by Bostonians who found the depiction of a nude and intoxicated woman dancing with her infant an affront to decency and motherhood. The statue was moved to New York, where it occupied a "place of honor" in the entrance hall of the Metropolitan Museum of Art.[138]

This greater cultural consensus about art left the leaders of the Boston anti-vice society free to devote more time to problems such as prostitution, which made sexual impropriety available to respectable youths, rather than to conflicts over upper-class culture. But it is also the case that the New England society seemed reluctant to enter controversies over art that did arise in Boston. In 1884 the patrons and leaders of the Museum of Fine Arts were considerably exercised about a painting by Regnault entitled *Automedon and the Horses of Achilles*. The painting depicted an almost naked Automedon holding two rearing and prancing horses; in contrast to the total undress of most female nudes, however, Automedon donned a cloak. The museum's art students were so enthused about the painting that they raised a subscription fund and bought it for the museum. One defender of the painting, Ralph Wormeley Curtis, commented on the painting by claiming: "As to diet, we firmly believe that juicy (underdone, if you will) porterhouse steak, broiled on red-hot coals, by Henri Regnault, is more 'healthful pabulum' than mushy *tête de veau* art boiled in Preraphaelite tepid water."[139]

The NESSV made no comment about this controversy, either in their Executive Committee *Minutes* or in the *Annual Reports*. In spite of their willingness to censure literature, albeit privately, the NESSV did not venture an opinion on an artistic exhibit until 1891, when it published a complaint in the *Evening Transcript* about a painting exhibited in the Boston Art Club. They did not say what painting was at issue, but their rhetoric was Comstockian:

> The limits of moral purity in art are not easily defined. Protests against special instances of indelicacy are not to be confounded with indiscriminate condemnation of the nude. The real issue is between the modest and the immodest, whether draped or undraped. Lofty genius and elevation of spirit may redeem any representation of the human form from sensuality. The Venus di Milo conspicuously illustrates this. But that there is an ideal treatment of the nude in painting and sculpture, by no means proves that nudity is always pure and innocent. There are works which no respectable exhibition committee would tolerate for an instant. Such committees always have their standards of propriety. Our complaint is that this standard is often inadequate.
>
> At the winter exhibition of the Boston Art Club there was admitted a painting which we believe to have been immodest, indecent, and wholly objectionable. It was unfit for the place. Its natural destination would have been the liquor saloon or the brothel. It was an affront to those invited to the gallery. . . .
>
> We have a right to expect of exhibition committees that they reject works of art which will make every modest woman blush, or inflame a man's coarser passions; we have a right to ask those who provide models, whether living or in marble or plaster, for our art classes, especially for those made up of women, that they carefully cherish those instincts of maidenly innocence and reserve which we all revere; and in these and all departments of art or literature we bear in mind that the only effectual safeguard for the moral purity of the young or old is the panoply of intuitive delicacy and moral sensitiveness.[140]

Two things are especially notable about this protest. First, it came after the fact—the wording of it indicates that the painting was already gone. This might have been an attempt to avoid attracting attention to the painting. Certainly the NESSV would not have wanted to create a mob anxious to look at the painting, as happened when Leeds protested against the exhibit in Philadelphia. Second, two days after this notice appeared a member of the Executive Committee resigned. Blodgett's letter of resignation reveals his misgivings about the society's policies:

> To be frank with you, I haven't the kind of stuff in me that makes me desire to help other people against their own wishes, and our Society's work seems to be largely an attempt to benefit a public which is at best irresponsive, and more frequently flatly opposed to help in the quarter where we offer it. The impossibility of dealing satisfactorily with such a public on questions of purity, where the morbid puritan self-consciousness makes their very discussion unwelcome, and where the modern distrust of the old aestheticism is—with good reason—prevalent, has made me feel that I at any rate am not adapted for that work.[141]

Blodgett had been a member of the Executive Committee since 1885, and he had stayed with the NESSV through prosecutions of brothel owners, gamblers, and vendors of "vile books."[142] Blodgett's resignation did not, however, dissuade the leaders of the anti-vice society from continuing their campaign against impurity in the theater.

## Art and Theater in Boston

The first campaign against the theater launched by the NESSV involved a play called *The Clemenceau Case*. The license of Boston's Park Theatre was revoked on account of the play, although the NESSV was not explicit about their role in this action. The play went to Lynn, pursued by agent Henry Chase, who was intent on preventing its performance. The pressure of the NESSV forced the company to expunge all objectionable material and, after three performances, return to New York.[143] Six months later the NESSV tried to close a play at the Howard Athenaeum. Although their original complaint to the Board of Aldermen is lost, the reply they received from H. S. Carruth, chairman of the Board of Aldermen, reveals that the NESSV had been instrumental in getting the aldermen to act against the Park Theatre. It also discloses criteria invoked in censoring plays.

> Your request to Ald. Stacey that the Board should visit the Howard Athenaeum in order to ascertain the character of the play there being produced was communicated to me by the alderman, and on Monday night a majority of the Board, of which I was one, visited the place. I had been led to expect from the bills posted upon the streets that the performance was of a decidedly questionable character, but upon exam-

ination at the theatre itself it was developed that the play was one of a class vulgar and objectionable, in a certain sense, but not such as would warrant any action on the part of the authorities. The play is vastly superior to the advertisements, and no such exposure of the person appears on the stage as one would be led to expect from the bills. The advertisement that a certain character would appear in costume, or lack of costume, which was used in the model scene of "The Clemenceau Case," failed to materialize. No such scene was produced on the stage.

I regret, as much as you can, the necessity which seems to exist for having such places of amusement, but the public temper, while it may sustain a Board of Aldermen in the revocation of a license for the production of such a play as "The Clemenceau Case," would unquestionably not do so in the case of the present play at the Howard. The character of the audience was such as usually assembles at that place and at the dime museums in that vicinity. It was almost exclusively composed of the male sex, with here and there a solitary woman, but there was no uproarious behavior on the part of the audience as was the case at "The Clemenceau Case," and no such direct appeals to the lower passions. I shall be happy at all times so long as I remain a member of the Board of Aldermen to exercise all the power that resides in me as a member of that board for the protection of the public morals, and at any time you have reason to believe that any play is being given or to be given which in its character demands investigation, I shall be most happy to do so, even at the risk of being called a prude.[144]

Theater censorship was aimed at the amusements of the working class, not of Boston's elite. The criterion for censorship was "uproarious behavior" of the crowd, apparently incited by the clothing or lack thereof of actresses. Like Comstock, the aldermen were guided in their judgments by lack of clothes of the players and by the social class and behavior of the audience who gazed at the spectacle.

This letter points to some differences in the censorship of books and theater, and between censorship in Boston and New York. First, censorship of Boston theater involved gaining the cooperation of the aldermen, while the censorship of books involved making direct threats to booksellers. As late as 1891 the NESSV complained of books that it could not censor; in spite of the suppression of Whitman, the reputation of Boston as a book-banning city was secured during the 1890s. By 1895 booksellers asked the Watch and Ward about possible prosecutions before selling possibly objectionable books.[145] However, the fate of *The Clemenceau Case* implies that the NESSV was able to exercise a much heavier hand against the theater than the NYSSV wielded in New York. Furthermore, the stated willingness of Carruth to cooperate with the NESSV—in spite of the imputation of "prudery" to his actions—suggests that in Boston the censors received much more cooperation from the aldermen than Comstock gained in New York. Still, as in New York, it was easier to censor low culture than high, that is, to use the law against the cultural tastes of the poor rather than against those of the rich.

## Censorship, Class, and the Control of Culture

The issue of art censorship illustrates both the role of class in determining the nature of "high" culture and the interaction of structural and ideological factors in creating consensus about its content. When the anti-vice societies attempted to censor "culture," they engaged an issue that struck at the heart of what it meant to be upper class. When the anti-vice societies addressed problems such as the sale of obscenity on the streets or police protection of gamblers who tempted youths to squander either their wages or their fortunes, they focused on issues that had sizable potential support among parents of all classes. Comstock, as we have seen, gave a particular slant to the issue of corruption in educational institutions when he focused on the threat obscenity posed to students in private schools. Thus he made a particular appeal to upper-class parents, although the moral corruption of children by pornography was not an issue confined to the upper class. But art censorship engaged the issue of the role of high culture in creating upper-class identities—and these identities were hotly contested, especially in New York. New York's upper class was particularly fragmented, and the city was home to the Four Hundred, a group keenly attuned to European culture and aesthetics. When Comstock arrested Knoedler for selling reproductions of Salon art, he attacked the tastes of a faction of the upper class; he also argued that a significant threat to the morality of children came from within the upper class itself.

Successful censorship, especially in New York City, happened when public ire and the law were arrayed against a polluting influence emanating from the lower classes. Thus Comstock's prosecution of Muller for selling photographic reproductions of Salon art passed virtually unnoticed. Because Muller sold his pictures in the Bowery, a neighborhood notorious for vice, their suppression was not seen as an attack on the tastes or practices of the upper class. Unfortunately for Comstock, the arrest of Knoedler was.

# 8

## CONCLUSION: FOCUS ON THE FAMILY

IN THE 1870s Comstock embarked on a censorship campaign that became one of the most successful and ultimately notorious in American history. Comstock's concern about moral purity extended his censorship of common pornography into other realms: to the censorship of art, including the arrest of one of the country's leading art dealers and the suppression of Walt Whitman's poetry; the suppression of abortion and the death of the country's most notorious abortionist; the arrest and imprisonment of persons who distributed birth control, as well as those who advocated women's emancipation through the elimination of marriage; and, finally, to raids on gambling dens. At the heart of Comstock's rhetoric, I argue, was concern about the moral corruption, and social downfall, of upper- and middle-class children. Comstock was successful because this rhetoric resonated with the concerns of powerful people, in particular, their fear that their own children would be excluded from social contacts and networks vital to their future success.

In playing on the possible failure of children, Comstock touched a recurring fear in the lives of parents and family members. But to organize a campaign against obscenity, Comstock had to mobilize and target this fear. He did this by linking the possible corruption of children by obscenity to changes threatening the family from within and without. Children were threatened by sexuality, by their own unleashed desire. The damage wrought by lust linked sexual vices to gambling, the latter resulting from uncontrolled lust for riches. Disordered desire had two causes that redefined it from a permanent state of the human condition to a problem with specific causes. These causes locate the problem of lust corrupting children in a social, historical, and political context. First, Comstock linked the corruption of children to changes occurring within the middle- and upper-class Victorian family. These included the changing role of women, in particular, the increasing demand that women be responsible for orchestrating the consumption practices that cloaked her family with the status of the middle class. In increasingly anonymous cities, one's character was judged by appearance, and women were responsible for these appearances. This meant that women's role in family reproduction changed during the nineteenth century. Farm families demanded labor, including the labor of children, which required women to spend much of their lives bearing and rearing a large family. Urbanization changed the value of children, and thus the role of women, who, in the middle and upper classes, were expected to produce fewer children, who were accorded great emotional value and who were a considerable economic expense. It was this investment in the family's future that was threatened by vice, Comstock argued, but combatting the threat required women to watch more vigilantly their children rather than spend time displaying themselves in public.

Families were threatened by changes from outside as well as within. The threat of sexual corruption of children was caused, Comstock argued, by a growing sexual subculture manifested in the availability of pornography on the streets and in the increasing presence of prostitutes in the city's neighborhoods. Having located a problem, Comstock pointed at its source, blaming the spread of sexual perversion on the growing immigrant population. Immigrants threatened elite families in a variety of ways. Not only did they seek to sexually corrupt children, they potentially usurped the social niche children were being prepared to occupy. The threat of immigrants became most apparent when Comstock attempted to shut down gambling parlors, where the sons of respectable families were plied with drink and stripped of their wages, inheritance, and dignity. An obsession with gambling, as with sex, destroyed self-control and thus manliness. In the background lurked immigrant policemen, who shielded gamblers from the proper execution of justice, and immigrant politicians, who headed and profited from corrupt city governments. Dirty politicians fleeced taxpayers, extracting taxes to support jobs for legions of city employees. Poor immigrants were a public burden and danger, as the armies of criminals created by gambling required imprisonment at taxpayers' expense.

The arguments that children's futures are endangered by the presence and vices of immigrants and the poor, that children will be harmed by sexual ideas thrust upon them, that the family is failing to protect children, in part because of women's increasing presence outside of home, which also causes its breakdown from within, are hardly the sole province of quaint Victorians like Comstock. An observer of American politics at the end of the twentieth century can hardly fail to notice the echoes of Comstock's arguments in contemporary political rhetoric. Some issues addressed in recent years directly mirror Comstock's concerns about sexuality and the corruption of youth: attempts to increase parents' control over their children's consumption of music by labeling music with allegedly obscene lyrics, to restrict sex education or the distribution of contraceptives in schools, to remove textbooks from curriculums or books from school libraries because of their messages about sexuality or religion, and to pass laws mandating parental consent before a minor can receive an abortion are all issues that, in slightly altered form, the anti-vice societies addressed a century ago. The most startling echo of Comstock's nineteenth-century crusade came in February 1996, when Congress passed the Communications Decency Act. This legislation borrowed language from the 1873 Comstock Act to make it a felony to transmit "indecent" information, including information about abortion, over the Internet. Comstock's claims that children were being corrupted by materials coming into homes without parents' knowledge were reiterated a century later in discussions of children accessing "cyberporn" through computer networks.

Sometimes the sexual corruption of children is the subtext of another issue; for example, attempts to repeal legislation prohibiting discrimination against homosexuals often imply that children will be persuaded to become homosexual. Other issues in contemporary political discourse mirror nineteenth-century concerns about the changing roles of women; for example, the abortion debate can be seen as a conflict over motherhood as women's primary role, while periodic horror stories about day-care workers and centers suggest that when women leave home, they endanger their children. And finally, the defense of children becomes an issue in political matters that have little to do with sex. For example, anti–affirmative action activists have argued that affirmative action threatens their children's chances in the labor force, and campaigns to restrict illegal immigration have argued that educating the children of illegal aliens takes resources from citizens' children.

These parallels between the late-nineteenth century and the late-twentieth raise two questions. The first concerns how movements to protect children emerge from a political and social context. The second, obvious from contemporary campaigns that employ rhetoric about children and promote the interests of whites and the native born, is whether language about protecting children represents an actual concern about young people or if it is cover for racist and classist social movements.

We assume that parents love their children, that they want to do what is best for them and provide them with whatever opportunities they can. Yet if this is so, if parents seek to affirm and extend their identities through raising children, then concern that children will fail should not be confined to Comstock's time, or our own. Indeed, concern about the future of one's children should be something of a constant, an ever-available source of anxiety to be tapped by moral reformers. It is important to recognize that the future of children is a fundamental concern: the question "What's the matter with kids today?" is a perennial one, yet while concerns about children are omnipresent, moral crusades are not. The question, then, is how concerns about children get connected to larger political and social issues and anxieties, so that a moral crusade seems a plausible response to a threat to children or to the family that has its source in a larger social conflict. Concern about one's children is a constant, but its expression varies according to historical context. In Comstock's time, anxiety about children was expressed in a context in which women's roles in the family were changing, in which the meaning of marriage changed as romantic love became sexualized and divorce more common, and where large numbers of immigrants threatened the political power of the native born. In our time, a variety of moral reform movements have arisen in a context in which women's family roles are changing, in which the family has been fundamentally altered by divorce, in which movements for gay and women's rights have struggled to change the social meanings of gender and sexuality, and in which there is widespread concern about the effects on society of immigrants and the poor. It may be happenstance that the end of the twentieth century has found us facing a situation so similar to the end of the nineteenth. I would not argue that moral crusades concerning themselves with children always occur at a point when concerns about gender and ethnicity converge. However, although history rarely repeats itself, there is one clear lesson to be learned from Comstock: people's claims that they are trying to protect children constitute real politics. The separation of material from symbolic politics makes little sense when talking about children's futures, because much of reproducing children's material futures involves cultural processes. We should pay attention to claims about the need to protect children and the social conflicts they reference. While the expression of concern about children varies, the concern is real.

Which leads to the second question. How do we distinguish actual concerns about children from the cynical use of rhetoric about children, often employed to justify reactionary or self-interested actions? It is apparent that rhetoric about "children" does not refer to all children. Deciphering whose children are at issue in moral rhetoric provides vital clues about the source of these politics. Rhetoric about the harm of heavy metal and rap music prevalent in the late 1980s is illustrative in this regard. Leaders of the Parent's Music Resource Center argued that heavy metal posed a threat to "our own kids," encouraging them to consider inappropriate sexual behavior, drug and alcohol use, and suicide. Rhetoric about rap music, however, argued that the music's consumers were a threat to society; arguments about rap music conjured images of menacing packs of black and Hispanic teenagers creating mayhem. Anti-rap rhetoric was devoid of concern that the music would cause its listeners to harm themselves.[1] But even if privileged whites use rhetoric about "children" that refers to only their own children, this does not mean that the futures of these children, including conferring on children parents' privileges, is not a vital concern of these parents. Movement leaders may use rhetoric about children to gain supporters, but this does not mean that supporters do not have genuine concerns about their children. It is more fruitful to accept these expressions of concern as valid and try to decipher their social source.

What is particularly unfortunate about the claim that expressed concerns about children mask real desire to reproduce racial and class inequalities is that it blinds us to what might be a principal mechanism through which racial and class inequalities are reproduced—namely, by parents seeking to pass their privileges to their children. The nineteenth-century upper class, remember, founded boarding schools to shield their children from the vices of the cities, created exclusive dance classes and balls in order to ensure that their children would marry from an appropriate pool, and founded high culture institutions partly with the hope that their children would become more sophisticated cultural consumers. The institutions established by the upper class in the nineteenth century carry on this mission in the twentieth, albeit with selective inclusion of the historically disadvantaged by some elite schools.[2] In the late-twentieth century, parents who express no stated desire to reproduce racial and class inequalities do precisely that when they choose where to live based on the quality of the public schools, which is largely determined by the wealth of the community. Given that middle-class children's futures depend on the quality of the education they receive, parents' search for the best public schools is understandable. It should not be attributed to underlying racial or class motives, even if in doing so they reproduce racial and class inequalities. The motive is the future of one's children; the outcome is the reproduction of privilege.

But this opens a final question about the use of the history of a nineteenth-century moral crusade to understand events in this century: namely, if cultural markers are used to reproduce class privilege, why would people who do not enjoy class privilege support contemporary moral reform movements? A compelling answer to this question obviously would involve intensive interviews with contemporary moral reform supporters, but there is reason to believe that the desire to see one's children improve on one's own class position is an important concern of working-class parents. In *The Hidden Injuries of Class*, Sennett and Cobb tell the stories of many working men whose hopes for the future lie in their children.[3] Their interviews were aggregated into tales of "representative," although fictitious, persons. One of these was an immigrant named Kartides, who left Greece with a teaching credential but could find work only as a janitor in the United States. Although Kartides believes that he will be a janitor for the rest of his life, "he is not resigned, for there seems one path of hope left: his children. It is they who can acquire dignity in anyone's eyes, if they increase their freedom by moving up to a higher class."[4] Kartides is a strict disciplinarian, demanding that his children give him the respect that others do not, "and they're going to learn how to behave in the way I behave."[5]

The desire to have children behave in accordance with parents' standards is motivated not only by the need to feel respected, although such respect is compensation to men and women who endure degrading labor in the hopes of making a better life for the people they love. These parents demand respect because they want their children to grow up to be persons with very different lives than theirs:

> Working class fathers . . . see the whole point of sacrificing for their children to be that the children *will* become unlike themselves; through education and the right kind of peer associations, the kids will learn the arts of rational control and acquire the power to make wide choices which in sum should make the kids better armed, less vulnerable in coping with the world than the fathers are. If the child succeeds in becoming better armed, the father does so only by proxy: his sacrifice does not end in his own life the social conditions that have made him feel open to shame, prey to feelings of inadequacy.[6]

Sennett and Cobb's work was written in 1972, in an era of economic prosperity. Two decades later, working-class men find themselves unable to earn a paycheck large enough to allow their wives to stay at home, while parents fear what place their children will find in a stagnant economy that has taken a particular toll on the manufacturing sector.[7] This fear is shared by middle-class parents. The 1994 elections witnessed a simultaneous concern about the fate of white children and a blaming of immigrants and the presumably immoral poor for economic woes, both in California and nationwide. In commenting on the 1994 election Anthony Lewis noted,

> Most American families today depend on two incomes. They are working harder, but they feel they are hardly holding their own. They don't know how they are going to send their children to college, or how those children will find jobs that will put them in the middle class—or keep them there.[8]

This suggests that one could profitably study contemporary moral crusades by considering the problems of reproducing the family in a declining economy, in a situation where the economy has forced changes in women's roles, and where these issues are understood by using a language of moral decline and racial division rather than one of economic stagnation.

## Reconsidering Status
## and Class Politics

Focusing on family reproduction suggests a previously unconsidered mechanism for understanding class and status politics, as well as a reconsideration of the relationship between class and status as systems of social privilege. It suggests as well, as I have argued, a new way of thinking about the dynamics of moral reform movements.

Moral crusades have convulsed American politics, but these issues have incited little scholarship among sociologists. The dominant understandings of moral reform movements have been remarkably untouched by revolutions in the field of sociology; the vast amount of work done on classes, class cultures, and class conflict since the late 1960s has been virtually ignored by scholars of moral reform movements. For their part, and with more unfortunate consequences for sociological theory, scholars of classes and class conflict have largely failed to consider what the ruckus about family politics might suggest about their models.

The primary culprit for the state of moral reform theory has been a reading of Weber that is wholly antagonistic to Marxist interpretations. The rigid separation of "class" from "status" explanations has removed explanations of moral reform from considerations of group conflict and from the structural dynamics that generate antagonistic social groups. And for their part, Marxist scholars' focus on the mode of production, on conflicts of interests generated by relations of production, and on the formation of classes predicated on the ownership and/or control of the means of production has largely blinded them to the importance of the families that produce laborers and that the labor of men and women reproduce.

The history of the anti-vice societies, and the support given them by the wealthy and privileged, suggests a need to rethink both theories of moral reform and of existing approaches to class and status. First, I will discuss the existing approaches to moral reform movements and the problematic ways they have used Weber's discussion of class and status. Then I will turn to Marxist approaches to moral reform, specifically asking how work on class formation might inform a theory of moral reform. I will then turn to a discussion of how status and class interests can be integrated into such a theory. This discussion will rely heavily on the work of Pierre Bourdieu, but Bourdieu's theory, I argue, is plagued by a lack of attention to family politics. Moral reform movements, I argue, are properly seen as struggles over class reproduction.

## Status Frustrations, Lifestyle Politics, and Moral Reform

Between 1960 and 1978 scholarship on moral reform focused primarily on status frustration as the impetus for moral reform movements. This literature had two strands: status discontent models and status discrepancy models. What these literatures shared were the beliefs that status systems and class systems were separate systems of social classification, that moral reform movements concerned themselves with status, and not class, politics, and that the political issues addressed in moral reform movements were symbolic of underlying status discontent.

Probably the most influential book in the field of moral reform is Joseph Gusfield's *Symbolic Crusade: Status Politics and the American Temperance Movement*. In this now thirty-year-old work, Gusfield interpreted the temperance movement as a struggle between status groups. His argument is based on a reading of Weber that explicitly separates the dynamics of status from those of class. A class, argued Gusfield, "is a sociological group in the sense that its members, by virtue of their common placement in the economic structure, share common interests. They are subject to a similar fate on the market."[9] A status group, on the other hand, shares a common claim to social prestige. Furthermore, Gusfield asserted, not only are status groups and classes not equivalent, instead "the two dimensions of class and status make up two analytically separate orders of the social structure."[10] Class is the distribution of economic power based on the economic division of labor, but status is a distribution of prestige based on group qualities.

This reading of Weber goes considerably beyond what Weber appeared to mean when he separated class from status. Weber argued that the shared lifestyles characteristic of a status group are ultimately based on a shared economic, meaning class, position.[11]

> But selection is far from being the only, or the predominant, way in which status groups are formed: Political membership or class situation has at all times been at least as frequently decisive. And today the class situation is by far the predominant factor, for of course the possibility of a style of life expected for members of a status group is usually conditioned economically.[12]

While Gusfield conceded that class might ultimately "limit the existence of status," his theory of moral reform was based on conflict between these two principles of stratification and on the existence of social conflicts that were not related to class (that is, economic) conflict. Instead, "the thrust of status politics lies precisely in identifying non-economic segments as crucial in certain social and political conflicts."[13]

Gusfield was correct in arguing that important social conflicts can have noneconomic roots. However, in his formulation, status politics are not only unrelated to classes, they are a peculiar sort of politics engaged in by a particular sort of people. Status politics symbolize the lifestyles of the groups engaged in them. Persons engaging in symbolic politics are not pursuing instrumental ends; instead, symbolic politics bolster the prestige of the group supporting them. Temperance was a fight between small-town Protestants and urban Catholic immigrants, and the prestige of the native born was at stake in the temperance crusade. Thus, "in symbolic behavior the action is ritualistic and ceremonial in that the goal is reached in the behavior itself rather than in any state it brings about."[14] Gusfield argued that temperance crusaders did not care that immigrants stopped drinking so much as they wanted it acknowledged that it was morally wrong to drink. In the passage of the Eighteenth Amendment, temperance crusaders saw symbolic legitimation of the prestige of their abstemious lifestyle.

In addition to contributing the idea of symbolic politics to the moral reform literature, Gusfield also introduced the notions of cultural modernism and cultural fundamentalism. Status politics were typically engaged in by cultural fundamentalists, persons who held values emanating from the rural "old middle class."

> The cultural fundamentalist is the defender of tradition. Although he is identified with rural doctrines, he is found in both city and country. The fundamentalist is attuned to traditional patterns as they are transmitted within family, neighborhood, and local organizations. His stance is inward, towards his immediate environment. The cultural modernist looks outward, to the media of mass communications, the national organizations, the colleges and universities, and the influences that originate outside the local community. Each sees the other as a contrast. The modernist reveres the future and change as good. The fundamentalist reveres the past and sees change as damaging and upsetting.[15]

While Gusfield's explanation of the temperance movement was sensitive to cultural conflicts between the native born and immigrants that arose at a particular historical moment, his theory was modified by Zurcher and Kirkpatrick into an ahistorical model of status discrepancy. While Gusfield contended that status groups attempted to alter a disputed prestige order through symbolic politics, Zurcher and Kirkpatrick drew on Lenski's work on status inconsistency to argue that persons who were status inconsistent—meaning those whose prestige was not congruent with their economic rewards—would be most likely to support moral reform movements. Among over one hundred hypotheses tested in their analysis of pro- and antipornography groups in two sites were predictions that antipornography activists would not only be status discrepant, but that they would tend to be poorly educated, from small towns, and cultural fundamentalists.[16]

Status discontent and status discrepancy models have been harshly criticized for two failings. First, as Wallis has noted, both Gusfield and Zurcher and Kirkpatrick failed to find an identifiable status group. Gusfield's data show that by 1885 over 30 percent of the leadership of the WCTU were wives of working-class husbands, which undermines his argument that the WCTU was composed of the "old middle class." Zurcher and Kirkpatrick have the same problem, but in this case they defined the "status group" solely on the basis of support or opposition to pornography, which, Wallis asserts, is not a trait that defines a group with similar life chances. Wallis proposed that the theory of status defense be abandoned in favor of cultural defense, defined as the politics of attempting to preserve a style of life that people believe is respectable and moral, and that moral issues no longer be understood as an attempt to alter an underlying prestige system.[17]

Page and Clelland proposed in 1978 that moral reform movements be understood as "the politics of lifestyle concern," and utilized this notion to analyze a conflict over school textbooks in West Virginia. By abandoning the idea that status politics were attempts to alter the prestige system, Page and Clelland freed the politics of moral reform from analyses that had deemed such politics irrational and (merely) symbolic. However, they replaced status politics with the notion that protest movements such as the textbook controversy represented " 'a vertical cleavage in the status arrangement' between 'cultural fundamentalists' and 'cultural modernists' which cuts across economic and educational class or strata lines," a notion borrowed directly from Gusfield.[18]

Page and Clelland made a significant contribution to the moral reform literature by acknowledging that participants in moral reform movements are organizing around issues whose outcomes they care about, but by importing the idea of a "cultural fundamentalism" that cuts across class lines, they forced themselves to ignore aspects of their data suggesting that underlying class dynamics were at issue in the textbook controversy.[19] What Page and Clelland specifically precluded by making cultural fundamentalism the center of their theory was a discussion of how moral reform movements might be an aspect of class conflict. When challenged on this point, Page and Clelland argued that "any movement which ignores economic exploitation, control of the work situation, and the differential impact of schools on life chances can hardly be viewed as 'the mobilization of class-consciousness' in the traditional Marxist usage."[20] By defining class conflict as solely conflict over wages and work, Page and Clelland precluded reconsidering the relationship between class and status.[21]

Page and Clelland's reliance on cultural fundamentalism as an explanatory principle also introduced a serious problem into the field of moral reform. Cultural fundamentalism was nothing more than adherence to conservative beliefs (as defined by modern sociologists), and identification with this belief system was both divorced from group conflict and not predictable by membership in any class (or status group). This weakness in Page and Clelland's formulation became more glaring in its next incarnation, which came in 1984 when Wood and Hughes argued that moral reform movements "are an outgrowth of socialization processes and an expression of cultural values." What Wood and Hughes proposed was that people support moral reform movements because they subscribe to the principles being defended by the movements. This rather self-evident proposition is an improvement over the assertion that moral reform movements are an unconscious and irrational expression of prestige envy. But these variations on the theme of cultural fundamentalism left students of moral reform with two basic problems: how to explain why cultural fundamentalist values are important to certain groups of people, and why movements to defend cultural fundamentalist values arise at some times rather than others.[22]

Scholarship on moral reform remains trapped in arguments about status defense versus cultural fundamentalism. Recent works on moral reform have argued that the anti-abortion campaign in Britain represents a concern over cultural values and not status defense, and similar results were found in an examination of support for the Moral Majority; at the same time, others have argued that status politics do not explain the politics of the Christian Right but do explain support for the Equal Rights Amendment. These studies indicate that conceptualizations of moral reform have remained stagnant. The problem is the separation of "class" from "status" and "culture" in these theories, and the way out is to understand how culture (and the defense of cultures) is related to class. But to do that we must first consider how work on moral reform movements might be dealt with using existing Marxist paradigms.[23]

## Structural Marxism and Moral Reform Movements

Students of moral reform movements have largely failed to consider what Marxist approaches might contribute to the study of moral reform. This has happened, in part, because they are caught in debates about whether moral reform movements are about prestige systems or whether the participants are really concerned about the values their movements advance; in addition, they have accepted unquestioningly Gusfield's characterization of "class" movements as centered around the workplace. At the same time, Marxist scholars' widespread blindness about families and gender issues has made their theoretical approaches seem irrelevant to the study of moral reform.

It is easy to see why sociologists who study moral reform have ignored Marxist approaches. It was not only Gusfield who considered "class conflict" to be concerned with work relations, for many Marxists have done the same. Most Marxist sociologists have understood a "class" to be a position in the means of production, and "class interests" as determined by this position. The exemplar of this approach is Erik Olin Wright, who defines the class structure as

> a structure of relationally defined positions filled by individuals (or families) that determines the objective class interests of those individuals. . . . The concept of class structure designates a set of positions distinct from the human individuals who occupy these positions. This does not mean, of course, that the positions exist independently of people per se, but simply that they exist independently of the specific incumbents of positions.[24]

Wright argues that class interests are determined by position in the class structure, and that " 'objective class interests' are defined with respect to mechanisms of material exploitation."[25] In his schema, "class" interests are solely concerned with economic exploitation. Furthermore, other potentially exploitive but "nonclass" relations, such as those between races and genders, do not shape what classes are (as this is determined by the economic structure) but instead operate within parameters set by "class" relations.[26] Awareness of class interests, or class consciousness, is measured by Wright in answers to statements such as "Big corporations have far too much power in society today" and "If given the chance, the non-management employees at the place where you work could run things effectively without bosses."[27] While Wright acknowledges in his definitions that families, and not just individuals, have class positions, clearly nothing about those families determines class interests. Furthermore, not only does the family have no role in determining what classes and class interests are, the role of history is slighted as well. Interests in Wright's analysis are determined by static structures and not as an ongoing process of defining both class identities and class interests.[28] Wright's schema implies that moral reform movements have no relation to class struggle; to scholars of class conflict, moral reform movements are thus intrinsically unimportant.

Given the blindness to "noneconomic" conflicts built into structural versions of Marxism, it is not surprising that few attempts have been made to use Marxist approaches to explain moral reform. An attempt by Brian Elliott and David McCrone shows how the mandate to make changes in economic relations the "real" cause of anything socially interesting can warp explanations of social movements (which is the flip side of status theorists' insistence that "class" has nothing to do with morality movements). Elliott and McCrone attempt to explain the rise of the New Right in Britain with a Marxist model, arguing that the New Right, made up of small businessmen and some conservative capitalists, rebelled simultaneously against the power of the Labour Party and the changes in the occupational structure that created increasing numbers of professionals and semi-professionals, which greatly expanded the public sector and brought increasing numbers of women into the labor force.[29] With changes in the economic structure came cultural changes, particularly the rebellion of youth and changes in women's family roles, wrought partly by the feminist movement and partly by the demands of the labor market. Elliott and McCrone acknowledge that these changes in the family generated considerable anxiety among all classes, but assert, "At the heart of the struggle lie real, material interests. Property and property rights constitute the battlefield and that could be clearly seen in the conflicts of the late 1970s."[30] Elliott and McCrone label the issues of sexual morality and religion espoused by the New Right as "ideological work" performed by Thatcherites. This "ideological work . . . ensured much popular consent for a programme that greatly increases state power and is deeply hostile to the material interests of manual workers."[31] Thus it seems that working-class support of Thatcher can be explained only by false consciousness, because such support flies in the face of workers' "real, material" interests. In their model the family is principally an institution for the accumulation and inheritance of property (which the working class does not have) and for the transmission of values that sustain private property, so attempts to defend the family primarily serve to defend the interests of capitalists—indicating even more strongly that working-class Thatcher supporters acted counter to their "real" interests.

The New Right is a complex movement, involving both class and family conflict in a period of national economic decline. The explanation of this movement offered by Elliott and McCrone seems convoluted because they are so intent on asserting that the heart of the New Right is a struggle between workers and capitalists over economic issues. Family issues are, in this model, epiphenomenal. The problem with this sort of Marxist explanation is that "real" interests concern those defined by labor relations, and the family is subsumed to the needs of the labor market. The alternative is to consider how classes and class issues are historically constructed, so that they are no longer solely determined by the mode of production, which gives the family a potential place in class formation and class politics.

## Working-Class Formation and
## Upper-Class Formation

An alternative to the Marxists' static categories exists in the writings of
E. P. Thompson, whose *Making of the English Working Class* fundamentally redefined the nature of labor history. Rejecting structural approaches to defining classes, Thompson situated class in the historical
experience of class actors: "Class is defined by men as they live their own
history, and, in the end, this is its only definition."[32] But Thompson also
defined class in terms of class consciousness, which is ultimately based on
interests determined by the relations of production.

> Class happens when some men, as a result of common experiences (in-
> herited or shared), feel and articulate the identity of their interests as
> between themselves, and as against other men whose interests are differ-
> ent from (and usually opposed to) theirs. The class experience is largely
> determined by the productive relations into which men are born—or
> enter involuntarily.[33]

Thompson's work has generated an enormous amount of debate and
scholarship. One of the most important critiques comes from those who
argue that this account slights the roles of gender and family in the production of class relations and class consciousness. For example, Sewell
argues that Thompson ultimately relies on productive relations to produce consciousness, and asserts that he is mistaken in relegating everything that is not reducible to the mode of production to the realm of
experience, instead of allowing "crypto-structures" such as kinship, religion, ideology, and law to have their own dynamics and interact with
productive systems.[34] A number of scholars have raised the issue that
family and gender dynamics are an essential aspect of the development of
class identities.[35] The family life of the working class has been an essential
component of the reproduction of this class, with women often serving
simultaneously as producers of waged labor, as producers of waged laborers, and as organizers of the home, where reproduction of both takes
place.[36] Recent historical studies on working-class politics show that the
struggle for family survival leads to strategies about future work roles for
children and political action when these roles are threatened, suggesting
that the problem of middle- and upper-class family reproduction that I
have outlined is an equally vexing problem for the poor, although the
problem occurs in a different form.[37]

Much work on class formation has focused on the working class, and
on the question, When do workers become conscious of their oppression

and thus able to unite in organizations that try to alter (or overthrow) the class system that oppresses them? For example, Scott McNall, a sociologist who utilizes Thompson's historical approach to class formation, argues that politics have been central to class mobilization in American society because

> one of the ways that people have learned about the nature of their oppression and about how to articulate the values they wish to protect, is through their participation in class organization. In mobilizing, in trying to actually change the economic and political system, people create themselves as a class. Politics, broadly defined, is not secondary but central to the process of class formation in American society.[38]

McNall is probably right to include political struggles as part of class formation, particularly in the nineteenth century, a context where almost all white men could vote. But learning about "the nature of their oppression" can hardly be a hallmark of class formation for the oppressors. Sociologists who have theorized about and done historical work on upper-class formation have tended to concern themselves with the formation of the dominant class as an economic class. This approach suggests that it is through social institutions that the specific, historic form of ownership and control of the means of production is reproduced.[39] For example, Roy argues that in the late-nineteenth century, members of the "corporate segment" of the capitalist class "organized themselves as a class" by forming a network of men's clubs, private schools, and "institutions of symbolic representation," meaning high culture, that facilitated cohesion within the upper class and fostered a sense of class superiority.[40] What is not clear in Roy's account, however, is the driving force behind this class-forming (actually, association-forming) activity. Roy writes about the proliferation of upper-class associations as a conscious strategy of the members of the corporate segment: "Looking at the total pattern of organizational affiliations of corporate officials around the turn of the century, it appears that the strategy adopted by the emerging corporate class segment was that of class cohesion as the first priority."[41] Roy assumes in this argument that "class formation" strategies of the dominant classes concerned economic domination. Rather than assuming that capitalists engaged in a conscious strategy of forming themselves as a class, which assumes that they had a clearly defined and accurate notion of what their class interests were, I suggest that capitalists formed many of the institutions that furthered class cohesion because of their interest in furthering the social position of their families, and in particular, in creating a family dynasty. This required more than great wealth, for it demanded acceptance in social networks that granted prestige, or creation of new ones that could. To focus on the economic aspects of class and ignore the social, or to artificially separate "class" from "status," leads to misapprehension of how class works and of the role of families in the formation and reproduction of classes, and to blindness about the source of moral politics.

## Culture as a Class Weapon: The Work of Pierre Bourdieu

The work of Pierre Bourdieu makes culture central to both the formation and reproduction of classes. Furthermore, while most theorists of class formation have focused on the working class, Bourdieu emphasizes the reproduction of the upper classes. His greatest contribution is his attempt to dissolve the boundary between class and status systems that has resulted from a specifically anti-Marxist reading of Weber. Instead, Bourdieu argues that culture is a form of power, and that culture is used both to define and reproduce classes and to exclude people from the dominant class. This means that struggles over the meaning of cultural symbols are integral to, not separate from, class politics. Central to Bourdieu's theory is the idea of "cultural capital," which is cultural knowledge. This cultural knowledge is to some extent measured by education and can be understood (and measured) as knowledge of the arts, of literature, and of such lifestyle symbols as fine food and wine. But cultural capital is simultaneously a basis of an individual's sense of self. Cultural capital creates lifestyles, expressed both in tastes and prejudices and in ways of apprehending the world.

There are three other kinds of capital in Bourdieu's schema: economic capital (i.e., wealth); social capital, that is, the networks of persons to which one has access and the resources gained through social connections; and symbolic capital, which is the power to define the worth and legitimacy of the various forms of capital.[42] While Bourdieu ultimately defines class position by occupation, access to many occupations is gained through mobilizing cultural and social resources acquired through social networks and in the educational system.[43] Much of class power is the power to exclude others from privileged positions. Here the family becomes crucially important in class reproduction, for success in the educational system is largely a product of the cultural capital, especially styles of self-presentation, that children acquire at home.[44] Indeed, part of the cultural knowledge that constitutes cultural capital cannot be measured by educational degrees at all, for the style of appropriation of culture, such as ways of seeing and discussing art, is learned within the family.[45]

But cultural capital is not a static commodity. Instead classes, especially the dominant class, continually struggle over the meaning of various cultural symbols. These struggles take place in various fields of endeavor—the arts, sports, and fashion, to name a few. While each field has autonomy from other fields, they all become sites of symbolic conflict between classes who seek to establish the legitimacy (and thus power) of their cultural symbols.[46]

While Lamont has shown that morality is a potential basis of social exclusion, in Bourdieu's schema morality is not a basis of cultural politics or class identities.[47] Nor is morality a legitimate arena of political struggle:

> When the questions posed are in the intermediate area between morality and politics, the contamination of politics by morality and the slippage from moral indignation to political reaction is most clearly seen—especially in those whose position in social space predisposes them to a moral perception of the social world, such as the petite bourgeoisie and especially its declining fractions or individuals. Resentment is clearly the basis of the reactionary or conservative-revolutionary stances of the declining petit bourgeois who are anxious to maintain order on all fronts, in domestic morality and in society, and who invest the revolt against the worsening of their social position in moral indignation against the worsening of morals.[48]

This passage raises several important points about Bourdieu's schema. Most obviously, the statement that moral reform is the domain of the petit bourgeois clearly cannot account for the late-nineteenth-century anti-vice movement, which was supported by some of America's wealthiest and most socially prominent people. Instead, Bourdieu offers an assessment of the causes of moral reform that is no different from Gusfield's assertion that moral reform movements represent the status indignation of an "old middle class." Bourdieu's implied separation of "morality" and "politics" looks especially strange when read in a country whose recent politics have concerned "family values" and a "war on drugs." But the problem with Bourdieu's statement is not only its empirical inadequacy. What this statement points to is the lack of a politics of the family in Bourdieu's work.

This is a fairly extraordinary omission, because in Bourdieu's schema the family is the central institution for reproducing classes. While much of *Distinction* is devoted to consumption that takes place within families, and most of its illustrations are scenes of domestic life, Bourdieu never discusses the roles of the people in these families, or how power might influence the interactions of the people within them.

Bourdieu does not ignore the issue of gender altogether. Gender enters his models in both constructing classes and determining the class position of individuals. For example, while Bourdieu determines the class position of individuals largely by their occupations, he acknowledges that significant gender and ethnic groupings take place within these classes.

> The individuals grouped in a class that is constructed in a particular respect (that is, in a particularly determinant respect) always bring with them, in addition to the pertinent properties by which they are classified, secondary properties which are thus smuggled into the explanatory model. This means that a class or class fraction is defined not only by its position in the relations of production, as identified by indices such as occupation, income or even educational level, but also by a certain sex-ratio, a certain distribution in geographical space (which is never socially neutral) and by a whole set of subsidiary characteristics which may function, in the form of tacit requirements, as real principles of selection or exclusion without ever being formally stated (this is the case with ethnic origin and sex).[49]

Bourdieu appears to be making two contradictory arguments about the relationship between class and gender. In one, occupations structure classes, and gender is merely "smuggled in" as a subsidiary characteristic of people in a class. But at the end of this passage Bourdieu seems to argue that discrimination based on race and sex is a factor that structures classes themselves. This implies that racism and sexism exist independently of the cultural and economic matrix that structures classes. But Bourdieu never discusses where racism and sexism come from or what structures (or ideologies), beyond economic discrimination, sustain them.

The confusion increases when Bourdieu discusses how classes are constructed. Bourdieu argues that classes are not defined by a property or by a "chain of properties strung out from a fundamental property (positions in the relations of production)," but are defined by the "structure of relations between all pertinent properties."[50] One of the "pertinent properties" that affects the class position of an individual is the class position of a person's spouse.[51] Thus families produce children and give children a class position, while spouses determine, in part, the class position of their mates. Bourdieu's failure to understand moral reform movements, I suggest, ultimately stems from his blindness to the dynamics of gender and his failure to perceive that gender interacts with, but does not arise from, class categories. Given the importance of the family in class reproduction, I argue that morality is a legitimate arena of class struggle that often takes the form of moral reform movements.

# The Family, Class Reproduction, and Moral Reform

Bourdieu's insight that cultural symbols are an aspect of class power, and that struggles over these symbols are an essential facet of both class formation and class reproduction, is, I believe, essential to understanding moral reform movements. Equally important is Lamont's insight that moral values are a basis of social inclusion or exclusion. The sharing of cultural symbols, moral values, and views of the world is essential in forming social relationships and social networks. It is also through the use of cultural markers that people are excluded from the (potentially) interconnected social networks that constitute the dominant class. The insight that culture is power dissolves the separation of class and status that has plagued work on moral reform movements. If class boundaries are drawn, in part, on the basis of shared moral values, then struggles over morality are potentially also struggles over class boundaries. This implies that moral crusades are integral to, not separate from, class conflict.

Bourdieu also provides a crucial insight in recognizing that the family is a central institution for the reproduction of class cultures. This means that "class" is not just something that happens in "the economy" or in factories, that "class conflict" is concerned not only with wage labor, and that the family is not to be consigned to the realm of the superstructure but is centrally implicated in the process of class formation. While Bourdieu correctly places the family in the center of his theory, he does not consider the power dynamics operating within and around the family. When alterations in these power dynamics threaten family reproduction, moral crusades are likely to result.

Families become an issue in class struggle because classes are formed around families. We should consider the discourses about family, culture, and class that were used by the people who were actually engaged in the process of class formation. Both the nature of classes and the meaning of class advancement involve a significant cultural or ideological component. But they involve, most crucially, a family component. Family politics are a critical part of the contemporary political landscape. To understand moral crusades, we must understand the role of families in creating and reproducing social privilege. And if we are to understand the dynamics of social inequality, we must also focus on the family.

# NOTES

## CHAPTER 1
## INTRODUCTION

1. Anthony Comstock, *Traps for the Young* (1883; reprint, Cambridge: Harvard University Press, Belknap Press, 1967).

2. The best extant discussions of the history of censorship in Boston are Paul S. Boyer, *Purity in Print: The Vice Society Movement and Book Censorship in America* (New York: Scribner's, 1968); and Ralph E. McCoy, "Banned in Boston: The Development of Literary Censorship in Massachusetts" (Ph.D. diss., University of Illinois, 1956).

3. See E. Digby Baltzell, *Puritan Boston and Quaker Philadelphia* (Boston: Beacon Press, 1979); and Boyer, *Purity in Print*.

4. Rosalind Petchesky, *Abortion and Women's Choice* (New York: Longman, 1984); Suzanne M. Marilley, "Francis Willard and the Feminism of Fear," *Feminist Studies* 19 (Spring 1993): 123–146.

5. See Michael P. Hanagan, "New Perspectives on Class Formation: Culture, Reproduction, and Agency," *Social Science History* 18 (Spring 1994): 77–94; and *Nascent Proletarians: Class Formation in Post-Revolutionary France, 1840–1880* (Oxford: Basil Blackwell, 1989).

6. In the late-twentieth century, one way parents do this is by choosing where to live based on the quality of the public schools, which is largely determined by the wealth of the community. This reproduces both class privilege and, to the degree that wealth is disproportionately held by white people, racial segregation. The ability to pursue the strategy of giving children opportunities by moving to areas with excellent public education systems depends on the wealth of parents, but poor parents also have made residential decisions based on the quality of schools. Grossman argues that one factor driving black migration from the South to the North was the search for educational opportunities for children. See James R. Grossman, *Land of Hope: Chicago, Black Southerners, and the Great Migration* (Chicago: University of Chicago Press, 1989).

7. On moral boundaries, see Michele Lamont, *Money, Manners, and Morals* (Chicago: University of Chicago Press, 1992).

8. See David I. Macleod, *Building Character in the American Boy* (Madison: University of Wisconsin Press, 1983); Mary P. Ryan, *Cradle of the Middle Class* (New York: Cambridge University Press, 1981); and Stuart S. Blumin, *The Emergence of the Middle Class* (New York: Cambridge University Press, 1989).

9. The literature on cultural capital is vast. The most important recent works are Pierre Bourdieu, *Distinction* (Cambridge: Harvard University Press, 1984); and Lamont, *Money, Manners, and Morals*. The concept of cultural capital is reviewed in Michele Lamont and Annette Lareau, "Cultural Capital: Allusions, Gaps, and Glissandos in Recent Theoretical Development," *Sociological Theory* 6 (1988): 152–168.

10. Susan A. Ostrander, *Women of the Upper Class* (Philadelphia: Temple University Press, 1984); Betty G. Farrell, *Elite Families: Class and Power in Nineteenth-Century Boston* (Albany: State University of New York Press, 1993); G. William Domhoff, *Who Rules America?* (Boston: Beacon Press, 1968); Nelson W. Aldrich, Jr., *Old Money* (New York: Vintage Books, 1988).

11. William M. Reddy makes a similar argument about eighteenth-century France, arguing that most merchants began investing in land, which yielded less profit, but through which they played the "game of family advancement."

> Profits from the first game served as a ticket of entry into the second. Within this second game, by following the prescribed course, with careful planning and a little luck, it was possible to manage a gradual social assent, slowly transferring the family's wealth out of trade into land and ennobling office. . . . merchants may have played the game of family advancement with less self-consciousness than historians usually assume. But there is no doubt that the game's existence and the rules that governed it were known to all.

Reddy, *Money and Liberty in Modern Europe* (New York: Cambridge University Press, 1987), 38.

12. Nathaniel Burt, *The Perennial Philadelphians* (Boston: Little, Brown, 1963).

13. On the efforts of the Boston elite to ensure appropriate marriages for their children see Farrell, *Elite Families.*

14. Aldrich, *Old Money,* 56.

15. On the difference between economic and social classes, and the problems within Marxist theories on the relationship between the two, see Anthony Giddens, *The Class Structure of the Advanced Societies* (New York: Harper and Row, 1973).

16. Annette Lareau, *Home Advantage: Social Class and Parental Intervention in Elementary Education* (London and New York: Falmer Press, 1989).

17. Mark S. Granovetter *Getting a Job: A Study of Contacts and Careers* (Cambridge: Harvard University Press, 1974).

18. While parents may want their children to "get ahead," meaning to attain a better class position, parents dread having their children fall lower than they are in the class system. As a result, working-class parents teach their children habits of obedience and conformity, which they imagine prepare them for the work world and which do, indeed, allow them to survive in working-class jobs. However, these behaviors are not valued in professional occupations and so are a hindrance in gaining access to middle-class jobs. See Melvin L. Kohn, *Class and Conformity* (Homewood, Ill.: Dorsey Press, 1969).

19. On women's role in social reproduction, see Barbara Laslett and Johanna Brenner, "Gender and Social Reproduction: Historical Perspectives," *Annual Review of Sociology* 15 (1989): 381–404; Johanna Brenner and Barbara Laslett, "Social Reproduction and the Family," in *Sociology from Crisis to Science?* vol. 2, *The Social Reproduction of Organization and Culture,* ed. Ulf Himmelstrand, (London: Sage, 1986), 116–131; and Leonore Davidoff and Catherine Hall, *Family Fortunes: Men and Women of the English Middle Class, 1780–1850* (Chicago: University of Chicago Press, 1987).

20. See Kristin Luker, *Abortion and the Politics of Motherhood* (Berkeley: University of California Press, 1984). Faye D. Ginsburg makes a similar argument about the economic interests of homemakers versus career women in *Contested Lives* (Berkeley: University of California Press, 1989), although her work focuses more on the rhetoric used by activists, and the construction of identities within this rhetoric. See Ginsburg, "The 'Word-Made' Flesh: The Disembodiment of Gender in the Abortion Debate," in *Uncertain Terms*, ed. Faye Ginsburg and Anna Lowenhaupt Tsing (Boston: Beacon Press, 1990), 59–75; and "Gender Politics and the Contradictions of Nurturance: Moral Authority and Constraints to Action for Female Abortion Activists," *Social Research* 58 (Fall 1991): 653–676.

21. See Janet Farrell Brodie, *Contraception and Abortion in Nineteenth-Century America* (Ithaca: Cornell University Press, 1994); and Carroll Smith-Rosenberg "The Abortion Movement and the AMA, 1850–1880," in *Disorderly Conduct* (New York: Oxford University Press, 1985), 217–244.

22. See Timothy Gilfoyle, *City of Eros* (New York: W. W. Norton and Co., 1992).

23. See Karen Lystra, *Searching the Heart* (New York: Oxford University Press, 1989).

24. Children's lack of economic success may be attributed to their moral failings even when economic changes preclude reproduction of parents' lifestyles. Twentieth-century baby boomers' failure to prosper as did their parents is attributed (by their parents) to their inability to delay gratification, rather than to the GI Bill, cheap housing loans, and the postwar economic boom that made the Depression generation prosperous. See Katherine S. Newman, *Declining Fortunes* (New York: Basic Books, 1993).

25. Baltzell, *Puritan Boston and Quaker Philadelphia*.

26. On the formation of high culture see Paul DiMaggio, "Cultural Entrepreneurship in Nineteenth-Century Boston: Part I, The Creation of an Organizational Base for High Culture in America," *Media, Culture and Society* 4 (1982): 33–50; and "Cultural Entrepreneurship in Nineteenth-Century Boston; Part II, The Classification and Framing of American Art," *Media, Culture, and Society* 4 (1982): 303–322; and Lawrence Levine, *Highbrow/Lowbrow: The Emergence of Culture Hierarchy in America* (Cambridge: Harvard University Press, 1988). On the formation of boarding schools see James McLachlan, *American Boarding Schools: A Historical Study* (New York: Charles Scribner's Sons, 1970). William Roy discusses the class formation activities of the upper class in "Institutional Governance and Social Cohesion: The Internal Organization of the American Capitalist Class, 1886–1905," *Research in Social Stratification and Mobility* 3 (1984): 147–171. Roy argues that capitalists built exclusive institutions to forge class cohesion; I suggest that concerns about families and children were the more immediate impetus for institution building.

27. Viviana A. Zelizer, *Pricing the Priceless Child* (New York: Basic Books, 1985); Brodie, *Contraception and Abortion in Nineteenth-Century America*; Linda Gordon, *Woman's Body, Woman's Right* (New York: Penguin, 1990).

28. See John F. Kasson, *Rudeness and Civility* (New York: Hill and Wang, 1990). In her essay "The Abortion Movement and the AMA, 1850–1880,"

Carroll Smith-Rosenberg argues that in the late-nineteenth century middle-class wives served as status symbols for their husbands.

29. Elaine S. Abelson, *When Ladies Go A-Thieving* (New York: Oxford University Press, 1989), 25–26; on women's role in capitalism, see Laslett and Brenner, "Gender and Social Reproduction."

30. Dr. N. Allen, "Changes in Population," *Harper's Magazine*, February 1869, 390.

31. "Shopping," *New York Times*, June 13, 1881, p. 4, quoted in Abelson, *When Ladies Go A-Thieving*, 30.

32. See Abelson, *When Ladies Go A-Thieving*, chap. 1.

33. See Smith-Rosenberg, "The Abortion Movement and the AMA, 1850–1880."

34. G. William Domhoff, who has done the most extensive inventory of the contemporary upper class, labels a person upper class if they or an immediate family member attended one of a number of elite schools, was a member of an elite club, or was listed in the *Social Register*. If one were able to find the membership lists and school rosters for the large number of elite schools and clubs that marked someone as being a member of upper-class social circles, and could cross-reference these lists with the memberships of the New York and New England anti-vice societies, then almost surely one would find that more than one-quarter to one-third of the anti-vice supporters were members of the upper class. My estimate is a conservative one based on readily available data. On upper-class membership in the contemporary United States see G. William Domhoff, *The Higher Circles* (New York: Vintage Books, 1971).

35. Cleveland Amory, *Who Killed Society?* (New York: Harper and Brothers, 1960).

36. Mrs. John King Van Rensselaer, *The Social Ladder* (New York: Henry Holt and Co., 1924), 157–158.

37. Ward McAllister, *Society as I Have Found It* (1890; reprint, New York: Arno Press, 1975), 157.

38. Ibid., 214.

39. Ibid., 215.

40. Ibid.

41. Ibid., 119.

42. See Mary Cable, *Top Drawer* (New York: Atheneum, 1984), 6–10.

43. Van Rensselaer, *The Social Ladder*, 139.

44. Quoted in Amory, *Who Killed Society?* 25.

45. Van Rensselaer, *The Social Ladder*, 35.

46. Aldrich, *Old Money*, 30.

47. Van Rensselaer, *The Social Ladder*, 171.

48. Ibid., 204.

49. Junius Henri Browne, *The Great Metropolis: A Mirror of New York* (1869; reprint, New York: Arno Press, 1975), 522.

50. Van Rensselaer, *The Social Ladder*, 239.

51. See Frederic Cople Jaher, "Style and Status: High Society in Late-Nineteenth-Century New York," in *The Rich, the Well-Born, and the Powerful*, ed. Frederic Cople Jaher (Urbana: University of Illinois Press, 1973), 282; and Van Rensselaer, *The Social Ladder*, 186–187.

52. On the importation of European habits, see McAllister, *Society as I Have Found It*, 127.

53. Aldrich, *Old Money*, 58.

54. Richard Grant Wright, "Class Distinctions in the United States," *North American Review* 137 (August 1883): 241.

55. Maureen E. Montgomery, *Gilded Prostitution: Status, Money, and Transatlantic Marriages, 1870–1914* (London and New York: Routledge, 1989); Jaher, "Style and Status," 281.

56. On myths about prostitutes see Gilfoyle, *City of Eros*.

57. Edward Crapsey, *The Nether Side of New York, or The Vice, Crime, and Poverty of the Great Metropolis* (New York: Sheldon and Co., 1872), 144.

58. James D. McCabe, Jr., *New York by Gaslight* (1882; reprint, New York: Greenwich House, 1984), 476–482.

59. Crapsey, *The Nether Side of New York*, 143.

60. Howard Crosby, Society for the Prevention of Crime, *Third Annual Report*, 1879, 20–21, quoted in Gilfoyle, *City of Eros*, 237. George Ellington, *The Women of New York, or The Under-world of the Great City* (Burlington, Iowa, 1869), 220–21, quoted in Gilfoyle, *City of Eros*, 102.

61. Gilfoyle, *City of Eros*, 198.

62. McCabe, *New York by Gaslight*, 59.


## CHAPTER 2
### THE CITY, SEXUALITY, AND THE SUPPRESSION OF ABORTION AND CONTRACEPTION

1. "The Evil of the Age," *New York Times*, August 23, 1871, p. 6. Quotations on the Bowlsby case are taken from the *New York Times*, August 27, 1871, p. 1; August 30, 1871, p. 8; and August 31, 1871, p. 8. Rosensweig's trial was covered in the *New York Times* on October 29, 1871.

2. James C. Mohr, *Abortion in America* (New York: Oxford University Press, 1978), 197.

3. James Mohr's pathbreaking study, *Abortion in America*, remains the best source on the practice of abortion in the nineteenth century. While Mohr notes that public opinion about abortion changed during the nineteenth century, he does not explain the causes of this change. Methods of abortion and the frequency of the practice are discussed by Mohr on pp. 53–82. See also Ely Van de Warker's *Detection of Criminal Abortion and a Study of Foeticidal Drugs* (Boston: James Campbell, 1872), which reports on Van de Warker's experiments with available abortifacient preparations.

4. *New York Times*, October 27, 1871, p. 2.

5. The *World* reported:

It was well known in Paterson that Walter Conklin had been paying attentions to Alice Bowlsby for some months past. He was a dashing, well-appearing young man, and, if report be true, a great favorite with the ladies. About a year ago he returned from Russia, whither he went in the capacity of an engineer. On his return, it is said, he found a young lady to whom he had been engaged to be married already wedded, and that he at once proceeded to make things even by making love to the sister-in-law of the woman who had disappointed him. At the same time he began a series of flirtations, which he kept up almost to the hour of his death. He was what is commonly known as a "ladies man." (September 1, 1871, p. 5)

See also the *New York Evening Post*, September 1, 1871, p. 1; and the *Sun* September 1, 1871, p. 1.

6. *New York Times*, October 29, 1871.

7. Augustus K. Gardner, *Conjugal Sins against the Laws of Life and Health and their Effects Upon the Father, Mother, and Child* (New York: J. S. Redfield, 1870), 112.

8. *New York Times*, August 30, 1871, p. 8; and August 31, 1871, p. 8. Perry was convicted of fourth-degree manslaughter and sentenced to two years in prison. His accomplice, a woman named Madame Van Buskirk, was also tried, but the jury could not agree on a verdict, and she was released. See the *New York Times*, September 24, 1871, p. 3; October 4, 1871, p. 5; and January 16, 1872, p. 5.

9. *New York Times*, December 23, 1874, p. 1.

10. Lystra, *Searching the Heart*, 64.

11. For discussions of sexuality in the nineteenth century, see Lystra, *Searching the Heart*; John D'Emilio and Estelle B. Freedman, *Intimate Matters: A History of Sexuality in America* (New York: Harper and Row, 1988); Nancy F. Cott, "Passionlessness: An Interpretation of Victorian Sexual Ideology, 1790–1850," *Signs* 1, no. 2 (1978): 219–236; Ellen Rothman, "Sex and Self-Control: Middle-Class Courtship in America, 1770–1870," in *The American Family in Social-Historical Perspective*, 3d ed., ed. Michel Gordon (New York: St. Martin's Press, 1983), 393–410; and Charles E. Rosenberg, "Sexuality, Class, and Role in Nineteenth-Century America," *American Quarterly* 25, no. 2 (May 1973): 131–153.

12. Crapsey, *The Nether Side of New York*, 148.

13. Ibid.

14. *New York Times*, February 18, 1879, p. 5. The death of Georgiana Shiras was announced with a similar headline: "A Victim of Malpractice: A Girl Twenty Years of Age Dies in Trying to Hide Her Shame." *New York Times*, July 27, 1877, p. 8.

15. Hugh Hodge, "Foeticide, or Criminal Abortion: A Lecture Introductory to the Course on Obstetrics, and Diseases of Women and Children," University of Pennsylvania, Philadelphia, 1869, in *Abortion in America*, ed. Charles Rosenberg and Carroll Smith-Rosenberg (New York: Arno Press, 1974), 38.

16. *New York Times*, December 24, 1878, p. 1.

17. Gardner, *Conjugal Sins*, p. 112; Mohr, *Abortion in America*.

18. Andrew Nebinger, "Criminal Abortion: Its Extent and Prevention; Read before the Philadelphia County Medical Society, February 9, 1870" (Philadelphia, 1870), in *Abortion in America*, ed. Charles Rosenberg and Carroll Smith-Rosenberg (New York: Arno Press, 1974), 14. This argument was elaborated by Van de Warker: "Generally, married women have a wholesome fear of criminal interference after the fourth month, from the belief that foetal life is then fully

developed. This idea is the balm in Gilead to the conscience of every married women; and the prevalent theory among 'nice' women is, that before that time 'no particular harm is done.' *The Detection of Criminal Abortion*, 9.

19. Nebinger, "Criminal Abortion," 29.

20. Ibid., 16.

21. "The Evil of the Age," *New York Times*, August 23, 1871, p. 6. In *The Nether Side of New York*, Crapsey quoted this interview in a discussion of how women rid themselves of illegitimate children by giving them to women who would take their children for a fee. On this practice, known as "baby farming," see Sherri Maxine Broder, "Politics of the Family: Political Culture, Moral Reform, and Family Relations in Gilded Age Philadelphia" (Ph.D. diss., Brown University, 1988).

While adulterous women were clearly sinners, their fall was sometimes attributed to male lust fed by prostitution. For example, Cook argued that women's sexual ignorance combined with men's sexual training in brothels to doom marriages, destroying love and passion.

> Lost indeed for the poor creature left mangled and terrified—nay, infinitely disgusted! Love, affection even, are well-nigh crushed out of the stricken woman, whose mental ejaculation, "O, that I had not married!" is the keynote to her whole after-existence. . . . Again and again these nights of horror are repeated, each, if possible, more hateful than the first, until her *monster* rests from sheer exhaustion, and nature cicatrizes the wounds of body and soul. The wounds are serious indeed. Passion is forever killed, or, if capable of resuscitation, it is not at the hands of him who destroyed it.

This first conjugal act, condemned by the author as "legalized rape," made wives more vulnerable to adulterous affairs that reawakened passions destroyed by brutal husbands. Thus the fall of an adulterous wife was caused by a bestial and callous man. N. F. Cook, *Satan in Society* (New York: Edward F. Hovey, 1878), 140–141. Italics in original.

22. Brodie, *Contraception and Abortion in Nineteenth-Century America*.

23. Dr. N. Allen, "Changes in Population," *Harper's Magazine*, 387–389.

24. Nebinger, "Criminal Abortion," 20–26.

25. Lookup Evans "came from Scotland about twenty years ago." Dr. Asher, the alias of the soon to be notorious Rosensweig, "claims to be a Russian, but his voice has the twang of a German Jew," an ethnicity shared by Jacoby, whose alias was Dr. Franklin. *New York Times*, August 23, 1871, p. 6.

26. *New York Times*, August 30, 1871, p. 8.

27. *New York Times*, February 14, 1873, p. 6.

28. Mohr, *Abortion in America*, chap. 6; Luker, *Abortion and the Politics of Motherhood*, chap. 2.

29. *New York Times*, August 23, 1871, p. 6.

30. Mohr, *Abortion in America*, 239. There is little evidence on how dangerous abortions were in the nineteenth century. In 1866 one writer asserted that, when skillfully performed, the operation had a fatality rate of less than one in a thousand. Edwin M. Hale, *A Systematic Treatise on Abortion*, quoted in Mohr, *Abortion in America*, 77.

31. *New York Times*, October 27, 1871, p. 2.

32. *New York Times*, August 23, 1871, p. 6.

33. *New York Times*, February 12, 1878, p. 5. "The wickedest woman in New York" from Browne, *The Great Metropolis*, 582.

34. *New York Times*, January 26, 1871.

35. Gardner, *Conjugal Sins*, 128.

36. Richard C. Johnson, "Anthony Comstock: Reform, Vice, and the American Way" (Ph.D. diss., University of Wisconsin, 1973), 16–23; Heywood Broun and Margaret Leech, *Anthony Comstock: Roundsman of the Lord* (New York: Literary Guild of America, 1927), 46–47.

37. Broun and Leech, *Anthony Comstock: Roundsman of the Lord*, 59–61.

38. Ibid., 82.

39. Ibid., 84–85; Johnson, "Anthony Comstock," 59.

40. Leta Hollingsworth, "Social Devices for Impelling Women to Bear and Rear Children," *American Journal of Sociology* 22 (1916): 19–29.

41. Smith-Rosenberg, "The Abortion Movement and the AMA, 1850–1880," 236; Brodie, *Contraception and Abortion in Nineteenth-Century America*.

42. "Obscene Literature," *New York Times*, March 15, 1873, p. 3.

43. Comstock, *Traps for the Young*, xiii. While using the mails to spread obscene materials was made a misdemeanor, it carried a potentially heavy penalty: a fine of not less than one hundred or more than five thousand dollars, or imprisonment at hard labor for from one to ten years.

44. "Obscene Literature," *New York Times*, March 15, 1873, p. 3.

45. NYSSV, *Second Annual Report*, 1876, 5.

46. NYSSV, *Fourth Annual Report*, 1878, 10.

47. Cook, *Satan in Society*, 151.

48. Gardner, *Conjugal Sins*, 109.

49. Cook, *Satan in Society*, 163. Gardner made a very similar argument: "the woman will remember, if virtue ever succumbs, the lessons which she has received, for deceiving nature and assuring herself impunity while odiously violating her conjugal faith, the palladium of the family." *Conjugal Sins*, 75.

50. NYSSV, *Second Annual Report*, 1876, 9.

51. *New York Times*, February 13, 1879, p. 8; and March 29, 1879, p. 8.

52. *New York Times*, February 13, 1879, p. 8; on Whitehead's past, see *New York Times*, March 29, 1879.

53. *New York Times*, February 12, 1878, p. 5; and February 13, 1878, p. 8.

54. Reagan notes that single male defendants in abortion cases soon learned that claiming that they had offered to marry the victim was obligatory for acquittal. See Leslie J. Reagan "'About to Meet Her Maker': Women, Doctors, Dying Declarations, and the State's Investigation of Abortion, Chicago, 1867–1940," *Journal of American History* (March 1991): 1240–1264. For Berger's trial, see *New York Times*, April 1, 1879, p. 8; April 2, 1879, p. 8; April 3, 1879, p. 8; and April 15, 1879, p. 3. Cosgrove's trial was covered by the *New York Times* on April 25, 1879, p. 9; April 26, 1879, p. 2; April 27, 1879, p. 12; April 30, 1879, p. 8; June 26, 1879, p. 8; and July 6, 1879, p. 2. The report of sentencing appeared on July 9, 1879, p. 8.

55. Anthony Comstock, *Frauds Exposed* (1880; reprint, Montclair, N.J.: Patterson Smith, 1969), 417–418.

56. Records of the New York Society of the Suppression of Vice, Library of Congress, vol. 1: Mancher case, pp. 5–6; Jacoby case, pp. 15–16; Andrews case, pp. 17–18; Bass case, pp. 57–58. A case similar to that of Morris Bass was the arrest of Leander Fox, who in 1873 was arrested for mailing obscene books and circulares. In this case Comstock seized "1000 rubber articles and various other vile articles, 100 photos, [and] 50 books." Fox was sentenced to one year in the county jail. The most curious case of the sale of a rubber article was the arrest of Joseph Kendall, who, under the pseudonym of "Goodyear India Rubber Glove Co." sold what Comstock called "a substitute for a Dildoe." Kendall, who seems to have been merely a clerk who sold this article, was convicted and fined $250 (in addition to the time he had spent in jail awaiting trial). Comstock noted that this was an important test case. This case appears on pp. 20–21 of Comstock's arrest records.

57. The Davis case appears on pp. 21–22 of the NYSSV *Records*. The Bradford case is discussed on pp. 113–114. Victoria Connors's death was yet another case that aroused horrified attention in the press: her decaying body was discovered buried in a barrel on Staten Island. There were a number of arrests in this case: Bradford for performing the abortion, Dr. Clarence Baker for having signed the death certificate, and Miss Connors's mother, who was arrested as an accomplice. Also arrested were two young men who were her lovers. One of these was a young physician named Dr. Frederic H. Lay, who was the son of a doctor and a recent graduate of Bellevue Hospital Medical College. Bradford was sentenced to fourteen years and six months in prison. See *New York Times*, September 16, 1878, p. 8; October 2, 1878, p. 2; December 5, 1878, p. 3; December 6, 1878, p. 3; December 7, 1878, p. 3; and December 14, 1878, p. 3. Comstock's complaint about corruption in the district attorney's office in dealing with obscenity cases was repeated often in his records but never in public. Comstock made these charges publicly when he began arresting gamblers, which will be discussed in chap. 5.

58. Comstock's activities are discussed in the *New York Times,* on August 31, 1872, p. 5; April 24, 1873, p. 2; and November 17, 1876, p. 8. The 1876 article bore the headline "Comstock's Western Raid: Good Work in the Suppression of Vice."

59. *Sun*, February 12, 1878, p. 1.

60. *New York Times,* February 12, 1878, p. 8.

61. Records of the New York Society for the Suppression of Vice, Library of Congress, volume 1, pp. 111–112. This passage is remarkable for suggesting that Comstock saw himself in the role of Christ.

62. "The Suicide of Ann Lohman," *World*, April 2, 1878, p. 4. For discussions of Restell's suicide see the *Daily Tribune*, April 2, 1878, p. 1; and the *New York Times,* April 2, 1878, p. 1.

63. *Sun*, April 2, 1878, 2.

64. NYSSV, *Fifth Annual Report*, 1879, 11.

65. Comstock, *Traps for the Young*, 155.

CHAPTER 3
MORAL REFORM AND THE PROTECTION OF YOUTH

1. Thus Bourdieu argues that the impetus for moral reform crusades comes from "declining fractions of the petit bourgeois," while Gusfield located the source of the nineteenth-century temperance crusade in the "old middle class," meaning Protestants who resided in small towns. See Bourdieu, *Distinction*, 435; and Joseph R. Gusfield, *Symbolic Crusade: Status Politics and the American Temperance Movement* (1963; reprint, Urbana: University of Illinois Press, 1986), 140.

2. Stephan Thernstrom, *The Other Bostonians* (Cambridge: Harvard University Press, 1973), 290.

3. Anthony Comstock, "The Suppression of Vice," *North American Review* 135 (November 1882): 484–485. Of the seventeen founders, ten of the men or their wives appeared in the 1892 *Social Register*. These included Morris K. Jesup, Howard Potter, William E. Dodge, Jr., J. Pierpont Morgan, J. M. Cornell, Charles E. Whitehead, Cephas Brainerd, Thatcher M. Adams, W. H. S. Wood, and Cornelius R. Agnew. NYSSV, *Second Annual Report*, 1876.

4. The surnames of supporters of the New England Society for the Suppression of Vice who are included as being from "social register families" in this calculation are: Abbott, Ames, Beebe, Bigelow, Bradford, Coolidge, Frothingham, Glover, Houghton, Hubbard, Kimball, Lawrence, Lowell, Loring, Merriam, Putnam, Sears, Shattuck, and Ware. The surnames of supporters of the New York Society for the Suppression of Vice who are included as being from "social register families" are: Alexander, Aspinwall, Atterbury, Auchincloss, Barnes, Benedict, Chandler, Colgate, Cornell, Delano, Dodge, Eaton, Ely, Hoyt, Lawrence, Livingston, Lord, Ludlow, Marquand, Morgan, Noyes, Parsons, Prime, Rhodes, Stillwell, Stoakes, Stokes, Sturges, Talmadge, Trask, Van Rensselaer, Van Stantvoort, and Wickes.

5. The *Tribune* list is the only extant source on the wealthy in the cities studied here. While a reputational list obviously does not report actual wealth, a better source of income data was not available. Too few of the NYSSV supporters were reported in the R. G. Dunn credit records to use them as a source; wills would have provided data on wealth at death and not necessarily during the years of NYSSV support. For a discussion of the limitations of the *Tribune* millionaires list, see Frederic Cople Jaher, *The Urban Establishment* (Urbana: University of Illinois Press, 1982), 94.

6. Each reason that Comstock gave for suppressing obscenity for the years 1873 through 1884 was counted. Each sentence in the *Annual Report* could yield multiple reasons for suppressing obscenity, although only one mention of each reason was counted for each sentence.

7. NYSSV, *Third Annual Report*, 1877, 6. Italics in original.

8. NYSSV, *Thirteenth Annual Report*, 1887, 9

9. Comstock, *Traps for the Young*, 136.

10. NYSSV, *Fourth Annual Report*, 1878, 10–11.

11. NYSSV, *Sixth Annual Report*, 1880, 9.

12. NYSSV, *Tenth Annual Report*, 1884, 27.

13. R. P. Neuman, "Masturbation, Madness, and the Modern Concepts of Childhood and Adolescence," *Journal of Social History* 8 (1975): 1–27; John S. Haller and Robin M. Haller, *The Physician and Sexuality in Victorian America* (Urbana: University of Illinois Press, 1974); E. H. Hare, "Masturbatory Insanity: The History of an Idea," *Journal of Mental Science* 108 (1962): 1–2; Robert H. MacDonald, "The Frightful Consequences of Onanism: Notes on the History of a Delusion," *Journal of the History of Ideas* 28 (July–September 1967): 423–431.

14. Cook, *Satan in Society*, 97–98.

15. NYSSV, *Seventh Annual Report*, 1881, 9.

16. NYSSV, *Fifth Annual Report*, 1879, 12; NYSSV, *Sixth Annual Report*, 1880, 10–11.

17. NYSSV, *Sixth Annual Report*, 1880, 11.

18. Comstock, *Traps for the Young*, 50.

19. On prostitution in late-nineteenth-century New York City, and the attempts of Comstock and Parkhurst to eradicate it, see Gilfoyle, *City of Eros*, 181–306.

20. NYSSV, *First Annual Report*, 1875, 10–11.

21. NYSSV, *Fifth Annual Report*, 1879, 12; see also NYSSV, *Fourth Annual Report*, 1878, 6.

22. Comstock, *Traps for the Young*, 134; Young Men's Christian Association, "Private and Confidential Report of the Committee for the Suppression of Vice," 1874, 6; NYSSV, *First Annual Report*, 1875, 11; NYSSV, *Fourth Annual Report*, 1878, 6–7.

23. NYSSV, *Second Annual Report*, 1876, 15; on obtaining names, see NYSSV, *First Annual Report*, 1875, 11.

24. NYSSV, *Fifth Annual Report*, 1879, 15.

25. Comstock, *Traps for the Young*, 139; NYSSV, *Ninth Annual Report*, 1883, 6–7.

26. On Gaulier's distribution of obscenity see NYSSV, *Third Annual Report*, 1877, 8. The information on Gaulier's arrest for sodomy appeared in the Sotheby's sale catalog, New York, October 29, 1986. Item number 27 included the letter from Comstock to Alonzo Cornell. My thanks to Edward Weber, former curator of the Labadie Collection at the University of Michigan, for bringing this source to my attention.

27. NYSSV, *Seventh Annual Report*, 1881, 10.

28. NYSSV, *Second Annual Report*, 1876, 11.

29. Neuman, "Masturbation, Madness, and the Modern Concepts of Childhood and Adolescence," 4.

30. NYSSV, *Fourth Annual Report*, 11.

31. NYSSV, *Seventh Annual Report*, 1881, p. 9.

32. McLachlan, *American Boarding Schools*, 178.

33. E. Digby Baltzell, *Philadelphia Gentlemen: The Making of a National Upper Class* (1958; reprint, Philadelphia: University of Pennsylvania Press, 1979); William G. Roy, "Institutional Governance and Social Cohesion: The Internal Organization of the American Capitalist Class, 1886–1905" *Research in Social Stratification and Mobility* 3 (1984): 147–171; and William G. Roy, "The Organization of the Corporate Class Segment of the American Capitalist Class at

the Turn of the Century," in *Bringing Class Back In: Contemporary and Historical Perspectives*, ed. Scott G. McNall, Rhonda F. Levine, and Rick Fantasia (Boulder, Colo.: Westview Press, 1991): 139–163.

34. NYSSV, *Third Annual Report*, 1877, 8–9.

35. Comstock, *Traps for the Young*, 27.

36. Ibid.

37. Ibid., 30–32.

38. Ibid., 151.

39. Ibid., 52.

40. Ibid., 53.

41. See Karen Halttunen, *Confidence Men and Painted Women* (New Haven: Yale University Press, 1982), 37–39.

42. NYSSV, *Tenth Annual Report*, 1884, 7–8.

43. NYSSV, *Seventh Annual Report*, 10.

44. For example, in *Eight Hours for What We Will*, Roy Rosensweig argues that "many industrialists tended to focus on the ways that drinking and the saloon subverted work discipline and thereby impinged on the pursuit of profits" (New York: Cambridge University Press, 1983), 224; while Conley argues that conflicts between workers and capitalists arise when "consumption practices interfere with the reproduction of labor power, that is, with the quality of the commodity capitalists are purchasing." See James R. Conley, "More Theory, Less Fact? Social Reproduction and Class Conflict in a Sociological Approach to Working-Class History," *Canadian Journal of Sociology* 12 (1988): 80. While Comstock's arguments appealed to capitalists' interests in controlling their workforce, his arguments about the control of children, of all classes, imply that the upper class had an interest in social reproduction that transcended labor-force issues.

45. NYSSV, *Sixth Annual Report*, 1880, 6.

46. Ibid., 6–7.

47. Ibid., 7.

48. Ibid.

49. This rhetorical tactic is in use in the late-twentieth century as well. In her article "Constructing Racial Rhetoric: Media Depictions of Harm in Heavy Metal and Rap Music," *American Sociological Review* 58 (December 1993): 753–767, Amy Binder shows how crimes committed by black youths have been blamed on their consumption of rap music.

50. NYSSV, *Sixth Annual Report*, 1880, 8.

51. NYSSV, *Seventh Annual Report*, 1881, 15–16.

52. Comstock, *Traps for the Young*, 135–136.

53. Ibid., 56.

54. Ibid., 57.

55. Ibid., 129–130.

56. NYSSV, *Third Annual Report*, 1877, 7–8, italics in original.

57. NYSSV, *Seventh Annual Report*, 1881, 24.

58. NYSSV, *Third Annual Report*, 1877, 9. The role of morality and dependency in constructing the citizen, who is gendered male, is discussed in Gwendolyn Mink, "The Lady and the Tramp: Gender, Race, and the Origins of the

American Welfare State," in *Women, the State, and Welfare*, ed. Linda Gordon (Madison: University of Wisconsin Press, 1990): 92–122.

59. NYSSV, *Second Annual Report*, 1876, 3.

60. Ibid., 8.

61. Stephen Nissenbaum, *Sex, Diet and Debility in Jacksonian America: Sylvester Graham and Health Reform* (Westport, Conn: Greenwood Press, 1980).

62. NYSSV, *First Annual Report*, 1875, 10–11.

63. NYSSV, *Sixth Annual Report*, 1880, 25.

64. Ibid., 26.

65. Ibid., 11.

66. Comstock, *Traps for the Young*, 18.

67. Ibid., 18.

68. Ibid., 245.

69. Ibid.

70. Ruth Birgitta Anderson Bordin, *Women and Temperance: The Quest for Power and Liberty, 1873–1900* (Philadelphia: Temple University Press, 1981); David Pivar, *Purity Crusade: Sexual Morality and Social Control, 1868–1900* (Westport, Conn.: Greenwood Press, 1973); Judith Walkowitz, *Prostitution and Victorian Society*, (New York: Cambridge University Press, 1980).

71. Josiah Woodward Leeds, *Scrapbooks*, Quaker Collection, Haverford College, vol. 3, p. 37 (hereafter *Leeds*).

72. NYSSV, *Twelfth Annual Report*, 1886, 12.

73. NYSSV, *Thirteenth Annual Report*, 1887, 31–36; NYSSV, *Seventeenth Annual Report*, 1891, p. 3.

74. Mrs. Charles Merritt to F. B. Allen, April 4, 1891, in *Letters to the New England Society for the Suppression of Vice* (hereafter *Letters*).

75. Zelizer, *Pricing the Priceless Child*.

76. Blumin, *The Emergence of the Middle Class*, chaps. 5 and 8.

77. See Newman, *Declining Fortunes*, chap. 5.

78. Ibid., chap. 6.

CHAPTER 4
ANTHONY COMSTOCK VERSUS FREE LOVE

1. On Beecher's renown see *New York Times*, July 30, 1874, p. 4; and "Henry Ward Beecher's Church," *Atlantic Monthly*, January 1867, 41–42. On Beecher and Tilton's involvement with suffrage, see Clifford E. Clark, Jr. *Henry Ward Beecher* (Urbana: University of Illinois Press, 1978), 202–204.

2. See Richard Wightman Fox, "Intimacy on Trial: Cultural Meanings of the Beecher-Tilton Affair," in *The Power of Culture*, ed. Richard Wightman Fox and T. J. Jackson Lears (Chicago: University of Chicago Press, 1993), 123.

3. Works on the Beecher affair include Fox, "Intimacy on Trial"; Altina L. Waller, *Reverend Beecher and Mrs. Tilton: Sex and Class in Victorian America* (Amherst: University of Massachusetts Press, 1982); and A. Cheree Carlson, "The Role of Character in Public Moral Argument: Henry Ward Beecher and the

Brooklyn Scandal," *Quarterly Journal of Speech* 77 (February 1991): 38–52. The changing culture of romance is studied by Lystra, *Searching the Heart.*

4. Rumor also had it that these friendships were not platonic.

5. Arlene Kisner, ed., *"Woodhull and Claflin's Weekly": The Lives and Writings of Notorious Victoria Woodhull and Her Sister Tennessee Claflin* (Washington, N.J.: Time Change Press, 1972), 9–10, 27–28; Waller, *Reverend Beecher and Mrs. Tilton,* 4; John C. Spurlock, *Free Love: Marriage and Middle-Class Radicalism in America, 1825–1860* (New York: New York University Press, 1988), 212 (on ties to communism).

6. Ann Braude, *Radical Spirits* (Boston: Beacon Press, 1989), 56.

7. Ibid., 170.

8. "Intelligent Motherhood," *Word,* December 1872, 1–2.

9. *Word,* December 1872, 1–2.

10. Kisner, *"Woodhull and Claflin's Weekly,"* 43.

11. Gilfoyle, *City of Eros,* p. 234.

12. The arrests and trials are covered in the *New York Times,* November 3, 1872, p. 1; November 5, 1872, p. 2; November 10, 1872, p. 3; December 4, 1872, p. 2; January 10, 1873, p. 5; January 22, 1873, p. 8; and January 23, 1873, p. 8. Comstock's notes in the *Arrest Records of the New York Society for the Suppression of Vice* 1:16. Blatchford's charge in the *New York Times,* June 28, 1873, p. 2.

13. On Tilton's motivations, see *New York Times,* June 25, 1874, p. 8; on the Committee of Inquiry, see *New York Times,* July 11, 1874.

14. Fox, "Intimacy on Trial," 119–125.

15. *New York Times,* July 24, 1874, p. 1.

16. In the letter from Elizabeth that her husband claimed included her admission of infidelity, she wrote, "Your opinions are not restful or congenial to my soul." *New York Times,* July 22, 1874, p. 5.

17. See Waller, *Reverend Beecher and Mrs. Tilton,* p. 121.

18. *New York Times,* July 22, 1874, p. 1.

19. Fox, "Intimacy on Trial," 119.

20. Waller, *Reverend Beecher and Mrs. Tilton,* 28–29.

21. Both Charles Beecher and Isabella Beecher Hooker were Spiritualists, and Harriet Beecher Stowe took seriously, and investigated, Spiritualists' claims. Henry and Harriet's father, the famed cleric Patrick Lyman Beecher, "taught his children that their dead mother, Roxanna, watched over them from heaven and continued to play an active role in their spiritual development," thus encouraging in his children both a more liberal theology and a belief in Spiritualism. See Braun, *Radical Spirits,* 27 and 50.

22. Fox, "Intimacy on Trial," 119–120.

23. *New York Times,* July 22, 1874, 5.

24. Fox, "Intimacy on Trial," p. 126.

25. "A Bewildering Dialect," *New York Times,* July 24, 1874, p. 4.

26. Lystra, *Searching the Heart,* p. 246.

27. *New York Times,* July 22, 1874, p. 5. In another letter, reprinted in the same *Times* article, Elizabeth made a similar statement, equating the role of God in her life to that of her husband, family, and friends: "I am conscious of three jets

to the fountain of my soul—to the Great Love and yourself—to whom as one I am eternally wedded; my children; and the dear friends who trust and love me."

28. Thomas S. Munnell, "Beecherism and Legalism," *Christian Quarterly* 4 (January 1872): 25.

29. Munnell, "Beecherism and Legalism," 25, 31, 32.

30. Noah Davis, "Marriage and Divorce," *North American Review* 139 (July 1884):30.

31. Ibid., 33.

32. Ibid., 34–35.

33. Ibid., 35.

34. *Word*, August 1874, 2.

35. "Beecher's Brutality," *Word*, November 1874, 4.

36. "National Gag-Law," *Word*, February 1876, 2. Italics in original.

37. "Constitution of the National Liberal League," 1–5; minutes of the National Liberal League, July 4, 1876, 43–44. National Defense Association Papers, Harvard Archives, Harvard University.

38. Ezra H. Heywood, *Cupid's Yokes, or, The Binding Forces of Conjugal Life* (Princeton, Mass.: Co-operative Publishing Co., 1877), 4.

39. Ibid., 5.

40. Ibid., 8.

41. Ibid., 19.

42. Ibid., 9.

43. Ibid., 21.

44. Ibid., 18.

45. Ibid., 21.

46. Heywood argued that intercourse was likely to result in conception from six to eight days before menstruation until ten to twelve days afterward. Thus Heywood located the approximately eight days a month that were a "safe" period almost exactly at the point of ovulation.

47. Heywood, *Cupid's Yokes*, 20–21.

48. Ibid., 22.

49. Ibid., 11–12.

50. Hal D. Sears, *The Sex Radicals: Free Love in High Victorian America* (Lawrence: Regents Press of Kansas, 1977), 167.

51. NYSSV, *Fourth Annual Report*, 7.

52. D. M. Bennett, *An Open Letter to Jesus Christ* (New York: Truth Seeker, 1875), 5, 20.

53. Ibid., 23–24.

54. Ibid., 24–27.

55. Martin Henry Blatt, *Free Love and Anarchism* (Urbana: University of Illinois Press, 1989), 115–118.

56. Sears, *The Sex Radicals*, 169.

57. Ibid., 168–169.

58. Anthony Comstock, "Lawlessness of the Liberal Leagues," *Our Day* 1 (May 1888): 395. Comstock also discusses the repeal efforts in *Frauds Exposed*, 398–415. Comstock's account of the activities of the National Defense Association is one of the most detailed available, and it is from an obviously biased

source. The petition that Comstock mentions appears to have been lost, so this is the only available source of the wording of the NDA's appeal to the Senate. In the *Our Day* article Comstock reports the response of the Senate Committee on Revision of Laws. His quotation of the available committee records is accurate, so this gives one more faith in the accuracy of Comstock's report of the petition.

59. House of Representatives Report #888, in *House Reports 834–1017, Second Session, Forty-fifth Congress*, 1826.

60. *Constitution of the National Defense Association*, Denton Family Papers, Labadie Collection, University of Michigan, p. 1; *Proceedings of the Indignation Meeting held in Faneuil Hall, Thursday Evening, August 1, 1878, to Protest Against the Injury done to the Freedom of the Press by the Conviction and Imprisonment of Ezra H. Heywood* (Boston: Benj. R. Tucker, 1878), 4.

61. *Proceedings of the Indignation Meeting*, 38–39.

62. Ibid., 62.

63. Ibid.: "anniversary," p. 3; "Fugitive Slave Act," 42; "Dred Scott," 33.

64. Ibid.: "Anthony Comstock . . ." 40; "Mr. Colgate . . ." 50.

65. Ibid., 53; on Hull see Sears, *The Sex Radicals*, 88.

66. T. Harry Williams, ed., *Hayes: The Diary of a President, 1875–1881* (New York: D. McKay, 1964), 183–184.

67. Sears, *The Sex Radicals*, 171.

68. Comstock, *Traps for the Young*, 163.

69. On the NDA, see NYSSV, *Thirteenth Annual Report*, 1887, 21; "long haired men" in Comstock, *Frauds Exposed*, 424; on NLL, see *Frauds Exposed*, 443; on Rawson, see *Frauds Exposed*, 475–484.

70. "The power possessed by Congress embraces the regulation of the entire postal system of the country. The right to designate what shall be carried necessarily involves the right to determine what shall be excluded. . . . Under the power to establish post-offices and post-roads, it must be held that Congress had the right to prescribe what it will carry along the post-roads as part of the mail, and what it will not carry, and to render this enactment efficient by punishing the offence of violating it. Whether certain things shall be excluded or not, is a matter for the sound discretion of Congress." Comstock, *Traps for the Young*, 218.

71. Ibid., 232.

72. Ibid., 205.

73. Ibid., 200–203.

74. Ibid., 202.

75. Ibid., 159.

76. Ibid., 162.

77. Ibid., 158, 205.

78. Ibid., 226–227.

79. Blatt, *Free Love and Anarchism*, 142–145.

80. "Irresponsible Parentage," *Word*, June 1878, 2.

81. Jesse F. Battan " 'The Word Made Flesh': Language, Authority, and Sexual Desire in Late-Nineteenth-Century America," *Journal of the History of Sexuality* 3 (1992): 223–244; Comstock, *Traps for the Young*, 163.

82. "A Woman's View of It—No. 1," *Word*, January 1883, 2.

83. "A Woman's View of It—No. 3" *Word*, March 1883, 3. In this article she also faulted Comstock's methods of gathering evidence for his prosecutions, arguing that they were proof of Comstock's own misguided sensuality: "If Comstock's own penis was well-informed & behaved he would not sign himself 'Anna E. Ray' a Washington Treasury clerk three months on with child wanting to procure abortion; he would not sin in ill-famed houses for 'Christ's sake'; he would not as 'Mrs. Farnsworth' or 'J. A. Mattocks' skulk in bed-chambers to supervise the processes of coition, or invade, again & again, the sanctity of my home to promote the scandalous libel on Human Nature which he calls 'religion' and 'morality.' "

84. "A Woman's View of It—No. 4," *Word*, April 1883, 2–3.

85. Blatt, *Free Love and Anarchism*, 144–147.

86. Angela Heywood was to be charged as well for authoring the articles. She was far along in pregnancy at the time, and charges were not brought against her.

87. Blatt, *Free Love and Anarchism*, 148.

88. Ibid., 164–165.

89. Ibid., 169–171.

90. Ibid., 110–111.

91. Edward Bliss Foote, Jr., to W. and E. M. F. Denton, 20 October 1890. Denton Family Papers, Labadie Collection, University of Michigan.

## CHAPTER 5
### IMMIGRANTS, CITY POLITICS, AND CENSORSHIP
### IN NEW YORK AND BOSTON

1. NYSSV, *First Annual Report*, 1875, 6.

2. NYSSV, *Second Annual Report,*, 1876, 11.

3. Thomas J. Archdeacon, *Becoming American: An Ethnic History* (New York: Free Press, 1983).

4. Edward Self, "The Abuse of Citizenship," *North American Review* 136 (June 1883): 541–556.

5. NYSSV, *First Annual Report*, 1875, 9.

6. NYSSV, *Second Annual Report*, 1876, 7.

7. Johnson, "Anthony Comstock," 190. Comstock did not report the parentage of his arrestees, so the proportion of those who were second-generation immigrants is unknown.

8. NYSSV, *Fourth Annual Report*, 1878, 11.

9. Archdeacon, *Becoming American*, 73.

10. Ibid.; John Higham, *Strangers in the Land* (1955; reprint, New Brunswick, N.J.: Rutgers University Press, 1988): 39.

11. Crapsey, *The Nether Side of New York*, 6.

12. Broun and Leech, *Anthony Comstock: Roundsman of the Lord*, 202.

13. Eighteen seventy-eight was a fruitful year for seizing "circulars, catalogues, songs, poems, etc."; Comstock seized 1,005,172 of these; see NYSSV, *Fifth Annual Report*, 1879, 19. Material was even scarcer in 1879, when he seized only 985 pounds of books and no obscene pictures or indecent rubber articles; see NYSSV, *Sixth Annual Report*, 1880, 18.

14. NYSSV, *Sixth Annual Report,* 1880, 12.

15. Ibid.

16. Ibid., 12–13.

17. NYSSV, *Seventh Annual Report,* 1881, 12.

18. NYSSV, *Sixth Annual Report,* 1880, 13.

19. O. B. Frothingham, "The Ethics of Gambling," *North American Review* 135 (August 1882): 166.

20. Ibid., 168. Frothingham, as well as Comstock, reiterated a number of anti-gambling themes voiced by reformers earlier in the nineteenth century. See Ann Fabian, *Card Sharps, Dream Books, and Bucket Shops* (Ithaca: Cornell University Press, 1990), 12–107.

21. NYSSV, *Seventh Annual Report,* 1881, 10–11.

22. NYSSV, *Sixth Annual Report,* 1880, 12.

23. Ibid., 13. In 1880 Comstock published his first book, entitled *Frauds Exposed,* which discussed lotteries and mentions gambling but did not mention the problem of governmental corruption. Gambling was linked to governmental corruption in the NYSSV, *Annual Report,* published that year. *Frauds Exposed* is a litany of complaints against bogus bankers and quack nostrum dealers, and is probably best read as a chronicle of Comstock's search for new vices to combat.

24. NYSSV, *Seventh Annual Report,* 1881, 14

25. Alexander B. Callow, *The Tweed Ring* (London: Oxford University Press, 1965); Seymour J. Mandelbaum, *Boss Tweed's New York* (New York: John Wiley and Sons, 1965).

26. Crapsey, *The Nether Side of New York,* 7.

27. Francis Parkman, "The Failure of Universal Suffrage," *North American Review* 263 (July–August 1878): 1–20.

28. Higham, *Strangers in the Land,* 60; Archdeacon, *Becoming American.*

29. McCabe, *New York by Gaslight,* 124.

30. John I. Mitchell, "Political Bosses," *North American Review* 135 (October 1882): 363–373.

31. Arthur Blake Ellis, "Municipal Finance," *Harper's New Monthly Magazine* 69 (October 1884): 779–787.

32. For example, see Martin Shefter, "Trade Unions and Political Machines: The Organization and Disorganization of the American Working Class in the Late-Nineteenth Century," in *Working Class Formation,* ed. Ira Katznelson and Aristide Zolberg (Princeton: Princeton University Press, 1986), 197–276; and John Bodnar, *The Transplanted: A History of Immigrants in Urban America* (Bloomington: Indiana University Press, 1985). For critiques of the "machine" version of urban political history, see Terrence J. McDonald, "The Problem of the Political in Recent American Urban History: Liberal Pluralism and the Rise of Functionalism," *Social History* 10 (October 1985): 323–345; and Jon C. Teaford, *The Unheralded Triumph* (Baltimore: Johns Hopkins University Press, 1984).

33. Teaford, *The Unheralded Triumph,* 4.

34. Ibid., 39–40.

35. Ibid., 18. While these reforms further diminished the power of New York City's aldermen, this did not quell the ethnic conflict that found its expression in city politics. In 1888, New York's Mayor Abram Hewitt, who was native born,

quarreled with the Board of Alderman over whether the shamrock flag would fly over city hall on St. Patrick's Day. His subsequent refusal to attend the St. Patrick's Day parade ultimately ended his political career. See Higham, *Strangers in the Land*, 41; and Teaford, *The Unheralded Triumph*, 52.

36. E. L. Godkin, "The Alderman and the Appointing Power," *Nation* 38 (February 21, 1884): 158–159.

37. Teaford, *The Unheralded Triumph*, 18–19.

38. Ibid., 48.

39. Godkin, "The Alderman and the Appointing Power," 158–159.

40. Geoffrey Blodgett, "Yankee Leadership in a Divided City: Boston, 1860–1910," in *Boston, 1700–1980: The Evolution of Urban Politics*, ed. Ronald P. Formisano and Constance K. Burns (Westport, Conn: Greenwood Press, 1984), 87–110; Teaford, *The Unheralded Triumph*, 49.

41. Blodgett, "Yankee Leadership in a Divided City"; Teaford, *The Unheralded Triumph*.

42. Teaford, *The Unheralded Triumph*, 182–183.

43. E. L. Godkin "The Constitutional Amendment on City Government," *Nation* 26 (February 14, 1878): 109.

44. Parkman, "The Failure of Universal Suffrage," 2.

45. Ibid., 4–5.

46. Ibid., 7.

47. Ibid., 14–15.

48. NYSSV, *Eighth Annual Report*, 1882, 10–11 and 14–15.

49. Comstock, *Traps for the Young*, 53–54.

50. *New York Times,* November 10, 1882, p. 8, cited in Teaford, *The Unheralded Triumph*, 33; see also Bodnar *The Transplanted*, 203. Teaford argues that the protection offered by having a position on the city council might have encouraged saloon owners to run for office, and that their position at the center of the community, and consequent knowledge of both community affairs and likely voters, may have made bar owners more likely to be elected. Teaford, *The Unheralded Triumph*, 34.

51. Callow, *The Tweed Ring*.

52. Comstock, *Traps for the Young*, 53–55.

53. NYSSV, *Ninth Annual Report*, 1883, 12–13.

54. NYSSV, *Tenth Annual Report*, 1884, 13.

55. NYSSV, *Eleventh Annual Report*, 1885, 11.

56. NYSSV, *Twelfth Annual Report,* 1886, 14.

57. NYSSV, *Eighth Annual Report*, 1882, 16.

58. Higham, *Strangers in the Land*; Barbara M. Solomon, *Ancestors and Immigrants* (Cambridge: Harvard University Press, 1956).

59. NESSV, *Annual Report* (hereafter *Report*), 1879–1880, 1.

60. Ibid., 2.

61. Ibid., 3.

62. Ibid., 3.

63. New England Society for the Suppression of Vice, *Minutes of Executive Committee*, private collection (hereafter *Minutes*), May 27, 1879, June 30, 1879, and October 28, 1879.

64. *Minutes*, January 27, 1880, and February 24, 1880; NESSV, *Report*, 1879–1880, p. 3.

65. *Minutes*, March 14, 1881.

66. *Minutes*, May 1, 1882.

67. NESSV, *Report*, 1881–1882, 4.

68. *Minutes*, February 6, 1882.

69. McCoy claims that the NESSV finally admitted to censoring Whitman in 1895. McCoy, "Banned in Boston," 95.

70. Homer B. Sprague, "Societies for the Suppression of Vice," *Education* (September 1882): 70.

71. *Minutes*, December 4, 1882, and January 1, 1883.

72. *Minutes*, March 5, 1883.

73. NESSV, *Report*, 1882–1883, 2.

74. *Minutes*, December 17, 1883.

75. *Minutes*, February 4, 1883; NESSV, *Report*, 1883–1884, 3–4.

76. NESSV, *Report*, 1883–1884, 13.

77. *Minutes*, September 8, 1884.

78. *Minutes*, January 5, 1885.

79. Blodgett, "Yankee Leadership in a Divided City."

80. *Transcript*, March 5, 1880, quoted in Solomon, *Ancestors and Immigrants*, 43. On the importance of the *Transcript* in elite Boston social circles, see Jaher, *The Urban Establishment*, 90.

81. Solomon, *Ancestors and Immigrants*, 53; Teaford, *The Unheralded Triumph*, 74.

82. NESSV, *Report*, 1881–1882, 3; NESSV, *Report*, 1883–1884, 15.

83. NESSV, *Report*, 1885–1886, 6.

84. Letters to the NESSV (hereafter *Letters*), January 26, 1885.

85. *Minutes*, March 1, 1886, and April 5, 1886; NESSV, *Report*, 1885–1886, 7.

86. "The Immoral Skating Rink," unlabeled newsclipping in *Letters*.

87. NESSV, *Report*, 1884–1885, 8.

88. NESSV, *Report*, 1885–1886, 7.

89. NESSV, *Report*, 1886–1887, 6.

90. *Letters*, June 6, 1886.

91. *Minutes*, January 10, 1887.

92. *Minutes*, June 6, 1887, and November 7, 1887.

93. F. B. Allen to Whiting, January 3, 1888, in *Letters*.

94. *Minutes*, February 6, 1888.

95. NESSV, *Report*, 1887–1888, 15.

96. *Letters*, February 27, 1888.

97. NESSV, *Report*, 1887–1888, 15; McCoy, "Banned in Boston," 27. Neil Schumsky has argued that the presence of "red light" districts in cities such as Boston at the end of the nineteenth century shows that elites tolerated prostitution because segregated vice districts helped delimit the boundaries between acceptable and unacceptable behavior. If the elites wanted to rid the cities of prostitution, Schumsky argues, they could and would have. Central to this argument is the assumption that upper classes control that the state and the

state acts to further the interests of the dominant class and to do its bidding. Such arguments do not take account of the fact that "the state" in the Gilded Age was fragmented and operated at three distinct levels—local, state, and national. Furthermore, such arguments are oblivious to the cries of nineteenth-century urban elites who sought to regain control of both the city government and the police. Schumsky is clearly mistaken in his assumption that the "city fathers" tolerated prostitution either out of the belief that prostitution served as a safety valve for an untamed male sexuality or that they saw segregated vice districts as a useful illustration of their own moral categories. In Boston the "city fathers" were unable to impose their moral categories on the city's prostitution business because the police force would not cooperate. While the unwritten policy of the police that so exercised the leaders of the NESSV conforms to Schumsky's ideas about why prostitution was tolerated, it is important to distinguish between the policy of the police and that of the upper class. See Neil Larry Schumsky, "Tacit Acceptance: Respectable Americans and Segregated Prostitution, 1870–1910," *Journal of Social History* 19 (Summer 1986): 665–680. On the levels of the state in the late-nineteenth century, see Stephen Skowronek, *Building a New American State* (New York: Cambridge University Press, 1982).

## CHAPTER 6
### CENSORIUS QUAKERS AND THE FAILURE
### OF THE ANTI-VICE MOVEMENT
### IN PHILADELPHIA

1. Boyer, *Purity in Print*; Baltzell, *Puritan Boston and Quaker Philadelphia*.
2. NYSSV, *Third Annual Report*, 1877, 12.
3. NYSSV, *Fourth Annual Report*, 1878, 13.
4. United States Department of the Interior, *Report on the Population of the United States at the Eleventh Census: 1890, Part I* (Washington, D.C.: Government Printing Office, 1895), clxii.
5. John S. Billings, *Vital Statistics of Boston and Philadelphia: Covering a Period of Six Years Ending May 31, 1890*, Department of the Interior, Census Office (Washington, D.C.: Government Printing Office, 1895), 116–119; Alan N. Burstein, "Immigrants and Residential Mobility: The Irish and Germans in Philadelphia, 1850–1880," in *Philadelphia: Work, Space, Family, and Group Experience in the Nineteenth Century*, ed. Theodore Hershberg (New York: Oxford University Press, 1981). Boston's immigrants were crowded into miserable tenements, with an average of 8.3 persons living in each dwelling in 1880, while in Philadelphia, the "city of homes," the figure was 5.8; see United States Department of the Interior, Census Office, *Compendium of the Tenth Census*, Part II (Washington, D.C.: Government Printing Office, 1883); and John F. Sutherland, "Housing the Poor in the City of Homes: Philadelphia at the Turn of the Century," in *The Peoples of Philadelphia: A History of Ethnic Groups and Lower-Class Life, 1790–1990*, ed. Allen F. Davis and Mark H. Haller (Philadelphia: Temple University Press, 1973). Slums took a grim toll of immigrant lives, with immigrant death rates for every age group in Boston exceeding those in Philadel-

phia between 1885 and 1890; see Billings, *Vital Statistics of Boston and Philadelphia*, 5–6; and Richard A. Meckel, "Immigration, Mortality, and Population Growth in Boston, 1840–1880," *Journal of Interdisciplinary History* 15 (1985): 393–418.

6. Dennis Clark, *The Irish in Philadelphia* (Philadelphia: Temple University Press, 1973); Stephanie W. Greenberg, "Industrial Location and Ethnic Residential Patterns in an Industrializing City: Philadelphia, 1880," in *Philadelphia: Work, Space, Family, and Group Experience in the Nineteenth Century*, ed. Theodore Hershberg (New York: Oxford University Press, 1981).

7. Dennis Clark, "The Philadelphia Irish: Persistent Presence," in *The Peoples of Philadelphia: A History of Ethnic Groups and Lower-Class Life, 1790–1940*, ed. Allen F. Davis and Mark H. Haller (Philadelphia: Temple University Press, 1973), 141–142.

8. Stephen P. Erie, *Rainbow's End: Irish-Americans and the Dilemmas of Urban Machine Politics, 1840–1985* (Berkeley: University of California Press, 1988).

9. Teaford, *The Unheralded Triumph*, 36.

10. Lincoln Steffens, "Philadelphia: Corrupt and Contented" *McClure's Magazine* 21 (1903): 249–263.

11. Howard F. Gillette, Jr., "Corrupt and Contented: Philadelphia's Political Machine, 1865–1887," Ph.D. diss., Yale University, 1970.

12. Jaher, *The Urban Establishment*, 261–262.

13. *The Union League and the Political Situation in Philadelphia*, by a Republican member of the League. Philadelphia, March 1873. Library of Congress.

14. Comstock to Leeds, *Leeds Scrapbooks*, Quaker Collection, Haverford College (hereafter *Leeds*), vol. 3, p. 37, April 20, 1885.

15. There are conflicting dates for Leeds's birth. A memorial published by the Philadelphia Friends' Book Store reports that he was born in 1841; an obituary in the Leeds Papers at Haverford College reports that he was born in 1838.

16. "Philadelphia's Duty to Her Centennial Guests," *Christian Neighbor*, April 12, 1875, in *Leeds* 1:6.

17. Joseph Lesley to Leeds, November 13, 1878, in *Leeds* 1:31.

18. Isaac Hinckley to Leeds, January 2, 1879 in *Leeds* 1:30.

19. Note on letter from R. C. Brown and Co. to Leeds, April 12, 1881, in *Leeds* 1:63.

20. R. C. Brown to Leeds, April 12, 1881, in *Leeds* 1:63.

21. Leeds to R. C. Brown and Co., April 16, 1881, *Leeds* 1:63.

22. *Philadelphia Inquirer*, June 4, 1884, in *Leeds* 2:87.

23. *Ledger*, June 19, 1884, in *Leeds* 2:87.

24. Leeds originally sent his request to the postmaster general but learned that the stands were under the jurisdiction of the secretary of the treasury. See *Christian Statesman*, July 3, 1884, in *Leeds* 2:89; and the note from Leeds attached to Leeds to Gresham, June 28, 1884, in *Leeds* 2:93.

25. Coon to Leeds, July 15, 1884, in *Leeds* 2:93. The custodian in question wrote to Leeds requesting a meeting so that he could learn what "matter is objectionable . . . it being difficult for me to draw the line" (Huidekoper to Leeds, July 15, 1884, 2:97). There is no report of this meeting in Leeds's papers.

26. Leeds to Smith, September 20, 1884, in *Leeds* 2:103. A news clipping stating that the mayor removed the poster at the request of Leeds is appended to the corner of Leeds's letter.

27. Leeds to Scattergood, September 29, 1884, in *Leeds* 2:109.

28. Scattergood to Leeds, October 3, 1884, in *Leeds* 2:109.

29. If Leeds received such a letter, it is not included in his scrapbook.

30. Leeds to Board of Education, November 10, 1884, in *Leeds* 2:111.

31. Leeds to John H. Graham, member of the Select Council, and Thomas Meehan, member of the Common Council, November 12, 1884, in *Leeds* 2:111.

32. Resolution from the Board of Education, clipping from the *Press*, November 12, 1884, in *Leeds* 2:110.

33. *Philadelphia Inquirer*, December 5, 1884, in *Leeds* 2:114.

34. A friend of Leeds, who was employed at Baldwin, offered to do what he could to support the initiative, and Leeds responded by suggesting that the men in the countinghouse and shops be read the resolution, and that a member of the firm, someone who worked in the countinghouse, and one of the shop workers sign the document on behalf of the rest. Macfernan responded by telling Leeds that he would get everyone he could in the office and the shops to sign Leeds's address. Macfernan to Leeds, November 17, 1884, in *Leeds* 2:114; Leeds to Macfernan, November 24, 1887, in *Leeds* 2:115; Macfernan to Leeds, November 26, 1884, in *Leeds* 2:115.

35. *Press*, November 17, 1884, in *Leeds* 2:112.

36. Ibid.

37. Leeds had gone against the mayor's advice in pursuing the legislation when he did. Mayor Smith had told Leeds that since it was the end of the year, councils would be busy with appropriations bills, so there was not time to pass a law in 1884. Leeds decided to go ahead because the attention of the people was then on the subject and he feared that, given time, the opposition could organize itself. Leeds to Macfernan, November 24, 1884, in *Leeds* 2:115.

38. Walker to Leeds, December 4, 1884, in *Leeds* 2:119; "General City News," clipping labeled *Press*, December 10, 1884, in *Leeds* 2:120. It is not clear that Leeds ever responded to Walker's offer, although the Baptist and Methodist ministers publicly endorsed the anti-obscenity legislation.

39. *Press*, December 10, 1884, in *Leeds* 2:120.

40. Unlabeled clipping in *Leeds* 2:121.

41. Baltzell, *Philadelphia Gentlemen*, 244–245.

42. "An Ordinance," *Philadelphia Inquirer*, November 22, 1884, in *Leeds* 2:113.

43. *Philadelphia Inquirer*, December 10, 1884, in *Leeds* 2:121.

44. *Philadelphia Inquirer*, December 10, 1884; and *Ledger*, December 10, 1884, in *Leeds* 2:121; unlabeled clippings in *Leeds* 4:47.

45. Walker to Leeds, February 3, 1885, in *Leeds* 3:10.

46. Leeds to J. G. Walker, February 9, 1885, in *Leeds* 3:10.

47. Walker to Leeds, March 4, 1885, in *Leeds* 3:18; see also *Leeds* 3:34. The chairman of the Citizens' Representative Committee was Samuel C. Brown, the secretary Theodore Barrett, and the treasurer George I. Bodine; see *Leeds* 3:3.

48. "To Repress Vice," unlabeled clipping, April 12, 1885, in *Leeds* 3:26.

49. "The Citizen's Representative Committee of Philadelphia," in *Leeds* 3:34.

50. As the Friends had declined formal representation, Leeds served as one of these individuals.

51. It does not seem that Leeds was ever formally made chairman of this group. That he claimed the title in this letter indicates that he must have been confident of his influence in the organization.

52. *Leeds* 3:35. Leeds had written a suggested penalty for persons defying the mayor, but struck this out on the advice of District Attorney Graham.

53. Leeds to George Graham, April 15, 1885, in *Leeds* 3:35.

54. Section 2 of "An Act to prevent and punish the making and dissemination of obscene literature and other immoral and indecent matter" made illegal the sale of papers "principally made up of criminal news, or pictures and stories of deeds of bloodshed, lust or crime" to minors. While this potentially gave Leeds recourse against the *Police Gazette*, his records do not indicate that he used it. More important for Leeds was a clause in the law that exempted art, which Leeds did not know about until after it became law. *Laws of the General Assembly of the State of Pennsylvania Passed at the Session of 1887* (Harrisburg: Edwin K. Meyers, State Printer, 1887), 85.

55. *Philadelphia Inquirer,* May 13, 1885, in *Leeds* 3:38. Gilmore was convicted by Judge Biddle and fined one hundred dollars; see *Leeds* 3:63.

56. *North American*, July 8, 1885, in *Leeds* 3:46; *Press*, July 8, 1885, in *Leeds* 3:46.

57. Leeds to Graham, October 20, 1885, in *Leeds* 3:63; Bennett to Leeds, November 12, 1885, in *Leeds* 3:67; *Press*, March 22, 1889, in *Leeds* 5:22.

58. An attempted consolidation of the CRC with the Law and Order Society and the Citizen's State Law and Order League was postponed because an agent from the Law and Order Society had been taking bribes from saloon keepers; see *Ledger*, March 16, 1886, in *Leeds* 3:83. The CRC united with the Law and Order Society two months later.

59. "The Suppression of Unclean Displays," *Christian Statesman*, May 24, 1888, in *Leeds* 4:81. On tobacco cards, see Dolores Mitchell, "Images of Exotic Women in Turn-of-the-Century Tobacco Art," *Feminist Studies* 18 (Spring 1992): 327–350.

60. *Christian Statesman*, December 18, 1890, in *Leeds* 6:84.

61. Meehan to Leeds, May 12, 1892, in *Leeds* 7:61.

62. Leeds to Biddle, March 23, 1886, in *Leeds* 3:89; Biddle to Leeds, March 24, 1886, in *Leeds* 3:89.

63. *Evening Bulletin*, July 6, 1887; *Press*, July 1, 1887; and *Ledger*, July 7, 1887 in *Leeds* 4:39.

64. Graham to Leeds, July 7, 1887, in *Leeds* 4:41.

65. Note from Leeds, in *Leeds* 4:48.

66. "Beauty Unadorned," *New York Herald*, November 19, 1887, p. 3, col. 2.

67. Clipping labeled *Press*, January 17, 1888, and unlabeled clippings in *Leeds* 4:66. On the law, see *Laws of the General Assembly of the State of Pennsylvania*, 86. A discussion of this case in the *Christian Statesman* quoted Leeds as saying that when he received a copy of this law it did not contain any reference

to "works of art," although an examination of the law as written revealed that art was indeed exempted. See "A Work of the Devil's Art," *Christian Statesman*, n.d., in *Leeds* 4:66.

68. Comstock to Leeds, March 30, 1888, in *Leeds* 4:75.

69. "The Telegraph Pictures," unlabeled clipping, in *Leeds* 4:74.

70. The attempt to blame censorship on Leeds rather than on the police was not confined to the press. One editorial noted that the assistant district attorney had claimed that because he had argued for Knoedler's acquittal, the religious papers attacked him. He held Leeds and Comstock responsible for the attack. The editorial continued: "As Mr. Leeds has never met Comstock, and had nothing whatever to do with the 'attacks,' this was a very injurious remark and apparently emboldened the counsel for the newsmen to also bring in Mr. Leeds name at numerous times and connecting it with Comstock's, against whom the New York newspapers have succeeded in raising a decided prejudice." See "Newspaper High Art," *Guide*, n.d., in *Leeds* 4:74.

71. *Ledger*, February 28, 1891, and March 6, 1891, in *Leeds* 6:106.

72. "Purity in Art Exhibits," *Philadelphia Inquirer*, March 6, 1891, in *Leeds* 6:108.

73. The letter was signed by Mrs. Samuel Clements, Mrs. Rene Guillon, Mrs. Wilbur F. Paddock, Mrs. William F. Biddle, Mrs. Wilbur F. Watkins, Mrs. William Burnham, Mrs. William G. Moorhead, Mrs. J. E. Whitney, Mrs. J. C. Hunter, Mrs. R. Redfield, Mrs. Walter Erben, Mrs. A. Van Harlingen, "Representing, by actual count, over 500 of the Christian women of Philadelphia." "Pictures of the Nude," clipping in *Leeds* 6:106.

74. Ibid.

75. "Purity in Art Exhibits," *Inquirer*, March 6, 1891, in *Leeds* 6:108.

76. "The Nude Pictures at the Academy," *Philadelphia Inquirer*, March 9, 1891, in *Leeds* 6:106.

77. *Philadelphia Inquirer*, March 23, 1891, in *Leeds* 6:109.

78. *Leeds* 6:108.

79. "For a Pure, Fine Arts Display at the Columbian Exposition," undated clipping, in *Leeds* 7:62.

80. "Protests against the Nude," *Washington Star*, n.d., in *Leeds* 6:108.

81. Leeds to Department of Treasury, November 13, 1891, in *Leeds* 7:17; Spaulding to Leeds, November 17, 1891, in *Leeds* 7:17

82. *Commercial Advertiser*, n.d., in *Leeds* 7:18.

83. *Bulletin*, November 21, 1891, in *Leeds* 7:19.

84. "A Pestiferous Crank," unlabeled clipping, in *Leeds* 7:19.

85. The figures for Comstock are calculated from Johnson, "Anthony Comstock: Reform, Vice, and the American Way," table 12, p. 195.

86. Leeds to Isaac Sharpless, July 16, 1884, in *Leeds* 2:97.

87. "Protesting against the Ballet," *Philadelphia Inquirer*, January 25, 1887, in *Leeds* 4:4.

88. *Christian Statesman*, February 10, 1887, in *Leeds* 4:8.

89. *Christian Statesman*, June 16, 1887, in *Leeds* 4:34.

90. "Concerning the Charity Ball," pamphlet in *Leeds*, vol. 2.

91. M. W. B. Davis to Leeds, December 15, 1885, in *Leeds* 3:69.

92. Leeds to Wanamaker, May 14, 1886, in *Leeds* 3:97; Wanamaker to Leeds, May 29, 1886, in *Leeds* 3:96.

93. Wanamaker to Leeds, February 15, 1890, in *Leeds* 6:17.

94. Baltzell, *Puritan Boston and Quaker Philadelphia*, 49–53, 103.

95. "Against Flash Papers," clipping in *Leeds* 2:120; "Letter to the Select and Common Councils of the City of Philadelphia," *Leeds* 3:8.

96. See Leeds's note on Baldwin to Leeds, May 14, 1886, in *Leeds* 3:96.

97. Comstock to Leeds, April 16, 1885, and "Private and Confidential," April 27, 1885, in *Leeds* 3:37.

98. Stevenson to Leeds, March 8, 1887, in *Leeds* 4:20.

99. Leeds to the Collector of Customs, Toronto, March 8, 1889, in *Leeds* 5:39.

100. Leeds to Wanamaker, March 25, 1889, in *Leeds* 5:39.

101. Tyner to Wanamaker, April 8, 1889, in *Leeds* 5:39.

102. NYSSV, *Twelfth Annual Report*, 1886, 12.

103. Hickey to Leeds, February 21, 1885, in *Leeds* 3:11; Leeds to Holmes, March 6, 1885, in *Leeds* 3:16. Holmes wanted one thousand copies, but she was not yet clear about the best place for literature in her department; see Holmes to Leeds, March 11, 1885, in *Leeds* 3:20.

104. Willard to Deborah Leeds, and note by Josiah Leeds on back of letter dated June 6, 1887, in *Leeds* 4:35.

105. Smith to Josiah and Deborah Leeds, October 17, 1887, in *Leeds* 4:49.

106. Woodbridge to Deborah Leeds, November 24, 1887, in *Leeds* 4:51.

107. Note on letter from Gordon to Leeds, December 15, 1887, in *Leeds* 4:54.

108. Deborah Leeds, "Dealing with Demoralizing Literature," in *Leeds* 4:92.

109. Office of the President of the WCTU to Leeds, March 19, 1891, in *Leeds* 6:115.

110. "Protest against Immoral Agencies in Philadelphia," in *Leeds* 6:128. Leeds was elected to the Board of Directors of the Social Purity Alliance in May 1886, although he was not there for his election and was informed of it afterward; see Stevenson to Leeds, in *Leeds* 3:100. He was elected as "Friends Orthodox Representative" to the same organization in 1887, which honor he was also informed of by mail; see Mary J. Gawthorp to Leeds, October 29, 1887, in *Leeds* 4:49. The alliance publicly protested against the theater in 1888 by signing an appeal printed in the *Episcopal Recorder*. This appeal was written by Leeds, and he signed it as a vice president of the organization; see "To the Law-Abiding, Purity-Loving People of Philadelphia," *Episcopal Recorder*, January 5, 1888, in *Leeds* 4:56.

111. This information appeared in Josiah Leeds's obituary, an unlabeled clipping entitled "Josiah W. Leeds, Vice Fighter, Dead" in the Quaker Collection at Haverford College.

112. "Steel's 'Saint Anthony,'" clipping labeled the *Press*, January 17, 1888, in *Leeds* 4:66. The clipping in Leeds's scrapbook has the lines about his weeping crossed out.

113. "Supplementary Considerations upon Purity in Fine Arts Exhibits," March 26, 1891, in *Leeds* 6:113. Leeds's Quakerism may partially account for his

support of women's rights. See Nancy A. Hewitt, "Feminist Friends: Agrarian Quakers and the Emergence of Women's Rights in America," *Feminist Studies* 12 (Spring 1986): 27–49.

114. In the 1880s and 1890s Francis Willard, a professor at Northwestern University, became a leading women's rights advocate, a suffragist, and a friend of Terrance Powderly, head of the Knights of Labor. As president of the WCTU she worked for the six-day workweek, supported the right of labor to strike, and supported prison reform. See Gusfield, *Symbolic Crusade*, 77–78.

115. See Kathleen D. McCarthy, *Women's Culture* (Chicago: University of Chicago Press, 1991), chap. 5.

116. On the formation of museums of art in Boston, Philadelphia, and New York, see Nathaniel Burt, *Palaces for the People* (Boston: Little, Brown, and Co., 1977); Winifred E. Howe, *A History of the Metropolitan Museum of Art* (New York: Metropolitan Museum of Art, 1913); Jaher, *The Urban Establishment*; Elizabeth McFadden, *The Glitter and the Gold* (New York: Dial Press, 1971); Lillian B. Miller, *Patrons and Patriotism* (Chicago: University of Chicago Press, 1966); George Roberts and Mary Roberts, *Triumph on Fairmount* (Philadelphia: Lippincott, 1959); and Calvin Tomkins, *Merchants and Masterpieces* (New York: E. P. Dutton and Co., 1970).

117. Baltzell, *Philadelphia Gentlemen*; Domhoff, *The Higher Circles*; Jaher, *The Urban Establishment*; McLachlan, *American Boarding Schools*, 214, 343. Anti-vice leaders had more than a passing interest in elite education. Groton, one of the country's most prestigious prep schools, was founded in 1884, when Phillips Brooks, vice president of the Boston anti-vice society, suggested to Endicott Peabody that he start a boarding school; see Solomon, *Ancestors and Immigrants*, 47. Brooks then served as president of Groton's board of trustees. J. P. Morgan, a founder of the New York Society for the Suppression of Vice, was also a Groton trustee; see McLachlan, *American Boarding Schools*, 251.

## CHAPTER 7
## MORALS VERSUS ART

1. Paul DiMaggio, "Cultural Entrepreneurship in Nineteenth-Century Boston," *Media, Culture, and Society*, pts. 1 and 2, 4 (1982): 33–50 and 303–322; Martin Green, *The Problem of Boston* (New York: W. W. Norton and Co., 1966); Alan Trachtenberg, *The Incorporation of America* (New York: Hill and Wang, 1982).

2. Quoted in Calvin Tomkins, *Merchants and Masterpieces* (New York: E. P. Dutton and Co., 1970), 84.

3. Metropolitan Museum of Art, *Annual Report, of the Trustees of the Association*, 1875, 66.

4. Trachtenberg, *The Incorporation of America*.

5. *Proceedings at the Opening of the Museum of Fine Arts*, 1876 (Boston: Alfred Mudge and Son), 6.

6. Burt, *Palaces for the People*; Elizabeth Johns, "The Farmer in the Work of William Sidney Mount," *Journal of Interdisciplinary History* 17 (1986): 257–281.

7. Metropolitan Museum of Art, *Annual Report of the Trustees of the Association*, 1880, 178.

8. Metropolitan Museum of Art, *Annual Report of the Trustees of the Association*, 1875, 65.

9. Metropolitan Museum of Art, *Annual Report of the Trustees of the Association*, 1874.

10. NYSSV, *Fifth Annual Report*, 1879, 16.

11. Ibid.

12. Ibid., 17

13. Levine, *Highbrow/Lowbrow*.

14. Comstock, *Traps for the Young*, 171.

15. Ibid., 170.

16. NYSSV, *Fifth Annual Report*, 1879, 16.

17. NYSSV, *Ninth Annual Report*, 1883, 8.

18. NYSSV, *Fifth Annual Report*, 1879, 16.

19. Comstock, *Traps for the Young*, 174.

20. NYSSV, *Fifth Annual Report*, 1879, 16.

21. NYSSV, *Ninth Annual Report*, 1883, 7.

22. Ibid., 8.

23. Comstock, *Traps for the Young*, 179.

24. NYSSV, *Twelfth Annual Report*, 1886, 12.

25. NYSSV, *Eighth Annual Report*, 1882, 6.

26. *Minutes*, February 6, 1882.

27. *Minutes*, March 6, 1882.

28. Thomas B. Harned, "Whitman and His Boston Publishers," *Conservator* (January 1896): 163.

29. Ibid.

30. "Whitman's 'Leaves of Grass,' " *New York Times*, May 22, 1882, 1.

31. McCoy, "Banned in Boston."

32. NESSV, *Report*, 1881–1882, 4.

33. McCoy, "Banned in Boston," 95.

34. Blatt, *Free Love and Anarchism*. The extent of opposition to the suppression of Whitman's poems is disputed. Blatt asserts that Benjamin Tucker challenged the censorship of Whitman by obtaining several copies of *Leaves of Grass* and selling them openly, but another source claims that the threat of prosecution made Boston book dealers circulate the book as secretly as possible. See William S. Kennedy, "Suppressing a Poet," *Conservator* (January 1895): 169–171.

35. *Boston Evening Transcript*, May 22, 1882, p. 1. A week later the *Transcript* reprinted an editorial from the *Saturday Evening Gazette* that criticized Whitman's defenders.

Since the revolt of decency against Mr. Whitman's literary improprieties, he has found admirers ready to rush into print with arguments in his favor. Their theory seems to be that Mr. Whitman should not be suppressed because the Bible and Shakespeare are allowed to go their way unchecked by law. But there is a maximum of poetry and a minimum of dirt in both the Bible and Shakespeare, whereas in "Leaves of Grass" the order is reversed.

... It is a cause for general felicitation that "Leaves of Grass" must no longer be published, and we may hail its disappearance with the familiar and homely sentiment, "A good riddance to bad rubbish." (*Boston Evening Transcript*, May 29, 1882, p. 4)

36. Sprague, "Societies for the Suppression of Vice," 72–73.

37. Ibid., 74, italics in original.

38. Walt Whitman, "A Woman Waits for Me," in *Leaves of Grass* (New York: Bantam Books, 1983), 83.

39. Whitman to William O'Connor, cited in Blatt, *Free Love and Anarchism*, 143.

40. Walt Whitman, "A Memorandum at a Venture," *North American Review* 134 (May 1882): 548.

41. William Douglas O'Connor, "Another Recovered Chapter in the History of 'Leaves of Grass,'" *Conservator* 7, no. 7 (September 1896): 99.

42. Jane Clapp, *Art Censorship: A Chronology of Proscribed and Prescribed Art* (Metuchen, N.J.: Scarecrow Press, 1972); *New York Tribune*, November 12, 1887, p. 3; *World*, November 13, 1887, p. 1.

43. Burt, *Palaces for the People*, 83.

44. See *Morning Journal*, November 13, 1887, p. 1; *World*, November 13, 1887, p. 1; *New York Tribune*, November 12, 1887, p. 3; *New York Evening Post*, November 17, 1887, p. 4; *New York Herald*, November 13, 1887, p. 4; *New York Times*, November 17, 1887, p. 9.

45. NYSSV, *Annual Report*, 1884, 11.

46. Clapp, *Art Censorship*, 158; Anthony Comstock, *Morals versus Art* (New York: J. S. Ogilvie and Co., 1887), 24.

47. Edward de Grazia, ed., *Censorship Landmarks* (New York: R. R. Bowker Co., 1969), 43.

48. NYSSV, *Tenth Annual Report*, 1884, 11.

49. *World*, November 17, 1887, p. 8.

50. *New York Herald*, November 13, 1887, p. 4.

51. Clapp, *Art Censorship*, 133; Burt, *Palaces for the People*.

52. *New York Herald*, November 13, 1887, p. 4.

53. *World*, November 20, 1887, p. 13.

54. *New York Herald*, November 15, 1887, p. 4.

55. *New York Herald*, November 14, 1887, p. 10.

56. *New York Herald*, November 15, 1887, p. 4.

57. *World*, November 17, 1887, p. 8.

58. *Evening Post*, November 17, 1887, p. 4.

59. Ibid., November 18, 1887, p. 4.

60. *New York Tribune*, November 12, 1887, p. 3.

61. *New York Times*, December 16, 1887, p. 4.

62. *New York Herald*, November 13, 1887, p. 4.

63. *World*, November 13, 1887, p. 1.

64. Ibid.

65. The artists signing this petition included William M. Chase, Augustus St. Gaudens, J. Alden Weir, Kenyon Cox, John La Farge, Wyatt Eaton, D. W. Tryon, and numerous others.

66. *World*, November 17, 1887, p. 8. I have found only one dissent to this statement from an artist. The letter appeared in the *Evening Post*, and asked,

> Do the artists know that the class of pictures referred to not only violate a proper sense of decency, but that they are painted for just this degrading ministry? Why is it that the female nude is always, or mostly always, the medium of the "innocent," "ennobling," and "refining" ministry so dear to the gentlemen who are constrained to vocal indignation to secure this "greatest educational benefit to the community"?

The letter is signed by "James Fairman, A.M., Artist." See *New York Evening Post*, December 5, 1887, p. 9.

67. *Evening Post*, November 17, 1887, p. 4.

68. *New York Herald*, November 15, 1887, p. 4.

69. Timothy J. Clark, *The Painting of Modern Life* (Princeton: Princeton University Press, 1984); Hollis Clayson, *Painted Love* (New Haven: Yale University Press, 1991); Peter Brooks, *Body Work* (Cambridge: Harvard University Press, 1993); Albert Boime, *The Academy and French Painting in the Nineteenth Century* (New Haven: Yale University Press, 1971).

70. *Evening Telegram*, November 15, 1887, p. 4.

71. *New York Herald*, November 13, 1887, p. 4.

72. *New York Herald*, November 14, 1887, p. 10.

73. British artists sometimes represented French culture as a direct threat to the family. It is not clear why this existing counterdiscourse, which could have given some legitimacy to Comstock's claims about the effects of French culture, was never invoked during the debate about French nudes. It is understandable that Comstock would be ignorant of it, and perhaps that artists were so oriented to the French Academy that they would ignore British examples, but it is curious that no members of America's anglophile upper class invoked the example of the British in this debate. See Lynda Nead, *Myths of Sexuality: Representations of Women in Victorian Britain* (New York: Basil Blackwell, 1988).

74. *New York Herald*, November 14, 1887, p. 10.

75. See the *New York Daily Tribune*, November 12, 1887, p. 3; *New York Herald*, November 13, 1887, p. 4; *Star*, November 17, 1887, p. 1.

76. *Star*, November 17, 1887, p. 1.

77. *Art Amateur*, January 1888, 28.

78. Ibid.

79. Comstock did, however, write to the *Evening Post* in response to a letter printed under the pseudonym "Broad Brim" that claimed that a New Jersey man was convicted, "in default of proper defense by counsel," of selling "classical works which can be bought in any first-class booksellers store." *Evening Post*, November 21, 1887, p. 4. Comstock's letter responding to this and other charges made by "Broad Brim" was printed by the *Evening Post*, on November 28, 1887, p. 5.

80. *New York Times*, December 13, 1887, p. 2.

81. *New York Herald*, November 13, 1887, p. 4.

82. *World*, November 20, 1887, p. 13.

83. *New York Herald*, November 13, 1887, p. 4.

84. Comstock, *Morals versus Art*, 8–9.

85. In 1880 the *Art Amateur* published a series of critiques of the policies of the Metropolitan Museum of Art. Responding to the trustees' appeal for more public funds for the museum, the *Art Amateur* noted that taxpayers had already paid for the museum building and added, "Another point should be insisted on before one dollar of the quarter of a million is subscribed. This is that the Museum should be opened on Sunday afternoons. That day is the only one on which the working public can visit it." See "Public Rights in a Public Museum," *Art Amateur* 2, no. 6 (May 1880): 112–113.

86. Comstock, *Morals versus Art*, 11.

87. Clapp, *Art Censorship*, 159. Clapp incorrectly dates this incident and *Life* magazine's response to it, reporting that it happened between 1887 and 1893 and that *Life* responded with a satirical drawing of the painting as Comstock would have it—with the horses wearing pants. *Life* published this cartoon in January of 1888, nearly a decade after the incident, in the midst of the furor over Knoedler's. See Broun and Leech, *Anthony Comstock: Roundsman of the Lord*, 239.

88. NYSSV, *Fifth Annual Report*, 1879, p. 17.

89. "My Note Book," *Art Amateur* 1, no. 4 (September 1879): 69.

90. *New York Evening Post*, November 18, 1887, p. 4; *New York Herald*, November 19, 1887, p. 3.

91. *New York Times*, November 24, 1887, p. 3.

92. *New York Herald*, November 14, 1887, p. 10.

93. Clark, *The Painting of Modern Life*, 123. It has also been described as "a heated, orgiastic struggle," by Horst de la Croix and Richard G. Tansey in *Gardner's Art through the Ages*, 8th ed. (New York: Harcourt, Brace, Jovanovich, 1986), 853.

94. "My Note Book," *Art Amateur* 16, no. 4 (March 1887).

95. *Evening Post*, December 5, 1887, p. 9.

96. Comstock, *Morals versus Art*, 11.

97. NYSSV, *Eighth Annual Report*, 1882, 6–7.

98. Comstock, *Morals versus Art*, 6.

99. Ibid.

100. Ibid., 7.

101. Ibid., 9.

102. NYSSV, *Fourteenth Annual Report*, 1888, 32.

103. Ibid., 25.

104. "The Nude in Art," *Appleton's Journal* 32 (February 1879): 183.

105. "The Nude in Art Once More," *Appleton's Journal* 40 (October 1879): 375.

106. Comstock, *Traps for the Young*, 34.

107. Ibid., 9.

108. Ibid., 11.

109. NYSSV, *Thirteenth Annual Report*, 1887, 13.

110. Comstock, *Morals versus Art*, 10.

111. Ibid., 4.

112. *World*, November 13, 1887, p. 1.

113. *Evening Telegram*, November 15, 1887, p. 4.

114. Comstock, *Traps for the Young*, 180. Leeds would have concurred with these sentiments, but I have found no evidence that he wrote them.

115. NYSSV, *Fourteenth Annual Report*, 1888, p. 32.

116. *Evening Telegram*, November 16, 1887, p. 1.

117. Comstock, *Morals versus Art*, 22–24; de Grazia, *Censorship Landmarks*, 42–44.

118. *New York Herald*, November 13, 1887, p. 4.

119. NYSSV, *Thirteenth Annual Report*, 1887, 34–41.

120. *Star*, November 18, 1887, p. 4.

121. *New York Herald*, November 20, 1887, p. 10.

122. Comstock to Leeds, November 21, 1887, in *Leeds* 4:51.

123. *New York Herald*, March 24, 1888, p. 3. It is not clear if they were ever tried. Most histories of the case claim that the defendants were fined three hundred dollars, which was the amount of their bail, so perhaps Knoedler and his assistant decided to forgo a trial. See Clapp, *Art Censorship*, 161; and Theodore A. Schroeder, *Free Speech Bibliography* (New York: H. W. Wilson Co., 1922), 188.

124. These were *La Asphyxie*, by Cherubino Pata; *After the Bath*, by Joseph Wencker; *La Baigneuse*, by Leon Jean Basile Perrault; and *La Repose*, by Chambord. Clapp, *Art Censorship*, 157.

125. *New York Herald*, March 24, 1888, p. 3.

126. Ibid.

127. *Morning Journal*, March 25, 1888, p. 4.

128. *New York Times*, March 24, 1888, p. 4.

129. *Star*, March 25, 1888, p. 4.

130. Ibid. The coincidence of the Knoedler raid with the hanging of the Haymarket anarchists prompted the *Star* to write an editorial comparing two of their enemies: the imprisoned anarchist Most, and Comstock.

> It is pretty hard to say whether Herr Most or Anthony Comstock is the bigger public nuisance. We have always been inclined to give the palm to the Anarchist, but we must admit that the weight of opinion is against us. Herr Most makes a great many threats, but Comstock acts as well as talks. Most warns that he will invade the homes and stores of our best merchants, but he has never done so, which Comstock has. Finally, Johann is locked up in the penitentiary occasionally and we have a period of peace and quiet, but Anthony rolls on forever. (*Star*, November 19, 1887, p. 4)

131. NYSSV, *Fifteenth Annual Report*, 1889, p. 15.

132. Dr. Howard Crosby quoted in "The Nude in Art," *Catholic Presbyterian* 2, no. 10 (October 1879): 304.

133. Boyer, "Banned in Boston," 95.

134. *New York Tribune Monthly*, June 1892.

135. Jaher, *The Urban Establishment*, 270–271.

136. E. P. Richardson, *Painting in America* (New York: Thomas Y. Crowell, 1965). The nouveau riches of Paris are credited with the proliferation of nudes there as well; see Clark, *The Painting of Modern Life*, 130.

137. Walter Muir Whitehill, *Museum of Fine Arts, Boston: A Centennial History*, vol. 1 (Cambridge: Harvard University Press, Belknap Press 1970), 31.

138. Clapp, *Art Censorship*; Trevor J. Fairbrother, *The Bostonians: Painters of an Elegant Age, 1870–1980* (Boston: Museum of Fine Arts, 1986).

139. Cited in Whitehill, *Museum of Fine Arts, Boston*, 81.

140. *Boston Evening Transcript*, April 1, 1891, in NESSV, *Reports*, 1890–1891, 19–20.

141. Warren K. Blodgett, Jr., to F. B. Allen, *Letters*, April 3, 1891.

142. *Minutes*, December 5, 1887.

143. NESSV, *Reports*, 1890–1891, 6–7.

144. H. S. Carruth to F. B. Allen, *Letters*, April 15, 1891.

145. NESSV, *Reports*, 1890–1891, 7; McCoy, "Banned in Boston," 133.

## CHAPTER 8
## CONCLUSION

1. Binder, "Constructing Racial Rhetoric."

2. See Peter W. Cookson and Caroline Hodges Percell, *Preparing for Power: America's Elite Boarding Schools* (New York: Basic Books, 1985); Caroline Hodges Percell and Peter W. Cookson, "Chartering and Bartering: Elite Education and Social Reproduction," *Social Problems* 33 (December 1985): 14–29; Richard L. Zweigenhaft and G. William Domhoff, *Blacks in the White Establishment* (New Haven: Yale University Press, 1991); Ostrander, *Women of the Upper Class*.

3. My thanks to Jane Mansbridge for directing me to this source.

4. Richard Sennett and Jonathan Cobb, *The Hidden Injuries of Class* (New York: Vintage Books, 1972), 49.

5. Ibid., 50.

6. Ibid., 128. On sacrificing for the people one loves, see p. 101–102 and 124.

7. Kathleen Gerson, *No Man's Land* (New York: Basic Books, 1993); Newman, *Declining Fortunes*.

8. Anthony Lewis, "Anger and Reality," *New York Times*, November 1994.

9. Gusfield, *Symbolic Crusade*, 14.

10. Ibid., 15.

11. Reinhard Bendix, "Inequality and Social Structure: A Comparison of Marx and Weber," *American Sociological Review* 39 (1974): 149–161.

12. Max Weber, "Class, Status, Party," in *Class, Status, and Power*, ed. Reinhard Bendix and Seymour Martin Lipset (Glencoe, Ill: Free Press, 1953), 63–75.

13. Gusfield, *Symbolic Crusade*, 18.

14. Ibid., 21.

15. Ibid., 140.

16. Louis A. Zurcher and R. George Kirkpatrick, *Citizens for Decency: Antipornography Crusades as Status Defense* (Austin: University of Texas Press, 1976); Gerhard E. Lenski, "Status Crystallization: A Non-Vertical Dimension of Status," *American Sociological Review* 19 (1954): 405–413; and "Social Participation and Status Crystallization," *American Sociological Review* 21 (1956):

458–464. The data presented in this book on support of the anti-vice society by various segments of the upper class do not support the predictions of status discrepancy or status discontent theories, as support for the anti-vice society was highest among those who were both Social Registrants and millionaires. I discuss this in more detail in "Class, Culture, and Campaigns against Vice in Three American Cities, 1872–1892," *American Sociological Review* 55 (February 1990): 44–62.

17. Roy Wallis, "A Critique of the Theory of Moral Crusades as Status Defense," *Scottish Journal of Sociology* 1 (1977): 195–203.

18. Ann L. Page and Donald A. Clelland, "The Kanawa County Textbook Controversy: A Study in the Politics of Lifestyle Concern," *Social Forces* 57 (September 1978): 267.

19. Page and Clelland found that persons protesting against the books had, on average, 10.9 years of education, while defenders of textbooks averaged 14.2 years of education. Instead of attempting to explain this significant difference, Page and Clelland made the spurious argument that because anti-textbook males averaged 11.9 years of education while pro-textbook females averaged 12.3 years of education, the conflict over textbooks was not "simply a dispute between members of educational strata." Page and Clelland, "The Kanawa County Textbook Controversy," 273.

20. Ann L. Page and Donald A. Clelland, "Kanawha County Revisted: Reply to Billings and Goldman," *Social Forces* 57 (September 1980): 282.

21. Dwight Billings and Robert Goldman, "Comment on the Kanawa County Textbook Controversy," *Social Forces* 57 (1979): 1393–1398.

22. Michael Wood and Michael Hughes, "The Moral Basis of Moral Reform: Status Discontent versus Culture and Socialization as Explanations of Anti-Pornography Social Movement Adherence," *American Sociological Review* 49 (1984): 86–99.

23. See Alan Clarke, "Moral Protest, Status Defence and the Anti-Abortion Campaign," *British Journal of Sociology* 38 (1987): 235–253; Joseph Tamney and Stephen Johnson, "Explaining Support for the Moral Majority," *Sociological Forum* 3 (1988): 234–255; Michael C. Moen, "Status Politics and the Political Agenda of the Christian Right," *Sociological Quarterly* 29, no. 3 (1988): 429–437; Wilbur J. Scott, "The Equal Rights Amendment as Status Politics," *Social Forces* 64 (1985): 499–506.

24. Erik Olin Wright, Carolyn Howe, and Doonmoo Cho, "Class Structure and Class Formation: A Comparative Analysis of the United States and Sweden," in *Cross-National Research in Sociology*, ed. Melvin L. Kohn (Newbury Park, Calif.: Sage Publications, 1989), 186.

25. Ibid., 187.

26. Eric Olin Wright, *Classes* (London: Verso Press, 1985), 29. Thus, when writing *Classes* Wright ignored almost two decades of feminist organizing and feminist scholarship. In doing so he evaded the knotty problem of trying to determine the class position of married women, whether in the labor force or not, and the class position of men who are married to employed women. Wright and Shin tried to address the latter problem by studying the subjective class identities of

married men and women; see Erik Olin Wright and Kwang-Yeong Shin, "Temporality and Class Analysis: A Comparative Study of the Effects of Class Trajectory and Class Structure on Class Consciousness in Sweden and the United States," *Sociological Theory* 6 (1988): 58–84. An excellent review of the debate on class and gender, which focuses on implications of gender theory for Wright's work, is Rosemary Crompton's "Class Theory and Gender," *British Journal of Sociology* 40 (December 1989): 565–587.

27. Wright and Shin, "Temporality and Class Analysis," 69.

28. Wright and Shin have attempted to take account of E. P. Thompson and the scholars who have been influenced by him, but this has not altered Wright's scheme for determining class interests. Instead, Wright and Shin propose that class identities might be the product of history but that class interests are still determined by class structures. Wright and Shin, "Temporality and Class Analysis."

29. Brian Elliott and David McCrone, "Class, Culture, and Morality: A Sociological Analysis of the New Conservatism," *Sociological Review* 35 (1987): 490.

30. Ibid., 503.

31. Ibid., 506

32. E. P. Thompson, *The Making of the English Working Class* (New York: Vintage Press, 1963), 11.

33. Ibid., 9.

34. William Sewell, Jr., "How Classes are Made: Critical Reflections on E. P. Thompson's Theory of Working-Class Formation," in *E. P. Thompson: Critical Perspectives*, ed. Harvey J. Kaye and Keith McClelland (Oxford: Polity Press, 1990), 50–77.

35. See Joan Wallach Scott, *Gender and the Politics of History* (New York: Columbia University Press, 1988); Kathleen Canning, "Gender and the Politics of Class Formation: Rethinking German Labor History," *American Historical Review* 97 (1992): 736–768.

36. Sonya Rose, *Limited Livelihood: Gender and Class in Nineteenth-Century England* (Berkeley: University of California Press, 1992); Brenner and Laslett, "Social Reproduction and the Family."

37. See Hanagan, *Nascent Proletarians*, and "New Perspectives on Class Formation."

38. Scott G. McNall, *The Road to Rebellion: Class Formation and Kansas Populism, 1865–1900* (Chicago: University of Chicago Press, 1988).

39. See William G. Roy, "Institutional Governance" and "The Social Organization of the Corporate Class Segment"; Maurice Zeitlin, "Corporate Ownership and Control: The Large Corporation and the Capitalist Class," *American Journal of Sociology* 79 (1974): 1073–1119. Zeitlin argues, "The concepts of kinecon group and of social class are therefore integrally related; both refer to the fusion of the kinship and property systems—and this fusion, in turn, tends to reproduce (literally and figuratively) the existing dominant class over time." *Landlords and Capitalists: The Dominant Class of Chile* (Princeton: Princeton University Press, 1988), 7.

40. Roy, "The Social Organization of the Corporate Class Segment," 25, 29.

41. Ibid., 31.

42. Bourdieu, *Distinction*; and "What Makes a Social Class: On the Theoretical and Practical Existence of Groups," *Berkeley Journal of Sociology* 32 (1987): 1–17.

43. See Bourdieu, *Distinction*, 101–102.

44. Lareau, *Home Advantage*; Paul DiMaggio and John Mohr, "Cultural Capital, Educational Attainment, and Marital Selection," *American Journal of Sociology* 90 (1985): 1231–1261.

45. Bourdieu, *Distinction*.

46. Ibid.; and Bourdieu, "The Social Space and the Genesis of Groups," *Theory and Society* 14 (1985): 723–744.

47. Lamont, *Money, Manners, and Morals*.

48. Bourdieu, *Distinction*, 435.

49. Ibid.

50. Ibid., 106. Leslie McCall analyzes gender issues in Bourdieu's work in "Does Gender *Fit*? Feminism, Bourdieu, and Conceptions of Social Order," *Theory and Society* 21 (November 1992): 837–867.

51. Bourdieu, *Distinction*, 108.

# BIBLIOGRAPHY

Abelson, Elaine S. 1989. *When Ladies Go A-Thieving*. New York: Oxford University Press.

Aldrich, Nelson W., Jr. 1988. *Old Money*. New York: Vintage Books.

Amory, Cleveland. 1957. *The Proper Bostonians*. New York: E. P. Dutton and Co.

———. 1960. *Who Killed Society?* New York: Harper and Brothers.

Arch-deacon, Thomas J. 1983. *Becoming American: An Ethnic History*. New York: Free Press.

Baltzell, E. Digby. [1958] 1979. *Philadelphia Gentlemen: The Making of a National Upper Class*. Philadelphia: University of Pennsylvania Press.

———. 1979. *Puritan Boston and Quaker Philadelphia*. Boston: Beacon Press.

Barker-Benfield, Ben. 1978. "The Spermatic Economy: A Nineteenth-Century View of Sexuality." In *The American Family in Socio-Historical Perspective*, 2d ed., edited by Michael Gordon. New York: St. Martin's Press

Battan, Jessie F. 1992. "'The Word Made Flesh': Language, Authority, and Sexual Desire in Late-Nineteenth-Century America." *Journal of the History of Sexuality* 3:223–244.

Becker, Howard S. 1963. *Outsiders*. New York: Free Press of Glencoe.

Beisel, Nicola. 1990. "Class, Culture, and Campaigns against Vice in Three American Cities, 1872–1892." *American Sociological Review* 55:44–62.

———. 1993. "Morals versus Art: Censorship, the Politics of Interpretation, and the Victorian Nude." *American Sociological Review* 58:145–162.

Bendix, Reinhard. 1974. "Inequality and Social Structure: A Comparison of Marx and Weber." *American Sociological Review* 39:149–161.

Benjamin, Walter. 1969. "The Work of Art in the Age of Mechanical Reproduction." In *Illuminations*, edited by Hanna Arendt, 217–251. New York: Schocken Books.

Bennett, D. M. 1875. *An Open Letter to Jesus Christ*. New York: The Truth Seeker.

Billings, Dwight, and Robert Goldman. 1979. "Comment on the Kanawha County Textbook Controversy." *Social Forces* 57:1393–1398.

Billings, John S. 1895. *Vital Statistics of Boston and Philadelphia: Covering a Period of Six Years Ending May 31, 1890*. Department of the Interior, Census Office. Washington, D.C.: Government Printing Office.

Binder, Amy. 1993. "Constructing Racial Rhetoric: Media Depictions of Harm in Heavy Metal and Rap Music." *American Sociological Review* 58:753–767.

Blatt, Martin Henry. 1989. *Free Love and Anarchism*. Urbana: University of Illinois Press.

Blodgett, Geoffrey. 1984. "Yankee Leadership in a Divided City: Boston, 1860–1910." In *Boston, 1700–1980: The Evolution of Urban Politics*, edited by Ronald P. Formisano and Constance K. Burns, 87–110. Westport, Conn.: Greenwood Press.

Blumberg, Paul M., and P. W. Paul. 1975. "Continuities and Discontinuities in Upper Class Marriages." *Journal of Marriage and the Family* 37:63–77.

Blumin, Stuart S. 1989. *The Emergence of the Middle Class*. New York: Cambridge University Press.

Bodnar, John. 1985. *The Transplanted: A History of Immigrants in Urban America*. Bloomington: Indiana University Press.

Boime, Albert. [1971] 1986. *The Academy and French Painting in the Nineteenth Century*. New Haven: Yale University Press.

Bordin, Ruth Birgitta Anderson. 1981. *Women and Temperance: The Quest for Power and Liberty, 1873–1900*. Philadelphia: Temple University Press.

*The Boston City Directory*. 1885–1892. Boston: Sampson and Murdock Co.

Boswell, Peyton. 1937. "September Morn." *Art Digest* 11 (June): 4.

Bourdieu, Pierre. 1984. *Distinction*. Cambridge: Harvard University Press.

———. 1985a. "The Market of Symbolic Goods." *Poetics* 14:13–44.

———. 1985b. "The Social Space and the Genesis of Groups." *Theory and Society* 14:723–744.

———. 1987a. "The Historical Genesis of a Pure Aesthetic." *Journal of Aesthetics and Art Criticism* 46:201–210.

———. 1987b. "What Makes a Social Class? On the Theoretical and Practical Existence of Groups." *Berkeley Journal of Sociology* 32:1–17.

———. 1989a. "Flaubert's Point of View." In *Literature and Social Practice*, edited by Phillipe Desan, Pricilla Parkhurst Furguson, and Wendy Griswold, 211–234. Chicago: University of Chicago Press.

———. 1989b. "Social Space and Symbolic Power." *Sociological Theory* 7: 14–25.

Boyer, Paul S. 1968. *Purity in Print: The Vice Society Movement and Book Censorship in America*. New York: Scribner's.

Brandmeyer, Gerard A., and R. Serge Denisoff. 1969. "Status Politics: An Appraisal of the Application of a Concept." *Pacific Sociological Review* 12:5–11.

Braude, Ann. 1989. *Radical Spirits*. Boston: Beacon Press.

Brenner, Johanna, and Barbara Laslett. 1986. "Social Reproduction and the Family." In *Sociology from Crisis to Science? vol. 2. The Social Reproduction of Organization and Culture*, edited by Ulf Himmelstrand, 116–131. London: Sage.

Broder, Sherri Maxine. 1988. "Politics of the Family: Political Culture, Moral Reform, and Family Relations in Gilded Age Philadelphia." Ph.D. dissertation, Brown University.

Brodie, Janet Farrell. 1994. *Contraception and Abortion in Nineteenth-Century America*. Ithaca: Cornell University Press.

Brooks, Peter. 1993. *Body Work*. Cambridge: Harvard University Press.

Broun, Heywood, and Margaret Leech. 1927. *Anthony Comstock, Roundsman of the Lord*. New York: Literary Guild of America.

Browne, Junius Henri. [1869] 1975. *The Great Metropolis: A Mirror of New York*. New York: Arno Press.

Brubaker, Rogers. 1985. "Rethinking Classical Theory: The Sociological Vision of Pierre Bourdieu." *Theory and Society* 14:745–775.

Brumberg, Joan. 1984. "'Ruined Girls': Changing Community Responses to Illegitimacy in Upstate New York, 1890–1920." *Journal of Social History* 18:247–272.

Burstein, Alan N. 1981. "Immigrants and Residential Mobility: The Irish and Germans in Philadelphia, 1850–1880." In *Philadelphia: Work, Space, Family, and Group Experience in the Nineteenth Century*, edited by Theodore Hershberg, 174–203. New York: Oxford University Press.

Burt, Nathaniel. 1963. *The Perennial Philadelphians: The Anatomy of an American Aristocracy*. Boston: Little, Brown.

———. 1977. *Palaces for the People*. Boston: Little, Brown and Company.

Cable, Mary. 1984. *Top Drawer*. New York: Antheneum.

Callow, Alexander B. 1965. *The Tweed Ring*. London: Oxford University Press.

Canning, Kathleen. 1992. "Gender and the Politics of Class Formation: Rethinking German Labor History." *American Historical Review* 97:736–768.

Carlson, A. Cheree. 1991. "The Role of Character in Public Moral Argument: Henry Ward Beecher and the Brooklyn Scandal." *Quarterly Journal of Speech* 77:38–52.

Citizen's Association of Boston. 1889. *First Annual Report*. Boston.

Clapp, Jane. 1972. *Art Censorship: A Chronology of Proscribed and Prescribed Art*. Metuchen, N.J.: Scarecrow Press.

Clark, Clifford E., Jr. 1978. *Henry Ward Beecher*. Urbana: University of Illinois Press.

Clark, Dennis. 1973a. *The Irish in Philadelphia*. Philadelphia: Temple University Press.

———. 1973b. "The Philadelphia Irish: Persistent Presence." In *The Peoples of Philadelphia: A History of Ethnic Groups and Lower-Class Life, 1790–1940*, edited by Allen F. Davis and Mark H. Haller, 135–154. Philadelphia: Temple University Press.

Clark, Kenneth. 1953. *The Nude: A Study in Ideal Form*. New York: Pantheon Books.

Clark, Timothy J. 1980. "Preliminaries to a Possible Treatment of 'Olympia' in 1865." *Screen* 21 (Spring): 18–41.

———. 1984. *The Painting of Modern Life*. Princeton: Princeton University Press.

Clarke, Alan. 1987. "Moral Protest, Status Defence, and the Anti-Abortion Campaign." *British Journal of Sociology* 38:235–253.

Clawson, Mary Ann. 1989. *Constructing Brotherhood: Class, Gender, and Fraternalism*. Princeton: Princeton University Press.

Clayson, Hollis. 1991. *Painted Love*. New Haven: Yale University Press.

Comstock, Anthony. [1880] 1969. *Frauds Exposed*. Montclair, N.J.: Patterson Smith.

———. 1882. "The Suppression of Vice." *North American Review* 135 (November): 484–489.

———. [1883] 1967. *Traps for the Young*. Cambridge: Harvard University Press, Belknap Press.

———. 1887. *Morals versus Art*. New York: J. S. Ogilvie and Co.

———. 1888. "Lawlessness of the Liberal Leagues." *Our Day* 1 (May): 393–398.

Conley, James R. 1988. "More Theory, Less Fact? Social Reproduction and Class Conflict in a Sociological Approach to Working-Class History." *Canadian Journal of Sociology* 12:73–102.

Cook, N. F. 1878. *Satan in Society.* New York: Edward F. Hovey.

Cookson, Peter W., Jr., and Caroline Hodges Persell. 1985. *Preparing for Power: America's Elite Boarding Schools.* New York: Basic Books.

Cott, Nancy F. 1978. "Passionlessness: An Interpretation of Victorian Sexual Ideology, 1790–1850." *Signs* 1, no. 2: 219–236.

Crapsey, Edward. 1872. *The Nether Side of New York, or The Vice, Crime, and Poverty of the Great Metropolis.* New York: Sheldon and Company.

Crompton, Rosemary, 1989. "Class Theory and Gender." *British Journal of Sociology* 40 (December): 565–587.

Davidoff, Lenore, and Catherine Hall. 1987. *Family Fortunes: Men and Women of the English Middle Class, 1780–1850.* Chicago: University of Chicago Press.

Davis, Noah. 1884. "Marriage and Divorce." *North American Review* 139 (July): 30–41.

Degler, Carl N. 1980. *At Odds.* New York: Oxford University Press.

de Grazia, Edward, ed. 1969. *Censorship Landmarks.* New York: R. R. Bowker Co.

de la Croix, Horst, and Richard G. Tansey. 1986. *Gardner's Art through the Ages.* 8th ed. New York: Harcourt Brace Jovanovich.

D'Emilio, John, and Estelle B. Freedman. 1988. *Intimate Matters: A History of Sexuality in America.* New York: Harper and Row.

DiMaggio, Paul. 1979. "Review Essay: On Pierre Bourdieu." *American Journal of Sociology* 6:1460–1474.

———. 1982a. "Cultural Entrepreneurship in Nineteenth-Century Boston: Part I, The Creation of an Organizational Base for High Culture in America." *Media, Culture, and Society* 4:33–50.

———. 1982b. "Cultural Entrepreneurship in Nineteenth-Century Boston: Part II, The Classification and Framing of American Art." *Media, Culture and Society* 4:303–322.

DiMaggio, Paul, and John Mohr. 1985. "Cultural Capital, Educational Attainment, and Marital Selection." *American Journal of Sociology* 90:1231–1261.

DiMaggio, Paul, and Michael Useem. 1978. "Social Class and Arts Consumption: The Origins and Consequences of Class Differences in Exposure to the Arts in America." *Theory and Society* 5:141–161.

Domhoff, G. William. 1968. *Who Rules America?* Boston: Beacon Press.

———. 1971. *The Higher Circles: The Governing Class in America.* New York: Vintage Books.

Dubois, Ellen Carol, and Linda Gordon. 1983. "Seeking Ecstasy on the Battlefield: Danger and Pleasure in Nineteenth-Century Feminist Thought." *Feminist Studies* 9:7–25.

Durham, Martin. 1986. "Class, Conservatism, and the Anti-Abortion Movement: A Review Essay." *Berkeley Journal of Sociology* 31:167–182.

Elliott, Brian, and David McCrone. 1987. "Class, Culture and Morality: A Sociological Analysis of the New Conservatism." *Sociological Review* 35: 485–515.

Ellis, Arthur Blake. 1884. "Municipal Finance." *Harper's New Monthly Magazine* 69 (October): 779–787.

Ellis, John. 1980. "Photography/Pornography/Art/Pornography." *Screen* 21: 81–108.

Erie, Steven P. 1988. *Rainbow's End: Irish-Americans and the Dilemmas of Urban Machine Politics, 1840–1985.* Berkeley: University of California Press.

Fabian, Ann. 1990. *Card Sharps, Dream Books, and Bucket Shops.* Ithaca: Cornell University Press.

Fairbrother, Trevor J. 1986. *The Bostonians: Painters of an Elegant Age.* Boston: Museum of Fine Arts.

Farber, Bernard. 1971. *Kinship and Class.* New York: Basic Books.

Farrell, Betty G. 1993. *Elite Families: Class and Power in Nineteenth-Century Boston.* Albany: State University of New York Press.

Fox, Richard Wightman. 1993. "Intimacy on Trial: Cultural Meanings of the Beecher-Tilton Affair." In *The Power of Culture*, edited by Richard Wightman Fox and T. J. Jackson Lears, 103–132. Chicago: University of Chicago Press.

Fraser, Nancy. 1989. *Unruly Practices: Power, Discourse and Gender in Contemporary Social Theory.* Minneapolis: University of Minnesota Press.

Freedman, Estelle B. 1982. "Sexuality in Nineteenth-Century America: Behavior, Ideology, and Politics." *Reviews in American History* 10:196–215.

Frith, Simon. 1986. "Art versus Technology: The Strange Case of Popular Music." *Media, Culture, and Society* 8:263–279.

Frothingham, O. B. 1882. "The Ethics of Gambling." *North American Review* 135 (August): 162–174.

Gamson, William A., and Andre Modigliani. 1989. "Nuclear Discourse and Public Opinion on Nuclear Power: A Constructionist Approach." *American Journal of Sociology* 95:1–37.

Gardner, Augustus K. 1870. *Conjugal Sins against the Laws of Life and Health and their Effects Upon the Father, Mother, and Child.* New York: J. S. Redfield.

Gerson, Kathleen. 1993. *No Man's Land.* New York: Basic Books.

Giddens, Anthony. 1973. *The Class Structure of the Advanced Societies.* New York: Harper and Row.

Gilfoyle, Timothy. 1992. *City of Eros.* New York: W. W. Norton and Co.

Gillette, Howard F., Jr. 1970. "Corrupt and Contented: Philadelphia's Political Machine, 1865–1887." Ph.D. dissertation, Yale University.

Ginsburg, Faye D. 1989. *Contested Lives.* Berkeley: University of California Press.

———. 1990. "The 'Word-Made' Flesh: The Disembodiment of Gender in the Abortion Debate." In *Uncertain Terms*, edited by Faye Ginsburg and Anna Lowenhaupt Tsing, 59–75. Boston: Beacon Press.

———. 1991. "Gender Politics and the Contradictions of Nurturance: Moral Authority and Constraints to Action for Female Abortion Activists." *Social Research* 58 (Fall): 653–676.

Godkin, E. L. 1878. "The Constitutional Amendment on City Government." *Nation* 26 (February 14): 109.

Godkin, E. L. 1884. "The Alderman and Appointing Power." *Nation* 38 (February 21): 158–159.

Goffman, Erving. 1951. "Symbols of Class Status." *British Journal of Sociology* 2:294–304.

Gordon, Linda. 1990. *Woman's Body, Woman's Right*. New York: Penguin Books.

———. 1982. "Why Nineteenth Century Feminists Did Not Support 'Birth Control' and Twentieth Century Feminists Do: Feminism, Reproduction, and the Family." In *Rethinking the Family: Some Feminist Questions*, edited by Barrie Thorne and Marilyn Yalom, 40–53. New York: Longman.

Gottdiener, M. 1985. "Hegemony and Mass Culture: A Semiotic Approach." *American Journal of Sociology* 90:979–1001.

Granovetter, Mark S. 1974. *Getting a Job: A Study of Contacts and Careers*. Cambridge: Harvard University Press.

Green, Martin. 1966. *The Problem of Boston*. New York: W. W. Norton and Company.

Greenberg, Stephanie W. 1981. "Industrial Location and Ethnic Residential Patterns in an Industrializing City: Philadelphia, 1880." In *Philadelphia: Work, Space, Family, and Group Experience in the Nineteenth Century*, edited by Theodore Hershberg, 204–239. New York: Oxford University Press.

Grossman, James R. 1989. *Land of Hope: Chicago, Black Southerners, and the Great Migration*. Chicago: University of Chicago Press.

Gusfield, Joseph R. [1963] 1986. *Symbolic Crusade: Status Politics and the American Temperance Movement*. Urbana: University of Illinois Press.

Hall, Peter Dobkin. 1978. "Marital Selection and Business in Massachusetts Merchant Families, 1700–1900." In *The American Family in Socio-Historical Perspective*, 2d ed., edited by Michael Gordon, 101–114. New York: St. Martin's Press.

Haller, John S., and Robin M. Haller. 1974. *The Physician and Sexuality in Victorian America*. Urbana: University of Illinois Press.

Halttunen, Karen. 1982. *Confidence Men and Painted Women*. New Haven: Yale University Press.

Hanagan, Michael P. 1989. *Nascent Proletarians: Class Formation in Post Revolutionary France, 1840–1880*. Oxford: Basil Blackwell.

———. 1994. "New Perspectives on Class Formation: Culture, Reproduction, and Agency," *Social Science History* 18 (Spring): 77–94.

Hare, E. H. 1962. "Masturbatory Insanity: The History of an Idea." *Journal of Mental Science* 108:1–2.

Harned, Thomas B. 1895, 1896. "Whitman and His Boston Publishers." *Conservator* (December 1895): 150–153; (January 1896): 163–166.

Harring, Sidney. 1983. *Policing a Class Society: The Experience of American Cities, 1865–1915*. New Brunswick, N.J.: Rutgers University Press.

Herford, Oliver. 1915. "The Passing of St. Anthony." *Harper's Weekly* 61 (July 3): 11.

Hershberg, Theodore, ed. 1981. *Philadelphia: Work, Space, Family, and Group Experience in the Nineteenth Century*. New York: Oxford University Press.

Hewitt, Nancy A. 1986. "Feminist Friends: Agrarian Quakers and the Emergence of Women's Rights in America." *Feminist Studies* 12 (Spring): 27–49.

Heywood, Ezra H. 1877. *Cupid's Yokes, or, The Binding Forces of Conjugal Life*. Princeton, Mass.: Co-operative Publishing Co.

Higham, John. [1955] 1988. *Strangers in the Land*. New Brunswick, N.J.: Rutgers University Press.

Hobson, Barbara Meil. 1987. *Uneasy Virtue: The Politics of Prostitution and the American Reform Tradition*. New York: Basic Books.

Hodge, Hugh. [1869] 1974. "Foeticide, or Criminal Abortion: A Lecture Introductory to the Course on Obstetrics, and Diseases of Women and Children." University of Pennsylvania, Philadelphia. In *Abortion in America*, edited by Charles Rosenberg and Carroll Smith-Rosenberg. New York: Arno Press.

Hogan, David John. 1985. *Class and Reform: School and Society in Chicago, 1880–1930*. Philadelphia: University of Pennsylvania Press.

Hollingsworth, Leta. 1916. "Social Devices for Impelling Women to Bear and Rear Children." *American Journal of Sociology* 22:19–29.

Howe, Winifred E. 1913. *A History of the Metropolitan Museum of Art*. New York: Metropolitan Museum of Art.

Humphries, Jane, and Jill Rubery. 1984. "The Reconstitution of the Supply Side of the Labour Market: The Relative Autonomy of Social Reproduction." *Cambridge Journal of Economics* 8:331–346.

Iseman, Myre St. Wald. 1912. *Race Suicide*. New York: Cosmopolitan Press.

Jaher, Frederic Cople. 1973. "Style and Status: High Society in Late-Nineteenth-Century New York." In *The Rich, the Well Born, and the Powerful: Elites and Upper Classes in History*, edited by Frederic Cople Jaher, 258–284. Urbana: University of Illinois Press.

————. 1982. *The Urban Establishment*. Urbana: University of Illinois Press.

Jenson, Jane. 1986. "Gender and Reproduction: Or, Babies and the State." *Studies in Political Economy* 20 (Summer): 9–46.

Johannsen, Albert. 1950. *The House of Beadle and Adams and Its Dime and Nickel Novels: The Story of a Vanished Literature*. Norman: University of Oklahoma Press.

Johns, Elizabeth. 1986. "The Farmer in the Work of William Sidney Mount." *Journal of Interdisciplinary History* 17:257–281.

Johnson, Richard C. 1973. "Anthony Comstock: Reform, Vice, and the American Way." Ph.D. dissertation, University of Wisconsin.

Joppke, Christian. 1986. "The Cultural Dimensions of Class Formation and Class Struggle: On the Social Theory of Pierre Bourdieu." *Berkeley Journal of Sociology* 31:53–78.

Kasson, John F. 1990. *Rudeness and Civility*. New York: Basic Books.

Katznelson, Ira, and Aristide Zolberg, eds. 1986. *Working Class Formation: Nineteenth Century Patterns in Western Europe and the United States*. Princeton: Princeton University Press.

Kennedy, William S. 1895. "Suppressing a Poet." *Conservator* (January): 169–171.

Kisner, Arlene, ed. 1972. *"Woodhull and Claflin's Weekly": The Lives and Writings of Notorious Victoria Woodhull and Her Sister Tennessee Claflin.* Washington, N.J.: Time Change Press.

Kohn, Melvin L. 1969. *Class and Conformity.* Homewood, Ill.: Dorsey Press.

Lamont, Michele. 1992. *Money, Manners, and Morals.* Chicago: University of Chicago Press.

Lamont, Michele, and Annette Lareau. 1988. "Cultural Capital: Allusions, Gaps, and Glissandos in Recent Theoretical Development." *Sociological Theory* 6:153–168.

Lareau, Annette. 1989. *Home Advantage: Social Class and Parental Inrtervention in Elementary Schooling.* London and New York: Faler Press.

Laslett, Barbara, and Johanna Brenner. 1989. "Gender and Social Reproduction: Historical Perspectives." *Annual Review of Sociology* 15:381–404.

*Laws of the General Assemby of the State of Pennsylvania Passed at the Session of 1887.* 1887. Harrisburg: Edwin K. Meyers, State Printer.

Leeds, Josiah Woodward. 1878–1892. *Scrapbooks.* Quaker Collection, Haverford College. (The scrapbooks contain many newsclippings that Leeds collected and dated. I have included his dates but cannot attest to their accuracy.)

Lenski, Gerhard E. 1954. "Status Crystallization: A Non-Vertical Dimension of Status." *American Sociological Review* 19:405–413.

———. 1956. "Social Participation and Status Crystallization." *American Sociological Review* 21:458–464.

Levine, Lawrence W. 1988. *Highbrow/Lowbrow: The Emergence of Cultural Hierarchy in America.* Cambridge: Harvard University Press.

Library Company. N.d. Photocopy of booksellers list, advertising "rich, rare, and racy books," such as Comstock condemned.

Luker, Kristin. 1984. *Abortion and the Politics of Motherhood.* Berkeley: University of California Press.

Lystra, Karen. 1989. *Searching the Heart.* New York: Oxford University Press.

MacDonald, Robert H. 1967. "The Frightful Consequences of Onanism: Notes on the History of a Delusion." *Journal of the History of Ideas* 28 (July–September): 423–431.

Macleod, David I. 1993. *Building Character in the American Boy.* Madison: University of Wisconsin Press.

Mandelbaum, Seymour J. 1965. *Boss Tweed's New York.* New York: John Wiley and Sons.

Marilley, Suzanne M. 1993. "Francis Willard and the Feminism of Fear." *Feminist Studies* 19 (Spring): 123–146.

McAllister, Ward. [1890] 1975. *Society as I Have Found It.* New York: Arno Press.

McCabe, James D., Jr. [1882] 1984. *New York by Gaslight* (originally published as *New York by Gaslight and Sunlight*). New York: Greenwich House.

McCall, Leslie. 1992. "Does Gender *Fit*? Feminism, Bourdieu, and Conceptions of Social Order." *Theory and Society* 21 (November): 837–867.

McCarthy, Kathleen D. 1991. *Women's Culture.* Chicago: University of Chicago Press.

McCoy, Ralph E. 1956. "Banned in Boston: The Development of Literary Censorship in Massachusetts." Ph.D. dissertation, University of Illinois.

McDonald, Terrence J. 1985. "The Problem of the Political in Recent American Urban History: Liberal Pluralism and the Rise of Functionalism." *Social History* 10 (October): 323–345.

————. 1986. *The Parameters of Urban Fiscal Policy*. Berkeley: University of California Press.

McFadden, Elizabeth. 1971. *The Glitter and the Gold*. New York: Dial Press.

McGerr, Michael E. *The Decline of Popular Politics: The American North, 1865–1928*. New York: Oxford University Press.

McLachlan, James. 1970. *American Boarding Schools: A Historical Study*. New York: Charles Schribner's Sons.

McNall, Scott G. 1988. *The Road to Rebellion: Class Formation and Kansas Populism, 1865–1900*. Chicago: University of Chicago Press.

Meckel, Richard A. 1985. "Immigration, Mortality, and Population Growth in Boston, 1840–1880." *Journal of Interdisciplinary History* 15:393–418.

Metropolitan Museum of Art. 1874–1887. *Annual Reports of the Trustees of the Association*. New York.

Miller, Lillian B. 1966. *Patrons and Patriotism*. Chicago: University of Chicago Press.

Mink, Gwendolyn. 1990. "The Lady and the Tramp: Gender, Race, and the Origins of the American Welfare State." In *Women, the State, and Welfare*, edited by Linda Gordon, 92–122. Madison: University of Wisconsin Press.

Mitchell, Dolores. 1992. "Images of Exotic Women in Turn-of-the-Century Tobacco Art." *Feminist Studies* 18 (Spring): 327–350.

Mitchell, John I. 1882. "Political Bosses." *North American Review* 135 (October): 363–373.

Moen, Michael C. 1988. "Status Politics and the Political Agenda of the Christian Right." *Sociological Quarterly* 29, no. 3: 429–437.

Mohr, James C. 1978. *Abortion in America*. New York: Oxford University Press.

Montgomery, Maureen E. 1989. *Gilded Prostitution: Status, Money, and Transatlantic Marriages, 1870–1914*. London and New York: Routledge.

Munnell, Thomas. 1872. "Beecherism and Legalism." *Christian Quarterly* 4 (January): 21–35.

"My Note Book." 1888. *The Art Amateur* 18, no. 2 (January): 28.

Nead, Lynda. 1988. *Myths of Sexuality: Representations of Women in Victorian Britain*. New York: Basil Blackwell.

————. 1990. "The Female Nude: Pornography, Art, and Sexuality." *Signs* 15:323–335.

Nebinger, Andrew. [1870] 1974. "Criminal Abortion: Its Extent and Prevention; Read before the Philadelphia County Medical Society, February 9, 1870." In *Abortion in America*, edited by Charles Rosenberg and Carroll Smith-Rosenberg. New York: Arno Press.

Neuman, R. P. 1975. "Masturbation, Madness, and the Modern Concepts of Childhood and Adolescence." *Journal of Social History* 8:1–27.

Newman, Katherine S. 1993. *Declining Fortunes*. New York: Basic Books.

New England Society for the Suppression of Vice. 1878–1879, 1881–1882 through 1891–1892. (Renamed the Watch and Ward Society in 1890). *Annual Reports*. Boston.

———. 1878–1888. *Minutes of Executive Committee Meetings*. Private Collection.

New England Society for the Suppression of Vice. *Letters to the New England Society for the Suppression of Vice*. Private Collection.

New York Court of Appeals. [1884] 1969. "The People of the State of New York, Respondent, v. August Muller, Appellant." In *Censorship Landmarks*, edited by Edward de Grazia, 42–44. New York: R. R. Bowker Co.

New York Social Register Association. 1890. *Social Register, Boston*. New York: Social Register Association.

———. 1892a. *Social Register, New York*. New York: Social Register Association.

———. 1892b. *Social Register, Philadelphia*. New York: Social Register Association.

New York Society for the Suppression of Vice. 1874–1892. *Annual Reports*. New York. (The report issued in 1874 is the report of the Young Men's Christian Association's Committee on the Suppression of Vice).

New York Society for the Suppression of Vice. *Records of the New York Society for the Suppression of Vice*. Manuscripts Division, Library of Congress.

*New York Tribune Monthly*. "American Millionaires." June 1892.

Nissenbaum, Stephen. 1980. *Sex, Diet, and Debility in Jacksonian America: Sylvester Graham and Health Reform*. Westport, Conn.: Greenwood Press.

Ostrander, Susan A. 1980. "Upper Class Women: The Feminine Side of Privilege." *Qualitative Sociology* 3:23–44.

———. 1984. *Women of the Upper Class*. Philadelphia: Temple University Press.

Page, Ann L., and Donald A. Clelland. 1978. "The Kanawha County Textbook Controversy: A Study in the Politics of Lifestyle Concern." *Social Forces* 57:265–281.

———. 1980. "Kanawha County Revisited: Reply to Billings and Goldman." *Social Forces* 57 (September).

Parkman, Francis. 1878. "The Failure of Universal Suffrage." *North American Review* 263 (July–August): 1–20.

Persell, Caroline Hodges, and Peter W. Cookson, Jr. 1985. "Chartering and Bartering: Elite Education and Social Reproduction." *Social Problems* 33 (December): 14–29.

Petchesky, Rosalind P. 1984. *Abortion and Women's Choice*. New York: Longman.

Pivar, David. 1973. *Purity Crusade: Sexual Morality and Social Control, 1868–1900*. Westport, Conn.: Greenwood Press.

Platt, Anthony. 1969. *The Child-Savers: The Invention of Delinquency*. Chicago: University of Chicago Press.

Priest, T. B. 1984. "Elite and Upper Class in Philadelphia, 1914." *Sociological Quarterly* 25 (Summer): 319–331.

*Proceedings at the Opening of the Museum of Fine Arts, with the Reports for 1876*. Boston: Alfred Mudge and Son.

*Proceedings of the Indignation Meeting held in Faneuil Hall, Thursday Evening, August 1, 1879, to Protest Against the Injury done to the Freedom of the Press by the Conviction and Imprisonment of Ezra H. Heywood.* Boston: Benj R. Tucker, 1878.

Reagan, Leslie J. 1991. "'About to Meet Her Maker': Women, Doctors, Dying Declarations, and the State's Investigation of Abortion, Chicago, 1867–1940." *Journal of American History* (March): 1240–1264.

Reddy, William M. 1987. *Money and Liberty in Modern Europe.* Cambridge: Cambridge University Press.

Rentoul, Robert Reid. 1906. *Race Culture or Race Suicide? (A Plea for the Un-born).* London and New York: Walter Scott Publishing Company.

Richardson, E. P. 1965. *Painting in America.* New York: Thomas Y. Crowell.

Roberts, George, and Mary Roberts. 1959. *Triumph on Fairmount.* Philadelphia: Lippincott.

Robinson, Robert V. 1984. "Reproducing Class Relations in Industrial Capitalism." *American Sociological Review* 49:182–196.

Rose, Sonya O. 1992. *Limited Livelihoods: Gender and Class in Nineteenth-Century England.* Berkeley: University of California Press.

Rosenberg, Charles E. 1973. "Sexuality, Class and Role in Nineteenth-Century America." *American Quarterly* 25, no. 2 (May): 131–153.

Rosensweig, Roy. 1983. *Eight Hours for What We Will.* New York: Cambridge University Press.

Rothman, Ellen. 1983. "Sex and Self-Control: Middle Class Courtship in American, 1770–1870." In *The American Family in Social-Historical Perspective*, 3d ed., edited by Michael Gordon, 393–410. New York: St. Martin's Press.

Roy, William G. 1984. "Institutional Governance and Social Cohesion: The Internal Organization of the American Capitalist Class, 1886–1905." *Research in Social Stratification and Mobility* 3:147–171.

———. 1991. "The Organization of the Corporate Class Segment of the U.S. Capitalist Class at the Turn of the Century." In *Bringing Class Back In: Contemporary and Historical Perspectives*, edited by Scott G. McNall, Rhonda F. Levine, and Rick Fantasia, 139–163. Boulder, Colo.: Westview Press.

Ryan, Mary P. 1981. *Cradle of the Middle Class.* New York: Cambridge University Press.

Sanger, Margaret. 1928. *Motherhood in Bondage.* New York: Brentano's.

Schroeder, Theodore A. 1922. *Free Speech Bibliography.* New York: H. W. Wilson Co.

Schumsky, Neil. 1986. "Tacit Acceptance: Respectable Americans and Segregated Prostitution, 1870–1910." *Journal of Social History* (Summer): 665–680.

Scott, Joan Wallach. 1988. *Gender and the Politics of History.* New York: Columbia University Press.

Scott, Wilbur J. 1985. "The Equal Rights Amendment as Status Politics." *Social Forces* 64:499–506.

Sears, Hal D. 1977. *The Sex Radicals: Free Love in High Victorian America.* Lawrence: Regents Press of Kansas.

Self, Edward. 1883. "The Abuse of Citizenship." *North American Review* 136 (June): 541–556.

Sennett, Richard, and Jonathan Cobb. 1972. *The Hidden Injuries of Class.* New York: Vintage Books.

Sewell, William H., Jr. 1990. "How Classes Are Made: Critical Reflections on E. P. Thompson's Theory of Working-Class Formation." In *E. P. Thompson: Critical Perspectives,* edited by Harvey J. Kaye and Keith McClelland, 50–77. Oxford: Polity Press.

Shefter, Martin. 1986. "Trade Unions and Political Machines: The Organization and Disorganization of the American Working Class in the Late-Nineteenth Century." In *Working Class Formation,* edited by Ira Katznelson and Aristide Zolberg, 197–276. Princeton: Princeton University Press.

Sheldon, George William. 1888. *Recent Ideals of American Art.* New York: D. Appleton and Co.

Skowronek, Stephen. 1982. *Building a New American State.* New York: Cambridge University Press.

Smith-Rosenberg, Carroll. 1985. *Disorderly Conduct: Visions of Gender in Victorian America.* New York: Alfred A. Knopf.

Sokolow, Jayme A. 1983. *Eros and Modernization: Sylvester Graham, Health Reform, and the Origins of Victorian Sexuality in America.* Rutherford, N.J.: Fairleigh Dickinson University Press.

Solomon, Barbara M. 1956. *Ancestors and Immigrants.* Cambridge: Harvard University Press.

Sprague, Homer B. 1882. "Societies for the Suppression of Vice." *Education* (September): 70–81.

Spurlock, John C. 1988. *Free Love: Marriage and Middle-Class Radicalism in America, 1825–1860.* New York: New York University Press.

Stansell, Christine. 1982. "Women, Children, and the Uses of the Streets: Class and Gender Conflict in New York City, 1850–1860." *Feminist Studies* 8 (Summer): 309–336.

———. 1987. *City of Women: Sex and Class in New York, 1789–1860.* Urbana: University of Illinois Press.

Steffens, Lincoln. 1903. "Philadelphia: Corrupt and Contented." *McClure's Magazine* 21:249–263.

Stuart, Ardemus. 1905. *A Digest of the Statute Law of the State of Pennsylvania from the year 1700 to 1903.* Philadelphia: George T. Bisel Co.

Sutherland, John F. 1973. "Housing the Poor in the City of Homes: Philadelphia at the Turn of the Century." In *The Peoples of Philadelphia: A History of Ethnic Groups and Lower-Class Life, 1790–1940,* edited by Allen F. Davis and Mark H. Haller, 175–202. Philadelphia: Temple University Press.

Tamney, Joseph, and Stephen Johnson. 1988. "Explaining Support for the Moral Majority." *Sociological Forum* 3:234–255.

Teaford, Jon C. 1984. *The Unheralded Triumph.* Baltimore: Johns Hopkins University Press.

Thernstrom, Stephan. 1973. *The Other Bostonians.* Cambridge: Harvard University Press.

Thompson, E. P. 1963. *The Making of the English Working Class*. New York: Vintage Press.

Tomkins, Calvin. 1970. *Merchants and Masterpieces*. New York: E. P. Dutton and Co.

Trachtenberg, Alan. 1982. *The Incorporation of America*. New York: Hill and Wang.

Trow City Directory Company. 1872–1892. *Trow's New York City Directory*. New York: Trow City Directory Company.

"The Union League and the Political Situation in Philadelphia," by a Republican member of the League. Philadelphia, March 1873. Library of Congress.

United States Department of the Interior, Census Office. 1883. *Compendium of the Tenth Census, Part II*. Washington, D.C.: Government Printing Office.

———. 1895. *Report on the Population of the United States at the Eleventh Census: 1890. Part I*. Washington, D.C.: Government Printing Office.

Van de Warker, Ely. 1872. *The Detection of Criminal Abortion and a Study of Foeticidal Drugs*. Boston: James Campbell.

Van Rensselaer, Mrs. John King. 1924. *The Social Ladder*. New York: Henry Holt and Co.

Veblen, Thorstein. 1931. *The Theory of the Leisure Class*. New York: Viking Press.

Vogel, Lise. 1974. "Fine Arts and Feminism: The Awakening Conscience." *Feminist Studies* 2:3–37.

Wacquant, Loic J. D. 1989. "Towards a Reflexive Sociology: A Workshop with Pierre Bourdieu." *Sociological Theory* 7:26–63.

Walkowitz, Judith. 1980. *Prostitution and Victorian Society*. New York: Cambridge University Press.

Waller, Altina L. 1982. *Reverend Beecher and Mrs. Tilton: Sex and Class in Victorian America*. Amherst: University of Massachusetts Press.

Wallis, Roy. 1977. "A Critique of the Theory of Moral Crusades as Status Defense." *Scottish Journal of Sociology* 1:195–203.

Weber, Max. 1953. "Class, Status, Party." In *Class, Status and Power*, edited by Reinhard Bendix and Seymour Martin Lipset, 63–75. Glencoe, Ill.: Free Press.

Weeks, Joseph D. 1886. *Report of Statistics of Wages in Manufacturing Industries, with Supplementary Reports on the Average Retail Prices of the Necessities of Life and on Trade Societies, Strikes, and Lockouts*. Washington, D.C.: Government Printing Office.

Whitehill, Walter Muir. 1970. *Museum of Fine Arts, Boston: A Centennial History*. Vol. 1. Cambridge: Harvard University Press, Belknap Press.

Whitman, Walt. 1882. "A Memorandum at a Venture." *North American Review* 134 (May): 546–550.

Whitman, Walt. 1983. *Leaves of Grass*. New York: Bantam Books.

Williams, T. Harry, ed. 1964. *Hayes: The Diary of a President, 1875–1881*. New York: D. McKay.

Willis, Paul. 1977. *Learning to Labor: How Working-Class Kids Get Working-Class Jobs*. New York: Columbia University Press.

Wood, Michael, and Michael Hughes. 1984. "The Moral Basis of Moral Reform: Status Discontent versus Culture and Socialization as Explanations of Anti-Pornography Social Movement Adherence." *American Sociological Review* 49:86–99.

Wright, Erik Olin. 1985. *Classes*. London: Verso Press.

Wright, Erik Olin, and Kwang-Yeong Shin. 1988. "Temporality and Class Analysis: A Comparative Study of the Effects of Class Trajectory and Class Structure on Class Consciousness in Sweden and the United States." *Sociological Theory* 6:58–84.

Wright, Erik Olin, Carolyn Howe, and Donmoon Cho. 1989. "Class Structure and Class Formation: A Comparative Analysis of the United States and Sweden." In *Cross-National Research in Sociology*, edited by Melvin L. Kohn, 185–217. Newbury Park, Calif.: Sage Publications.

Wright, Richard Grant. 1883. "Class Distinctions in the United States," *North American Review* 137 (August): 231–246.

Young Men's Christian Association, New York. 1874. "Private and Confidential Report of the Committee for the Suppression of Vice."

Zeitlin, Maurice. 1974. "Corporate Ownership and Control: The Large Corporation and the Capitalist Class." *American Journal of Sociology* 79:1073–1119.

———. 1988. *Landlords and Capitalists: The Dominant Class of Chile*. Princeton: Princeton University Press.

Zelizer, Viviana A. 1985. *Pricing the Priceless Child*. New York: Basic Books.

Zurcher, Louis A., and R. George Kirkpatrick. 1976. *Citizens for Decency: Antipornography Crusades as Status Defense*. Austin: University of Texas Press.

Zweigenhaft, Richard L., and G. William Domhoff. 1991. *Blacks in the White Establishment*. New Haven: Yale University Press.

# INDEX

PRINCETON STUDIES IN AMERICAN POLITICS:
HISTORICAL, INTERNATIONAL, AND COMPARATIVE PERSPECTIVES

*Labor Visions and State Power: The Origins of Business
Unionism in the United States* by Victoria C. Hattam

*The Lincoln Persuasion: Remaking American Liberalism*
by J. David Greenstone

*Politics and Industrialization: Early Railroads in the
United States and Prussia* by Colleen A. Dunlavy

*Political Parties and the State: The American Historical Experience*
by Martin Shefter

*Prisoners of Myth: The Leadership of the Tennessee
Valley Authority, 1933–1990* by Erwin C. Hargrove

*Bound by Our Constitution: Women, Workers, and the Minimum Wage*
by Vivien Hart

*Experts and Politicians: Reform Challenges to Machine Politics in
New York, Cleveland, and Chicago* by Kenneth Finegold

*Social Policy in the United States: Future Possibilities in
Historical Perspective* by Theda Skocpol

*Political Organizations* by James Q. Wilson

*Facing Up to the American Dream: Race, Class, and the Soul
of the Nation* by Jennifer L. Hochschild

*Classifying by Race* edited by Paul E. Peterson

*From the Outside In: World War II and the American State*
by Bartholomew H. Sparrow

*Kindred Strangers: The Uneasy Relationship between Politics
and Business in America* by David Vogel

*Why Movements Succeed or Fail: Opportunity, Culture, and
the Struggle for Woman Suffrage* by Lee Ann Banaszak

*The Power of Separation: American Constitutionalism and
the Myth of the Legislative Veto* by Jessica Korn

*Party Decline in America: Policy, Politics, and the Fiscal State*
by John J. Coleman

*The Origins of the Urban Crisis: Race and Inequality in Postwar Detroit*
by Thomas J. Sugrue

Printed in the United States
200789BV00003B/4/A

9 780691 027784